Jewish Translation, Translating Jewishness

Jewish Translation, Translating Jewishness

Edited by
Magdalena Waligórska and Tara Kohn

DE GRUYTER

This volume was made possible thanks
to the generous support of:

Alexander von Humboldt
Stiftung / Foundation

The publication has been prepared in cooperation with:

 and

ISBN 978-3-11-068321-9
e-ISBN (PDF) 978-3-11-055078-8
e-ISBN (EPUB) 978-3-11-055019-1

Library of Congress Cataloging-in-Publication Data

Names: Waligórska, Magdalena, editor. | Kohn, Tara, 1983- editor.
Title: Jewish translation, translating Jewishness / edited by Magdalena
  Waligórska and Tara Kohn.
Description: Berlin ; Boston : Walter de Gruyter, GmbH, [2018]
Identifiers: LCCN 2018006871 | ISBN 9783110547641 (hardcover)
Subjects: LCSH: Jews--Languages--Translating. | Jewish
  literature--Translations--History and criticism. | Translating and
  interpreting--Social aspects. | Jews--Civilization.
Classification: LCC PJ5067 .J49 2018 | DDC 418/.02089924--dc23 LC record
  available at https://lccn.loc.gov/2018006871

Bibliographic information published by the Deutsche Nationalbibliothek
The Deutsche Nationalbibliothek lists this publication in the Deutsche Nationalbibliografie;
detailed bibliographic data are available on the Internet at http://dnb.dnb.de.

© 2019 Walter de Gruyter GmbH, Berlin/Boston
This volume is text- and page-identical with the hardback published in 2018.
Cover image: Karen Underhill
Printing and binding: CPI books GmbH, Leck

www.degruyter.com

Acknowledgements

The authors would like to thank the Alexander von Humboldt Foundation for generously supporting this project through a post-doctoral grant to Magdalena Waligórska and a subsidy to publish the present volume.

We are also indebted to *Przekładaniec: A Journal of Translation Studies* and the Jagiellonian University Press in Kraków for granting us the permission to publish the English translation of eight of the essays featured here as well as interviews with authors and translators that first appeared in the Polish version as a theme issue of *Przekładaniec* (no. 29/2014). We would like to thank in particular the Chief Editor of *Przekładaniec*, Magdalena Heydel, as well as Head of the Jagiellonian University Press, Łukasz Kocój, for making this co-edition project possible. We would also like to extend our warmest thanks to *Przekładaniec*'s editorial team, especially Agata Hołobut and Elżbieta Wójcik-Leese, for encouragement and editorial counsel in the early stages of the project. The unwavering support, professionalism and kindness of the journal's Managing Editor, Zofia Ziemann, was essential for the completion of this project.

This volume has profited enormously from the mentoring advice and critical insights of Irmela von der Lühe (Free University Berlin), Vivian Liska (University of Antwerp), and Magdalena Marszałek (University of Potsdam), who also co-organized and co-hosted the public discussions with writers and translators that are recorded in the final section of the volume. This part of the book would not have been possible without Joanna Bator, Bożena Keff, Erica Fischer, Robert Schindel, Esther Kinsky, Michael Zgodzay, Katarzyna Weintraub and Jacek St. Buras, who agreed to share their experiences and insights in the interviews published here. Our very special thanks are also extended to Nina Müller and Marcin Piekoszewski of the Berlin Buch|Buch, which hosted the meetings with the authors and translators in 2013.

Our editorial assistant, Niklas Cohrs, was instrumental in putting the final manuscript of this volume in proper shape. We would also like to extend our gratitude to Jennifer Hunter for her expert guidance with aspects of the introductory text and Karen Underhill who, as one of few happy owners of a Yiddish typewriter, provided us with the cover image.

Last, but not least, we owe our debt of gratitude to our Acquisitions Editor, Sophie Wagenhofer, for her open-mindedness and enthusiasm for this book project, as well as to the editorial team at DeGruyter for their help and assistance in finalizing this project.

Contents

Magdalena Waligórska and Tara Kohn
Jewish Translation / Translating Jewishness —— 1

Around the Book

Wojciech Kosior
The Fallen (Or) Giants? The Gigantic Qualities of the *Nefilim* in the Hebrew Bible —— 17

Orr Scharf
Whose Bible is it Anyway? The Buber-Rosenzweig Translation as a Bible for Christian Readers —— 39

Borderlands and Bridges

Kenneth B. Moss
Not *The Dybbuk* but *Don Quixote:* Translation, Deparochialization, and Nationalism in Jewish Culture, 1917–1919 —— 67

Natalia Krynicka
Maneuvering around the "Great Wall of China": Translations of Yiddish Literature into Polish before the First World War —— 113

Marek Tuszewicki
Non-Jewish Languages of Jewish Magic: On Homeliness, Otherness, and Translation —— 135

Migrations and Inspirations

Joachim Schlör
"Da wär's halt gut, wenn man Englisch könnt!" Robert Gilbert, Hermann Leopoldi and the Role of Languages between Exile and Return —— 153

Na'ama Sheffi
The Politics of Translation: The German-Hebrew Case —— 173

Mahmoud Kayyal
Hegemony and Ideology in the Translations between Arabic and Hebrew Literatures in Modern Times —— 193

Agnieszka Podpora
The Saint of Socialist Palestine: Yosef Haim Brenner in Polish Translation —— 213

Translation after the Shoah

Dorota Glowacka
The Tower of Babel: Holocaust Testimonials and the Ethics of Translation —— 237

Iwona Guść
Ania's Diary: The Polish Translation of the Diary of Anne Frank: Its History, First Publication, and Reception in Post-Stalinist Poland —— 259

Tara Kohn
Translation and Re-Vision: On the Resurgence and Resurfacing of Alter Kacyzne's Photographic Texts —— 279

Authors and Translators in Conversation

Magdalena Waligórska
The Boundaries of Translation: Polish-Jewish-German Literary Borderlands —— 303

Joanna Bator and Esther Kinsky
On a Jew in the Attic and Hybrid Identity —— 311

Robert Schindel and Jacek St. Buras
On Naming the Dead and Splinters of Truth —— 319

Bożena Keff and Michael Zgodzay
On Mother, Fatherland, and the Judeo-Communist Nation —— 327

Erica Fischer and Katarzyna Weintraub
On Searching for the Truth and Translation that Gets under the Skin —— 337

Contributors —— 347

Index —— 351

Magdalena Waligórska and Tara Kohn
Jewish Translation / Translating Jewishness

> "Translation is a process of self-creation and of mutual creation; ... but if translation creates the translated text, it also translates the translator."
> (Bauman 1999, xlvii)

In his writings on his work as a translator, the poet Edwin Honig reflects on his youthful absorption of many languages, suggesting that his ability to move across and between linguistic systems was rooted in the depths of his ancestral heritage and Jewish upbringing. He became multilingual instinctively and almost inadvertently, in a way that was "nonsystematic, pre-adolescent, and half-hatched in the family nest." (Honig 1985, 1–2) The intertwining strands of what became, for him, "internal languages"— English, Yiddish, Polish, German, Hebrew, Spanish, Italian, and French—wove the textures of his familial past and shaped who he became as a writer (Roskies 2004, 262; Honig 1985, 1). For Honig, as for many Jewish authors, the act of translation was one of return and rediscovery: to the fragments of the languages that he remembered from his childhood; to words that were deeply intimate, unfixed in meaning, and a source of constant invention; to his own writerly voice as it was "echoed back" to him through lines of text written by someone else. In shaping new works out of old words, Honig notes, he found ways to simultaneously deepen his understanding of himself and the Other, to move both inward and outward—across borders and cultural divides (Honig 1985, 2, 7).

This volume considers Jewish translation, to borrow Honig's words, as a means of heightening both self-awareness and "self-transcendence," as "another version of the paradox: to know yourself, lose yourself in the other." (Honig 1985, 8) The title of this volume reflects our double lens on this issue: we explore both the cultural and political resonances of Jewish translating efforts and the ways the Jewish experience has been translated by others. Defining our area of interest in this way brings up important questions. Can we even speak of "Jewish translation" if the very definition of "Jewish literature" is not obvious? Which languages would have to be taken into consideration to fully document the scope of "Jewish translation"? Can we speak of a specifically Jewish school or philosophy of translation? How should we treat various non-Jewish attempts at translating Jewish texts?

Gideon Toury, the outstanding Israeli translation scholar, defined Jewish translation as comprising not only those efforts involving Hebrew or other Jewish languages (such as Yiddish, Ladino, Judeo-Arabic or Judeo-Persian) but also translations between two non-Jewish languages, if their subject or the actors involved had "a Jewish character." (Toury 2002, x) Naomi Seidman, in turn, in her *Faithful Renderings*, lists the "uniquely strong connection to the original language" of the Scriptures and the willingness to bring the reader through the translation towards the source text as the characteristics of the specifically Jewish approach to translation (Seidman 2006, 14–17). Seidman also notes that Jews, because of their mobility and the nomadic experience on the fault lines of different cultures, social groups and classes, have always carried meaning across the borders. "The Jew—almost by definition—is Europe's translator," she concludes (16). Not only did translation, therefore, play a central role in Jewish life over the centuries, but Jews have made a considerable contribution to the discipline of translation.

The history of Jewish translation is directly correlated with the history of Jewish migration and the shifting topographies of Jewish cultural life. Probably the most influential early Jewish translation project was the Septuagint, the first Greek translation of the Hebrew Bible—and the first translation project of any kind at this scale—likely produced over the course of two or three centuries and across many locations (Jobes and Silva 2001, 19, 30). Scholars have suggested that in their approach to these ancient and sacred texts, translators were inevitably influenced by the theological and political concerns of their own time. The Septuagint, then, "translates the translator"—or, in Honig's view, recasts the translator's vision through the words of the Other—and transforms the Hebrew text in a way that offers insight both into the nuances of the original biblical passages and into the way they were interpreted between 250 and 150 BCE (Baumann 1999, xlvi; Honig 1985, 2; Jobes and Silva 2001, 21–22, 89). These complex processes of translation evolved into a legend about seventy Jewish scholars who, working separately for seventy days, created identical versions of the Greek translation. This myth, significant in the way that it frames the Greek translation, like the Hebrew version, as a divinely-inspired text, has fascinated contemporaries as much as the strategies of translation that the text reveals (Jobes and Silva 2001, 36; see Kosior and Scharf in this volume).

The early translations from Hebrew into Greek and Latin in many ways demonstrate the progressive ideals of Jewish intellectuals during the age of Greek philosophy. Indeed, during the Hellenistic period, the Septuagint was as—if not more—widely known as the Hebrew Bible. Perhaps in response to the rise of Christianity, however, its status began to wane among rabbis and Jewish thinkers. According to the most common scholarly explanation of this trend, language became one of the central ways that Jews articulated their religious difference; as Greek-speaking Christians embraced the Septuagint, followers of Judaism reverted back to the Hebrew texts.[1] This shift influenced the intensity of translation enterprises in the Jewish world for many centuries (Seidman 2006, 12; Toury 2002, xiii). In the Middle Ages, as many Christian theologians began to study Hebrew in order to recover meanings in the original biblical passages —often in consultation with rabbis and scholars entrenched in Judaism—there was a widespread revival in Jewish teaching and translation (d'Alverny 1982, 427). For religious scholars in the context of twelfth- and thirteenth-century England and Northern France, translation often became a means of expressing theological authority; the act of reworking and re-interpreting sacred texts became central to dialogues and debates between Christians and Jews (Nisse 2017, 3–6). The vectors of translation changed not only in response to biblical study, but also because of new forms of learning across linguistic barriers and in response to the shifting social and cultural needs of European Jews (d'Alverny 1982, 426). When, as a consequence of migrations, for example, Jews lost their command of Arabic, Jewish scholars launched a project of translating Arabic-language scholarly works and legal treatises written by Jews in Muslim Spain and North Africa (Toury 2002, xix).

In the period of the Renaissance, when Italy emerged as "a new center of multilingual Jewish culture," translators did not endeavor to replicate, or mimic the textures of the original with accuracy, but rather to appropriate the text and transform it (Toury 2002, xix; Russell 2001, 29). Often, translation was a form of invention designed to transmit ideas from one culture to another (Russell 2001, 29). It was really only the *Haskalah* movement that brought with it a true expansion of Jewish translation efforts, which were now inspired by German culture. Translators began to think of their work, in Honig's words, as a form of "minding, mending, emending, and transcending a text" rather than transforming it to fit the needs of the reader (Honig 1985, 7). Moses Mendelssohn, one of the most prominent Jewish philosophers of the era, for example, reflects on his approach to translation by considering the careful choices he made as he selected each word: "I believe I can account for every one of my deviations," he writes, "and wherever I have been unfaithful to the text, the error lies in my understanding, not my will." (Gottlieb 2011, 180) During this period, Jewish scholars and translators believed that the German language was an essential medium for the Jewish Enlightenment. French and English literature was translated into Hebrew through German, and children's literature in Hebrew followed the Ger-

---

[1] In her recent study *Translation and Survival: The Greek Bible of the Ancient Jewish Diaspora*, Tessa Rajak complicates this idea, calling into question the well-accepted narrative that Jews abandoned the Septuagint in response to the rise of Christianity. See particularly her chapter "The Septuagint Between Jews and Christians," 278–314.

man model (see Na'ama Sheffi in this volume). It was also in Germany that the discipline of Jewish translation studies developed within the framework of the *Wissenschaft des Judentums* (Toury 2002, xxv).

During the nineteenth century, there was a shift eastwards, with Russia rising as center of the new Jewish translation projects. The revival of Hebrew that commenced then benefited greatly from the creative injection provided by the translation of Russian literature (Toury 2002, xxvi). Translations from Russian into Hebrew and Yiddish catalyzed change both on the linguistic level and in the realm of philosophy and politics, inspiring, for example, Jewish nationalism (see Moss in this volume).

The wave of pogroms that has swept through the Russian Empire at the turn of the nineteenth and twentieth centuries, the Bolshevik Revolution, and both world wars reconfigured the map of Jewish translation again. Migration to the United States and the *Yishuv* opened new vectors of translation (see Kayyal and Schlör in this volume). Jewish writers and translators wandering between two or more worlds, like Walter Benjamin, Yosef Haim Brenner, or Robert Gilbert both exemplified the predicament of European Jews in exile and reflected in their work on the process of translation itself (see Glowacka, Podpora and Schlör in this volume).

After the Shoah, as literature of the Holocaust became, with the exeption of the Torah, the largest and most important body of texts in Jewish languages to reach a non-Jewish audience, translation faced new challenges and opened new opportunities (Seidman 2006, 13). Monumental projects of translating trauma, conveyed in both literary works and oral testimonies, such as David Boder's oral history interviews with survivors from 1946, or much later recordings by Claude Lanzmann, opened the question of the translatability of the Jewish experience (Rosen 2010; Felman 1991). The debates on whether translation can serve as a strategy of witnessing the unspeakable and whether a testimony in a neutral language could have a therapeutic effect on the traumatized victims have profoundly transformed the field (Glowacka 2012; see Kohn, Guść, and Glowacka in this volume).

One central issue that has always loomed large in the discussions around Jewish translations was that of identity. It was, after all, often the wish to serve their community that propelled Jewish translators and, at times, the desire to confirm one's own stereotypes about the Other that attracted readers to translated Jewish texts. According to Naomi Seidman, "translation discourse has often served as barely concealed Jewish-Christian polemic." (Seidman 2006, 31) The fact that translation gives the promise of understanding an outgroup while defining canons, boundaries and spheres of influence makes it into a particularly powerful tool of constructing a collective identity. On the one hand, it helps to define what Seidman calls "a map of ... Jewish-Christian difference." (30) On the other, translation is a process that challenges the existing dichotomies. To Zygmunt Bauman, translation constitutes "[t]he meeting ground, the frontierland, of cultures" where "boundaries are constantly obsessively drawn only to be continually violated and re-drawn again and again." (Bauman 1999, xlviii) Mapping one's own domain and exploring the areas shared with the Other unavoidably transforms the participants involved, as Bauman theorized. Translation therefore destabilizes as much as it defines boundaries.

Translation studies, therefore, is a very resonant discipline in deepening our understanding of the relations between Jews in the Diaspora and their host societies. One of the founding mothers of the field, Susan Bassnett, proposed to treat translation as a "laboratory situation" to study cultural interaction (Bassnett 2007, 19). Similarly, Wolfgang Iser observes that translation "enacts one culture in terms of the other" and thus "organizes an interchange between cultures." (Iser 1996, 262–63) Understanding this process gives us a useful framework to investigate the connections between different cultures and the gains and losses incurred in the transfer of a given motif from one culture to another (Venuti in Rubel and Rosman 2003, 11). And, given that the act of translation is "fundamentally ethnocentric" and therefore never simply "communication between equals," (Venuti 1998, 11) the dynamics involved in it reflect both power relations and the strategies of contesting them. Natalia Krynicka, looking at nineteenth century translations from Yiddish into Polish, compellingly illustrates the ambivalence of such efforts where "fascination always verges on derision" and translators do not refrain from censorship, or even caricature (Krynicka, p. 116).

Analyzing such power relations, we need to remember that, as Lawrence Venuti put it, translation is a "double-edged" tool:

> As translation constructs a domestic representation for a foreign text and culture, it simultaneously constructs a domestic subject, a position of intelligibility that is also an ideological position, informed by the codes and canons, interests and agendas of certain domestic social groups ... [Hence] a translation can be powerful in maintaining or revisiting the hierarchy of values in the translating language. (Venuti 1998, 68)

Consequently, even distortions and misrepresentations that we commit vis-à-vis the translated Other reveal our own traumas and conflicts, or what Slavoj Žižek names "the Real of social antagonism." (2009, 367) In the attempt to interpret the words of Others, we inevitably reveal aspects of our self-knowledge and our own value system. Thus an act of ascribing beliefs to someone else—which is part of the process of translation—delivers a diagnosis of our own beliefs (Jones 2003, 51). So when an anonymous author of the preface to Sholem Ash's translation into Polish speaks about Yiddish in terms of "a premeditated barrier or a strategic ruse that is intended to keep the Polish neighbours in the dark," (Krynicka, p. 125) this translation tells us more about the rising influence of ethnic nationalism in the early twentieth-century Poland than about Jews themselves.

But if the divides between Jews and non-Jews have been attracting the attention of historians and sociologists for a long time, the processes that have aimed to bridge this intergroup boundary, such as translation, have only recently began to be theorized (Bronner 2014; Glenn and Sokoloff 2010; Fellous 2010; Nisse 2017; Šiaučiūnaitė-Verbickienė 2017). Examining cultural translation in pre-World War II Poland, Eugenia Prokop-Janiec compares the divide between Jews and non-Jews to a see-through fence that allowed a "mutual visibility." (2013, 29) This visibility is in the focus of the authors of this volume—even though they often have to conclude that the gaze through the fence is rarely objective. The German theoretician of translation, Wolfgang Iser, puts forward a thesis that absorbing the elements of another culture via translation is a way to counteract the deficits and a sense of loss in the target culture (Iser 1996, 262). So, even though the translated text may be marred by shortcomings or distortions, the quest for "translatability" is, according to Iser, always therapeutic:

> If the experience of crises, issuing into a critique of one's own culture, is meant to balance out the deficiencies diagnosed, recourse to other cultures proves to be a means of therapy for a growing awareness of cultural pathology. The latter can be counteracted not just by taking over features and attitudes from different cultures, but first and foremost by instilling a self-reflexivity into the stricken culture, thus providing scope for self-monitoring. Translatability is motivated by the need to cope with a crisis that can no longer be alleviated by the mere assimilation or appropriation of other cultures. (Iser 1996, 248)

Perhaps the most literal illustration of "therapy by translation" are the Eastern European (Jewish and non-Jewish) magical practices that have often borrowed from each other, appropriating, for example, distorted elements of the Other's language (see Tuszewicki in this volume). The demand for translations of "the Jewish voice" in contemporary Germany, manifested, for example, by the heightened interest in translating works on Jewish topics, likewise illustrates how the market of translations reflects social needs (see the interview section at the end of the volume).

If translation is like a "border crossing" between "us" and "them" that allows both friendly explorations and hostile incursions, the figure of the translator is equally ambivalent (Budick 1996, 11). One such protagonist we get to know in this volume is Józef Szofman, who consciously manipulated the literary strategies of Yosef Haim Brenner in order not to threaten the appeal of Zionism in Poland (see Podpora in this volume). Klemens Junosza, in turn, the first translator of Mendele Moykher Sforim's works into Polish, used the translation as a vehicle to communicate his own views on the "Jewish question." (Krynicka, pp. 116, 121) Examples of this kind demonstrate how "translator's conduct will never be innocent." (Alvarez and Vidal 1996, 5) The translator crosses the borders, but can also violate them (Rubel and Rosman 2003, 13).

The authority of the translator both allows her to commit strategic mistranslations and invests her with the capacity to examine her own culture and its mechanisms of exclusion (Venuti 1998, 83). Such a critical stance towards one's own collective identity, which Venuti also labeled as the "ethics of difference," is particularly common in the case of Jewish translators, who were often exposed to the painful experience of migration. According to the data of the Pew Forum on Religion and Public Life, a quarter of the Jewish population worldwide was not born in the country of its residence; in comparison, only five percent of Christians find themselves in the same situation (Bronner 2014, 13). As Robert Gilbert, a refugee from Nazi Germany, continued his songwriting career in the USA, he had to reconcile his nostalgia for Berlin and the emotional attachment to the German language with the bitter awareness of having been rejected by his home country. However, after Gilbert had returned to Munich after the war to translate Broadway musicals for a German spectator, it was his "split nationality" that enabled him to build bridges across the Altantic (Schlör, p. 166). Similarly, Imre Kertész, who declared his "homelessness" in any language, decided to write about the Holocaust in his native Hungarian, but only because the sense of alienation he felt while using this language corresponded to the "rupture of language 'after Auschwitz.'" (Glowacka, p. 241) Paradoxically, here, the alienation of the translator becomes the means for building bridges.

Among the contributors to this volume are translation scholars, literary and cultural scholars, as well as historians and theologians, who discuss processes of cultural translation in many different dimensions, ranging from art and literature, to politics and popular magical practices. The common denominator for all these interdisciplinary explorations is, however, the role of translation as a tool in constructing the image of the Other and one's own group identity. The project revolves around four main themes: the translations of the foundational text of Judaism—the Torah, the Jewish/non-Jewish cultural borderlands, migration, and translation in the aftermath of the Shoah. Poland, Germany, Russia, Israel and the United States, as the modern centers of Jewish translation, are the main geographical reference points of the collection, but the texts will take us to a number of other countries too.

The essays in the first section of the volume explore the sacred biblical texts, framing complexities and ambiguities that are foundational to the broader study of Jewish translation. Wojciech Kosior explores these questions through a study of the Septuagint. Analyzing motifs from the Hebrew and Greek mythology, and their partly overlapping semantic fields, the author points to the untranslatability of certain parts of the Scriptures. Through his fascinating microstudy of the Hebrew term *nefilim* and the ways it emerges in the Septuagint, Kosior suggests that this methodological approach—the reflection on a singular word or phrase— reveals the multifaceted and often paradoxical nature of translation: the way the transmission of language across cultural boundaries often obscures as much as it unveils.

Orr Scharf's contribution centers on Martin Buber's and Franz Rosenzweig's version of the Hebrew Bible, a translation that, in many significant ways, resists conventions of language and format. He argues that their unorthodox layout— their choice, for example, to omit the divisions between chapters and verses—signals not only an attempt to expand their audience and to open interfaith debate, but also the ways in which, for the translators, the Hebrew language opened a channel into the spiritual core of Judaism. Rather than transforming the language into German phrases and idioms, Scharf notes, Buber and Rosenzweig delved deeply into the intricacies of the Hebrew verse, offering lines of text in their translation that were designed to resonate for Jewish readers in profound ways.

Part Two of the volume, devoted to cultural borderlands, addresses the issue of how translation enables the creation and daily maintenance of intergroup boundaries and helps to nurture collective identities. Kenneth Moss investigates one of the most politically charged projects of this kind—the translation of Russian literature into Hebrew and Yiddish in post-revolutionary Russia. For many Jewish nationalists of the period, the systematic translation of Russian literary texts was to serve as a source of innovation for the Jewish languages and a way to strengthen the communal bonds. Transformed to frame Romantic and secular nationalist values, he argues that traditional Jewish literary works formed, in this context, an aesthetic and ethical foundation for modern Jewish culture.

Natalia Krynicka deals with the opposite direction of such efforts—looking at the translations of Yiddish literature into Polish at the turn of the twentieth century. The stormy debates on the Jewish assimilation and dissimilation that accompanied such translation projects were just as important here as the ambivalent position of the translators themselves—often converts who wished to distance themselves from the traditional, Yiddish-speaking Jewry and, at the same time, had a unique chance to mediate between the Polish and Yiddish-language realm. At the time when both the Haskalah and the wave of fascination in folk cultures seemed to foster a curiosity towards the culture and writings of

Eastern European Jews, Polish pre-World War I translations of Yiddish classics, often prefaced with highly biased introductions, only solidified the Polish prejudice towards the Jewish "jargon" and its users. Instead of building bridges, such translations would sometimes cause considerable damage to intergroup relations.

While translations of high-brow literature resonated basically exclusively among the intelligentsia, perhaps the most popular realm of translation were the magical practices. Marek Tuszewicki introduces us to this sphere of Jewish/non-Jewish relations, marked by intensive mutual borrowing. Slavic folklore appropriated elements of Jewish healing spells, granting the Jewish Other both the status of a sorcerer and a healer. But Jewish magical tradition was also not hermetically sealed from alien influences. And so, amulets with the name of Jesus, or images of the Virgin Mary would occasionally appear in the Jewish magical repertoire. This intensive cultural transfer, nonetheless, only strengthened the intergroup boundary. The magical nature of the Other relied on the undomesticated otherness; it was the "pollution" associated with the Other that secured the magical effect. How deeply ingrained and persistent such othering strategies have been is demonstrated by the recent anthropological research which shows that ascribing magical or demonic features to Jews has not ceased even after the Shoah and has had very serious consequences for the Jews (Cała 1992; Cała 2012; Tokarska-Bakir 2008; Żyndul 2011; Lehrer 2014).

Part Three of this volume, devoted to migrations and cultural transfers, concentrates on the Jewish experience of exile, as well as the Zionist project and its consequences. Joachim Schlör opens this section with the story of two German-speaking Jewish artists, the songwriter Robert Gilbert and Herman Leopoldi, pianist and composer, who fled from Nazi persecution to the United States and struggled to find themselves in a new culture. Their feeling of uprootedness and Gilbert's attempt at returning to post-war Germany become the starting point for a more universal reflection on the Jewish experience of migration and the role of translation as a stepping stone between mental homelessness and integration. Translation helps migrants achieve social mimicry, for example, by means of changing a Jewish-sounding surname, but it also nurtures a particular state of mind. The ability to translate fuels the adventurous resolve to cross borders and creatively re-negotiate one's own group identity—like Gilbert, who claimed of himself that he became not only American, but an "American Indian." (Schlör, p. 162)

The remaining texts of this section concentrate on Hebrew, pointing to the complex ways in which the Zionist project of reviving the language both relied on the literary inspiration drawn from other sources and required the maintenance of clear-cut group boundaries. The experience of the Jewish pioneers from the *Yishuv* is in focus of Agnieszka Podpora's chapter on Yosef Haim Brenner. The Polish translations of Brenner's often bitter Hebrew prose were addressed in particular at the Jewish youth and were successfully instrumentalized to idealize the Zionist writer and provide a slightly retouched narrative of the *aliyah*. The strategies of Brenner's translator, Józef Szofman, who defused the author's most drastic literary devices and purged his hybrid, Yiddish-inflected language, illustrate the political implications of translation. It also indicates to what extent translation can become a tool of utopia.

Na'ama Sheffi likewise reveals the sinews of politics behind translation. Looking at twentieth-century translations from German to Hebrew, she maps the interest in German-language literature in the country where German high culture both appealed to the German-educated intellectual elite and, after the Nazi's takeover of power and the Holocaust, became a taboo. The fascination with, and aversion to, German literature in the twentieth and twenty-first centuries, as Sheffi compellingly demonstrates in her text, have been triggered not only by the current political affairs but also migratory waves. The arrival of the first Holocaust survivors to Palestine, or the recent migration of Israelis to Germany both created new demand on the market for translated literature, and gave an impulse for the creation of new literature.

Mahmoud Kayyal contributes to this discussion by addressing the tangled connections between the conflict in the Middle East and the discourses that underpinned translations between Arabic and Hebrew. He traces a splintered web of perspectives on how translation can serve as a tool of deepening familiarity across hostile cultural divides, promoting new forms of understanding between Arabs and Israeli Jews, and shaping new narratives that counter deeply-rooted and damaging constructs of the Other. He suggests that each stage of the process of translation—from the selection of source material to the circulation of completed texts—emerged, in many ways, out of the ideological divides between the two cultures and in response to political unrest.

The last section of this volume addresses the challenges of Jewish translation and translating Jewishness in the aftermath of the Shoah. Dorota Glowacka investigates translation as an act of bearing witness to the atrocities of the Holocaust. Looking at the choice of language in which survivors decided to narrate their traumas, Glowacka examines the role of translation in the process of healing and reconfiguring one's identity in the aftermath of violence. Translation, she argues, can provide a "neutral language" and a "protective shield" for traumatized witnesses. The fact that "there is no national language in which the Holocaust story can truly be told" is, paradoxically, not an obstacle. The "translinguistic horizon" that conditions Holocaust testimonies prevents any national language from appropriating this narrative and foregrounds the imperative of bearing witness (Glowacka, p. 240).

In her contribution to the volume, Iwona Guść considers these questions about translation and trauma through her exploration of the first Polish version of the writings of one particular victim of the Holocaust: the well-known diarist Anne Frank. In her careful study of a singular, yet significant, iteration of this repeatedly-translated text—first published in Warsaw in 1957—Guść explores the meanings of the structural and linguistic choices in the context of postwar Poland. She argues that the translators and publishers, in conversation with Frank's father, altered the text to stress the childlike innocence of the young writer, syntactically heightening qualities and patterns of speech that would have been familiar to Polish readers. This translation of the diary, she suggests, worked to evoke empathy by strategically blurring the boundaries between Jewish and Polish suffering during World War II.

Tara Kohn focuses on these themes through the work of Alter Kacyzne, a Warsaw-based artist who emerged as a prolific photographer and writer in the 1920s, and who continued to translate his ideas across media until his brutal death at the height of Nazi terror. She contends that his writing—dense with vivid visual description and distinctly photographic in nature—is closely tied to a practice of image-making that was shaped, in turn, by his writerly approach to revision and translation. Kohn goes on to explore the additional translations of his photographs as they were published in New York's Yiddish language press and later re-circulated in the wake of the Holocaust, suggesting that they became not only traces of what was, for American viewers, a homeland left behind, but also evocations of catastrophic loss.

An appendix containing a series of interviews with authors and translators who reflect on the difficulties of transposing the experience of the Shoah into a literary language closes this volume, providing a follow up to many of the themes addressed in this collection of essays. In including this segment, we hope to incorporate the voices of practitioners of translation into our broader theoretical discussion of Jewish translation. The interviews with four Polish- and German-language authors: Joanna Bator, Robert Schindel, Bożena Keff and Erica Fischer, who all, by means of different genres, tried to render the Jewish experience of the Second World War and the way it became an inheritable trauma, speak to the wider debate on the translatability of trauma. Four translators, Esther Kinsky, Jacek St. Buras, Michael Zgodzay and Katarzyna Weintraub, in turn, speak of their strategies of translating these texts for a German- or Polish-speaking reader. Taken together, these conversations provide a fascinating perspective on the national mythologies, taboos and the limits of translation.

This collection in no way exhausts the subject or is meant as a comprehensive history of Jewish translation. Instead, it points to translating practices as a platform of Jewish/non-Jewish relations and proposes translation theory as a useful analytical tool to examine them. Considering intergroup contact through the lens of translation sharpens our perspective because it is through what Honig describes as the "transformation ... generated through the raw materials of the original" that boundaries between groups are negotiated and disputed (Honig 1985, 3). Homi Bhabha sees translation as a space of hybridity (*third space*) where borders between groups can be shifted and where new cultural products emerge that transcend the existing dichotomies (Bhabha 1995, 25). This volume introduces the reader into the borderland between Jewish culture and those that have surrounded it, demonstrating that the demarcation lines between them sometimes run a surprising course. The potential of this space, which inspires but also transforms its protagonists, remains both that of opportunity and a challenge. "To learn from translators," in Honig's words, "opens a new terrain" where "word-by-word minutiae" lead us into deeper, more textured cultural understandings (Honig 1985, 8).

Bibliography

Alvarez, Roman, and M. Carmen-Africa Vidal. 1996. "Translating: A Political Act." In *Translation, Power, Subversion*, edited by Roman Alvarez and M. Carmen-Africa Vidal, 1–9. Clevedon: Multilingual Matters.

Bassnett, Susan. 2007. "Culture and Translation." In *A Companion to Translation Studies*, edited by Piotr Kuhiwczak and Karin Littau, 13–23. Clevedon: Multilingual Matters.

Bauman, Zygmunt. 1999. *Culture as Praxis*. London: Sage.

Bhabha, Homi. 1995. *The Location of Culture*. London: Routledge.

Bronner, Simon J. 2014. "Framing Jewish Culture." In *Framing Jewish Culture: Boundaries and Representations*. Vol. 4, *Jewish Cultural Studies*, edited by Simon J. Bronner, 1–29. Oxford: The Littman Library of Jewish Civilization.

Budick, Sanford. 1996. "Crises of Alterity: Cultural Untranslatability and the Experience of Secondary Otherness." In *The Translatability of Cultures: Figurations of the Space Between*, edited by Sanford Budick and Wolfgang Iser, 1–22. Stanford: Stanford University Press.

Cała, Alina. 1992. *Wizerunek Żyda w polskiej kulturze ludowej*. Warszawa: Wydawnictwa Uniwersytetu Warszawskiego.

Cała, Alina. 2012. *Żyd – wróg odwieczny? Antysemityzm w Polsce i jego źródła*. Warszawa: Wydawnictwo Nisza.

d'Alverny, Marie-Therese. 1982. "Translations and Translators." In *Renaissance and Renewal in the Twelfth Century*, edited by Robert Louis Benson et al., 421–462. Cambridge, MA: Harvard University Press.

Even-Zohar, Itamar. 1978. "The Position of Translated Literature within the Literary Polysystem." In *Literature and Translation: New Perspectives in Literary Studies*, edited by James S. Holmes et al., 117–127. Louven: Acco.
Fellous, Sonia. 2000. "Cultural Hybridity, Cultural Subversion: Text and Image in the Alba Bible, 1422–33." *Exemplaria*, 12 (1): 205–229.
Felman, Shoshana. 1991. "In an Era of Testimony: Claude Lanzmann's Shoah." *Yale French Studies* 79: 39–81.
Glenn, Susan A., and Naomi B. Sokoloff, eds. 2010. *Boundaries of Jewish Identity*. Seattle: University of Washington Press.
Glowacka, Dorota. 2012. *Disappearing Traces: Holocaust Testimonials, Ethics and Aesthetics*. Seattle: University of Washington Press.
Gottlieb, Micah, ed. 2011. *Moses Mendelssohn: Writings on Judaism, Christianity, and the Bible*. Waltham, MA.: Brandeis University Press.
Honig, Edwin. 1985. *The Poet's Other Voice: Conversations on Literary Translation*. Amherst: The University of Massachusetts Press.
Iser, Wolfgang. 1996. "The Emergence of a Cross-Cultural Discourse: Thomas Carlyle's *Sartor Resartus*." In *The Translatability of Cultures: Figurations of the Space Between*, edited by Sanford Budick and Wolfgang Iser, 245–264. Stanford: Stanford University Press.
Jobes, Karen, and Moises Silva. 2001. *Invitation to the Septuagint*. Grand Rapids, MI: Baker Academic Press.
Jones, Todd. 2003. "Translation and Belief Ascription: Fundamental Barriers." In *Translating Cultures: Perspectives on Translation and Anthropology*, edited by Paula G. Rubel and Abraham Rosman, 45–73. Oxford: Berg.
Lehrer, Erica T., ed. 2014. *Na szczęście to Żyd: Polskie figurki Żydów / Lucky Jews: Poland's Jewish Figurines*. Kraków: Ha!Art.
Miłosz, Czesław. 2011. *Rodzinna Europa*. Kraków: Wydawnictwo Literackie.
Moss, Kenneth B. 2009. *Jewish Renaissance in the Russian Revolution*. Cambridge: Harvard University Press.
Nisse, Ruth. 2017. *Jacob's Shipwreck: Diaspora, Translation, and Jewish-Christian Relations in Medieval England*. Ithaca and London: Cornell University Press.
Prokop-Janiec, Elżbieta. 2013. *Pogranicze polsko-żydowskie: Topografie i teksty*. Kraków: Wydawnictwo Uniwersytetu Jagiellońskiego.
Rajak, Tessa. 2009. *Translation and Survival: The Greek Bible of the Ancient Jewish Diaspora*. Oxford: Oxford University Press.
Rosen, Alan. 2010. *The Wonder of Their Voices: The 1946 Holocaust Interviews of David Boder*. Oxford: Oxford University Press.
Roskies, David. G. 2004. "The Task of the Jewish Translator: A Valedictory Address." *Prooftexts* 14, no. 3 (Fall): 263–272.
Rubel, Paula G., and Abraham Rosman. 2003. "Introduction: Translation and Anthropology." In *Translating Cultures: Perspectives on Translation and Anthropology*, edited by Paula G. Rubel and Abraham Rosman, 1–22. Oxford: Berg.
Russell, Daniel. 2001. "Introduction: The Renaissance." In *The Politics of Translation in the Middle Ages and Renaissance*, edited by Renate Blumenfeld-Kosinsky et al., 29–36. Ottawa, ON and Tempe, AZ: University of Ottowa Press and Arizona Center for Medieval and Renaissance Studies.

Seidman, Naomi. 2006. *Faithful Renderings: Jewish-Christian Differences and the Politics of Translation*. Chicago: University of Chicago Press.
Šiaučiūnaitė-Verbickienė, Jurgita. 2017. "Translations and Self-Representation: Literature as a Tool for a Mutual Jewish-Lithuanian Acquaintance." *Jewish Culture and History* 18 (2): 190–208.
Tokarska-Bakir, Joanna. 2008. *Legendy o krwi: Antropologia przesądu*. Warszawa: WAB.
Toury, Gideon. 2002. "Translation and Reflection on Translation: A Skeletal History of the Uninitiated." In *Jewish Translation History: A Bibliography of Bibliographies and Studies*, edited by Robert Singerman, ix–xxxi. Amsterdam: John Benjamin Publishing.
Venuti, Lawrence. 1998. *The Scandals of Translation: Towards an Ethics of Difference*. London: Routledge.
Żyndul, Jolanta. 2011. *Kłamstwo krwi: Legenda mordu rytualnego na ziemiach polskich w XIX i XX wieku*. Warszawa: Cyklady.
Žižek, Slavoj. 2009. "Widmo ideologii." In *Žižek: Przewodnik Krytyki Politycznej*, edited by Maciej Kropiwnicki and Julian Kutyła, 323–374. Warszawa: Krytyka Polityczna.

Around the Book

Wojciech Kosior
The Fallen (Or) Giants? The Gigantic Qualities of the *Nefilim* in the Hebrew Bible

After the Babylonian Captivity, everyday spoken Hebrew was gradually replaced by various dialects of Aramaic and Greek. As such, in the fourth to third century BC it was partially relegated to the sphere of literature and liturgy and became the domain of the intellectual elite of the period.[1] In order to maintain ecumenical participation in the shared religious legacy, there arose the need to provide Jewish congregations with not only comprehensible but also meaningful renditions of the biblical text. Hence, the Greek translation of the Hebrew Bible (HB) known as the Septuagint (LXX), gradually emerged.[2] Its position among the other early renditions is extraordinary and far exceeds that of the Aramaic translations known as targums. The distinguished status enjoyed by the LXX is traditionally believed to originate from the divine inspiration of the seventy or seventy-two translators who had independently produced a coherent work.[3]

Whatever the legend surrounding the emergence of the LXX, the task performed by its translators must have been a demanding one. Obviously, as the spheres of language, religion and culture are inseparable, the textual message is always nested in a broader context. Accordingly, the process of translation is a multidimensional endeavor that includes a variety of aspects, and the larger the gap between the languages, cultures and religions, the more challenging the task itself. This was exactly the case with the Hellenistic and Semitic entourages. Since there is no absolute correspondence between different languages, as well as between cultures or religions, the task is far beyond the simple matching of particular words from the dictionary (Luzbetak 1990, 108–9, 115; Nida 1964,

---

[1] For the nuances of the process, see for example the book of de Lange (1996).
[2] The sole expression of "Hebrew Bible" is misleading as it assumes the existence of some structured corpus of writs providing the translators with the clearly defined framework. In fact however, the status and contents of the scriptures which are *nowadays* known as the HB back in three hundred BC is in many ways problematic. Analogically, the LXX should not be perceived as a one-off enterprise but rather as the effect of a gradual process of writing, compiling and redacting. Due to the brevity of space, this issue will not be addressed in the present paper. The interested reader can consult the work of Barrera (1998, 143–235).
[3] For the tradition concerning the origins of the LXX see: *Letter of Aristeas* 310–11; Eusebius, *Praeparatio evangelica* 13.12.1–2; Philo, *Life of Moses* 2.26–44; Josephus *Antiquities* 12.11–118 (Aejmelaeus 2007, 76; Wright 2010, 236). The story is retained in the Rabbinic sources, e.g. in BT Megillah 9a.

145; Nida 2003, 2–6). The hypothetical translators wishing to render the biblical text had to confront several issues. In front of them lay the text of the HB supplemented by its interpretations and expositions, which had been transmitted in oral form. By connecting these fundamental sources, the translators were able to reconstruct a fairly coherent and intelligible unit. Next, having understood the biblical text they needed to find the appropriate Greek words and phrases to transmit the biblical message as they had perceived it. And in order to fulfill this task, they had to be well acquainted with the target culture and religion.[4]

Some insight into the translators' work can be provided by an analysis of a particular word or phrase that undergoes the process of linguistic and cultural transmission. One such example comes in the form of the word *nefilim* which appears just three times in the Masoretic text of the HB in two verses: once in Gen 6:4 and twice in Num 13:33.[5] Even a quick glance at the parallel modern translations of said passages shows the vivid tendency: most renditions apply the word "giants" to both the mysterious antediluvian figures and to the primeval inhabitants of one of the Canaanite valleys.[6] What we have in front of us, then, is the bottom line of the centuries-old transmission of these fragments starting from the ancient LXX which speaks of *gigantes*. One could then ask: how did the Greek translators *know* that the *nefilim* denoted giants? The answer is: they did not. Yet, they had to *choose* an explanation that would not wander too far from the hypothetical primary meaning of the text or compromise the data existing in both cultures. As will become apparent, the Greek and Hebrew sources alike provided equally rich and varied descriptions of *nefilim* and *gigantes* so as to allow the translators to extract the necessary material and draw the connecting lines between their particular aspects. Thus, placed between the Scylla of preciseness and Charybdis of intelligibility, they had to reshape the hypothetical initial meaning of the *nefilim*. The main purposes of the present study are therefore (1) to follow the hypothetical process of interpretation and translation by (2) reconstructing the ancient Greek mythical complex of giants and by (3) an-

---

[4] Notwithstanding, for years scholars have assumed that the Greek translation was conceived with the literal purpose in mind, with no attempts at elucidation. Only the recent decades have seen a gradual change in the awareness of the interpretational aspect of the LXX (Aejmelaeus 2007, 60, 295).
[5] The scarcity of information concerning the biblical *nefilim* has been doubly interpreted as witnessing either the widespread familiarity with the term or complete unfamiliarity with it. Both have triggered flamboyant expositions aimed at filling the semantic gaps. (Hendel 2004, 11, 17; Kugel 1997, 181–82).
[6] Among the notable deviations in English renditions of Numbers 13:33 is Young's Literal Translation which speaks of "the fallen ones" and the New Living Translation reading the "giant Nephilites" into the text.

alyzing the biblical sources speaking about the *nefilim*. Such an endeavor will lead (4) to pointing out the factors that have contributed to this line of translation. Finally, by scrutinizing the issue of the *nefilim–gigantes* it will be possible (5) to present the ancient biblical translators' workshop on the particular example.[7]

1 The *Gigantes*

In all probability, the Greek mythical complex of giants was well known and widespread in the third century BC and as such can be reconstructed based on the traditional sources.[8] The most ancient texts that refer to the giants are Hesiod's *Theogony* and Homer's *Odyssey*. According to the former, (ll. 176–206) the giants were the serpent-footed entities who emerged from the genital blood of the castrated Uranos-Heaven spilt upon Gaia-Earth.[9] The later passages (ll. 687–712) tell of the conflict between the elder deities and the titans. Described as the earth-born (*gygenes*) in the latter, they are ultimately crushed by the stones hurled from the heavens (ll. 713–35) and pushed down to the gloomy depths of Tartaros (ll. 807–19).[10] Homer in his *Odyssey* (7.59, 206; 10.120) claimed that the giants were simply oversized humans, the autochthones dwelling in the volcanic areas of the far west. These insolent creatures were stirred by their mother, Gaia, against the Olympian gods and attempted to assault the heavens. They eventually failed and were annihilated along with Phaeacians, Cyclopes and Laestrygones (*Odyssey* 7.200). The latter identification of the mythical creatures with the specific tribes resembles the one supported by Herodotus (*History*

---

[7] The processes underlying the emergence of the LXX are shrouded in mystery, and the tools for verification of the scholarly assumptions have significant limitations. It is important to keep in mind that these texts have been conceived, reiterated and translated by a group of individuals, with each of them characterized by a separate set of motives, beliefs and assumptions. As a result, what we are left with are certain hypotheses with limited conclusions. As the word "hypothesis" implies, what follows in this paper is a hermeneutical proposal and as such is opened for discussion, comments and critique.

[8] For the list of sources see the works of Delcourt and Rankin (1965), Goff (2009, 150–51), Hendel (2004, 30–32) and Kraeling (1947, 203–4).

[9] The wording utilized here makes it difficult to discern whether a deity or a natural phenomena is intended. Either way, the earthly connections of *gigantes* find support in the etymology of the word, which is usually derived from *gygenys* meaning "{born} from earth."

[10] Sometimes transcribed as *Tartarus* which by itself is Latinized form, analogically to Greek *angelos* and Latin *angelus*.

8:55) who mentions the cult of Erechtheus the Earthborn present in Athens and later substituted by Poseidon (Goff 2009, 151).

This complex is supported by the texts from the second century BC. For instance, the *Bibliotheca* of Pseudo-Apollodorus speaks of the giants as the bulky offspring of Heaven and Earth, strong and terrifying. They challenge the "elder" gods but are ultimately defeated by Zeus' thunderbolts and Hercules' arrows (1:6:1–2). Diodorus Siculus, in the *Library of History* (4.21.5) acknowledges the birth from Gaia and the enormous size of the giants inhabiting the Phlegraean plains known for the seismic and volcanic activity. According to said author (5.71.4), the giants repressed humanity and were therefore punished by the deities. These images of giants are supplemented by authors living at the beginning of the Common Era. Philostratus in his *Life of Apollonius of Tyana* (5.16) acknowledges the existence of giants, "corroborated" by their bones excavated during his days. Yet, to assume that the giants had challenged the deities is, as he puts it, "madness to relate and madness to believe."[11] Ovid in *Metamorphoses* (1:151–62, 262–312) refers to the tradition that the giants were buried under the mountains which they had previously attempted to use in their assault on the heavens. From their remnants, a new race of the wicked humans had emerged and only later was partially blotted out by the flood sent by Jupiter while other giants were trapped in the underworld. Finally, Strabo in *Geography* (5.4.6) speaks of the whole district spoiled by the foul smell of sulfur given off the earth hollowed by thunderbolts—all of this being a reminder of the *gigantomachia* which took place ages before.[12]

These texts converge to leave us with a more or less coherent picture of giants conceived in a union between heaven and earth. These creatures, usually of towering physique and exceeding strength,[13] pose danger to the cosmic order established by the deities and as such represent the broadly understood forces of chaos.[14] Although defeated in the fierce battle, they are not completely annihilat-

---

11 Flavius Philostratus, *The Life of Apollonius*, tr. F.C. Conybeare, http://www.livius.org/ap-ark/apollonius/life/va_5_16.html, (accessed September 26, 2017).
12 It is worth noting here that some of the Greek traditions reemerge in much later rabbinic writings. For instance, the motif of Kronos castrating Uranos must have been well known to the early rabbis who hint at it in BT Sanhedrin 70a (Shinan and Zakovitch 2012, 135).
13 The modern common usage of the word "giant" emphasizes just one aspect of this semantic complex, namely the size. In other words, to describe something as "gigantic" rarely means "hybrid," "untamed" or "of earthly origins." Nevertheless, it is the former meaning which is often implicitly assumed in the absence of any other clues.
14 An interesting and useful distinction is introduced by Sonik, who offers two types of chaos: (1) the cosmogonic, manifested in the morally neutral amorphic primordial matter and (2) the

ed. Instead they are eternally trapped under earth or mountains, returned to the place from which they originated. With all probability this complex of ideas belonged to the totality of religious and mythical heritage of the Hellenistic world in the third century BC and was the point of reference for the translators of the HB into Greek.[15]

2 The *Nefilim*

At first glance the Hebrew word rendered as *gigantes* has nothing in common with its LXX counterpart. Notwithstanding the semantic mystery of the *nefilim*, the linguistic features of the word pose few problems. Although there are at least several candidates for its root, the most linguistically probable is נ.פ.ל.[16] Its basic meaning is "to fall", yet the semantic range is extremely broad and encompasses "prostrating," "dropping," "perishing," "failing," "becoming sad," etc.[17] The termination *-im* denotes the plural form of the word whereas the Ma-

---

kratogenic, which takes the form of the forces threatening the universal order, at the same time being within that order (Sonik 2013, 4, 8–11).

15 In search for the explanation for the emergence of the mythological idea of giants, one could turn to the family relations as the source domain of this metaphor. One of the most influential explanation is supplied by Bettelheim (2010, 28, 33–34, 62). Accordingly, the highly ambivalent relation between the child and his parents is transferred to the sphere of myth and fantasy. Portraying father and mother as the giants being outsmarted by the mythical hero protagonist thus allows to relieve the tension of the conflicting emotions without risking the consequences of challenging the parents in the "real" world. Acknowledging the insightfulness of this interpretation it seems worthy to supply a complementary parents' perspective. Accordingly, *gigantes* would resemble teenagers or the young adults—both being liminal figures. As such they are physically mature, grown up and strong, yet in between the orders: too young to be adult which is metaphorized as deity, yet, too old to be a child understood as human. These qualities are amplified by their overdeveloped impulses and uncontrollable appetites of various qualities: sex, hunger and aggression—just like the "unrest" giants of the Greek myths they vent their feelings on humans, their younger siblings. Still, they are not fully aware of their possibilities and what they possess in sheer strength and physical qualities, they lack in intelligence and wit. They challenge their parents and try to take over the territory which would allow for a certain level of independency and finally, they either become parents/gods themselves or are expelled and condemned to eternal immaturity.

16 Contra: Harris, Archer and Waltke [TWOT] who argue for the roots פ.נ.ל. or פ.ל.א. conveying the idea of wonderfulness (TWOT 1393). See also the similar problem in the phrase *'odkha 'al ki nora'ot nifleti* (Ps 139:14).

17 For more examples see the dictionaries of Brown, Driver and Briggs (1906 [BDB], 6237), Kohler and Baumgartner (2002 [HALOT], 5626) and TWOT 1392. In later and modern Hebrew the root is equally semantically potent (Klein 1987, 421–22).

soretic vocalization suggests the *pa'il* morphological pattern spelled *nafil* analogically to the words like *qadish*, *'aritz* or *bahir*. This form is used substantively with a passive meaning to denote duration in a state, and therefore *nefilim* would mean "those fallen and remaining so."[18] Meanwhile, in terms of sheer statistics, the standard Masoretic form, conveying the meaning of the "fallen one," is the active participle in binyan *pa'al*: *nofel* in singular and *nofelim* in plural.[19] This in general refers to the fallen warriors in the military narratives, for example in Josh 8:25; Judg 8:10; 20:46; 1Sam 20:46; 31:8; 2Sam 1:19, 25, 27; 1Chr 10:8; 2Chr 20:24 (Doak 2013, 621; Hendel 2004, 21–22). Among the instances of the *nofelim*, however, one group of occurrences seems to be distinguished due to its descriptive context. It appears in Ezekiel's vision of the underworld in chapter 32 and despite the grammatical form of the word evoking the associations with the defeated soldiers, the literary entourage of those *nofelim* sends back to the *nefilim* of Gen 6:4 and Num 13:33. En masse, there are three main interconnected text clusters that have contributed to the Greek translators' choice in rendering the *nefilim* as *gigantes*.[20]

Gen 6:1–4 is a short fragment that has provoked a plethora of hermeneutic proposals over the centuries. First and foremost, the text contains numerous linguistic challenges of a lexical and semantic nature. Not only does the passage swarm with extremely rare words and phrases, but it also uses grammatical structures that are atypical and ambiguous, thus hindering the possibility of producing one, coherent exposition.[21] Secondly, the varied vocabulary, different di-

---

18 Worth mentioning here is Goldberg's interpretation. He understands the root נ.פ.ל. in this context as conveying the meaning of not belonging to particular species or not falling under specific rule, thus making the *nefilim* the unsuccessful, amorphic organisms from the antediluvian times. Goldberg also remarks that the *pa'il* form implies that the state denoted by the root has been attained by way of one's own choice, contrary to the meaning of the *pa'ul* form (Goldberg 2012, 129, 131).
19 For the linguistic hypothesis concerning the accentual shift a>o and i>e. see the paper of Maclaurin (1965, 468–69).
20 A separate problem is the usage of the root נ.פ.ל. in later rabbinic literature which witnesses to the variety of meanings. For example, the phrase *ben nefilim* appears in Exod R. 15:28 or BT Hullin 127a where it most probably denotes a kind of a reptile; in BT Bekhorot 44b the phrase *ruah ben nefilim* refers to a malevolent spirit responsible for asthmatic spells; in Ruth R. 4:3 it is said that the union of *nafil* and *nefila'* produces a *gibbor*. Finally, the most widespread is the meaning of miscarriages (Heb. *nefalim*) as it appears in e.g. BT Bava Batra 101b, 102b; BT Pesahim 9a–b (Jastrow 1903, 923).
21 The literature concerning the linguistic difficulties evoked by Gen 6:1–8 is vast and an adequate presentation of all the peculiarities of the said passage would mean to go far beyond both the volume limitations of this paper as well as to deviate from its declared purpose. For further discussion, see the bibliography of the present study.

vine names and other narrative "fractures" suggest the composite nature of the text, which most probably contains the pieces witnessing to different traditions juxtaposed in the redactional endeavor. Traditional biblical scholars interpret this passage as incomplete: Wellhausen describes it as a "cracked erratic boulder" whereas Gunkel resorts to the metaphor of a limbless "torso" in his explication. In all probability then, some hypothetical primeval variant of the story has been reiterated so as to fit in here (Hendel 1987, 14). Finally, our passage is put in the broader framework of the antediluvian cycle of archetypal transgressions: disobedience in chapter 3 and jealousy in chapter 4, somewhat paralleled by the misdeeds of Ham in chapter 9, the people of Shineʿar in chapter 11 and the daughters of Lot in chapter 19 (Tomasino 1992, 128–30). As such it is often taken as explaining the roots of evil on earth, as apparent in later Jewish and Christian expositions.

We can safely assume that all these factors posed a significant challenge to the Greek translators. Notwithstanding the inherent ambiguity of the text, they had to decide for one coherent reading: the people multiply on earth; the sons of ʾelohim take the daughters of ʾadam and those give birth to their children;[22] Yahveh sees the wickedness of ʾadam and decides to wreak havoc on earth and thus to blot out his creation.[23] The *nefilim* themselves appear in verse 4 which in Hebrew reads: "the *nefilim* were on earth in those days and also afterwards when the sons of ʾelohim would come to the daughters of ʾadam and [they] would give birth to them; these are the mighty ones of the old, the {famous men}."[24] The vagueness of this verse is crucial and leads to two hermeneutic

---

22 Heb. *laqahat* is treated here as an old technical term, equivalent to the much later *linsoʾ*. This suggests the relatively early date of origin (Frevel and Conczorowski 2011, 30; Marzel 1981; Shinan and Zakovitch 2012, 224; BDB 4939; HALOT 4162; TWOT 1124).

23 In fact, although the flood finds three possible justifications in the text: (verses 5–7; 11–12; 13), neither makes any mention of *nefilim* or *bney ha-ʾelohim*. This fact along with other factors led some scholars to argue that the *nefilim* account had previously been a separate unit, only later inserted before the flood story so as to "accumulate" the transgressions and to justify Yahveh's decision (Darshan 2014, 144, 163). For the review of the problems connected with the flood in the broader context see e.g.: the works of Clines (2012, 74–84), Kraeling (1947, 194) and Parker (1999, 796).

24 All the source-texts are presented in author's own translation unless stated otherwise. The square brackets indicate the words introduced in translation, the curly brackets—the words translated freely, whereas the soft brackets—additional remarks. The priority of the translations was to maintain the inherent ambiguity of the text. In this particular case it is important to note the grammatical awkwardness of verse 4a which would sound far more natural had it commenced with the phrase *sons of* ʾelohim *came* (Hebr. *va-yavoʾ bney ha-ʾelohim*). Thus, the *nefilim* could be taken as a later addition placed here so as to provide the etiology for the *nefilim* of Num 13:33 (Darshan 2014, 145).

questions. First, are the *nefilim* some independent figures or the offspring of *bney ha-'elohim* and the *banot ha-'adam*? Second, do the "mighty ones" as well as the "{famous men}" refer to the sons of *'elohim* or the *nefilim*? Undoubtedly, the Greek translators had to deal with these issues and the final result of their struggle clearly shows that they interpreted (1) the *nefilim* as the offspring of a supernatural union, (2) being at the same time the mighty and famous men of a distant past. Assumably, they relied on the Greek tradition, which presented the giants as the progeny of Uranos and Gaia, being connected to the tribes inhabiting the particular regions. However, the hypothetical reasons for identifying the *nefilim* with *gigantes* go beyond this simple analogy and find support in the Hebrew text as well.

3 Between Gods and Humans

Given the wording of Gen 6:4 it is assumed that the *nefilim* are the offspring of the union of the sons of *'elohim* and the daughters of *'adam*. Accordingly, the uncovering of the identity of *nefilim* depends on how to interpret the status of their "parents." Whereas the latter of them pose little hermeneutical challenge, apart from assessing whether *'adam* refers to humanity in total or the patriarch Adam,[25] the former has troubled generations of exegetes. As a result, the interpretation of *nefilim* as well as the vibe of the whole pericope relies upon how to deal with the sons of *'elohim*. The phrase itself is doubtful already on the linguistic level. First and foremost, the problems have been caused by the word *'elohim* being the plural form of *'eloah*. This can denote deities, some lesser heavenly figures, or serve as a personal name of one of the gods of the HB.[26] Secondly, no less significant is the definite article *ha*, never preceding personal names. Its presence might help in judging whether the said phrase denotes the sons of a specific deity or a class of beings. Yet, although the article is connected to the second element of the *smikhut* phrase, according to the grammar of Biblical He-

---

[25] Those who argue that the term refers specifically to Adam the patriarch, do it on the grounds that it continues the story of Gen 4–5 (Harper 1894, 441). Cf. the rabbinic tradition talking about the enormous size, indefinite shape and androgynous nature of the first human present *inter alia* in Gen R. 8:1 and Lev R. 14:1. For the connections between the giants, first human and the figure of golem see the paper of Krawczyk (2007, 122–26).

[26] Some difficulties are caused by the fact that *'elohim* is sometimes applied to the deceased ancestors (1Sam 28:13), aristocracy (Exod 4:16; 7:11) or judges (Exod 21:6; 22:8–9). Yet, in terms of statistics it is the supernatural meaning that prevails over the mundane (Parker 1999, 794).

brew it may refer to the first one as well. In this particular case it is unknown whether *ha* refers to *banim* or *'elohim* and thus precludes the possibility of knowing which meaning of *'elohim* is in use here. Thirdly, the word *banim* is also ambiguous, literally "sons" yet often utilized in reference to the "close entourage" or "followers" as is witnessed by the phrase *bney ha-nevi'im*, in for example 2Kgs 2:7. The identity of *bney ha-'elohim* is therefore by all means mysterious.

Notwithstanding, the Greek translators have rendered it as *'uioi tou Theou* (Gr. "sons of god") and their decision must have been based on several factors. First, the very structure of Gen 6:1–4, stressing the dichotomy of *bney ha-'elohim* and *banot ha-'adam*, suggests interpreting both figures as representations of not only two sexes but two ontological orders, whatever the meaning of *'elohim* (Kugel 1997, 179–80). Secondly, the idea of human-divine cohabitation finds some support in the HB. This is apparent in the troublesome hint of Yahveh and Eve in Gen 4:1 or the euphemistic expressions describing the relations between the angel of Yahveh and the wife of Manoah in Judg 13:2–5.[27] Outside of the HB the concept is present, for example, in the *Epic of Gilgamesh* I.46 and IX:51, where the protagonist is said to be a hybrid, or in the Ugaritic myth *The Gracious and Most Beautiful Gods*, which describes El as begetting Shahar and Shalem with an earthly woman (Bercerra 2008, 51–56). Thirdly, the biblical usage of the *bney ha-'elohim*, however scarce it is, supports the translator's choice. Apart from Gen 6 and an equally troublesome occurrence in Deut 32:8 it is present in Job 1:6; 2:1; 38:7, where it denotes the members of the hypothetical divine court with time identified as angels as is suggested by the LXX rendition of those verses. In addition to this, the HB contains similar phrases like *bney 'Elyon* (Ps 82:6) and *bney 'elim* (Ps 29:1; 89:7) whose textual context suggests that they are to be read as denoting supernatural beings constituting the heavenly court.[28]

The relationship between *gibborim*, *'anshey ha-shem*, *nefilim* and *bney ha-'elohim* is also of interest.[29] As will become apparent, the translator's decision to treat the first two as describing the third one was established in the biblical semantics. First and foremost, the root ג.ב.ר. in general conveys the meaning of "being strong" or "strengthening." In binyan *hitpa'el* it means "to boast" (Isa 42:13; Job 15:25) and this particular aspect is transmitted in the word *gibbor*—"one who magnifies himself, behaves proudly, a tyrant." (BDB 1614) As

---

[27] As one scholar puts it: "the procreative context is the only one which allows for a direct communication between woman and YHWH (or his messenger)." (Havrelock 2007, 156)
[28] Other passages conveying this idea are: Pss 29:1; 82:6; 89:6; Job 1–2; 1Kgs 22:19–22; Isa 6:1–8 (Coxon 1999, 619; Neuer 1966; Parker 1999, 794).
[29] For the review of the possible options, see Kraeling 1947, 196.

such, the word is not seldom used in regards with Yahveh, a prototypical mighty male, waging war for his people.³⁰ Analogically, *gibbor* may be utilized to denote somebody attempting to challenge his deity, as is the case in Job 15:25; 36:9 or Isa 42:13 (TWOT 310). The default meaning however, in terms of statistics with most of the instances present in the so-called historical books, is that of a "strong, valiant man." a brave soldier (BDB 1619; HALOT 1381; TWOT 310). Interestingly enough, the instance of *gibborim* in Gen 6:4b had been given as *gigantes* in the LXX—just like the *nefilim* of verse 4a and against the usual rendition pattern (Gr. *anthropoi* or *dynatoi*), yet in connection with its primeval "boastful" meaning. By resorting to this particular wording, the translators managed to connect the concluding epithets with *nefilim–gigantes*, emphasizing their semi-divine nature and hinting at the haughtiness of these creatures.

The latter idea is additionally supported by the meaning of the *'anshey ha-shem*. Due to the density of the Genesis accounts traditionally interpreted as speaking about the humans' attempt to transgress their limitations, the present phrase is said to be reserved for the ones who rebel against the deity. Especially relevant in this context is the close account of the tower of Babel³¹ whose builders exclaim in Gen 11:4 "let us make ourselves a name" (Heb. *ve-na'aseh lanu shem*).³² As a result, the way the terms *gibborim* and *'anshey ha-shem* are utilized suggests they were taken as conveying the notion of a rebellion directed against the heavens, which neatly fits the analogical motive in case of the Greek giants. Thus the *nefilim* were understood by the translators as the mighty men of antiq-

---

30 E. g. Ps 24:8; 106:8; 145:4; Deut 10:17, Neh 9:32, Isa 10:21, Jer 32:18.
31 As is suggested by later expositions (e. g. Eusebius, *Praeparatio Evangelica* 9.8.12), the purpose of the tower of Babel may have been the refuge from another flood (Toorn and Horst 1990, 16).
32 As such Genesis 6:1–4 fits in the progression of Gen 3:22 and 11:1–8 in which Yahveh is being threatened by humans (Darshan 2014, 146). See also: Isa 63:12; Jer 32:20; Dan 9:16; Neh 9:10; 2Sam 7:9; 1Chr 17:8; 2Sam 8:13. The outside "rebellious" reading of Gen 6 is present in e. g.: Flavius, *Antiquities* 1:3:1; Philo, *On the Giants* 2:258, 1Enoch 6 and Jubilees 5 (Kraeling 1947, 197; Marzel 1981; Neuer 1966). Some more insight into the potentially blasphemous undertones of *'anshey ha-shem* is provided by the Azatiwada inscription: a Phoenician-Hieroglyphic Luwian text dated to the eighth or seventh century BC and discovered in the region of Cilicia. One part of the material (COS 2.31 iii 12-iv.1), interpreted by the scholars as the set of curses reads: "Now if a king among kings or a prince among princes, if a man who is a *man of renown* [my emphasis—W.K.], who shall erase the name of Azatiwada from this gate and shall place (his) name (on it) ... then shall Ba'al Shamem and El, creator of the earth, and Shemesh the eternal, and the whole group of the children of the gods erase that kingdom, and that king, and that man who is a man of renown." (Lawson-Younger 1997, 148–50)

uity, semi-divine figures being the offspring conceived by the representatives of heavens and earth, two separate and distant orders.³³

4 Between Myth and History

The Greek translators dealing with the story of Gen 6:1–4 must have had in mind the connections with the other explicit reference to the *nefilim* in Num 13:33. The background of this verse is a longer narrative in chapters 13–14 that describes the gradual conquest of Canaan. The most immediate context of the *nefilim* is the report brought by the spies sent to make reconnaissance in the land. In verse 28 the local inhabitants, "the children of ʿAnaq," are said to be strong whereas their cities are "great and fortified exceedingly"³⁴ while in verse 31 the spies refuse to confront this tribe, because "it is stronger {than us}."³⁵ Despite the remark concerning the unparalleled size of the fruits collected from the val-

---

33 The myth telling of the gigantic and disobedient creatures inhabiting the antediluvian earth appears in other places of the LXX as well. This is the case with Bar 3:26–28, Wis 14:5–6, 3Macc 2:4 and Sir 16:7. Apart from that, similar ideas appear in the New Testament, in itself being significantly influenced by the form and content of LXX. For instance, Pet 2:4 speaks of the angels who have been disposed to Tartaros while other allusions appear in Luke 10:18; 2Pet 2:4; Jude 1:6. Yet the story of Gen 6 finds its most elaborate and complex reiteration in 1Enoch 6–17. The tradition herein transmitted compromises various conflicting interpretations with a flamboyant and inventive twist of the Promethean aspect. The *bney ha-ʾelohim* are rendered as the "sons of heavens" (6:2) and later on interpreted as the band of angels led by Semjaza. The rebellious and haughty nature of the latter seems in turn to be a play on the motive of the divine riot conveyed in two famous passages of the HB; in Isa 14:12–15 the reader finds the story of the son of dawn (Heb. *helel ben shahar*; Lat. *Lucifer*) expelled from heavens whereas Ezek 28:12–19 speaks of the most distinguished cherub of Yahveh who has fallen in pride. The Enochian angels descend from above and take themselves the earthly women with whom they have the gigantic progeny (7:2–5; 9:9), who in turn are said to be annihilated (10:9), imprisoned along the rebellious angels in the "valleys of earth" (11:12–13) or turned into ever-malicious "spirits of earth" (15:9) (Coxon 1999, 619; Mussies 1999, 343–44). For the review of monotheistic interpretations of Gen 6 in the broader framework of the myth of the fallen angels see the paper of Jung (1925). Although the paper is definitely aged, plentiful important source references are provided.
34 See the biblical description of the cities like Hebron, Gath or Ashdod. Interestingly enough, Rashi ad. 13:18 cites Midrash Tanhuma 6 which claims that living in an open city is a sign of strength whereas inhabiting a fortress betrays weakness (Maclaurin 1965, 468–70).
35 The word ממנו can be read either as *mimmenu* or *mimmeno*—"from us" and "from him" respectively. This fact has given rise to the series of expositions (e.g. Rashi ad. loc.; BT Sotah 35a) explaining the spies' conviction that the inhabitants of the land are stronger than Yahveh himself (Leibowitz 1986, 139–40).

ley of Eshkol (verses 23–24, 27),[36] the Anaqites themselves are presented as valiant men, posing real, yet mundane danger to the invading Hebrews.[37]

Up to this moment the narrative seems to remain more or less within the rhetoric of the historical portions of the HB and only verses 32–33 bring in some perplexing statements. Verse 32 reads: "the earth we have passed through in order to spy it, is the land that devours its inhabitants, whereas the whole nation we have seen {over there}[38] are {men large in size}."[39] First and foremost, the idea of "devouring land" in the HB is scarce. The only other instance appears in Ezek 36:13–14 with the land of Israel being the addressee of the invocation. Somewhat more widespread is the parallel expression of earth that swallows (Heb. *livloʻ*) which is present in Exod 15:12, Num 16:32 (cf. 26:10) and Ps 106:17.[40] Second, to assess the meaning of the phrase is difficult also due to the relatively broad semantic range of the Hebrew word *'eretz* usually translated as the "land." The word appears approximately two and a half thousand times in the HB, and apart from the literal meaning it is sometimes taken to denote the inhabitants of the area by means of metonymy (1Kgs 2:2; 10:24; Ps 33:8), to be a personification (Deut 32:1; Jer 6:19; 22:9) or—analogically to the instances in other Semitic languages—to refer to the underworld (Job 10:21–22; BDB 864; HALOT 809; TWOT 167). In other words, it is far from obvious which of the senses had been initially intended. In result, there have been numerous attempts at interpreting the meaning of the reference to the land engrossing its dwellers: attributing the Canaanites with cannibalism, acknowledging the infertility and general insecurity of the region or, explaining that the challenges offered by the land resulted in the survival of the fittest (Allen 2002–2004; Kugel 1997,

---

36 The Greek translators have rendered the grapes (Heb. *'eshkol*) as *gigastou*—it is questionable whether the paronomasia with *gigantes* had been intended.
37 The very term used to denote the inhabitants of Canaan is interesting. First, the word *'anaq* in some places like Cant 4:9 or Prov 1:9 denotes "necklace" or "pendant" analogically to the Aramaic *'unqa'* or *'inqa.'* This meaning however seems to be derived from the more basic one, namely "neck" with time and by means of metonymy attributed to the jewelry worn thereon. See also the connection drawn by Ps 73:6 associating neck with pride (Even-Shoshan 1979, 1960–1961). Second, in this context it is interesting to ask, whether the Enochian (1Enoch 6–11 and 3Enoch 5) tradition of the fallen angels bringing down constellations and heavenly bodies was a variation of the heavenly jewelry motive (Reed 2001, 115–17; BDB 7266; HALOT 6438). Third, there is one more factor that may have contributed to the LXX interpretation of the Anaqites as giants and it is the homoiophony of the Hebrew *'anaq* and the Greek *anakh* denoting the authoritative ruler.
38 Heb. *betokhah*, literally "inside her." See the further part of the paper for the analogies with the underworld.
39 Heb. *'anshey middot*, literally "men of measures."
40 See also the distant image in Rev 12:16.

791; Leibowitz 1986, 141). All of these options, however, seem far from likely, given the remark about the size of the fruits brought forth by the spies, witnessing the favorable vegetation conditions.[41] Moreover, due to the close proximity of the story of Korah and his band being consumed by the mouth of earth in Num 16, we may assume that the statement in verse 32 can be read literally as intended at evoking the associations between Canaan and the underworld.[42]

Second, the acknowledgement of the size of the Anaqites finds its explication in verse 33: "and we saw there the *nefilim*; the sons of *ʿAnaq* are from the *nefilim*;[43] in our eyes we were like locust[44] and {like a gnat} we were in their eyes." Not only is the enormous size of the Anaqites acknowledged, but the direct connection with the *nefilim* is also drawn. In other words, the overgrown inhabitants of Canaan are portrayed as hailing from some semi-divine figures of the ancient, antediluvian times.[45] Of course, the context of this statement being in verse 32 explicitly termed as "rumor" (Heb. *dibbah*, HALOT 1705) wants us to believe that the reference to the *nefilim* might be similar to that of

---

41 The contradiction had been spotted already by the early expositors. Modern scholarship explains that two descriptions of Canaan in verses 25–30 and 31–33 contain distinct traditions with the latter being the more "mythical" one (Allen 2002–2004).
42 An interesting remark appears in Rashi's commentary to verse 32, who explains: "in every place we have passed through, we have found them burying the dead" (Cf. BT Sotah 35a) thus stressing the thanatological undertones of the verse.
43 Worth noting is the difference in the Greek rendering of Num 13:33. LXX reads: "And there we saw the giants, and we were before them as locusts." (tr. Brenton L.C.L.) Clearly, the gloss present in the Masoretic text is missing here and LXX conveys *lectio difficilior*. This may mean that the identification (*bney ʿAnaq min ha-nefilim*) has been introduced on the later stage only. Interestingly, the closest retelling of the story in Deut 1:28 makes no remark of *nefilim* whatsoever and neither does Amos 2:9–10 mention anything apart from acknowledging the excessive size of the Amorites (Goff 2010, 651).
44 Heb. *hagav* appears only five times and most probably denotes a non-flying species like a grasshopper. Its meaning is definitely ambivalent: although it is very small, the sheer number seems to pose a significant danger. Worth noting is that it appears as an agent of Yahveh's wrath in Exod 10, Isa 40:22 and 2Chr 7:13 (BDB 2813; TWOT 601; HALOT 2347; Lerner 1999, 548).
45 The question of how the *nefilim* managed to survive the flood and settle in Canaan has ignited the exegetes' imagination. It is said for example, that they had endured the cataclysm due to their height which allowed them to keep their heads over the surface of waters. The other variant explains that they had found refuge in the tower which was high enough to ensure security (Kugel 1997, 197; Stuckenbruck 2000, 356). In the context of Greek parallels it is worth referring to the myth of the Trojan War which somewhat resembles the ancient Near Eastern flood accounts. According to Hesiod's *Catalogue of Women* 204 M-W, Zeus devised to destroy humanity along the demigods in order to restore the initial order based on the basic division between humans and the divine (Hendel 1987, 18–19). The problem of the parallels between the demigods of *Catalogue* and the *nefilim* of Gen 6:1–4 is thoroughly addressed by Darshan 2014.

the "bogeymen and hobgoblins." (Allen 2002–2004) On the other hand however, the choice of the wording is significant: the Anaqites are designated with the same term that appears in Gen 6:4. Whereas some try to repel any connection between these two instances, insisting on the different nature of both *nefilim* (Marzel 1981), what ultimately counts is exactly this semantic ambiguity, which resembles that of the *gigantes*. As is apparent in the Greek sources, the giant features had also been attributed to the autochthonic people inhabiting the rural fringes of the Hellenistic world. No wonder then that the translators decided to transmit the *nefilim* of verse 33a as *gigantas*.[46]

Simply put, these *nefilim–gigantes* have been in a way historicized and placed in the heroic period of the pre-settlement Canaan (Coxon 1999, 618; Kraeling 1947, 195), which in turn was utilized by the Greek translator. The question remains however, what might have been the initial purpose of "incorporating" these figures in the rows of the hostile Canaanite army. One of the most widespread hypotheses tries to answer this question by resorting to the idea of etiology. The region of Canaan had been filled by huge stone monuments like dolmens, cairns or menhirs, as well as by the abandoned cities of stunning sizes, whose presence needed to be somehow explained. Thus, it was the astonishment of the wandering tribes who strived to elucidate the existence of the encountered artifacts by resorting to the idea of giant humanoid engineers responsible for building these facilities (Graves and Patai 1966, 106; Krauss 1947, 135–36, 139; Vidal 2007, 31, 37–39). This explanation, however compelling, does not deplete the hermeneutic possibilities. First of all, the giants are presented as factual and real creatures rather than some legendary primeval inhabitants. Moreover, notwithstanding the undeniable connections between the giants and chaos, the former are placed in the cities, *ex definitio* being the domain of the gods and the symbols of the cosmic order. From this perspective, the wandering Hebrews of the conquest narrative were the mythical chaos incorporated—a wild, untamed force coming from the desert and wreaking havoc in the Canaanite settlements. Obviously, such association was to be avoided so as to sustain the desired positive image of the Hebrews. The technological supremacy of the city dwellers could not be denied so the biblical writers may have resorted to the attribution of the chaotic qualities symbolized by the huge size to the inhabitants of Canaan and thus to portray the raiding Hebrews as the bringers of peace and order in the

---

[46] One of the later Rabbinic interpretations (Gen R. 26:7; 31:12; Pirqey de-rabbi Eliezer 34) retains the tendency similar to that of the LXX and puts the *nefilim* along all the encountered Canaanite tribes in one category.

domain of turmoil.⁴⁷ By utilizing this semantic castling, the confrontation between the people of Yahveh and the others clearly resembled the well-grounded motif of the so called *chaoskampf* in which a young and ambitious deity defeats a primeval chaotic monster and establishes the cosmic order. This is also analogous to the popular mythical motive of a hero descending to the underworld with the purpose of confronting the evil adversary residing therein. And just as the hostile creature offered the god or the protagonist an opportunity to earn his name so did the giants do to the Hebrews (Sonik 2013, 19). Consequently, in order to establish the *nomos* in the land, all the gigantic presence needed to be eradicated—and this in fact is one of the leading motifs of the conquest narrative in the HB.⁴⁸

5 Between the Dead and the Mighty

This complex of the chaotic and underworldly references, giant figures and the distinguished use of *nofelim* brings us to the last piece of the *nefilim–gigantes* puzzle, contained in Ezekiel's proclamation against Egypt (32:17–32). Even a quick glance at the structure and vocabulary of the passage allows us to discern several important facets. First, the land of the living (Heb. *'eretz haym*) is juxtaposed with the land below (Heb. *'eretz tahtiyot*) with the latter often interpreted as the deeper and distinguished level of Sheol. As such it clearly resembles the Greek Tartaros, a special quarters of the kingdom of Hades being the prison for the rebellious giants and titans. Second, this association is all the more valid as the *'eretz tahtiyot* is said to be inhabited by those "uncircumcised" (Heb. *'arelim*, 9 times), "pierced" (by the sword) (Heb. *halalim* or *haleley herev*, 15 times), "mighty" (Heb. *gibborim*, 2 times)⁴⁹ and "fallen" (Heb. *nofelim*, 4 times).⁵⁰ The presence and juxtaposition of the latter two terms, also in their Greek equivalents in the LXX, is significant as it evokes the associations with both Gen 6

---

47 As one scholar puts it, "all that is overgrown or physically monstrous represents a connection to the primeval chaos that stands as a barrier to creation and right rule." (Doak 2011, iii)
48 See for instance: Josh 11:21–22; 12:4–6; 13:12; 15:14; Judg 1:20; 2Sam 21:18–22 Chronicles 20:4–8. An interesting remark is also provided by Routledge. The said author argues that the inhabitants of Palestine (including the Hebrews) shared a "common history of movement, conquest and possession of their current territory": Ammon, Moab, Edom and Philistines captured Canaan in the same manner, by combating the autochthonic giants (Routledge 2004, 43–44).
49 Plus two instances of the word *gevurah*, "mightiness."
50 Interestingly enough, the LXX renders the *nofelim* literally as *peptokotes* whereas the Aramaic translation utilizes the word *qatil*, "murdered."

and Num 13. Third, all the instances of *nofelim* appear in a dense cluster in verses 22–27. Of particular significance is verse 27, containing, in this context, a unique word: *me'arelim* usually translated as "uncircumcised" and probably a scribal error.[51] This is corroborated by the LXX which renders the phrase as *apo aionos* meaning "of old" (Heb. *me'olam*)—the same wording that appears in the translation of Gen 6:4, suggesting the prehistoric era. In sum, the pericope draws a picture of the mighty ones of ancient times who were destroyed and fell into the underworld, where they inhabited special quarters. Even if to acknowledge the possibility of merging different traditions in the redactorial process, the final image, i.e. the one faced by the Greek translator, fits neatly the pattern supported by the presentation of the *nefilim* in Gen 6:4 and their identification with the *bney 'Anaq* in the land of Canaan in Num 13:32–33 (Doak 2013, 619–20; Marzel 1981).[52]

This particular "underworldly" case of the *nofelim–gigantes* needs to be understood in a broader scope—in relationship to the process of reading the giants into the biblical narratives by the Greek translators. There are over thirty-five instances of the word *gigas* in its various forms in the LXX counterparts of the HB, of which only two were used to translate the *nefilim*, with the rest divided more or less equally between the *gibbor(im)* and the *refa'(im)*.[53] The latter appears approximately thirty times in the HB and in most cases denotes one of the tribes encountered by the Hebrews during the conquest of Canaan. Just a couple of times it refers to the deceased inhabitants of the underworld.[54] At first glance these two groups could not be farther from each other, as nothing should connect the mighty autochthones, "men of measures," and the pale shades of the

---

51 The later rabbinic tradition connects the uncircumcised with Sheol and Gehennah on the basis of the apotropaic function of *brit milah*. See for instance Exod R. 19:4 or Tanhuma Tzav 14. I have scrutinized this problem elsewhere (Kosior 2013).
52 The connection with the latter is also supported by the associations between valleys and the idea of the underworld. This aspect is all the more significant given the ambivalent or even simply negative vibe of the depressions of the land in the HB. Some of them being the riverbeds (*nehalim*), would periodically become flooded with water and mud whereas the others, like the valley (*gaya'*) of the sons of Hinnom, served the purpose of a waste dump. See: Job 11:8; 12:22; Prov 9: 18; Josh 15:8; 18:6; 2Sam 5:18.22; Isa 17:5; Joel 4:2.12 (Pardee and Xella 1999, 605). These facets may have contributed to the semantic potential of valley on the mythical plane as the abode of the dead and otherwise expelled or as the domain of the chaotic watery monster.
53 All the calculations performed by means of the search module of the BibleWorks 8.0.
54 The notion of ambivalence is present in the very idea of Canaan. Whereas the promises given in Egypt speak of it as "the land of the patriarchs," the Hebrews themselves approach it as "the land of the others." The country is by all means *unheimlich* and so are the giants, "the distorted image of the patriarchs" and "the ghosts of the forefathers." (Pardes 2002, 101, 113–14)

dead. In fact, the LXX tries to solve this confusion by resorting to different, more specific terms relying on the textual context (Rouillard-Bonraisin 1999, 695). Thus for instance, when *refa'im* seem to refer to the particular group of the Canaanites, eight times a simple transliteration is involved and the word *Rafaim* or *Rafain* applied. This is the case for example in the Deuteronomic retelling of the conquest (Deut 2–3) and mentioning the giant king Og as the last of the *refa'im* (Kosman 2002, 5, 7–8). With regards to this tribe, however far more widespread and slightly exceeding in numbers (nine times), is the translation by means of the word *gigantes*. This option dominates in rendering the instances of *refa'im* in Josh and 1Sam. In addition, the word is translated twice as *titanes* in 2Sam 5. Finally, the LXX had to deal with those *refa'im* said to inhabit the underworld and in this sphere the most significant departure in meaning occurred as the word had been translated as *iatroi*, "physicians" (Ps 88:11; Isa 26:14) or *asebis*, "ungodly." (Isa 26:19) In this regard it is also interesting that twice (Prov 2:18; 9:18) does the LXX apply the word *gygenei*, "earthborn," thus closely tying the dead with the earth (Goff 2009, 146).

Notwithstanding the scarcity of appearance, the *refa'im*–shades introduces two interesting nuances to the question of giants. First, the word *refa'im* is the derivate of the root ר.פ.א., conveying the meaning of healing. However, some scholars go further and point at its ambiguous semantic potential, as this root is etymologically akin to ר.פ.ה., in its various grammatical forms meaning "being weak" and "powerless." It could be therefore said that the deceased have embraced the experience of death and accordingly are capable of healing (BDB 9242; HALOT 8014; TWOT 2198d). The *refa'im* would then be the departed heroes comprising the roles of the wounded healers.[55] Second, the Ugaritic literature provides some parallel instances. The word *rpum*, believed to be the semantic equivalent of the Heb. *refa'im*, appears for example in KTU 1.6 vi:45–46 in parallelism to *'ilnym* (Ug. "gods"), both of which are said to be submitted to the sun goddess. Even more significant is the so called "rephaim-text" in KTU 1:20–22 which clearly portrays *rpum* as the dead and deified royal ancestors (Lewis 1999, 223–31; Rouillard-Bonraisin 1999, 692). Such understanding is probably present also in Isa 26:14 or Ps 88:11 where *refa'im* are the dead consulted for knowledge.[56] In sum then, the Greek translators faced the word *refa'im* with its nuanced meaning comprising the hostile autochthonous tribe, men of large posture and the deceased heroic ancestors dwelling in the underworld.

---

[55] Against this assumption however is the fact that the only instance in the HB which connects the root ר.פ.א. to the idea of healing is Jer 8:22 (Hays 2009, 396).
[56] Cf. the ironic usage in Job 13:4 as the polemics against the power of the dead (Hays 2009, 394, 398).

All those elements seem to fit the description of the giants and the word *gigas* seemed a compatible term to denote the long-dead gigantic inhabitants of the land. This in turn provided the semantic background for the analogical rendering of *nefilim*.

6 Between the Revealed and the Concealed

In sum then, the Greek *gigantes* and the Hebrew *nefilim* as perceived by the translators shared several traits. First and foremost, both were liminal figures resulting from the union of the opposite orders and as such retained the unclear status between the human and divine. Similarly, dim was their moral designation and the sources witnessed to both awe and fascination with which these figures must have been looked upon. Secondly, both were presented as impersonating chaotic qualities and posing some serious danger to gods and humans. They appeared either in the prehistoric or early historical context, but in both cases they preceded the ordering of the cosmos. Lastly, both *gigantes* and *nefilim* were clearly connected with the underworld and were said to have originated from earth and as well end up closed therein. Obviously then, the Greek translators have chosen the term which was meaningful for their Hellenistic audience. However, was it the best solution?

Given the limitations of every translation, especially one aiming at bridging two distant cultures, it is crucial to acknowledge the ambivalent nature of this process. Undoubtedly, the translators strive to find the most appropriate term that evokes a similar set of associations without the need of any additional explanation. At the same time however, the particular decision reducing the semantic uncertainty blurs the other interpretative options. From the perspective of the anonymous translators, both *nefilim* and *gigantes* shared some traits like hybrid nature and enormous size. These however did not by any means exhaust the pool of qualities and by resorting to *gigantes*, the translators had to resign from what they perceived as the less important facets of the *nefilim*. In other words, whatever had been the initial interpretation of the mysterious *nefilim* in these passages, it was in a way overwritten and thus substituted by what came in the form of the Greek *gigantes*. Should the translators utilize the Greek literal equivalent of *peptokotes*, as they did in case of Ezek 32:22–27, or simply transcribe the word, as for example they did with the mysterious *serafin* in Isa 6,[57] they would have sustained the ambiguity and an invitation to specu-

---

[57] Interestingly enough however, the very same word appearing in other places of proto-Isaiah

late about the nature of the *nefilim*. Yet, they decided to resort to a far more familiar idea of the giants, even at the cost of forfeiting the antique meaning of the word in question. This particular example clearly shows the dual nature of translation: it simultaneously sharpens and blurs, adds and removes, reveals and conceals.

Bibliography

Aejmelaeus, Anneli. 2007. *On the Trail of the Septuagint Translators: Collected Essays.* Leuven: Peeters.

Allen, Ronald B. 2002–2004. *Numbers.* The Expositor's Bible Commentary. (CD-ROM). Grand Rapids: Zondervan.

Barrera, Julio T. 1998. *The Jewish Bible and the Christian Bible: An Introduction to the History of the Bible.* Leiden: Brill.

Bercerra, Daniel. 2008. "El and the Birth of the Gracious Gods." *Studia Antiqua* 6, no. 1: 51–56.

Bettelheim, Bruno. 2010. *The Uses of Enchantment: The Meaning and Importance of Fairy Tales.* New York: Vintage Books.

Brown, Francis, S. R. Driver, and Charles A. Briggs. 1906. *A Hebrew and English Lexicon of the Old Testament.* (CD-ROM). [BDB]. Oxford: Clarendon Press.

Budd, Philip J. 1991. *Numbers.* Word Biblical Commentary. (CD-ROM). Waco: Word Books.

Clines, David J. A. 2012. "The Failure of the Flood." In *Making a Difference: Essays on the Hebrew Bible and Judaism in Honor of Tamara Cohn Eskenazi*, edited by David J. Clines et al., 74–84. Sheffield: Sheffield Phoenix Press.

Cassuto, Moshe D. 1979. "Ma'aseh Bney ha-ʾElohim u-Banot ha-ʾAdam." In *Sifrut Miqraʾit ve-Sifrut Qanʿanit*, edited by Moshe Cassuto. Jerusalem: Magnes Press. http://lib.cet.ac.il/pages/item.asp?item=11748 (accessed September 26, 2017).

Coxon, Peter W. 1999. "Nephilim." In *Dictionary of Deities and Demons in the Bible*, edited by Karel van der Toorn, Bob Becking, and Pieter W. van der Horst, 343–346. Leiden and Boston: Brill [DDD].

Darshan, Guy. 2014. "Sipur Bney ha-ʾElohim u-Banot ha-ʾAdam (Bereshit 6:1–4) le-ʾOr Qatalog ha-Nashim ha-Hesyodi." *Shnaton* 23: 141–164.

Delcourt, Marie, and Robert L. Rankin. 1965. "The Last Giants." *History of Religions* 4, no. 2: 209–242.

Doak, Brian R. 2011. *The Last of the Rephaim: Conquest and Cataclysm in the Heroic Ages of Ancient Israel.* Massachusetts: University of Massachusetts Press.

Doak, Brian R. 2013. "Ezekiel's Topography of the (Un-)Heroic Dead in Ezekiel 32:17–32." *Journal of Biblical Literature* 132, no. 3: 607–624.

Even-Shoshan, Avraham. 1979. *Ha-Milon he-Hadash.* Jerusalem: Kiryat Sefer.

(14:29; 30:6) is rendered as *ofeis petomenoi* and *aspidon petomenon* respectively thus corroborating the preferred serpentine interpretation.

Frevel, Christian, and Benedikt Conczorowski. 2011. "Deepening the Water: First Steps to a Diachronic Approach on Intermarriage in the Hebrew Bible." In *Mixed Marriages: Intermarriage and Group Identity in the Second Temple Period*, edited by Christian Frevel, 15–45. New York: Bloomsbury T & T Clark.

Goff, Matthew J. 2009. "Subterranean Giants and Septuagint Proverbs: The 'Earth-born' of LXX Proverbs." In *With Wisdom as a Robe: Qumran and other Jewish Studies in Honour of Ida Fröhlich*, edited by Károly Dobos and Ida Fröhlich, 146–156. Sheffield: Sheffield Phoenix Press.

Goff, Matthew J. 2010. "Ben Sira and the Giants of the Land: A Note on Ben Sira 16:7." *Journal of Biblical Literature* 129, no. 4: 645–655.

Goldberg, Oskar. 2012. *Rzeczywistość Hebrajczyków*. Kraków: Nomos.

Graves, Robert, and Raphael Patai. 1966. *Hebrew Myths: The Book of Genesis*. London: Cassell.

Harper, William R. 1894. "The Sons of God and the Daughters of Men: Genesis VI." *The Biblical World* 3, no. 6: 440–448.

Harris, R. Laird, Gleason L. Archer, and Bruce K. Waltke. 2003. *Theological Wordbook of the Old Testament*. (CD-ROM). Chicago: Moody Press [TWOT].

Havrelock, Rachel. 2007. "The Myth of Birthing a Hero: Heroic Barrenness in the Hebrew Bible." *Biblical Interpretation* 16: 154–178.

Hays, Christopher. 2009. "What Sort of Friends? A New Proposal Regarding (רפא(ים and טפלי (ט) in Job 13,4." *Biblical* 90, Fasc. 3: 394–399.

Hendel, Ron S. 1987. "Of Demigods and the Deluge: Toward an Interpretation of Genesis 6:1–4." *Journal of Biblical Literature* 106, no. 1: 13–26.

Hendel, Ron S. 2004. "The Nephilim Were on Earth: Genesis 6:1–4 and its Ancient Near Eastern Context." In *The Fall of Angels*, edited by Christoph Auffarth and Loren T. Stuckenbruck, 11–34. Leiden and Boston: Brill.

Jastrow, Marcus. 1903. *Dictionary of Targumim, Talmud and Midrashic Literature*. New York: Judaica Treasury.

Jung, Leo. 1925. "Fallen Angels in Jewish, Christian and Mohammedan Literature: A Study in Comparative Folk-Lore." *The Jewish Quarterly Review* 15, no. 4: 467–502.

Klein, Ernest. 1987. *A Comprehensive Etymological Dictionary of the English Language for Readers of English*. Jerusalem: Carta.

Kohler, Ludwig, and Walter Baumgartner. 2002. *The Hebrew and Aramaic Lexicon of the Old Testament*. (CD-ROM). Leiden: Brill [HALOT].

Kosman, Admiel. 2002. "The Story of a Giant Story: The Winding Way of Og King of Bashan in the Jewish Haggadic Tradition." *Hebrew Union College Annual* 73: 157–190.

Kosior, Wojciech. 2013. "Brit milah: Some Remarks on the Apotropaic Meaning of Circumcision in Agadic Midrashes." *The Polish Journal of the Arts and Culture* 4, no. 1: 103–118.

Kraeling, Emil G. 1947. "The Significance and Origin of Gen. 6:1–4." *Journal of Near Eastern Studies* 6, no. 4: 193–208.

Krauss S. 1947. "Jewish Giants in the Gentile Folklore." *The Jewish Quarterly Review* 38, no. 2: 135–149.

Krawczyk, Mikołaj. 2007. "Golem—an Analysis of the Roots of the Modern Jewish Legend." *Studia Religiologica* 40: 119–133.

Kugel, James. 1997. *Traditions of the Bible: A Guide to the Bible As It Was at the Start of the Common Era*. Cambridge, MA and London: Harvard University Press.

Lange, Nicholas de. 1996. "The Revival of the Hebrew Language in the Third Century CE." *Jewish Studies Quarterly* 3, no. 4: 342–358.

Lawson-Younger, K. 2003. "The Azatiwada Inscription." In *The Context of Scripture*, edited by William W. Hallo, 148–150. Leiden and Boston: Brill.

Leibowitz, Nehama. 1986. *Studies in Bamidbar: In the Context of Ancient and Modern Jewish Bible Commentary*. Jerusalem: World Zionist Organization.

Leibowitz, Nehama. 1986. *Studies in Bereshit: In the Context of Ancient and Modern Jewish Bible Commentary*. Jerusalem: World Zionist Organization.

Lerner, Berel D. 1999. "Timid Grasshoppers and Fierce Locusts: An Ironic Pair of Biblical Metaphors." *Vetus Testamentum* 49, Fasc. 4: 545–548.

Lewis, Theodore J. 1999. "Dead." In DDD, 223–231.

Luzbetak, Louis J. 1990. "Contextual Translation: The Role of Cultural Anthropology." In *Bible Translation and the Spread of the Church: The Last 200 Years*, edited by Philip C. Stine, 108–119. Leiden: Brill.

MacLaurin, E.C.B. 1965. "Anak/'ανξ." *Vetus Testamentum* 15, Fasc. 4: 468–474.

Marzel, Yitzhaq. 1981. "Bney ha-'Elohim u-Banot ha-Adam, Hitpathut u-Kelayah." *Gilayon* 4. http://lib.cet.ac.il/pages/item.asp?item=8794 (accessed September 26, 2017).

Mussies, Gerard. 1999. "Giants." In DDD, 618–620.

Neuer, Menachem. 1966. "Ha-Nefilim Hayu ba-'Aretz (Bere[shit] 6,1–4)." *Gilayon* 3 (27). http://lib.cet.ac.il/pages/item.asp?item=7891 (accessed September 26, 2017).

Nida, Eugene A. 1964. *Toward a Science of Translating: With Special Reference to Principles and Procedures Involved in Bible Translating*. Leiden: Brill.

Nida, Eugene A., and Charles R. Taber. 2003. *The Theory and Practice of Translation*. Leiden: Brill.

Pardee, Dennis, and Paolo Xella. 1999. "Mountains and Valleys." In DDD, 604–605.

Pardes, Ilana. 2002. *The Biography of Ancient Israel: National Narratives in the Bible*. London: University of California Press.

Parker, Simon B. 1999. "Sons of (the) Gods." In DDD, 794–800.

Reed, Annette Y. 2001. "From Asael and Šemihazah to Uzzah, Azzah, and Azael: 3 Enoch 5 (§§ 7–8) and Jewish Reception-History of 1 Enoch." *Jewish Studies Quarterly* 8, no. 2: 105–136.

Rouillard-Bonraisin, Hedwige. 1999. "Rephaim." In DDD, 692–700.

Shinan Avigdor, and Yair Zakovitch. 2012. *From Gods to God: How the Bible Debunked, Suppressed, or Changed Ancient Myths and Legends*. Nebraska: Nebraska University Press.

Sonik, Karen. 2013. "From Hesiod's Abyss to Ovid's *rudis indigestaque moles:* Chaos and Cosmos in the Babylonian 'Epic of Creation'." In *Creation and Chaos: A Reconsideration of Hermann Gunkel's Chaoskampf Hypothesis*, edited by Jo Ann Scurlock and Richard H. Beal, 1–25. Winona Lake: Eisenbrauns.

Stuckenbruck, Loren T. 2000. "The 'Angels' and 'Giants' of Genesis 6:1–4 in Second and Third Century BCE Jewish Interpretation: Reflections on the Posture of Early Apocalyptic Traditions." *Dead Sea Discoveries* 7, no. 3: 354–377.

Tomasino, Anthony J. 1992. "History Repeats Itself: The 'Fall' and Noah's Drunkenness." *Vetus Testamentum* 42, Fasc. 1: 128–130.

Toorn, Karel van der, and Pieter W. van der Horst. 1990. "Nimrod before and after the Bible." *The Harvard Theological Review* 83, no. 1: 1–29.
Uehlinger, Christoph. 1999. "Nimrod." In DDD, 627–630.
Vidal, Jordi. 2007. "Tierra de Gigantes: La 'Protohistoria' de Transjordania Según la Tradición Cananea." *Habis* 38: 31–40.
Wenham, Gordon J. 1998. *Genesis*. Word Biblical Commentary. (CD-ROM). Waco: Word Books.
Wright, Benjamin G. III. 2010. "The Textual-Linguistic Character and Sociocultural Context of the Septuagint." In *Translation is Required: The Septuagint in Retrospect and Prospect*, edited by Robert J. V. Hiebert, 235–240. Atlanta: Society of Biblical Literature.

Orr Scharf
Whose Bible is it Anyway? The Buber-Rosenzweig Translation as a Bible for Christian Readers

For Jews, the translation of the Hebrew Bible has always been an internal affair. Ever since the emergence of its first translation in the second century BCE—the Greek Septuagint—translations of Tanakh have been produced in the local languages of exiled communities whose members could no longer read and understand holy writ in the Hebrew original.[1] In fact, this state of affairs is evident within the Biblical text itself. The Books of Daniel, Ezra and Nehemiah contain long passages in Aramaic, while the Book of Nehemiah lists the names of those who "caused the people [the returned exiles from Babylon gathered near the Temple's Water Gate in Jerusalem] to understand (*mevinim*) the Torah as the people stood in their places; and they read in the book of God's teachings interpreted (*meforash*) and they put their minds to it and they understood the Scriptures read." (Neh 8:7–8; see also verses 2, 9)[2] Rabbinic Judaism incorporated the reading of scripture in translation within the religious praxis as well: the weekly portion of the Torah is read at synagogues in Hebrew, yet the halachic prescription famously stipulates that "One shall always partake of public readings of [Torah] portions [by reading] the Holy Scripture twice and translation once [*shnayim miqra ve-ehad targum*]."[3]

The privileging of Targum—canonized Aramaic translation of the Torah attributed to Onkelos—was reiterated with the invention of print. The layout of

---

[1] Contemporary scholars tend to agree with Zecharia Frenkel's claim that that the prevalence and dominance of Aramaic Bible translations also exerted influence on the Septuagint's Greek (Joosten 2016, 149).
[2] The classic commentaries infer from different parts of the verses that the public reading by Levites was done in translation. According to Rashi "*hemavinim*" means "they translated [*metargemin*] words of Torah to the people," while Gersonides understands the very act of reading ("and they read in the book of God's teachings") to mean that, "The Levites read the words interpreted [*davar meforash*] in the book of God's teachings because they translated for them [the people], and not only did they translate it into readily understandable language [*be-lashon muvan*], they also put their minds and wisdom to the words in translation."
[3] BT Berachot, 8a. Nevertheless, the translation (*targum*) in question is into Aramaic, which enjoys a similar status of sanctity to Hebrew. BT Megillah 9a–9b discloses the sages' concerns regarding the translation of ritual scrolls on phylacteries and doorposts (*mezuzot*) into other languages, which are assuaged in relation to the translation of the Torah into Greek.

https://doi.org/10.1515/9783110550788-003

print editions of the *Miqra'ot Gedolot* (the standard Bible edition with the masoretic text and commentaries) from the very first edition until today (Venice 1525),[4] affixes the Targum in a small rubric next to the Hebrew of the masora, and places the classic commentaries underneath them both.

In Islam, early tradition granted primacy to the Arabic original; and while translations of the Koran proliferate, their authoritativeness continues to require justification over and against the *Urtext* (Pearson 1986, 429).[5] In Christianity, however, the opposite is true: the canonical version of the Holy Bible in the Catholic Church is Jerome's Latin translation, the Vulgate, rather than the Hebrew and Greek originals of the Old and New Testaments. One of the revolutionary contributions of the age of the Reformation was the introduction of vernacular Bible translations that replaced the inscrutable Latin and assumed its authority.[6]

The advent of Jewish emancipation and assimilation in the modern era only enhanced the need for Jewish vernacular translations of Tanakh offered to a Jewish readership. The age of Reformation had brought on an onrush of Christian Bible translations (the King James and Luther translations being seminal examples), which facilitated the access of emancipated Jews to their scriptures through the prism of Christian theology. Moses Mendelssohn's translation of the Pentateuch (called alternately *Sefer Netivot Hashalom* and the *Bi'ur*) was an important milestone in the evolution of modern Jewish Bible translations. The famed thinker's decision to render the Five Books of Moses (as well as Psalms in a separate volume) into modern German transliterated in Hebrew script was an attempt to reach out to a new type of Jewish readership—one whose language of worship was neither Hebrew nor a Jewish language (such as Yiddish, Aramaic or Judeo-Arabic)—but who remained within the fold of tra-

---

[4] The earliest Bible editions produced by Jewish printers in the Iberian Peninsula and Italy in the fifteenth and early sixteenth century were made strictly for a Jewish readership. The inclusion of Targum and commentaries in the Pentateuch edition of Jacob Ben Hayim Ibn Adoniya (Venice, 1525), *Miqra'ot Gedolot*, was a revolutionary innovation that became the golden standard of Jewish Pentateuch editions since (Goshen-Gottstein 1972).

[5] The Editor-in-chief of the first Muslim translation of the Koran into Hebrew describes the endeavor as no less than a personal risk: "We, at the 'Bayinat' Center, responsible for this translation, are aware that we are supposedly serving as mediators between Allah, may His name be exalted, and the Jewish reader, a highly sensitive and tremendously important task, because thanks to our faith we believe that we will indeed be asked by Allah, may His name be exalted, about this translation, and that we may be punished, if we lie in it [the translation] about Allah, by distorting the meaning of His words, or by neglecting to carry out the work to the best of our abilities." (Omar al Eis 2015, 7)

[6] For the rise of the vernacular Bible in the enlightenment see Sheehan 2007. For a comprehensive and convincing account of the emergence of the King James Bible see Hill 1994.

dition.⁷ This meant, among other things, retaining the conventional layout of Jewish editions of the Pentateuch (Hebrew verses in large font accompanied by a translation in the adjacent column)—occupying approximately one third of the page—with commentary underneath occupying the remaining two thirds of the page.

Raphael Samson Hirsch's best-selling German edition of the Pentateuch was similar in concept to Mendelssohn's (Hirsch 1899). The setting of the translation in Gothic script detracted little from the edition's traditional identity. To be sure, other Jewish translations of the Bible were set in layouts closer to the Christian counterparts, but they gestured towards the Jewish tradition by retaining Hebrew in the titles of the books of the Bible (Zunz 1935; Philippson 1858).

The Hebrew Bible translation of Martin Buber (1878–1965) and Franz Rosenzweig (1886–1929) defied the design conventions of its predecessors (Buber and F. Rosenzweig 1926a–j1930).⁸ Its small format, exclusive emphasis on the biblical text (the title pages do not include a year of publication, let alone any accompanying comments), and most conspicuously, its disregard towards the standard division into chapters and verses (shared by Jewish and Christian Bibles alike), signified its authors' highly unorthodox approach to the Bible.⁹ One of its most salient visual features is the absence of Hebrew or any other graphic link to the Jewish tradition of Bible publishing. The putatively "neutral" presentation therefore makes a clear attempt to offer the readers a Bible "with no strings attached," that is, a translation bereft of an overt denominational affiliation. That such an aspiration is a sheer impossibility was all the more true at the time of publication of the B-R translation, at the height of the Weimar Repub-

---

7 In his introduction to the translation, Mendelssohn describes the reasons for undertaking the project: "the sons of the Children of Israel who possess the mind to understand words of wisdom seek out God's word in the translations of Christian sages, because the Christians translate the Torah each and every generation into their national languages … indeed, this is the road that many members of our nation have tread, which is a terrible trap and obstacle to the ones who fall into them, and this has caused a great evil, because the Christian translators who are not learned in the teachings of our Sages of Blessed Memory and are not attuned to the words of tradition … with their renditions breach the wall of Torah, and any man may approach it and do with it as he pleases … to the extent of not reading what the Torah says, instead reading into it whatever they fancy." (Mendelssohn 1887, 16, unless noted otherwise, all translations are my own)
8 Buber completed the project of translating all 24 books of the Bible in 1961, republished 1992. *Die Schrift: Aus dem Hebräischen verdeutscht von Martin Buber gemeinsam mit Franz Rosenzweig.* Deutsche Bibelgesellschaft. This latter edition includes revisions and amendments of the work conducted with Rosenzweig.
9 To the best of my knowledge, the visual display of the B-R translation has not been dedicated a study of its own, a worthy topic that calls for further inquiry.

lic (1926–1930). Its authors chose such an idiosyncratic layout for their translation not only because they aimed to cultivate a readership that is not exclusively Jewish, but also because they sought to renegotiate the ways they presented their Jewish affiliation to their readers.

Buber's and Rosenzweig's stance in the Jewish-Christian Bible polemics oscillates between ambivalence and ambiguity. Their respect for and indebtedness to Christian theology was mingled with an entrenched suspicion of Christian supersessionism, but they reserved the consequential ressentiment largely for private correspondence and internal discussion. Thus, their insistence on engaging in dialogue with Christians on the Bible and its contemporary theological significance neither obscured nor mitigated their deep-seated concerns about the dangers of such discussion. Like the layout design of *Die Schrift*, Buber, in his essay "People Today and the Jewish Bible," (1994c) argues for a commitment to reflecting on the importance of the Bible in modernity, irrespective of creed, while holding fast to a perception of the Hebrew Bible as a Jewish scripture. The ambivalent and ambiguous underpinnings of their approach are also evident from the imbalance between the essay's title and content. The text is purged of any use of the word "Jewish" and it makes a single reference to Christianity by name (9–10). Buber's repeated reference to "contemporary man" (*der heutige Mensch*)[10] further emphasizes his wish to address a problem that surpasses denominational divisions. In order to help contemporary humanity out of the spiritual impasse it has reached, Buber strives to regain a sense of "biblical reality" (*biblische Wirklichkeit*), by which he (following Rosenzweig) means acknowledging and distinguishing between creation, revelation and redemption, as the formative elements of reality (9). To demonstrate how this may be achieved, Buber offers reflections on three biblical terms that represent divine creation and revelation: God's *ruach* (spirit, or *Geist*), and Tent of Meeting (*Ohel Mo'ed—Zelt der Offenbarung*) and the rest day of the Sabbath. In the current discussion, it is particularly noteworthy that Buber's references to other readings of the citations he provides are to non-Jewish authors (Friedrich Nietzsche, [Buber 1994c, 11] Hermann Gunkel, [15] Johann Wolfgang von Goethe [17]) or heterodox Jewish readings (Benedict Spinoza [15]), when in fact his own interpretations are heavily inspired by rabbinic exegesis.[11]

Returning to the essay's title, we may now gain some sense of Buber's (and Rosenzweig's) ambiguity and ambivalence: his announcement of the Jewish

---

10 Rosenwald and Fox translate the term as "people today."
11 On Buber's and Rosenzweig's reliance on rabbinical sources in the translation see Scharf 2014.

provenance of biblical reality is hardly supported by, or elaborated on, in the body of the text. What is more, Buber's indiscriminate concern for "contemporary man" is tinged with bitterness at Christianity's distancing itself from this reality through what he refers to as "dog's work [*Pfuschwerk*]," by which he means the impact of Marcionism on early Christian discourse (Buber 2012, 43).[12] This particular ambiguity in Buber's and Rosenzweig's writing about the Hebrew Bible is key to understanding their approach to Christian readers of their translation. It is reminiscent of Heidegger's interpretation of the ancient Greek term for truth—*aletheia*—as the constant movement between covering and uncovering. At the same time, one must recall that their joint translation venture began at the initiative of a young publisher, Lambert Schneider, whom Buber describes as being "of pure Christian ancestry." (1994a, 177) Awed by Martin Luther's translation, they initially contemplated creating a "revised" Luther Bible: as Rosenzweig put it in a letter to Buber in early 1925, a new Jewish-German translation of the Bible was not only impossible but strictly forbidden (F. Rosenzweig 1979b, 1021). It was only after trying such revision that they were forced to concede the futility of their attempt, and began working on the B-R translation as we know it today (Buber 1994a, 177–78). Luther's Bible maintained its dominant presence throughout the project, however, not only as an important reference, but also as a foremost example for Christian appropriations of the Bible.[13] Therefore, as a Bible for Christian readers the Buber-Rosenzweig translation has polemical elements that are hard to ignore, while certain other features, both visual and substantive, make it difficult for a critic to pinpoint the translators' contrarian reading of the Bible.

1 Between Moriah and Golgotha

The relationship between Rosenzweig and Eugen Rosenstock-Huessy (1888–1973)[14] was intense and tumultuous. Their initial encounter in January 1910 was followed by three years of close contact. Shortly after submitting his doctoral dissertation at the University of Freiburg in 1912, the twenty-six-year-old Rosenzweig came to Leipzig to take the class Rosenstock taught on medieval jurisprudence at the local university. Their intellectual-personal bond culminated in a

---

12 This expression is omitted from Rosenwald's and Fox's translation.
13 Rosenzweig considered the translation to "reign" over German, that is, to be the formative document of its modern written form (F. Rosenzweig 1994a, 51–53).
14 In 1914 Rosenstock added the last name of his wife, Margarit Hüssy, to his name. For convenience's sake I will refer to him here only as Rosenstock.

dramatic dispute on the night of 7 July, 1913, which came to be known as the *Leipziger Nachtgespräch*. Rosenstock, who had converted to Christianity from Judaism seven years earlier, mounted a relentless assault on the confounded Rosenzweig, who had reached an impasse in his search for a viable spiritual path, which he believed Judaism could not offer him. Rosenstock (and Franz's Christian-born cousin Rudolph Ehrenberg, who was also present on that fateful night) thus persuaded Rosenzweig to be baptized. Some three months later, however, Rosenzweig overturned his decision, famously writing to his cousin Rudi that he had decided to remain a Jew.[15]

This tempestuous period led Rosenzweig to distance himself from his Christian friend for almost three years, until Rosenstock initiated renewed contact in 1916. An infantry officer in Somme and Verdun, Rosenstock wrote to Franz, who was serving as an NCO at an artillery unit on the Balkan front. The correspondence that ensued has come to be hailed as a classic of modern Jewish-Christian dialogue.[16] Spanning from May through November or December of 1916, the epistolary exchange contains existential, theological and meta-historical arguments that shaped the two friends' later works, and have justifiably attracted scholarly attention. These arguments, however, rely on a historical substratum that has not received its due recognition: namely the period between the first and fourth centuries CE, the era of Christianity's emergence and the rise of the Church.[17]

As historians of ideas,[18] Rosenzweig and Rosenstock showed only slight interest in the emergent relationship between Judaism and Christianity, giving little, if any, consideration to the historical reality in which those texts were composed. Rather, as their correspondence from the year 1916 indicates, they based their dialogue on the Judeo-Christian canon (the Old and New Testaments, Patristic literature, mainly), offering distilled expressions of the essence of the two faiths. Thus, for example, when Rosenzweig remonstrates about Rosenstock considering both of them Jews, he refers to the New Testament to prove Rosenstock wrong:

---

15 Rosenzweig, letter to Rudolph Ehrenberg dated October 31, 1913 (F. Rosenzweig 1979a, 133).
16 The correspondence first appeared as a separate section in Rosenzweig's collected letters (F. Rosenzweig 1935; Rosenstock-Huessy 2016). If nothing else, the unusual, quadruple introduction to the English edition of their correspondence (by Harold Stahmer, Alexander Altmann, Dorothy Emmett and Rosenstock, who also added a postscript) is testament to the importance of this recorded dialogue.
17 A notable exception is Pollock 2014.
18 Rosenstock studied classical philology, history and law at Zurich and received his PhD in jurisprudence from the University of Heidelberg; Rosenzweig studied history with Friedrich Meinecke and wrote his dissertation on G.W.F. Hegel's concept of the state.

you are directly hindering me from treating my Judaism in the first person, in that you call yourself a Jew too. That is to me equally intolerable, emotionally and intellectually. For me you can be nothing else but a Christian ... Moreover, suppose you were really a Christian *ek ton peritomes* [a Jew since circumcision] (you are one, but, in spite of your brilliant Logion of Luke, only in your theoretical consciousness, not in the reality of your life before you were a Christian ...). But even if you were one, it would not make any difference to me, because I do not recognize this missionary-theological concept of "Christians from Israel," because it is positive and the Jew between the Crucifixion and the Second Coming can only have a negative meaning in Christian theology. (undated letter: Rosenstock-Huessy 2016, 98–99)

In this passage, Rosenzweig intimates that the claim that one may remain a Jew while being a practicing Christian is not only repugnant to him but also untenable in the light of the teachings of both Jesus and Paul. Rosenstock's self-perception as a Christian from birth is deceptive, his Jewish friend contends, not only on the grounds of his biography,[19] but also because of his subtle deviation from Paul's claim to having undergone a prenatal revelation of Christ in Galatians 1:13, 15–16: "For you have heard of my former life in Judaism ... But when he who had set me apart before I was born, and had called me through his grace, was pleased to reveal his Son to me, in order that I might preach him among the Gentiles..." By claiming he is a Christian since circumcision, Rosenstock emphasizes that he remains a Jew while accepting the teachings of Jesus Christ. By claiming that he was a Christian before birth, Paul, who was "advanced in Judaism beyond many of my own age among my people," (Gal 1:14) wishes to say that his life as a Jew was an empty shell that he shed once he was ready to spread the teachings of Christ among the Gentiles. To drive his point home, Rosenzweig concludes with a strictly negative view of the Jew between the Crucifixion and the Second Coming that inspired the infamous image of the Wandering Jew.[20] He argues that Judaism cannot be subsumed under Christianity because the younger faith, from its earliest days on, has considered such religious affiliation to be mutually exclusive: being Christian ruled out being Jewish.

Several weeks later, Rosenstock makes a distinction that pulls the rug from under his own argument. Invoking a well-trodden comparison between Abra-

---

19 In the letter Rosenzweig reminds Rosenstock that he might be a Christian from birth mentally, but "not in the reality of your life before you were a Christian; and I know that now because I know your parents' house." (Rosenstock-Huessy 2016, 99)
20 The sentence that refers to "The Jew *kat exokhen* [par excellence], the 'Ahasuerus' of Christian—and naturally Teutonic—lore..." (Rosenstock-Huessy 2016, 99)

ham's near-sacrifice of Isaac and Jesus' self-sacrifice, he points to the greater devotion of the Christian to God, which places him on the moral high ground:

> Abraham sacrifices his son; in the New Testament, he who brings the covenant with God sacrifices himself. That is the whole difference. Among the pagans, as with the Jews, everyone aspires to be founder, father, owner, testator, ancestor, guardian, master. Each one rules over a bit of the world. The Christian, on the other hand, knows a second kingdom of poverty, weakness, dependence, minority, shame, repentance, and shy childishness. Abraham sacrifices what he has, Christ what he is. (Rosenstock, letter to Rosenzweig dated October 30, 1916: Rosenstock-Huessy 2016, 124)

Rosenzweig counters this claim by pointing out Rosenstock's projection of Greek tragedy onto the Binding of Isaac:

> You have rightly put your finger on this difference in speaking of Moriah and Golgotha. But you have read your Genesis 22 badly. You have confused Abraham and Agamemnon. The latter indeed sacrificed what he had for the sake of something else that he wanted ... But Abraham did not offer something, not "a" child, but his only son, and what is more, the son of the promise and sacrificed him to the God of his promise ... not for nothing is this story associated with our highest festivals; it is the prototype of the sacrifice not of one's own person (Golgotha), but of one's existence in one's people, of the "son" and all future sons. (Rosenzweig, letter to Rosenstock dated November 7, 1916: Rosenstock-Huessy 2016, 133–34)

Unlike the King of Mycenae, Abraham the Patriarch did not use his progeny instrumentally as sacrifice. In fact, Rosenzweig maintains, Abraham's projected sacrifice, curbed at the very last minute, was greater than either Agamemnon's or Jesus'. In contrast with the tragic character, Abraham did not send one of several children to be sacrificed but an *only* child. Unlike the Son of God, the sacrifice Abraham made was not limited to himself, as it would have prevented the formation of God's nation, eradicating the fulfillment of divine promise. This error, Rosenzweig makes clear, derives from a gross misreading of the biblical narrative:

> The son [Isaac] is given back; he is now only the son of the promise. Nothing else happens, no Ilium falls, only the promise remains firm; the father was ready to sacrifice not for the sake of some Ilium, but for the sake of nothing. Agamemnon sacrifices something "that he had;" Abraham, all that he could be; Christ, all that he is. (Rosenstock-Huessy 2016, 134)

No doubt, Rosenstock's interpolation was tinged with supersessionist inclinations that surfaced in some of his statements. Among other things, Rosenstock describes the Jews as professing their commitment to God's revelation while doing everything they can to prevent it, to the point of being "the image on earth of Lucifer," and that "Israel's time as the people of the Bible has gone by. The Church ... is today the Synagogue." (Rosenstock-Huessy 2016, 125, 140)[21] To make things worse, he submits that "Today Christianity has a new Old Testament instead of your old one; namely, today its living Old Testament is Church History." (Rosenstock-Huessy 2016, 140) Setting aside the validity of Rosenstock's argumentation (or lack thereof), one must note that the statement reveals a crucial blind spot in his position. It is impossible to think of the Old Testament as irrelevant to the present and to read it seriously, which is exactly what Rosenzweig points out in his riposte. Commenting on the comparison between Abraham's and Jesus' sacrifices, Rosenzweig delineates the unbridgeable rift between the two faiths:

> Now that I want to continue, I find that everything that I want to write is something I can't express to you. For now I would have to show you Judaism from within, that is, to be able to show it to you in a hymn, just as you are able to show me, the outsider, Christianity. And for the very reason that you can do it, I cannot. Christianity has its soul in its externals; Judaism, on the outside, has only its hard, protective shell, and one can speak of its soul only from within. So it can't be done—and you must take my word for it that the, as it were, abstract character of the religious life is the same with us and with you. (Rosenzweig, letter to Rosenstock dated November 7, 1916: Rosenstock-Huessy 2016, 133)

It appears that Rosenzweig ascribes the impregnability of the Jewish experience for outsiders to its spiritual core, which is prayer. Since Judaism distances its practitioners from members of other religious communities, the spiritual sustenance of Judaism (which Rosenzweig calls "its soul") is palpable only to those who can experience it first-hand. If there were other aspects of religious life that Rosenzweig had in mind when he wrote this letter, language would be first on the list.

---

21 Admittedly, it is hard to pinpoint Rosenstock's view on Judaism, or even categorize it as either "positive" or negative." It has become a subject of renewed debate in the last two or three decades, as some scholars have protested against his designation as dismissive of Judaism, or even as anti-Semitic (Huessy 2015). See also Wayne Cristaudo, who laments that, "More often than not, the [1916] exchange has been read by people in a partisan manner and Rosenstock-Huessy is portrayed as an apostate hell-bent on converting his friend." (2009, 140) Cristaudo's formidable monograph (2012) forcefully argues for a personal and intellectual symbiosis between Rosenstock and Rosenzweig. For a more balanced assessment, see Zank 2003.

2 Haves and Have-nots

Both Rosenzweig and Rosenstock posited language as a fundamental element in their thought. The theory that emerged from their joint work on language, Speech Thinking (*Sprachdenken*), first came from Rosenstock, but gained more acclaim through Rosenzweig's writing.[22] For Rosenstock, the discovery that it is not language as such, but language as speech that serves as a lynchpin between the thinking subject and external reality (the natural world and God), animated him to develop his own system, the so-called "Cross of Reality."[23] The philosophical analysis of language as such can remain as abstract as conventional philosophical discourse. Language as speech forces philosophical reflection to take context into account without losing sight of the broader framework of the philosophical system: "In actual conversation, something happens; I do not know in advance what the other will say to me because I myself do not even know what I am going to say … To think here means to think for no one and to speak to no one … But to speak means to speak to someone and to think for someone; and this Someone is always a quite definite Someone." (F. Rosenzweig 2000, 126–27) The transition from language to speech, both thinkers reasoned, by necessity entailed dialogue, without which language would lose its fundamental communicative function. This insight was not only theoretical. Their dialogical thinking, which overlapped with Buber's *I and Thou*, the work of Ferdinand Ebner's *The Word and Spiritual Realities* and others,[24] found expression in attempts to establish forms of dialogue more conducive to human existence (with a group that identified itself as the Patmos Circle),[25] and to Jewish-Christian dialogue (with the interfaith journal *Die Kreatur* [Petuchowski 1995]). Without getting into the intricacies of Speech Thinking and its impact on the two intellectual circles, suffice it here to note that dialogue is premised on the existence of a common language between interlocutors. Without a common language, the prospect of com-

---

[22] After realizing that the *Star of Redemption* is misunderstood by the majority of its readers, Rosenzweig wrote an explanatory essay to offer a synoptic view of the work in the context of the contemporary problems faced by philosophy and theology. Positing Speech Thinking as the book's method, he points out its merit over abstract philosophical thought as being temporal, concrete and attached to the Other. In developing this method, Rosenzweig asserts, he is indebted most of all to Rosenstock (F. Rosenzweig 2000, 127).
[23] For a succinct and effective summary of the evolution of Rosenstock's conception of language see Stahmer 1968, 115–21.
[24] For a list of related works see Stahmer 1968, 123. Decades after its publication, Bernhard Casper's study (1967) of dialogical thinking in Rosenzweig, Buber and Ebner remains essential.
[25] For a historical sketch and bibliography see Stünkel 2015.

munication and mutual understanding is severally handicapped. And if we understand Rosenzweig's claim about the inaccessibility of Judaism to outsiders to be closely linked to non-Jews' lack of knowledge of Hebrew, then the language of the Hebrew Bible becomes a major obstacle on the road to Jewish-Christian understanding.[26]

Only a few months later, Rosenzweig wrote to his mentor, Hermann Cohen (1865–1918) a letter later published as "It is Time" (*Zeit ists*), in which he laid out a visionary education program for Germany's Jews (F. Rosenzweig 2002).[27] The young intellectual draws a dividing line, placing world nations and their relationship with their language on one side, and Jews' relationship with Hebrew on the other side. For the non-Jew, he contends, "knowledge of the words of a language does not necessarily imply 'possession' of its civilization," (29–30) that is: such a relationship is perfunctory and superficial. Judaism, however, "is rooted in the soul of the individual, with a language of its own." (30) This makes the relationship between Jews and the language of the Bible unique: "The German, and even the Jew qua German, can and will read the Bible as Luther, Herder or Moses Mendelssohn read it; the Jew can understand it only in Hebrew."(30) The relationship between the Jew and Hebrew culminates, however, in prayer: "of the language of Hebrew prayer we may state quite categorically: it cannot be translated." (30)

In *The Star of Redemption*, Rosenzweig elaborates on this conception of Hebrew as the holy tongue. The rootedness of Hebrew in the soul of the individual Jew, he submits, arises from the position of Jews as the eternal people among world nations. While the language of every other nation lives and dies according to the nation's historical fate, the Jews use the languages of other nations as their vernacular, while remaining free from land and detached from the historical cycle of triumph and defeat. And yet, Hebrew is not a dead language, as it is usually designated, because it is reserved for Jews' conversation with God (F. Rosenzweig 2007, 299–301).

---

26 This position is exposed to the counter-argument that in the course of exile knowledge of Hebrew among the Jews themselves became scant, and hence religious experience would have been equally inaccessible to them as to Christians. For Rosenzweig, however, the "material" quality of Hebrew, that is, its pronunciation and reading by Jews even without understanding the words uttered or read is sufficient for maintaining the bond between Jews and their sacred language. Commenting on the issue to Gershom Scholem, Rosenzewig said that "The Hebrew word not understood gives him [the Jew reading it] more than what the most beautiful of translations can." (Letter dated March 10th, 1921: F. Rosenzweig 1979b, 699)

27 Written on the Macedonian front, it was originally published in late 1917 by Verlag der Neuen Jüdischen Monatshefte. Now available in F. Rosenzweig 1984.

While this conception, certainly from a twenty-first century perspective, appears anachronistic and even simplistic, it convincingly underscores Hebrew's potential to make its speakers feel a special connection with a long and rich spiritual history. What Rosenzweig describes in "The New Thinking" as the moment when "the old words come," (2000, 131) Nahum Glatzer articulates more straightforwardly as Rosenzweig's belief "in the edifying power of its letters and in the Hebrew word as a vessel containing the echoes of the sounds that rose from Sinai and remain as delightful as on the day they issued out." (1959, 233) As Rosenzweig's foremost disciple and research assistant to him and Buber in the translation project, Glatzer was in a privileged position to suggest that for Rosenzweig, the translation of the Bible will not become poetry in another vernacular, but rather will remain Hebraic in its vernacular garb (233).[28]

Defying translational conventions by turning his attention away from German and instead toward the aesthetics and structure of Hebrew, Rosenzweig was far from considering the translation of Hebrew devotional texts as an internal Jewish affair. On the contrary, his first experimentations with translation—published around 1920–1922[29]—were designed to allow both Jewish and non-Jewish guests with no knowledge of Hebrew, to follow the ceremony at the Sabbath dinner table (Rosenzweig, letter to Gershom Scholem dated 10 March, 1921: F. Rosenzweig 1979b, 699). Nonetheless, the warm hospitality he showed to those guests and the friendly relations his translation helped maintain did little to cover up the unease, to the point of acrimony, which he experiences while confronting the "have-nots"—those possessing no Hebrew knowledge. For Rosenzweig, the necessity of translating for the "have-nots" always bears the risk of sliding down the slippery slope of Jewish apologetics, which he considered intolerable. He confided to his disciple Rudolph Hallo:

> For whom do I translate? Now for those who have no Hebrew knowledge. Along with them, also for those who do indeed know Hebrew, but until now through intentional (if unfortu-

---

[28] Mara Benjamin radicalizes this notion to claim that Rosenzweig "aimed to do nothing less than to demonstrate the hidden Hebraic foundation of German arts, letters and thought. The translation of the Bible into German that resulted from this effort simultaneously posited the essential contribution of Judaism to German culture and challenged the political and social agenda of classical ethical monotheism with an insistence on the difference of the Jewish contribution to, and the place within, German culture." (2009, 103)

[29] F. Rosenzweig 1920 is a translation of the Grace after Meals; F. Rosenzweig 1922 contains translations of songs traditionally sung on the eve of the Sabbath. He also published a hymn by master poet Rabbi Israel Najara (1555–1625) in F. Rosenzweig 1921–1922, 692. See Amir 2011, 4 n.14. In 1922 Rosenzweig also prepared an incomplete rendition of the famous Yom Kippur prayer *Kol Nidre* that he never published (Shahar 2016, 264).

nate) apologetically-tinged translations lost sight of the original ... And my Christian friends? And apologetics? Dear God—honestly, [the translations] naturally belong to the people with no knowledge of Hebrew as well as to the "Ehrenbergs and Rosenstocks." But when translating I have been thinking only about myself, about how the prayer [translated] sounds to me. In hindsight, for Christians I have done nothing else. Overall, do you mean to say that initially my Christian friends had something against my putting Teffilin, or fasting together with the Frankfurt community?

I believe that you see me facing up to a test that you have forced upon your Christian friends. I suspect this now. Because precisely the need to face up to Christian Christians is the test, without which there would be no need to make Judaism apologetic. [By undergoing this] test one comes to know also the pagans [who are only] Christian by name, through Idealism or Mysticism or whatever is the right name for it. Usually rather [we face] polemically our Jew of today as we do Christians. (Rosenzweig, letter to Rudolph Hallo dated 27 March, 1922: F. Rosenzweig 1979b, 765–66)

The letter distinguishes between three audiences that Rosenzweig feels the need to interact with by means of his translation: Christian friends (among whom he includes the "Ehrenbergs and Rosenstocks," that is, intimate friends and theological polemicists), apologetic Jews, and those he calls "pagan" Christians. What these three audiences share, despite their patent differences, is the inability to read a Hebrew text, either due to the lack of knowledge of the language, or long-term exposure to apologetic translations.

The same audiences continued to preoccupy Rosenzweig in his first major translation of poems by medieval thinker and bard Rabbi Yehuda Halevi (Letter to Margarete Susman dated 22 August, 1924: F. Rosenzweig 1979b, 982–83).[30] Rosenzweig never saw the translation of Hebrew texts for contemporary Germans as an opportunity to build bridges between languages, cultures, and faiths. Rather, it was a perilous trek along a precipice: rendering the holy tongue in German was more likely to play into the hands of hostile Christians or apologetic Jews than to facilitate understanding. This is why Rosenzweig emphasizes to Hallo, another near-convert who decided to return to the Jewish fold, that his translation of prayers is personal, and does not take into consideration the needs or expectations of an audience. The intimacy of Jewish spiritual life, which Rosenzweig had tried to explain in his response to Rosenstock, was a personal experience and that he sought to convey through his translations. Rendering Hebrew devotional texts into German, even as he knew that non-Jewish read-

---

[30] The translation of collected poems was published in two editions (F. Rosenzweig 1924; F. Rosenzweig 1927). The full edition, comprising 103 poem translations, was published in F. Rosenzweig 1983. English translation: Galli 1995.

ers would miss the spiritual intimacy that praying Jews understand, was, in Rosenzweig's eyes, a bold polemical act.

The decision to accept Buber's invitation to co-translate the Hebrew Bible in 1925 thus intersected with the trajectory of Rosenzweig's growing investment in a struggle to assert the legitimacy of the Jewish faith in the face of Christian de-legitimization. Along this trajectory, the Hebrew language occupied a pivotal role, as both a channel into the soul of Judaism, as Rosenzweig put it, and as the holy tongue that functions as the guarantor of Jews' bond with the eternal God. Hence, the translation of Hebrew into German, all the more so when it came to the Bible, could not be aimed to propitiate Christian readers; it had to convey something from the Hebraic spirit of the biblical Urtext in order to assert the inextricability of both the Hebrew and the Bible from Jewish life.

3 "Alles in der Schrift ist echte Gesprochenheit"

After Rosenzweig's death, Buber wrote an essay under a succinct title of "The Why and How of Our Translation of the Bible," which summarizes the two major preoccupations that shaped the authors' translation of the Hebrew Bible: their motivations and methodology.[31] Never losing sight of their agenda, they nonetheless made a heroic effort to leave the text as it stands, allowing the history of its reception to guide their translational choices. The ambivalence and ambiguity that appear to have shaped the layout of Buber's and Rosenzweig's *Die Schrift* also contributed to a Heideggerian tactic of concealment and revelation of their work process (Rosenwald 2007; Scharf 2016). The explanatory essays that the translators published as they progressed with their work, (Buber and F. Rosenzweig 1936)[32] tended to emphasize the conceptual principles that guided their translation while obscuring the penetrating depths of philological insight and research on the reception history of the Hebrew Bible that Buber and Rosenzweig carried out. Exposing the true dimensions of their scholarly endeavor therefore requires shedding more light on their "workshop," as

---

31 Rosenzweig was diagnosed with Amyotrophic lateral sclerosis in 1922 and was completely paralyzed by the time they began translating together. Communicating almost exclusively through his wife, Edith, Rosenzweig was able to insert his suggested corrections and critiques on Buber's initial drafts. It was clear to all that his chances of living to see the translation completed were less than nothing. On Buber's and Rosenzweig's working process see Batnitzky 1997.
32 Buber's essays are now available in HaCohen 2012; Rosenzweig's in R. Mayer and A. Mayer 1984. English translation may be found in Buber and F. Rosenzweig 1994.

Leora Batnitzky has called it, which would consist of a careful reconstruction of their working process on individual verses, words and phrases (1997).

An unexpected, new corpus of evidence on the translators' work process surfaced in recent years at the Martin Buber Archive at the National Library of Israel. Previously unpublished typescripts of two lecture cycles on Judaism and Christianity were found during the preparation of a new critical edition of Buber's writings, the *Martin Buber Werkausgabe*.[33] Alongside materials familiar from Buber's published works, the lectures contain new and detailed discussions on the relation between Judaism and Christianity in the first few centuries of the Common Era.

Delivered in 1930's Germany, Buber's lectures, *Vorlesungen über Judentum und Christentum*, engage sensitive questions regarding the shared historical and theological roots of the two faiths. While Buber relies on detailed historical-philological analyses of sources, the historical background of their delivery is also significant. Buber gave those lectures at a time when Germany's Jews were facing a growing threat of spiritual and cultural annihilation that later led to physical extermination. Although we know that at least one cycle was taught at Frankfurt's *Freies jüdisches Lehrhaus* after its reopening in 1933, studies about the Lehrhaus published in recent years contain few details about the lectures, while some of them even neglect to mention that they ever took place (Scharf 2017b; 2017a). Moreover, Buber does not appear to have mentioned these lectures anywhere in his writings and documents. The most natural place to do so would have been in his best-known work on Jewish-Christian relations, *Two Types of Faith* (Buber 2011).[34]

Both versions of the *Vorlesungen über Judentum und Christentum* are subdivided into three parts that bear the following titles: (1) *Jüdischer und christlicher Glaube* (Jewish and Christian Faith); (2) *Jüdischer und christlicher Erlösungslehre* (Jewish and Christian Teachings on Redemption); (3) *Jüdischer und christlicher Messianismus* (Jewish and Christian Messianism). Notably, this structural division distinguishes between two forms of salvation: redemption and messianism. Though these terms are often used interchangeably, based on the assumption that they are synonymous, Buber's insistence on discussing them separately emphasizes the fundamental difference between the two. Redemption is the fulfillment of the potential of being saved from this-worldly dross, which comes from sin. It must involve divine intervention but does *not* entail the necessary arrival of a redeeming figure. In contradistinction, messianism is a particular form of

---

33 The typescripts' call number at the archive is Arc. Ms. Var 350 bet f. Buber (Scharf 2017b).
34 In English translation: Buber 1951.

redemption, fulfilled by the coming of the Kingdom of God through the efforts of the figure of the *mashiah*, that is, "the anointed." In Judaism and Christianity, messianism shares these two fundamental elements, but diverges on the timing of the messianic process: while Christians maintain that it lies in the future, for "classical Judaism" it pertains to the historical conditions of the present (Buber 2017, 193–94).

Although the lectures' third and final part is titled "Jewish *and* Christian Messianism," it is dedicated almost exclusively to messianic figures in the Hebrew Bible, principally during the formation of Israelite kingship: the story of Gideon in Judges chapters 6–8; the Israelites' demand of a king from Samuel in I Samuel, chapters 7–9; the Song of Channa in I Samuel 2:1–11; King David's song in II Samuel 23:1–8 (Buber 2017, 198–230). In the penultimate lecture of the first cycle, Buber invokes three passages from Isaiah, enshrined in the New Testament as proof of Jesus' messianic calling, which marks the handing over of "chosenness" from Judaism to Christianity:

1. "For to us a child is born, to us a son is given; and the government will be upon his shoulder, and his name will be called 'Wonderful Counselor, Mighty God, Everlasting Father, Prince of Peace.'" (Isa 9:5)
2. "There shall come forth a shoot from the stump of Jesse, and a branch shall grow out of his roots. And the Spirit of the LORD shall rest upon him, the spirit of wisdom and understanding, the spirit of counsel and might, the spirit of knowledge and the fear of the LORD." (Isa 11:1–2)
3. The figure of the suffering servant (chapter 53).

Buber submits that, "we see in Isaiah, as well as in the pre-exilic prophets in general, this image [*Vorstellung*] of a man that accommodates God, so to speak, who in the encounter assumes the [divine] Spirit, and does what the Spirit orders … he will not stamp out or impose Redemption, so to speak, that is, the fulfillment of creation of the world [*Schöpfung der Welt*]; something of the redemptive power [*Erlösungsmächtigkeit*], of a redemptive claim [*Erlösungsverlangen*], of redemptive ripeness [*Erlösungsreife*] rises, out of the life of creature, man and the nations." (Buber 2017, 232) To begin with, Buber lowers the expectations towards the messiah figure in Isaiah: neither divine nor of divine descent, the messiah figure in the prophecies in question, he maintains, assumes the spirit of the Godhead and acquires certain redemptive qualities. Correspondingly, he qualifies the expectations towards the outcome of the messiah's actions: he will not bring about all-out salvation. The purpose of his arrival is linked to the specific historical circumstances surrounding the exile. While Isaiah prophesies before the conquest of Jerusalem, the aftermath of the Babylonian exile looms large on his orations, melding together the fears of foreign takeover by either the Babylonians or the Egyptians, with anxiety over the suffering that will ensue (Buber 2017, 232–33).

Buber opens the lecture with a rendering of Isaiah 9:5 that reproduces word for word the translation he authored together with Rosenzweig:

> "Seinen Namen, einen entrückten, ruft man:
> Ratsmann des Göttlichen,
> Held des Ewigvaters,
> Fürst des Friedens." (Buber and F. Rosenzweig, 39)[35]

He justifies the word choice as follows:

> That there are no divine epithets anymore, one sees with clarity, it is a man who has been sent by God, His representative, His prince of the kingdom of peace: to [effect] a more prosperous princedom and peace ... *You see, when one simply goes to the text ... when one turns to the text with sufficient genuineness, then the cocoon [Gespinste], the construct [Gebilde] [of] a deified Messiah disappears.* (Buber 2017, 230, my italics)

To recall Rosenzweig's conception of the Hebrew language, its vouchsafing of Israel's bond with God (put forth in the *Star*) impedes non-Jews' ability to understand Judaism (as may be surmised from his letter to Rosenstock). Yet, the Hebrew Bible forms the ground where non-Jews may come closer to Jews, and perhaps even partake in the same experience of scripture when they read Bible translations that retain the German idiom, such as Luther's or Mendelssohn's ("It is Time"). In essays describing the working process on *Die Schrift*, Buber connected this conception with striving for the genuine meaning of the biblical text:

> Everything in Scripture is genuine spokenness [*alles in der Schrift ist echte Gesprochenheit*], in comparison with which "content" and "form" seem only the result of a sham analysis; *Botschaft*,[36] then, even where it is expressed indirectly, must not be reduced to annotation or commentary. (Buber 1994d, 28; F. Rosenzweig 1994b, 135, 140)

And explained how this conception differs from other Bible translations:

> Even the most significant translations of the Bible that we possess—the Greek Septuagint, the Latin Vulgate, the German of Luther—do not aim principally at maintaining the original character of the book as manifested in word choice, in syntax, and in rhythmical articula-

---

[35] An English approximation of this and the following German translations appears below.
[36] Literally: message. Buber employs the term to capture to overarching meaning, impetus and impact of the biblical text.

tion. They aim rather at transmitting to the translators' actual community—the Jewish diaspora of Hellenism, the early Christian *oikumene*, the faithful adherents of the Reformation—a reliable foundational document. They accordingly carry over the "content" of the text into another language. They do not *a priori* ignore the peculiarities of its constituent elements, of its structure, of its dynamic; but they easily enough sacrifice those peculiarities when stubborn "form" seems to hinder the rendering of "content." (Buber 1994b, 74)[37]

In their translation, instead of striving to move from the Hebrew Urtext to a German idiom, Buber and Rosenzweig sank themselves as deep as possible into the verse. By that they not only unearthed the lexical meaning they wanted their translation to convey, but also the intricacies of the reality that begat the text, which it depicts:

For the prophets, deification of the Messiah was as implausible as the deification of a king, because for them messiah is indistinguishable from king, who becomes real only through anointing. *The prophets distinguish not between history and eschatology, reality and religious idea, and such like; rather, for them the Messiah was as real as only a king can be, which is why they waited for him out in the open, as though waiting for the king's son to accede to the throne.* (Buber 2017, 230–31, my italics)

But could the translators convey that? Israeli Bible scholar Benjamin Uffenheimer places Buber's reading of the verse in between two classic views of the messianic figure that Jewish commentaries espouse: (1) Rabbinical literature[38] and medieval exegetes[39] propound that the messiah is a concrete historical figure, identifying him with King Hezekiah of Judea; (2) The canonical Jewish translations of the Septuagint and Aramaic Targum Pseudo-Jonathan espouse an ideal messiah-king figure (Uffenheimer 1964, 107). According to Uffenheimer, "Buber takes a slightly different approach, to avoid ascribing the divine appella-

---

[37] Compare Rosenzweig's commendation of Luther's retention of the resonance of the Hebrew original: "[Luther] had the courage to import into the German the sentence construction of the Hebrew, even then cyclopean for the cultivated German consciousness of language … And Luther was permitted to translate because he possessed for this linguistic conquest the necessary courage as well as the necessary circumspection." (F. Rosenzweig 1995, 171)
[38] Especially in BT Sanhedrin 94a: "The Blessed Holy One wished to make Hezekiah messiah, when Sennacherib wreaked an all-out war. Said the Measure of Justice to the Blessed Holy One: Master of the World, You did not make David King of Israel messiah, who sang so many songs in your praise, and Hezekiah, for whom you've made all of these miracles and did not sing to You, him you will make messiah? Thus He said nothing. The earth immediately said to Him, Master of the World: I will sing to You instead of this righteous man; make him messiah."
[39] Rashi, Rabbi David Kimhi (Radak), Rabbi Abraham Ibn Ezra ad loc.

tions to the ideal king." (1964, 109)⁴⁰ The translation achieves this, he maintains, by changing the Hebrew noun *pele* (miracle) into an adjective. Notably, however, Uffenheimer does not mention that Buber and Rosenzweig's presentation of the appellations in the verse, which have the potential of denoting divinity, assert the complete submission of the messiah figure to God: *Ratsmann des Göttlichen* (counsel *of* the godly), *Held des Ewigvaters* (hero of the eternal Father), and *Fürst des Friedens* (prince of peace). This reading of their translation fits in with Uffenheimer's juxtaposition of the two possible Jewish readings of the verse with its possible Christian reading. Inspired by the sermon in Matthew 4:12–16, (1964, 107, 111)⁴¹ it considers the prophecy as referring to the future divine messiah, that is, Jesus Christ.

In the same lecture, Buber briefly mentions Old Testament theologian Hugo Gressmann (1877–1927) as a counterpoint to his own reading. He cites Gressmann's translation, which ascribes all four names in the verse to the messiah,⁴² and then asks rhetorically: "When one translates this way, it is no wonder when it is asked: is this the only way Isaiah could have intoned God's unparalleled grandeur? God alone can be great and over and against all else that is small. How could the same prophet let the messiah assume God's attributes?" (Buber 2017, 230) While Gressmann's translation indeed concertizes the divine attributes in the messiah figure, as Buber points out, the rationalization of his choices is actually quite close to Buber's. In his introduction to the study in which the translated verse that Buber cites appears, Gressmann stresses that while the religious-historical study of biblical prophecy is justifiably associated with religious life and ideas, in recent time it had become clear that the prophets were also attempting to pass religious-moral judgment on the political events of their era (1929, 14). He surmises that the calls for world rule (*Weltherrschaft*) voiced in the prophecies point at their pre-exilic roots, (198) and concludes his commentary on his own translation of Isaiah 9:5 as follows: "it is very impor-

---

40 Uffenheimer is relying on Buber's later revision that reads, "*Seinen Wundernamen ruft man*" ("One would call out his miraculous name.") The rendition together with Rosenzweig is slightly different: "*Seinen Namen, einen entrückten, ruft man*" = One would call out his enrapturing name.
41 The passage in Matthew reads: "Now when he heard that John had been arrested, he withdrew into Galilee; and leaving Nazareth he went and dwelt in Caper'na-um by the sea, in the territory of Zeb'ulun and Naph'tali,that what was spoken by the prophet Isaiah might be fulfilled: The land of Zeb'ulun and the land of Naph'tali, toward the sea, across the Jordan, Galilee of the Gentiles—the people who sat in darkness have seen a great light, and for those who sat in the region and shadow of death light has dawned."
42 "*Man nennet seinen Namen ein Wunder der Rat, Heldengott, Ewigvater, Friedenfürst.*" = One names his name miracle of advice, God's hero, eternal father, prince of peace.

tant that the names of the messiah of Isaiah 9:5 never reappear [in the Bible]; what was possible in the time of Isaiah, becomes impossible later on." (246)

How is this dissonance between Gressmann's interpretive perspective, as expressed in the commentary, and the theological implications of his translation possible? Why would he maintain, similarly to Buber and contrary to the widely held Christian reading, that Isaiah's prophecy refers to the time and place of its communication, and yet produce a translation so similar to Christological renditions of the verse?[43] Unlike Rosenstock, the Christian Bible translators whose work Buber and Rosenzweig were familiar with had excellent command of Hebrew, and they were well versed in the corpus of traditional Jewish exegesis. Therefore, in Gressmann's case it is not the lack of knowledge that we can blame for the discordant perspectives on the Bible and its message. It appears, then, that Rosenzweig's conception of Hebrew and Buber's emphasis on the inextricability of form and content in the biblical text point at a quality that Hebrew possesses, which cannot be reduced to linguistic structures and philological analysis. To put it in scientific terms, Buber and Rosenzweig, on the one hand, and Gressmann, on the other hand, based their work on similar premises and relied on comparable evidence, but reached diametrically opposed outcomes. Their methods, one is inclined to concede, must have been inspired by different motivations.

4 Conclusion: Whose Bible is it Anyway?

In the last twenty years or so, two books bearing very similar titles appeared: *Whose Bible is it Anyway?*, (Davies 1995) and *Whose Bible is it?* (Pelikan 2005) The former presents the reflection of a longtime Bible scholar on the hindrances of ideological bias to the academic study of the Bible, whereas the latter stakes out a common ground for Jews', Catholics' and Protestants' reading of the biblical text together without compromising on their own unique view on its sacredness. These books, and their titles especially, indicate that close to a century after Buber and Rosenzweig produced their translations, both believers and scholars of different faiths continue to suffer from lack of confidence in the face of counterclaims or competing interpretations of their scriptures.

---

[43] Compare, for example Luther: "er heißt Wunderbar, Rat, Held, Ewig-Vater Friedefürst"; and the rendition of Franz Delitzsch (who translated the New Testament into Hebrew as a missionary act): "und man nennt seinen Namen: Wunder, Berater, starker Gott, Ewig-Vater, Friede Fürst." (Delitzsch 1889, 167)

Philip Davies proposes a strict dichotomy between a discipline he calls Bible study, which seeks to establish a religious understanding of scripture as divine message, and the academic study of the Bible, which is interested in the text's evolution, problems and nuances (1995, 20–21). In contrast, Jaroslav Pelikan traces a broad common denominator that accommodates both the similarities and differences between the histories, premises and needs of the respective faiths (2005, 7–26). Both authors, in my view, inadvertently underscore the importance and relevance of Buber's and Rosenzweig's translation project, especially when read by Christians. Firstly, Davies' dichotomy leaves a crucial lacuna: translation. This activity involves both academic tools and skills, and spiritual investment. As I have tried to show, translators' devotional affiliation inescapably defines their reception of the text, while binding together the two approaches to the study of the Bible. Whereas Pelikan's accommodating view, worthwhile and commendable as it is, has the potential of concealing agendas and obscuring essential differences between the premises upon which each religion bases its readings of scripture. Buber's and Rosenzweig's endeavor, though partially camouflaging its own agenda and motivations, offers Christian readers access to the Jewish Bible: providing a sense of its resonance in the Jewish ear and the Jewish mind, and an idea of how this resonance is linked to the long and vibrant history of Jewish Bible exegesis. At the same time, it offers a reminder that dialogue can, and sometimes should, include an agreement to disagree.

Bibliography

Amir, Yehoyada. 2011. "'Toward the Source of Truthful Life': Franz Rosenzweig's Encounter with the Poetry of Rabbi Yehuda Halevi." In *Jehuda Halevi: Fünfundneunzig Hymnen und Gedichte Deutsch und Hebräisch mit einem Vorwort und mit Anmerkungen*, edited by Yehoyada Amir. 1–28. Jerusalem: Magnes.

Batnitzky, Leora. 1997. "Translation as Transcendence: A Glimpse into the Workshop of the Buber-Rosenzweig Bible Translation." *New German Critique* 70: 87–116.

Benjamin, Mara. 2009. *Rosenzweig's Bible: Reinventing Scripture for Jewish Modernity*. Cambridge: Cambridge University Press.

Buber, Martin. 1951. *Two Types of Faith*, trans. N.P. Goldhawk. London: Routledge; K. Paul.

Buber, Martin. 1994a. "From the Beginning of our Bible Translation." In Buber and Rosenzweig 1994, 176–183.

Buber, Martin. 1994b. "On Word Choice in Translating the Bible: In Memoriam Franz Rosenzweig." In Buber and Rosenzweig 1994, 73–89.

Buber, Martin. 1994c. "People Today and the Jewish Bible: From a Lecture Series." In Buber and Rosenzweig 1994, 4–21.

Buber, Martin. 1994d. "The Language of Botschaft." In Buber and Rosenzweig 1994.

Buber, Martin. 2011. "Zwei Glaubensweisen." In *Martin Buber Werkausgabe 9. Schriften zum Christentum*, edited by Karl-Josef Kuschel, 202–312. Gütersloh: Gütersloher Verlagshaus.
Buber, Martin. 2012. "Der Mensch von heute und die jüdische Bibel." In *Martin Buber Werkausgabe 14: Schriften zur Bibelübersetzung*, edited by Ran HaCohen. Gütersloh: Gütersloher Verlagshaus.
Buber, Martin. 2017. *Martin Buber Werkausgabe 5: Vorlesungen über Judentum und Christentum*, edited by Orr Scharf. Gütersloh: Gütersloher Verlagshaus.
Buber, Martin, and Franz Rosenzweig. *Die Schrift: Das Buch Jeschajahu. Zu Verdeutschung unternommen von Martin Buber gemeinsamen mit Franz Rosenzweig*. Berlin: Lambert Schneider.
Buber, Martin, and Franz Rosenzweig. 1926a–1930. *Im Anfang*. Die Schrift 1. Berlin: Lambert Schneider.
Buber, Martin, and Franz Rosenzweig. 1926b–1930. *Namen*. Die Schrift 2. Berlin: Lambert Schneider.
Buber, Martin, and Franz Rosenzweig. 1926c–1930. *Er Rief*. Die Schrift 3. Berlin: Lambert Schneider.
Buber, Martin, and Franz Rosenzweig. 1926d–1930. *In der Wüste*. Die Schrift 4. Berlin: Lambert Schneider.
Buber, Martin, and Franz Rosenzweig. 1926e–1930. *Reden*. Die Schrift 5. Berlin: Lambert Schneider.
Buber, Martin, and Franz Rosenzweig. 1926f–1930. *Jehoschua*. Die Schrift 6. Berlin: Lambert Schneider.
Buber, Martin, and Franz Rosenzweig. 1926 g–1930. *Richter*. Die Schrift 7. Berlin: Lambert Schneider.
Buber, Martin, and Franz Rosenzweig. 1926 h–1930. *Schmuel*. Die Schrift 8. Berlin: Lambert Schneider.
Buber, Martin, and Franz Rosenzweig. 1926i–1930. *Könige*. Die Schrift 9. Berlin: Lambert Schneider.
Buber, Martin, and Franz Rosenzweig. 1926j–1930. *Jeschajahu*. Die Schrift 10. Berlin: Lambert Schneider.
Buber, Martin, and Franz Rosenzweig. 1936. *Die Schrift und ihre Verdeutschung*. Berlin: Schocken.
Buber, Martin, and Franz Rosenzweig, eds. 1994. *Scripture and Translation*, trans. Lawrence Rosenwald with Everett Fox. Bloomington, IN: Indiana University Press.
Casper, Bernhard. 1967. *Das Dialogische Denken: Eine Untersuchung der religionsphilosophischen Bedeutung Franz Rosenzweigs, Ferdinand Ebners und Martin Bubers*. Freiburg: Herder.
Cristaudo, Wayne. 2009. "The Great Gift: The Impact of Franz Rosenzweig's Jewishness on Euegen Rosenstock-Huessy." In *The Cross and the Star: The Post-Nietzschean Christian and Jewish Thought of Eugen Rosenstock-Huessy and Franz Rosenzweig*, edited by Wayne Cristaudo and Frances Huessy, 139–162. Newcastle upon Tyne: Cambridge Scholars.
Cristaudo, Wayne. 2012. *Religion, Redemption, and Revolution: The New Speech Thinking of Franz Rosenzweig and Eugen Rosenstock-Huessy*. Toronto: University of Toronto Press.
Davies, Philip R. 1995. *Whose Bible is it Anyway?* Journal for the Study of the Old Testament Supplement Series 204. Sheffield: Sheffield Academic Press.
Delitzsch, Franz. 1889. *Commentar über Das Buch Jesaia*. Leipzig: Dörffling & Franke.

Galli, Barbara Ellen, ed. 1995. *Franz Rosenzweig and Jehuda Halevi: Translating, Translations and Translators*. Montreal, Kingston: McGill-Queen's University Press.

Glatzer, Nahum. 1959. "Languages and Hebrew in Particular in Rosenzweig's Thought." In *Yovel Shay: Essays in Honor of Shmuel Yosef Agnon upon Reaching Seventy on the 9th of Av, 5718*, edited by Baruch Kurzweil, 229–236. Ramat Gan: Bar Ilan University Press.

Goshen-Gottstein, Moshe. 1972. "Introduction." In *Biblia Rabbinica: A Reprint of the 1525 Venice Edition*, edited by Ben Hayim Ibn Adoniya, Jacob, 6–8. Jerusalem: Makor.

Gressman, Hugo. 1929. *Der Messias*. Göttingen: Vanderhoeck & Ruprecht.

HaCohen, Ran, ed. 2012. *Martin Buber Werkausgabe*. Schriften zur Bibelübersetzung 14. Gütersloh: Gütersloher Verlagshaus.

Hill, Christopher. 1994. *The English Bible and the Seventeenth-Century Revolution*. London: Penguin.

Hirsch, Samson Raphael. 1899. *Der Pentateuch: Übersetzt und erklärt von Samson Raphael Hirsch*. 3rd ed. 5 vols. Frankfurt a. M.: J. Kauffmann.

Huessy, Raymund. 2015. "Eugen and Margit Rosenstock-Huessy in 'Rosenzweig Studies': A Reflection on the Centennial of the 'Leipziger Nachtgespräch'." *Culture, Theory and Critique* 56 (1): 101–117.

Joosten, Jan. 2016. "How Old is the Targumic Tradition? Traces of the Jewish Targum in the Second Temple Period, and Vice Versa." In *The Text of the Hebrew Bible and Its Editions*, 143–159. Supplements to the Textual History of the Bible 1. Leiden: Brill.

Mayer, Reinhold, and Annemarie Mayer, eds. 1984. *Zweistromland: Kleinere Schriften zu Glauben und Denken*. Gesammelte Schriften 3. Dordrecht: Martinus Nijhoff.

Mendelssohn, Moses. 1887. "Light on the Path, which is a General Introduction to the Five Books." In *Sefer Netivot Hashalom:* 9–22. Warsaw: Alafin.

Omar al Eis, Zayed. 2015. *The Koran in Another Tongue*, trans. Subhi Ali Adawi. Aman: Bayinat.

Pearson, J. D. 1986. "Translations of the Kur'an." In *The Encyclopedia of Islam: New Edition*, edited by Bosworth, C. E. et al, 429. Leiden: Brill.

Pelikan, Jaroslav. 2005. *Whose Bible Is It? A History of the Scriptures Through the Ages*. New York: Viking.

Petuchowski, Elizabeth. 1995. "Die Kreatur, an Interdenominational Journal, and Martin Buber's Strange Use of the Term 'Reality' (Wirklichkeit)." *Deutsche Vierteljahrsschrift für Literaturwissenschaft und Geistgeschichte* 69 (4): 766–787.

Philippson, Ludwig. 1858. *Die Israelitische Bibel: Enthaltend: den Heiligen Urtext, die deutsche Uebertragung, die allgemeine, ausfürliche Erläuterung mit mehr als 500 englischen Holtzschnitten*. 2nd ed. 2 vols. Leipzig: Baumgärtner's Buchhandlung.

Pollock, Benjamin. 2014. *Franz Rosenzweig's Conversions: World Denial and World Redemption*. Bloomington, IN: Indiana University Press.

Rosenstock-Huessy, Eugen, ed. 2016. *Judaism Despite Christianity: The "Letters on Christianity and Judaism" between Eugen Rosenstock-Huessy and Franz Rosenzweig*. Tuscaloosa, AL: University of Alabama Press.

Rosenwald, Lawrence. 2007. "Between Two Worlds: Martin Buber's 'The How and Why of Our Bible Translation.'" *Jewish Studies Quarterly* 14: 144–151.

Rosenzweig, Franz. 1920. *Der Tischdank*. Berlin: Fritz Gurlitt.

Rosenzweig, Franz. 1921–1922. "Meister des All Du." *Der Jude* 6.

Rosenzweig, Franz. 1922. *Häusliche Feier: Deutsch von Franz Rosenzweig*. Frankfurt a. M. J. Kauffmann.
Rosenzweig, Franz. 1924. *Sechzig Hymnen und Gedichte des Jehuda Halevi*. Konstanz: Oskar Wöhrle.
Rosenzweig, Franz. 1927. *Zweiundneunzig Hymnen und Gedichte des Jehuda Halevi*. Berlin: Lambert Schneider.
Rosenzweig, Franz. 1935. "Franz Rosenzweig und Eugen Rosenstock: Judentum und Christentum." In *Briefe*, edited by Edith Rosenzweig and Ernst Simon, 638–720. Berlin: Schocken.
Rosenzweig, Franz. 1979a. *Franz Rosenzweig. Der Mensch und sein Werk. Gesammelte Schriften I: Briefe und Tagebücher 1. Band, 1900–1918*, edited by Rachel Rosenzweig, Edith Rosenzweig-Scheinmann, and Bernhard Casper. Haag: Martinus Nijhoff.
Rosenzweig, Franz. 1979b. *Franz Rosenzweig. Der Mensch und sein Werk. Gesammelte Schriften I: Briefe und Tagebücher 2. Band, 1918–1929*, edited by Rachel Rosenzweig, Edith Rosenzweig-Scheinmann, and Bernhard Casper. Haag: Martinus Nijhoff.
Rosenzweig, Franz. 1983. *Franz Rosenzweig. Der Mensch und sein Werk. Sprachdenken: Jehuda Halevi*, edited by Rafael Rosenzweig. Gesammelte Schriften IV. Hague: Martinus Nijhoff.
Rosenzweig, Franz. 1984. *Franz Rosenzweig. Der Mensch und sein Werk. Zweistromland: Kleinere Schriften zu Glauben und Denken*, edited by Reinhold Mayer and Annemarie Mayer, 461–482. Gesammelte Schriften 3. Dordrecht: Martinus Nijhoff.
Rosenzweig, Franz. 1994a. "Scripture and Luther." In Buber and Rosenzweig 1994, 47–69.
Rosenzweig, Franz. 1994b. "The Secret of Biblical Narrative Form." In Buber and Rosenzweig 1994, 129–142.
Rosenzweig, Franz. 1995. "Afterword." In *Franz Rosenzweig and Jehuda Halevi: Translating, Translations and Translators*, edited by Barbara E. Galli, 169–184. Montreal, Kingston: McGill-Queen's University Press.
Rosenzweig, Franz. 2000. "The New Thinking." In *Philosophical and Theological Writings*, edited by Paul W. Franks and Michael Morgan, 109–139. Indianapolis, IN: Hackett.
Rosenzweig, Franz. 2002. "It Is Time." In *On Jewish Learning*, edited by N. N. Glatzer, 27–54. Madison, WI: University of Wisconsin Press.
Rosenzweig, Franz. 2007. *The Star of Redemption*, trans. William Hallo. Notre Dame: University of Notre Dame Press.
Rosenzweig, Rachel, Edith Rosenzweig-Scheinmann, and Bernhard Casper, eds. 1979a. *Gesammelte Schriften I: Briefe und Tagebücher 1. Band, 1900–1918*. Haag: Martinus Nijhoff.
Rosenzweig, Rachel, Edith Rosenzweig-Scheinmann, and Bernhard Casper, eds. 1979b. *Gesammelte Schriften I: Briefe und Tagebücher 2. Band, 1918–1929*. Haag: Martinus Nijhoff.
Scharf, Orr. 2014. "'If One Translates a Verse Literally, He Is a Liar': On Dual Loyalties in the Buber-Rosenzweig Translation of the Bible." In *"Theocracy" and "Nation" in Jewish Thought: Past and Present*, edited by Ada Taggar-Cohen, 68–76. Kyoto: Doshisha University.
Scharf, Orr. 2016. "Clandestine Scholarship: The Septuagint as a Key into Martin Buber's and Franz Rosenzweig's Bible Translation." In *"Alles in der Schrift ist echte Gesprochenheit"*:

Martin Buber und die Verdeutschung der Schrift, 120–129. Martin Buber Studien 2. Hessen: Verlag Edition AV.

Scharf, Orr. 2017a. "Einzelkommentare." In Buber 2017, 330–332.

Scharf, Orr. 2017b. "Von 'Ecclesia et Synagoga' zu 'Zwei Glaubensweisen': Martin Bubers Vorlesungen über Judentum und Christentum." In Buber 2017, 11–49.

Shahar, Galili. 2016. *Bodies and Names: Readings in Modern Jewish Literature.* Tel Aviv: Am Oved.

Sheehan, Jonathan. 2007. *The Enlightenment Bible: Translation, Scholarship, Culture.* Princeton, NJ: Princeton University Press.

Stahmer, Harold. 1968. *Speak that I May See Thee! The Religious Significance of Language.* New York: Macmillan.

Stünkel, Knut Martin. 2015. "Eugen Rosenstock-Huessy's Early Symblysmatic Experiences: The Sociology of Patmos and Die Kreatur." *Culture, Theory and Critique* 56 (1): 13–27.

Uffenheimer, Benjamin. 1964. "For to us a child is born, to us a child is given.' (Isaiah 9:5): Readings in Isaiah's Eschatology." In *Sefer Segal: Presented in Honor of Prof. Moshe Zvi Segal by His Friends and Disciples*, edited by Yehoshua M. Grinz and Liver Ya'akov, 103–126. Jerusalem: Kiryat Sefer.

Zank, Michael. 2003. "The Rosenzweig-Rosenstock Triangle, or What Can We Learn from Letters to Grittli? A Review Essay." *Modern Judaism* 23 (1): 74–98.

Zunz, Leopold, ed. 1935. *Die vierundzwanzig Bücher der Heiligen Schrift nach dem masoretischen Texte.* trans. H. Arnheim, Julius Fürst, M. Sachs. 17th ed. Berlin: Leo Alterthum.

Borderlands and Bridges

Kenneth B. Moss
Not *The Dybbuk* but *Don Quixote*: Translation, Deparochialization, and Nationalism in Jewish Culture, 1917–1919

Writing in the weeks before the February Revolution in the Moscow newspaper *Ha-am*, the Zionist-Hebraist publicist A. Litai called for the creation of an organized, publicly funded program to translate "the famous works of the great figures of the nations of the world" into Hebrew (Litai 1917). There was nothing remarkable about Litai's interest in the translation of canonical foreign literary works per se. A concern for this sort of translation (as distinct from intentional adaptation, imitation, and other forms of literary importation) was by 1917 a normal feature of both the Hebrew and Yiddish literary spheres in Russia and beyond. In Russia's Hebrew literary sphere, the inauguration of a world literature series by the Hebrew writer Ben-Avigdor's Tushiyah publishing house in 1896 marked a shift from intermittent, idiosyncratic manifestations of interest in literary translation throughout the nineteenth century on the part of figures like Micha Yosef Lebensohn or the missionary/translator Y. Zalkinson to more sustained and normative attention (Miron 1987, 35–36). By 1911, there was a Hebrew publishing venture, Turgeman, devoted solely to translating the shared European canon of children's literature—Twain, Jules Verne, Mayne Reid, *1001 Nights*, and the like (Ofek 1984, 65–69; for the parallel case in the *Yishuv*, see Shavit and Shavit 1977, 48–51). Belated but parallel developments marked the individuating Yiddish literary sphere, where by 1913, the Yiddishist journal *Di yidishe velt* carried translations of Greek and Babylonian epic (Shulman 1965, 146–47).

But if Litai's interest in literary translation was not especially noteworthy, his proposal was striking for other reasons. Remarkable, first, was his vision of a grand program of encompassing literary translation run by a public body standing above the market and the idiosyncrasies of writers and publishers. Even more notable were the motivations underpinning it: in a rhetoric of cultural crisis usually reserved for more pressing matters than literary translation, Litai insisted that the very perpetuation of modern Hebrew culture and even "our national language" itself now depended on such an immediate, massive translation effort. Most remarkable of all was the extraordinary resonance and amplification these ideas—arrived at quite independently and simultaneously by other cultural actors—would enjoy in the Hebrew and Yiddish cultural spheres in the two explosive years to come.

Litai wrote at a critical juncture in the history of the Jewish nationalist intelligentsia's endeavor to create a new kind of Jewish culture. Since the turn of the century, growing numbers of young Russian Jews, locked in a dialectical relationship with the metropolitan Russian culture to which many of their peers were acculturating ever more fully, had come to share a vision of a modern Jewish 'high culture' in an (idealized) European mold. This putative culture was humanist, historicist, essentially secular, shot through with Romantic conceptions of language and nationhood, and predicated above all on the ideal of Art as the highest end of human individual and collective expression. Its adherents hoped that it would overcome traditional Jewish culture, displace market-driven Yiddish popular culture, compete with metropolitan Russian, Polish, and German cultures on their own terms, and reconstitute both a putative Jewish nation and the Jewish individual in the process. Though such dramatic achievements remained far out of reach—and though this cultural vision itself was increasingly sundered by tensions over language, political affiliation, and definitions of Jewish culture itself—there did emerge a distinct and substantial Jewish cultural sphere by 1914. By January 1917, when Litai called for his grand translation project, the situation seemed on the surface quite different: the war and wartime censorship had brutally snuffed out the key journals, publishing houses, and cultural organizations of this cultural endeavor (Slutsky 1961, xiv–xxiii). Yet the vision that had driven this institution-building remained a deeply internalized commitment for a substantial part of the East European Jewish intelligentsia. It drove Litai's pen at a moment when it seemed that the institutions of the cultural sphere were shattered for good, and it proved ready to reemerge full-blown under the right circumstances: the unprecedented freedoms of expression and institution-building offered by the Revolution of February 1917 opened the way for numerous Jewish intellectuals, activists, and artists to throw themselves once again into the task of creating the new culture (Moss 2009).

This return to cultural activity after two years of desperate silence drew added impetus from such post-February factors as the apparent triumph of secular nationalism in Jewish political life and the challenges of national revolution across Eastern Europe; the promise of cultural autonomy and state support for Jewish culture, especially in Ukraine; the perception that for good or for ill, the war had finally destroyed traditional Jewish society; the spontaneous burgeoning of new aesthetic trends in the arts at the hands of a host of newcomers to the Jewish cultural sphere; and, with the Bolshevik coup in October, the promise or specter of a more encompassing revolution, cultural as well as sociopolitical. But although 1917 is often treated as a point of fracture in Jewish cultural history, it is important to understand that these developments actually did *not* usher in a radical new beginning for the Jewish national cultural project, even on the Yiddishist left. Rather, they provoked an urgent cultural stocktaking and reassertion: across hardening divisions of political ideology, linguistic commitment, and cultural aspirations, the culturally engaged Jewish intelligentsia almost unanimously (if separately) seized this moment to reassert, expand, and realize cultural agendas long in the making. This consolidating sensibility derived impetus not only from the new opportunities but also from a widespread conviction that the future of this culture could only be secured by organized endeavor. Thus, in April 1917, the Hebraist patron-activist Hillel Zlatopolski called on Hebraists to obey "the commandment of this great hour" and "turn our spiritual energy to the work of national creation"; a year later, his Yiddishist opponents echoed the same mix of enthusiasm and urgency: "But in this time when it is possible for spiritual culture to develop freely, one begins to feel the need to unify our powers, to organize cultural work, ... to bind together all initiatives." ("Me-et Tarbut," 5)

One of the most striking manifestations of this process of consolidation was the intensification of prewar efforts to shape the new Jewish aesthetic culture by incorporating sources outside its definitional boundaries. Most famously, some Jewish cultural producers like Haim Nahman Bialik and S. An-ski renewed prewar efforts to recuperate indigenous Jewish sources, whether pre-modern Hebrew texts or East European Jewish "folk culture," so that they might serve as the cornerstone of a new, secular-national yet "authentic" Jewish culture (Moss 2003, 103–18; Moss 2009, ch. 3; Kiel 1991, 150–61; Rubin 2000). Wrested from their traditional moorings and reworked in accordance with secular nationalist and Romantic aesthetic values, these products of traditional Jewish creativity would provide a defining aesthetic and even ethical framework for modern Jewish culture. In recent years, these efforts to recuperate indigenous Jewish sources—which yielded, among other things, the most impressive flowering of Jewish plastic art in modern times in the work of figures like El Lissitzky and Iosif Tchaikov (Wolitz 1988; Bowlt 1988)—have begun to receive the scholarly attention they warrant (Roskies 1995, 1996; Kazovski 2003; Veidlinger 2000; Ivanov 1999; Kiel 1991; Rubin 2000). They have also come to define our understanding of modern Jewish culture as a whole: this negotiation between the modern self and pre-modern Jewish expression has come to seem *the* paradigmatic move of modern Jewish culture, with the recuperation of classical Hebrew sources the defining Hebraist cultural posture and folklorism, that of Yiddishism.

Yet an examination of Jewish cultural activity as a whole in the 1917–1919 period, rather than through the particular lens of such indigenizing strategies, yields a surprising finding: these continued efforts to recuperate pre-modern indigenous Jewish sources as the fundaments of the new Jewish culture were paralleled by, ideologically *overshadowed* by, and even vigorously denigrated in favor of a third, largely unexamined strategy of culture-building, namely, systematic, massive, immediate, and non-adaptive[1] literary translation of a posited unitary, universal canon of Western literature into Hebrew or Yiddish. When Litai echoed and amplified this argument the following year in the newly restored Hebraist journal *Ha-shiloah* (Litai ["A. Ben-Moshe"] 1918, 540–46), he was no longer a lone voice but one of a choir of intellectuals who shared his sense that a grand project of translation was perhaps the most pressing need of the cultural moment. This was, moreover, a remarkably strange choir: its members traversed the full range of political, linguistic, and cultural commitment, from uncompromising integral Zionist-Hebraists like Litai or *Ha-shiloah*'s editor Yosef Klausner to the Hebraist pro-Communist Eliezer Shteynman, from the Hebraist aesthete David Frishman to the revolutionary and radical Yiddishist Moyshe Litvakov.

This discourse on the centrality of translation intersected, moreover, with an increasingly predominant discourse in the Jewish cultural sphere that, far from valorizing traditional indigenous sources, declared them a secondary value or even an obstacle to the attainment of a compelling modern Jewish culture. Some of the proponents of translation wedded their plans to full-fledged attacks on strategies of recuperation, asserting that what Jewish culture needed was not the indigenous but precisely the alien. Others hewed a more compromising line, but the linkage between the discourse on translation and the outpouring of attacks on "parochialism" in Jewish culture by an ideologically varied cohort of cultural figures dramatizes the importance of rethinking what "Jewish culture" had come to mean by 1917 through the lens of translation.

These emphatic calls for placing organized translation at the center of Jewish cultural life found more concrete institutional expression in a new breed of Hebrew and Yiddish publishing houses that emerged in 1917–1918. The Hebraist Stybel and Omanut publishing houses and the Yiddishist Kiever-Farlag, Folks-Farlag, and Kultur-Lige Farlag (and numerous other small Yiddishist publishing ventures) understood themselves less as businesses than as shapers of Jewish culture as a whole in accordance with coherent overarching visions. Eclipsing veteran cultural publishers like Bialik's Moriah or the Yiddishist Kletskin Farlag, these new publishing ventures sought, as Stybel's chief editor Frishman put it in a letter to Bialik on June 9, 1917, to "build the Pithom and Ramses of a whole lit-

---

[1] By non-adaptive translation, I mean to distinguish an attitude toward the text as an integral unit and work of art from translation-as-adaptation, in which the alteration of contents (especially "Judaization") and even defining generic features was a matter of course (see Borovaia 2001, 149–68 for a ground-breaking account). The kind of translation I am dealing with is a polar opposite formally and, even more important, ideologically, as we shall see.

erature" (*Keneset* 1940, 26)—or, as the the Yiddishist Nokhem Shtif of the Folks-Farlag put it retrospectively in 1922, to "be *the* cultural institution to build our literary cultural work and chart a path." (Niger Collection, file 203) Significantly, almost all of these major publishing houses (and many smaller ones) made large-scale literary translation a defining feature of their programs. Thus, by 1918, Litai was no longer calling for action, but commenting on a massive translation program by the Stybel press, merely one of the most remarkable instances of an astonishing outpouring of translations and discourse about translation that convulsed Hebraist and Yiddishist cultural life at this juncture (Litai ["Ben-Moshe"], 1918; Litai ["A.B.M."] 1919).

This chapter examines the rhetoric and practice of translation in the post-February Jewish cultural sphere as a means to investigate several larger issues central to the history of the Jewish cultural project in Eastern Europe. It focuses on the key Jewish cultural circles of Moscow, Kiev, and Odessa, during the brief but critical period following February 1917 but prior to the decisive penetration of Bolshevik and Yevsektsiia power into Jewish cultural life from within and without, roughly late 1918 in Moscow and European Russia and mid-1919 in Ukraine and the borderlands. As I show at length elsewhere (Moss 2009), the re-emergent Russian Jewish cultural sphere of February 1917 was in most essential respects a continuation of prewar Jewish culture initially only marginally reshaped by immanent cultural-revolutionary drives; only later, between 1919 and 1921, was it dramatically transformed by the triumphant. Thus, the current chapter analyzes the Jewish cultural sphere at a juncture when its participants felt both free and compelled to clarify and reassert their longstanding cultural project but were not yet seduced or forced to dramatically recast their visions by the new revolutionary reality. Moving between conceptions of translation and other discourses and practices concerned with "Europeanizing" Jewish literary culture, it seeks to explain why a wide swath of the Jewish nationalist intelligentsia, Hebraists and Yiddishists both,[2] had come by 1917 to see wholesale incorporation of an imagined encompassing, unitary canon of Western literature, more than or even instead of the reincorporation of indigenous Jewish sources, as a key to the creation of a satisfactory modern Jewish secular culture. It argues that the driving force of this sensibility was a paradoxical form of Jewish cultural nationalism, found among both Hebraists and Yiddishists and across the political spectrum, which sought (in some respects out of necessity) to remake Jewish culture as a

---

2 Elsewhere I have analyzed the almost universal devaluation among Jewish nationalist intellectuals of Russian as a *target* language of Jewish cultural life in this period, even as the larger process of Russification continued apace (Moss 2009, 68–70). On Russian-language Jewish cultural publishing, see below.

branch of a posited multilingual "universal" (European) culture; it thus builds on the efforts of Benjamin Harshav, Yaacov Shavit, and Seth Wolitz, among others, to redefine our concepts of Jewish culture, Yiddishism and Hebraism, and Jewish nationalism by examining how they operated in league with rather than against "universal" culture for contemporaries (Harshav 1993; Shavit 1997, chap. 8; Wolitz 1978, 1981, 1991). At the same time, this chapter investigates how the dynamics of high culture itself and the sociological realities of Diaspora existence operated to reshape Jewish cultural nationalism.

1 Translation and the Future of Jewish Culture

Litai was, as noted, one of an array of intellectuals, critics, writers, and activists who separately articulated an explicit conception of what we might call programmatic translation in the 1917–1919 period. If Litai was the most rhetorically urgent of these, it was Moyshe Litvakov, the leading Yiddishist theorist of his day, who offered the most ramified expression of this stance in a 1919 essay in the Kiev Yiddishist cultural journal *Bikher-velt* entitled "The System of Translations." (Litvakov 1919b, 1919c) Litvakov argued that Yiddish literature had reached a stage of stagnation and decline beyond which it could move only by means of a massive, systematic program of translation from the "world poetry of all generations, peoples, and languages," especially the "living waters" of contemporary European literature (Litvakov 1919c, 37, 41). Such a project required planning, adherence to principles dictated by a larger vision of what Yiddish literature truly needed to become—namely, a self-sufficient, all-encompassing art-literature—and the leadership of the literary and intellectual elite. Litvakov emphasized both the critical significance of this undertaking and the model for it through an invocation of the early-nineteenth-century German literary sphere and to a lesser extent the nineteenth-century Russian literary sphere as exemplary instances in which literary elites had undertaken ramified programs of translation "as a type of national-cultural function on behalf of the vital interests of the national literature." (Litvakov 1919b, 12)

As a literary critic and theorist, Litvakov was an aggressive proponent of the most avant-garde literary streams of the day and an impatient, demanding critic of anything he deemed old-fashioned or epigonic. He was also, by mid-1919, a committed supporter of the Bolshevik Revolution; by the time the second half of this article was published in August 1919, he held a position in the Yiddish cultural institutions of the newly installed Bolshevik government in Kiev (the first half, published in January 1919, was written before the Bolshevik takeover).

Yet neither of these commitments found much echo in Litvakov's translation program:

> These must be translated: works which have had the most significant influence on the formation and development of our literary feelings, thoughts, and ways of speaking, whose images, symbols, figures, and expressions have made their way into our everyday lives [*tog-shteyger*]. Works which have called forth particular literary-social streams and become a jumping-off point for a new development. Works in which the eternal beauty of the artistic word is crystallized. The major epic works of the various peoples and lands. Works of writers who characterize or embody a significant epoch or interesting strata of society. Above all, works which represent boundary markers in the development of literary forms, genres, and tendencies. (Litvakov, 1919c, 42–43)

Indeed, Litvakov summarily dismissed any notion that this program of translation should suit itself to any immediate political needs or even the needs of Yiddish readers ("the masses") themselves; simultaneously, he just as explicitly asserted that translation *not* be organized to further any particular literary movement or aesthetic: "There are phases in the history of a national literature when neither this or that individual translator-devotee nor the public but rather [the literature] itself requires translation for its growth and development." (Litvakov 1919b, 10)

Not everyone made the same surprising double move; one reviewer for the same journal welcomed a Yiddish translation of Byron's *Heaven and Earth* in part because Byron's art was supposedly "a direct means of struggle ... with that world which the great Revolution has just outlived." (Gomlen 1919, 42) But the leading proponents of translation shared Litvakov's general views on both counts. Eliezer Shteynman—aggressively pro-Bolshevik though deeply Zionist, and committed to a vague but heartfelt program of revolution in Hebrew literature itself—numbered among the Stybel press's chief merits precisely the fact that it had no limiting aesthetic or political agenda: in the pages of the Hebrew anthology *Erets*, which yoked together Bolshevik sympathies, Zionism, and a call for "youth" revolution in Hebrew literature (Gilboa 1974, 17–19; Moss 2003, 215–16, 314–17), Shteynman praised the Stybel press's massive translation program for bringing "everything, everything to us: from the first fruits of realism, from the flowers of Romanticism, and from the grapes of modernism." (Shteynman 1919a) Litai propounded a slightly more focused agenda—opining that the Stybel press should translate fewer Decadent works and more Romantic ones in view of their salutary impact on Jewish consciousness—but also welcomed the grandly encompassing effort to bring "the literature of the world" into Hebrew all at once—and the absence of a political line in Stybel's *Ha-tekufah* (Litai 1918, 543).

The primary purpose of the envisioned global translation was less to reshape a general reading public (though these champions of translation certainly hoped that readers might benefit) than to reshape Hebrew or Yiddish literature themselves. One means by which translation would accomplish this feat was by catalyzing the development of a *neutral* literary language free of Jewish clichés. Litvakov made the avoidance of unwarranted Judaization in translation an explicit principle. The Yiddishist critic Nokhem Oyslender devoted close attention in his review of a Yiddish *Hiawatha* to the question of whether the translator had managed to avoid giving the "wigwam ... the smell of the Jewish study house." (Oyslender, 1919) By the same token, successful non-Judaized translation was deemed the ultimate test and symbol of the maturation of a literary language, and contemporaries responded to translations of the era as though they were referenda on the possibilities and achievements of Hebrew or Yiddish literature in their entirety. Yosef Klausner laid out clearly what was at stake in his jubilant comments on H. Taviov's translation of Wilde's *Picture of Dorian Gray* for the Stybel press. *Dorian Gray* was, in Klausner's view, not only a distinctly difficult "modern" work—a challenge for the translator under any circumstances—but also a "story which has no connection to Israel [Jewish matters]." Taviov's translation, which Klausner deemed possibly "the *first complete* Hebrew translation" of a work with no such Jewish connection, thus demonstrated that Hebrew had become a living language "sufficient to all the needs of feeling and thought and description of the modern person." (Klausner 1918b, 344) For Moyshe Kulbak, Max Weinreich's 1913 translation of book nine of Homer's *Iliad* was similar proof that Yiddish was a mature literary language, presumably because of the common assumption that the Homeric tradition was the very antithesis of classical Jewish literary expression (Kulbak [1918] 1962). The 1917 announcement that the great Hebrew poet and translator Shaul Tshernikhovsky would translate the same text into Hebrew generated great excitement in the Hebraist literary community, further suggesting how widespread this sensibility was (S. An-ski to Bialik 10/23 April 1918 in Ungerfeld 1974).

These two *Iliad* translations themselves enacted a translation poetics in deep accord with this sensibility. Both translators endeavored to hew to the complex dactylic hexameter of the original insofar as the respective poetic structures of ancient Greek, Hebrew, and Yiddish allowed it. Witness their translations of the famous first lines of book 9: "*Kokhoh hifkidu ha-Troyim shoymrehem; akh benei ho-Akhaim/retet akhozom vo-fakhad, ho-akhim li-eymoh u-mnusoh*"; "*Ot azoy hobn di Troyer gevakht: un a gvaldike eyme/hot di Akheer bafaln, gevorfn in ayzikn yeyish.*" (Tshernikhovsky, 1930; Shulman 1965, 147–48)[3] As Aminadav Dykman notes in his assessment of Tshernikhovsky's translation in relation to the original Greek, previous Hebrew translations, and the contemporary Hebrew literary "horizon of reception," this formal choice was not by any means a given in either earlier Hebrew *Iliad* translations nor, more important, in the Russian and German translations that Tshernikhovsky (and Weinreich) would have known (Dykman 1994, 429). Their attempts to capture the formal feel of the Homeric poetry thus reflects a very considered choice of form over "meaning" (or rather, a rejection of any such distinction in the name of a sovereign logic of poetry). Equally consonant with the sensibilities I have outlined was the translators' deployment of language organically related to existing registers yet distant from any particular spoken or textual register, which served to make the poems simultaneously compelling yet profoundly strange aesthetic objects. Thus, for instance, for the "many-fished sea" of book nine, Weinreich offered the syntactically natural yet stylistically alien "filfishikn fantos." In Tshernikhovsky's case, this involved trying to avoid the biblicization that characterized all previous Hebrew translations of Homer from that of the maskil Meir Halevi Letteris (1800–1871) to the 1898 attempt by Dovid Margolin (Dykman 1994, 447–55). As Dykman notes, to turn Greek epic into biblical epic was the culturally obvious choice for Hebrew translators (Erich Auerbach's famous emphasis on their difference notwithstanding) *if* one regarded translation as cultural mediation. Tshernikhovsky's decision to avoid it—and his efforts more generally to escape the gravity of any of the literary languages of the many-layered Hebrew textual tradition[4]—bespeak a will not to mediation but to the preservation of the aesthetic object's strangeness.[5] Tshernikhovsky and Weinreich sought instead to insert belated foundation stones beneath the rising edifice of modern, expansive Hebrew and Yiddish literary languages.

---

[3] I am of course trying to approximate Tshernikhovsky's Ashkenazic pronunciation; thus "oto ha-yam" becomes "oyso ha-yom," etc. My thanks to Daniel Moss for his guidance on the intricacies of meter in quantitative and accentual-syllabic verse.

[4] Of course, this could only be a relative escape. Dykman notes many structures and forms reminiscent of biblical, rabbinic, and liturgical corpora in Tshernikhovsky's translation. The key point here, however, is intentionality and the product it yielded: a translation in which what Dykman calls Hebraization was "immeasurably less than that in the translations of his predecessors and was not guiding foundational principle in the translation." (Dykman 1994, 456)

[5] Ironically, Dykman suggests that Tshernikhovsky believed—or came to believe—that in fact his translations recovered a historically real "Canaanite" affinity between ancient Greek and ancient Israelite culture (Dykman 1994, 463). But this does not alter the affinity of his translation technique to the larger non-Judaizing agenda examined here.

This concern about literary language was, in turn, part of a more global agenda that explains the concern to translate whole swaths of the European literary tradition (rather than selecting those works especially suited to some perceived need of the literary language): the desire to remake Hebrew or Yiddish literature as typical European literatures. For some, this may have had strong nationalist symbolic valence. The Hebraist patron and publisher Shoshana Persits entertained "an aspiration to see Hebrew culture in all of its manifestations stand on a level at least equal to the cultures of the great nations." (Tidhar 1947, 2825) Similar concerns seem to have animated Moyshe Kulbak's assertion that successful translation of Homer was not merely a vehicle for the maturity of a *"kulturshprakh,"* but also a sign of "a certain spiritual maturity on the part of that nation" (any nation) which translated it (Kulbak 1918, 238).

But, more important, there was a concretely literary goal: the translation programs of the day reflect the conviction that the creation of a compensatory literary tradition through translation was essential not merely as a point of pride and civilized status but as a means to make Jewish literature itself part of a shared, ever-more universal European literary culture. Thus, Litvakov's surprisingly catholic translation efforts were intended to transform Yiddish literature into "a big-city-universalist literature, with inclinations and orientations toward taking a place in world literature," not by emphasizing one particular aesthetic line but precisely by endowing it with world literature's entire panoply of forms and "fundamental motifs and moods, visions and images, symbols and figures, legends and myths." (Litvakov 1919c, 37–38, 43) Litai, Litvakov's polar opposite in political and linguistic-political terms, shared precisely the same vision of what literature was, how it worked, and what Jewish literature should be. He imagined the relationship among fully developed literatures like those of England, Germany, and Russia as a constant process of "mutual influence" through which these literatures "renew themselves and enrich themselves from day to day." To Litai, it was self-evident that "our literature," which by "a European measure is only at the beginning of its development," should aspire to join this company, and only programmatic translation could provide the necessary "universal" fundament (Litai 1918, 541).

Whereas each individual translation of merit might help transform Hebrew or Yiddish into more flexible literary languages, global translation was to bring about this transformation in the first instance by (re)educating the Jewish writer. Needless to say, none of the champions of translation hoped for a flood of imitations. On the contrary, they no doubt shared the hopes of another advocate of large-scale translation, Frishman, who maintained that such a body of translations would serve not as a source for mechanical imitation—indeed, he believed that only by translating these works accurately and making them an "integral part of Hebrew culture" could imitation be avoided—but provide inspiration, benchmarks, and an aestheticizing and Europeanizing influence on Hebrew writers.[6] Litvakov articulated a similar mechanism: "Should the future and even present Yiddish writer cleave spiritually and psychically to this wonder-world of great artworks, if he should reforge them in the flame of his intuition, our literature's 'Pale of Settlement' will be perforce abolished." (Litvakov 1919c, 38)

Translation was thus not pro forma—a matter of appearances—nor mere raw material; the European classics had to become central generative influences in Jewish literature by refining both the literary language and the authors who employed it. In a narrow sense, each individual translation had to be a genuine literary achievement. Although these critics were well aware of the formal challenges inherent in translation, they did not produce technical guides to translation like the *Printsipy khudozhestvennogo perevoda* (Chukovsky and Gumilev 1919), a guide to the "principles of artistic translation" created in the framework of Maxim Gorky's contemporary grand Russian world-translation program (on which see below). Nor did they produce penetrating philosophical meditations on language and translation like those of the Russian Symbolists before them or Benjamin and Buber-Rozenzweig after them.[7] Rather, whether due to lack of resources, talent, or leisure, these critics came at the issue piecemeal in individual reviews, as in Ezra Korman's formal comments on poetic translation in a review of Pushkin's "Poltava" in translation (Korman 1919a). One more potent means by which they hoped to overcome this challenge was harnessing the most talented Jewish writers themselves to translation. In the name of all Hebraists who wished for "the revival of our language," Litai hoped Bialik would undertake to translate "the classic foreign works." (Litai 1919, 605) Independently, David Frishman and the publisher-patron Avraham Yosef Stybel plied Bialik throughout April and May 1918 with requests that he

---

6 Frishman's investment in translation as a cultural strategy was part of a tightly linked set of convictions about the nature of literature, culture, and humanity as such centering around a transhistorical humanist conception of art implying a single universal though open literary canon. Here I am indebted to Iris Parush's painstaking reconstruction of Frishman's literary-cultural ideology (Parush 1992, 40–49, 70–75, 94, and infra). With regard to translation's role specifically, I disagree in part with Parush's contention that Frishman hoped that translation would transform Jewish cultural consciousness but had no particular hope to transform Jewish literature directly. By the 1917–1918 moment, at any rate, Frishman's translation praxis clearly bespeaks the hope that translation might indeed also have a direct influence on Hebrew literature, for instance generically—Frishman's preoccupation with translating great examples of the modern novel can hardly have been unconnected to his desire to see novels of "genius" in Hebrew literature, and translation was clearly intended in part to transform *writers* themselves.

7 My thanks to Ben Nathans and Gabriella Safran for this comparison.

translate *Evgenii Onegin* on the grounds that he was the "only one" who could do a good translation (*Kneset* 1940, 34–35; Beit Bialik Correspondence Collection, file *shin*-219). These hopes reflected a wholly Romantic notion of literature and authorial genius: as editor and children's writer M. Ben-Eliezer put it, "For a translation of a classic work of poetry, he only is qualified who is himself a poet and who has in his soul traces of the soul of the poet he is translating." (Ben-Eliezer 1917) In a more global sense, foreign literature could only have the requisite impact if imported whole, as a set of canons and genres, so that the Jewish writer might internalize the whole embodied history of a putatively universal literary development.[8] Hence the disgust of critic Ezra Korman with an anthology that purported to offer translations of the most important modern European poetry but merely proffered an unsystematic smattering organized not by national literature but by the Yiddish translator (Korman 1919b). Hence too the oft-repeated desire to see translation organized in some central fashion.

As the repeated references to the Stybel publishing house suggest, these visions were not confined to the realm of intention. This same conception of translation guided the grand program of this publishing house from its inception in Moscow in 1917. Its founder, the newly minted millionaire Hebraist Avraham Yosef Stybel, was utterly devoted to Hebrew literature and willing to expend a considerable part of his own fortune on the support of Hebrew writers materially and on the transformation of Hebrew literature itself (Amichay-Michlin 2000, 37–65). When in 1917 he placed the press with its million-ruble endowment entirely in the hands of his long-time hero, the Hebraist aesthete Frishman, he signaled his full agreement with Frishman's particular vision for Hebrew literature. Frishman and Stybel shared the view that Hebrew literature could not confine itself to any Jewish form of expression but must instead strive to be part of a posited universal literature, and that translation of the sort that intellectuals like Litai and Litvakov envisioned was the key means of facilitating this development (Tverski 1948, 14–18).[9]

Guided by Frishman and Stybel, the publishing house undertook a massive program of translation from European and world literature. Frishman's convic-

---

[8] Tellingly, writing in distant Palestine in 1919, the poet-critic Yaacov Steinberg voiced a similar notion of "gaps" in a putative universal literary structure (Shavit and Shavit 1977, 55).
[9] In point of fact, Litai criticized many of Frishman's specific choices as too much "cake" and not enough bread; in particular, he was unhappy that some of those he considered truly "universal" writers and works were being neglected in favor of writers who were merely "national" (like Chekhov!), and he was also irritated by the number of Decadent works being translated (Litai 1918, 542–43). But in so doing, Litai affirmed the larger shared principle of a "universal" literary substratum that had to be translated into all languages.

tion that the great works of literature were unique and unclassifiable expressions of a timeless human genius yielded an eclectic list of commissioned translations spanning genres and millennia: the range of works included a strong selection of Russian classic prose and poetry (Pushkin, Lermontov, Tolstoy, Dostoevsky, Chekhov); other giants of nineteenth-century prose (Dickens, Flaubert, Zola) and poetry (Mickiewicz, Heine); a strong representation of fin-de-siècle work (Wilde, Maeterlink, Ibsen, Hamsun, Przybysweski, France, Strindberg); and selections from the Greco-Roman tradition. The unifying principle of this list, though, was the supposed power of each work to jumpstart a worthwhile Hebrew literature.[10] The translations were to be done by writers, not mere translators. Stybel's first assistant, the newspaperman Ben-Tsion Katz, made particular efforts to recruit Tshernikhovsky (a doctor) to work full-time for the press. Frishman and at times Stybel himself solicited the participation of dozens of Hebrew writers both in revolutionary Russia and abroad, and Yehuda Slutsky noted that virtually every Hebrew writer in Russia took part in this endeavor in some way (Slutsky 1961, 25–30). Within roughly a year of its founding, the press had published five translated literary works, fifteen more were in production or ready to print, and over forty had been commissioned; translations also assumed a central place in the Stybel quarterly *Ha-tekufah* ("Hotsaat Stybel" 1918).

The distinctive features of the translation program collectively imagined by this disparate collection of Hebraists and Yiddishists may be thrown into sharper relief by comparison both to previous translation tendencies in Hebrew and Yiddish literary life and to contemporaneous tendencies in its co-territorial Russian literary sphere. First, the insistence that translation be organized primarily around the perceived formal needs of Hebrew or Yiddish literature themselves marked the triumph of a principle that had never been absent from Jewish literary life but that had been largely subordinate to conceptions of translation as a means for the direct (re)education of the Jewish *reader*. This held true for Hebrew literary life until the readership crisis of the first decade of the twentieth century

---

10 Though a variety of factors seem to have gone into the Stybel press's choice of writers, the list was strongly shaped by Frishman's distinctive vision of the European literary canon and the needs of Hebrew literature. Among those writers actively distributed for translation in the publisher's first year, Dostoevsky, France, Heine, Homer, Ibsen, Pushkin, Tolstoy, Wilde, and Zola occupied a central place in Frishman's canon. The press's call for translators who "know their strength" and were capable of translating Shakespeare, Goethe, Schiller, and Byron as well as the great playwrights and poets of ancient Greece and Rome also reflected Frishman's sense of what Hebrew literature truly needed, while Frishman himself had already undertaken Tagore and the Brothers Grimm (Parush 1992, 47–48, 146, and 146–47 n. 5; "Hotsaat Stybel" 1918).

—thus, Ben-Avigdor's pioneering conception of translation, though certainly concerned with the needs of Hebrew literature, was framed by a desire to leaven his readers' Jewishness with a putatively universal human wisdom (*klaliut*) (Ben-Avigdor 1895; Miron 1987, 33–35)—and even afterward in some quarters (for example, the Ha-Poel Ha-Tsair publishing house La-ʻam; cf. Shavit and Shavit 1977, 48). Translation into Yiddish was, naturally, even more tied to models of readership needs. The existence of a substantial popular market in Yiddish brought a flood of desultory translation-adaptations for a popular readership (Shmeruk 1983, 345–46) and Warsaw and New York publications of fashionable, accessible contemporary European prose writers (Hamsun, Maupassant, Chekhov) seem to have been linked to an as-yet unstudied middlebrow Yiddish readership akin to the emergent urban, middlebrow Russian readership analyzed by Jeffrey Brooks (Litvak 1919a, 13; Brooks 1978, 102–4, 114–16). More ideologically driven translation orientations were no less readership-centered: above all, translations produced within the broad range of progressive publishing in Yiddish were chosen according to an educative model. Thus, the Minsk publishing house "Kultur," founded by a left-leaning engineer in 1904, chose writers like Twain, Chekhov, and Korolenko who were of a piece with its diet of popular science, an almanac on "all lands and peoples," and a guide for emigrants by Alexander Harkavy (*Zamelbukh "Kultur"* 1905; Reyzen 1935, 85–86). Only in the last years of the prewar period did the pendulum begin to swing in the other direction, and it is this reorientation that came to full expression in the reemergent Hebrew and Yiddish literary spheres of 1917–1919.

This literature-centered translation sensibility also stands in illuminating contrast to its Russian parallel, Maxim Gorky's *Vsemirnaia Literatura* (world literature) project. Founded in September 1918, *Vsemirnaia Literatura* endeavored to create a "foundational library" of 1500 American, European, and Eastern literary works in Russian translation with the support of the Soviet state and with the participation of Russia's finest writers and scholars (Golubeva 1968, 96–99; Zaidman 1973, 141–42). This project, undertaken on a scale of which the Jewish champions of literary translation could only dream, was certainly intended on some level to serve Russian literature itself. In technical terms, the *Vsemirnaia literatura* project was more sophisticated than the visions of the Jewish cultural activists. Beyond the technical primer on translation by the Acmeist Nikolai Gumilev and the future dean of Soviet translators Kornei Chukovskii, it established a special poetic collegium, and conducted an ongoing practicum for its writer-translators. But the goals of its founder, Gorky, were first and foremost reader-centered: this *osnovnaia biblioteka* was meant to instill an internationalist humanism in the relatively educated Russian reader (it was paired with a *narodnaia biblioteka*, or folk library, aimed at the uneducated reader). Hence, Gorky pressed his translators—who included Russia's leading avant-garde writers—to serve a non-elite readership, and attacked some of their introductory essays as inaccessible (Golubeva 1968, 100, 110).

Thus, strangely, the concerns of these Jewish champions of translation, nationalist and radical activists by no means indifferent to the needs of the masses, bore less affinity with the sensibilities of the near-universally admired Gorky than they did with the most unabashed aesthetes of Russia's prewar Symbolist community.[11] Yet here, too, there was an illuminating difference. On the whole, the Symbolists and Decadents of the Russian fin-de-siècle sought to parley creative engagement with idiosyncratic assemblages of foreign cultural sources into literary fusion primarily *in and through* their own literary production, though some of them were also serious translators (Polonsky 1998, 1–22).[12] The Jewish translation advocates of the 1917 moment demanded something both less and more ambitious: not the slow, careful *processing* of foreign influences, but their brute insertion *en bloc* into the literary tradition.

In all these ways, as well in other tendencies out of step with the times (the concern, for instance, to have only literary writers do translations rather than professional translators), the Jewish discourse on translation at this juncture smacked of a previous age: the Russian and German literary spheres of the previous century—which Litvakov and others like David Frishman quite penetratingly invoked—with their multi-decade quest to master the literary powers of their neighbors to the west and the Western classical tradition (Friedberg 1997, 38, 48, 60; Frishman 1922, 6–7).[13] Even as individual Hebrew and Yiddish writers like Der Nister or Avigdor Ha-Meiri carried out creative recastings of external influences in ways no less sophisticated than their European counterparts—as in Nister's negotiation of Hans Christian Andersen or Ha-Meiri's negotiation of

---

11 As a model in the most general sense, Gorky's undertaking was perhaps of interest to these Jewish champions of translation, but many of the proposals and undertakings discussed here, especially the Hebrew ones, predate it, and I have seen no direct reference to it among Jewish national intellectuals except by Vladimir Jabotinsky—a figure quite distant from the Hebrew and Yiddish literary spheres in Russia at this juncture—who held it up as a model for a national translation program in the *Yishuv* (Shavit and Shavit 1977, 54).

12 Maurice Friedberg suggests that the Symbolists' shared conceptions of language saddled some of them with doubts about the possibilities of satisfactory translation as such and drove them toward either hyper-literal translation poetics or a tendency to remake the target poet as a Symbolist (Friedberg 1997, 63–64).

13 Greenleaf and Moeller-Sally offer a suggestive consideration of literary translation and its place in the formation of a national (but also imperial) literary sphere in early nineteenth century Russia Greenleaf and Moeller-Sally 1998, 2–8). Thanks to Anne Eakin Moss for bringing this source to my attention.

his Hungarian counterpart Edy Andre—the revolutionary-era Jewish advocates of translation were concerned not to enrich Hebrew or Yiddish literature but to *refound* it. Their vision was part of a self-consciously belated program of culture-building. Despite deep ideological differences, they shared a notion of a universal (or pan-European) Literature with a single if evolving structure of genres, styles, and sensibilities that Jewish literature in Hebrew or Yiddish had to encompass through translation (in part so that they would be able to grow beyond these). In so doing, Hebrew or Yiddish literature would necessarily emulate, as M. Ben-Eliezer put it, "all the young literatures which maintain themselves from translations." (Ben-Eliezer 1917, 319) Ben-Eliezer captured this sensibility in language drawn from the realm of capital: world literature in translation was "spiritual capital [*hon ruhani*]" that "the young peoples take on credit from their older neighbors" and that served "as the basis for the building of their national literature." This figuration of literary translation as a form of capital investment is profoundly revealing: literature may be qualitatively unique and irreducible, but it can also be transformed through translation into a form of reproducible capital that can be employed universally and serially by any investor nation.

These conceptions of literature stemmed not from naiveté nor lack of sophistication but, on the contrary, a firmly historicized and even coldly analytical perspective on what made for a strong national literature. These champions of translation saw that Russian and German literatures (the non-Jewish literatures they knew best) had become the distinctive literatures they were precisely and paradoxically through translation, and they saw similar practices among other young literatures. Furthermore, the modernism-inclined among them, like Litvakov, knew that literary revolutions were only possible when modernists could counterpose their literary experiments to a stable canon. And they knew that they were embarking on this project late, at a modernist moment when the very notion of a single Literature was under attack; but they saw this belated translation project as a necessity, even if it sat ill with their otherwise fairly radical cultural politics.

2 The Deparochializing Imperative

Running through some of these arguments for systematic, programmatic translation was a radical de-Judaizing strain. Some proponents of translation framed it not as an important supplement in the building of Jewish culture but as the sharp wedge of a larger effort to deparochialize it—to do away with any delimitation of Jewish literature in terms of some posited Jewish thematics or sources and to make it as encompassing of human experience as any other. It was this stance that Shteynman assumed when he declared that the massive importation of world literature would play a critical role in bringing Hebrew literature "off its narrow path, its side-track." (Shteynman 1919a) Tshernikhovsky, long identified with such pagan sensibilities, drily noted in his translation of Anacreon's poems that "there is no cultured nation which does not have in its literature something from those poems which are called Anacreonic .... These poems, poems of the pleasures of life ... are entirely absent only from our literature." (Tshernikhovsky 1920, 3)

The same assumptions drove many critics' evaluation of translations in terms of their implied reader. It was a given for most critics of the period that a translation had to assume and thus help construct not the (existing) parochial "Jewish reader" but a mature modern reader who could occupy any reader-position demanded by a work. Klausner praised Taviov in his review of the latter's *Dorian Gray* for making no cuts or changes reflecting assumptions that certain things would not be interesting to the Hebrew reader and could therefore be cut out, "as were wont to do even the 'Europeans' among our translators up to the present day." (Klausner 1918b, 343; Ben-Eliezer 1917) Shteynman poured scorn on prewar Hebrew publishers who, unlike Stybel, shaped their programs based on "their assumptions" that the needs of the Jewish reading public were "somehow special." (Shteynman 1919a) Litvakov put these sentiments more programmatically: the confidence to reject any sharp division between "'Jewishness-literature' and 'humanity-literature'" was the mark of a "living people, which speaks and thinks in a living language." (Litvakov 1919c, 42)

In his essay on translation and elsewhere, Litvakov insisted that contemporary Yiddish literature had to grow beyond its intimate attachment to Jewish folk culture. "Our literature," he wrote, "has by now almost entirely exhausted the spring of its traditional, national-Jewishy [*yidishlekhe*] themes and motifs, thoughts and feelings." What had been a necessary "small-town-provincial [*kleynshtetldik*]-nationalist phase" in the development of a modern Yiddish literature was now at an end—not because external circumstances (like the Revolution) dictated it, but because the literature itself had "exhausted" the specifically literary value of folk culture and its conceits and was left with mere folk "ornamentalism." Systematic, massive, and rapid translation, Litvakov argued, had proven its capacity in the German, Russian, and even Hebrew cases to drive a national literature beyond parochialism; it would now provide Yiddish literature and its future authors with a way out of their own literary-cultural dead end.

Strikingly, these and other radical advocates of deparochialization-through-translation tied their translation discourse to open rejections of the romantic-populist valorization of pre-modern Jewish folk culture or traditional culture as the essential basis of the new Jewish culture. Thus, Litvakov's aggressive vision of translation's task went hand in hand with a denigration of the place of folk culture in the new Yiddish culture that he hoped would come into being. The "emancipatory national-secular content" that Litvakov sought and found in Yiddish literature emerged precisely through its evolution beyond folk culture toward the self-consciously literary expression of the modern individual consciousness: it was not the folk but "individual creators and poets" who were the "fathers of the new tradition which has come to itself." (Litvakov 1918, 76, 98) This model captured a sensibility arguably more prevalent in the Yiddish cultural sphere (certainly the Yiddishist avant-garde) of the day than the valorization of Yiddish folklore as the fundament of Yiddish literature by figures like An-ski or the radical Nokhem Oyslender. Litvakov's colleague Dobrushin, while embracing the significance of folklore for children's books, saw the use of such elements in art-literature as a stage to be overcome (Dobrushin 1919a, 1919b).

Reflecting a parallel logic vis-à-vis *kinus* of classic Hebrew texts, Eliezer Shteynman, writing under the pseudonym Aleph, directly attacked Bialik's and Ahad Ha'am's elevation of the classical Hebrew tradition over modern Hebrew literature. Where Bialik found artistic greatness in the Talmud and midrashic tradition, Shteynman saw only crippling diminution in the interpretive rather than authorial-creative stance dictated by tradition: "We created 'Talmud,' which we called a sea—and we were lost among its waves; in our hands [we hold] many pearls and gems which are essential to no nation or language, and in a short while we too will not understand their language. Because we were merely interpreters. And this is our punishment." (Shteynman 1919a) Contemporary Hebrew writers had to demonstrate creative plenitude, not assume the stance of commentators—to pull the new literature not from the past, but "out of their finger," as Bialik had mockingly put it.

Those who clamored to free Jewish cultural creativity from the confines of privileged folk or classical sources were themselves responding to sallies by champions of the indigenizing strategy, especially Bialik. In the years before the Revolution, Bialik had repeatedly charged his contemporaries with abject internalization of pan-European conceptions of aesthetic value and a consequent failure to achieve a distinct Jewish national character in Jewish literature. Responding angrily to what he saw as his contemporaries' dismissal of the Jewish tradition's cultural richness, he insisted that "our poverty [lies] not only in what we *lack*, but in the fact that we do not properly use the possessions that we *do* have." (Bialik [1913b] 1955c, 218–19) Only a grounding in the indigenous tradition would allow modern Hebrew culture to cease "feeding on its own flesh" (dwelling on its own expressive dilemmas) and render it strong enough to absorb foreign works (like the translations that Bialik himself commissioned for Moriah) without being overwhelmed: "The language will 'make national' everything that it is given and all that enters its bounds." (Bialik [1913a] 1955b, 210, 217)

Bialik revisited these charges in his epochal "Halakhah ve-aggadah," delivered as a lecture in Odessa and Moscow in 1916–1917 and then published in Hebrew in 1917 and Russian in 1918. In the section of the essay devoted to drawing out the meaning of these two multilayered terms for modern Jewish literature specifically, Bialik challenged contemporary Hebrew writers to turn rabbinic cultural sources into epic: "a true artist, one who does not seek to draw 'the divine spirit' out of his thumb or from licking the dishes of an alien table, but draws it from the fathomless depths of the nation's soul and the mystery of its life—a true artist will find no insuperable difficulty in producing something great even from material such as this, if only the greatness which is in his own soul." (citing from Simon translation Bialik [1917] 2000, 79 with modifications from original Bialik [1917] 1955, 228). Immersion in classical texts, Bialik suggested, might allow Jewish artists to produce a distinctive "national epic" in place of "borrowed vessels and feeble imitation of ready-made alien forms." (Bialik [1917] 2000, 80)

Bialik's preeminent status ensured respectful attention to "Halakhah ve-aggadah," though contemporaries differed wildly on what this fertilely ambiguous essay meant (Moss 2009, 177–80). But at least for this important subset of the Jewish cultural sphere, by 1917 it had come to seem that not Bialik but another veteran cultural figure, Frishman, had his finger on the pulse of his generation. Frishman had long held that the Jewish tradition, with the partial exception of the Bible and the aggadic literature, offered only life-denying tendencies in the Nietzschean sense that were precisely to blame for the stifled creativity of the Jewish people. What Hebrew literature needed in order to become a contributing part of universal human civilization was not an imported European literary tradition *in addition to* but rather *instead of* a reworking of Jewry's own traditions. In 1913, he had dismissed Bialik's faith in the power of Jewish classical sources to compel the engagement of Jewish youth, who, he argued, were not ignorant of traditional Jewish genius, but rather saw it as having no bearing on "whether we still have the power to give birth." (Frishman [1913] 1932, 57–58). The much younger cohort of critics who echoed these ideas in 1917 seemed themselves to bear out his claim. M. Ben-Eliezer, who fell somewhere between these two poles, nevertheless respectfully rebuked those who "say ... that we do not need to bring within our literature the 'offspring of aliens, and that just as the Hebrew people did not exert itself to bring in converts, so it is fit that our Hebrew literature keep distant these creations which did not issue from the source of Israel." On the contrary, he insisted, there was no road to literary development except through translation: "But those who believe in the revival of Hebrew literature and its development, and see a great necessity in this, must follow after all the young literatures which maintain themselves from translations." (Ben-Eliezer 1917)

3 Deparochialization in Cultural Practice

How representative or influential were these attitudes about translation and deparochialization in the cultural sphere as a whole? We find striking resonances and repercussions of these attitudes in three central sites: the burgeoning critical discourse on Jewish literature overall; literary creativity itself; and the realm of literary publishing.

A survey of the vast corpus of frankly prescriptive literary criticism which flooded the Hebrew and Yiddish cultural sphere in the 1917–1919 period reveals that the operative cultural principles of the translation proponents extended well beyond their circle. Broad swaths of the literary intelligentsia across all spectra issued parallel calls for deparochializing and Europeanizing Jewish literary expression. In Kiev's Yiddishist circles, Litvakov—who even dared to question the continued significance of Y. L. Peretz on the grounds that he had posthumously "perhaps against his will" become a point of departure for "regurgitated old-Jewishy feelings, experiences, and images" (Litvakov 1919c, 37)—was more the norm than the exception. While Nahman Mayzl and Nokhem Oyslender both articulated suitably radical versions of folklorism as a Yiddishist cultural strategy, most of Kiev's Yiddishists, it seems, shared Litvakov's impatient sense that Yiddish literature needed to move beyond such parochialism. Not just Litvakov but many Yiddishist critics (Dobrushin, Ezra Korman, one P. Reyland) hailed the cohort of Yiddish modernist poets who made their debut in the literary circles of Kiev in 1918–1919 as pioneers of a new epoch in Yiddish literature in large part because much of their poetry seemed refreshingly free of Jewish themes and intertexts. Critics praised these poets for their "wantonness," their seemingly un-Jewish embrace of nature, their demonstrative inattention to the Jewish past and embrace of the here and now, and their invention of a wholly personal poetic persona in place of the conventional national elegist or folk voice (Wolitz 1978; Reyland 1919; Litvakov ["M. Lit"] 1919a). In a typical move, Dobrushin contrasted the love poetry of Dovid Hofshteyn with that of the more veteran Yiddish poet Dovid Eynhorn and with Bialik (Dobrushin 1919a, 94–95). Whereas Eynhorn's love poetry depended on Jewish folk motifs and Bialik's couched the speaker's erotic appeal in a language redolent of biblical love poetry, Hofshteyn transcended these parochial limitations: "I saw her in the naked joy of her flesh,/ in the disheveled crown of her fragrant hair,/ I heard from the depths of age-young years:/ —This is what one calls a wife!" (trans. Kronfeld 1996, 214) Significantly, Dobrushin attributed this capacity to Hofshteyn's mastery of what was "for us a new, truly European emotion-culture."

In a very different corner of the literary world, the noted Russian (ethnically Jewish) aesthete M. O. Gershenzon declared that Bialik's younger Hebrew contemporaries had already surpassed him because they had embraced a modern, universal voice while Bialik was "still almost entirely absorbed in Jewish matters—to him, it has still not been granted to go forth into the expanse of human freedom." (Gershenzon 1918, viii) It is perhaps unsurprising that an outsider to Jewish national cultural concerns like Gershenzon should take this stance. But strikingly parallel contentions can be found in the works of unvarnished cultural nationalists, and in fact predominated in contemporary *Hebrew* criticism across the political and aesthetic spectrum. Thus, Klausner demonstrated no less of an obsession with overcoming the supposed parochialism of Jewish literature in the name of "universal" literary value and chose the same target. Insisting that "every true poet is also a pantheist," Klausner compared Bialik unfavorably to Shakespeare, Goethe, and Pushkin because whereas these "world-embracing spirits" had drawn on all materials of world civilization to address "truly great and deep general-human problem[s]," Bialik (ostensibly) remained mired in parochial Jewishness (Klausner 1917, 453).

Klausner had propounded these views, and distinguished himself with them, before the war. But by 1917, they had become the dominant stance in the Hebrew literary sphere as a whole. Almost all the younger Hebrew poets and literary critics who staked out a stance in the period argued that Hebrew literature had to break decisively with the "parochial" and "Jewish" conventions that had defined modern secular Hebrew poetry since its birth in the nineteenth century, such as foregrounding themes of national destiny and structuring the poem in creative tension with biblical and talmudic texts. Many echoed Klausner's attack on their beloved Bialik in these very terms. Tellingly, even some of those who defended Bialik's literary preeminence actually shared the same set of anti-parochial standards. In *Ha-Tekufah*, Natan Grinblat (later Goren) attacked those who claimed that Bialik was "more Hebrew that European" and that "a book of Bialik's poems is not a *sefer hitzoni*"—that is, those who praised Bialik for the very obdurate Jewishness that drove critics like Klausner to distraction. Grinblat insisted instead that Bialik's poetry was in its "very essence ... none other than that art which is entirely '*hitzonit*' [foreign to the Jewish tradition]," that is, modern European lyric poetry (Grinblat 1918, 673).

The younger Hebrew writers of the day cast about for more suitable canonical forebears and lodestars. Tellingly, numerous Hebrew poets and critics across the political and aesthetic spectrum hailed the "pagan," "European" Tshernikhovsky as the new fundament of Hebrew literary and cultural consciousness. Eliahu Meitus declared that whereas Bialik had "opened windows to the sun for us," Tshernikhovsky "brought us outside and gave us the sun and the moon and the stars ... and taught us to love—to love everything ... to love man, and to love life, the world and all it contains, without any accounting." (Meitus 1917) This claim was echoed with little variation by contemporaries like Y. Karni and Y. Elsharif. Even the hard left Zionist Sh. Tsemah posited Tshernikhovsky as the "the necessary and logical phenomenon who shows the way which we have traversed and reveals also the new life and the new heavens stretching before us." (Tsemah 1919, 581) What all found compelling about Tshernikhovsky was an apparent literary-cum-psychic wholeness that inhered especially in his rejection of any distinction between Jewish and non-Jewish culture. As Klausner put it, "the main thing" was that Tshernikhovsky was a *European* poet who attained to "a level on which stand the more perfect poets of Europe"; yet Tshernikhovsky's very Europeanness and humanism were not at odds with a poetry of Jewish revival, but in fact represented it in the fullest sense as an incarnation of what the nation had to strive to become. Tshernikhovsky was "a poet who is himself entirely Revival [*meshorer, she-hu kulo tehiyah*]." (Klausner 1918a, 104–5)

For all this talk about "Judaizing" and "Europeanizing" tendencies in literature, we might well ask whether these sentiments found any purchase in the arts themselves. Many writers of the day moved fluidly between these ostensibly opposed tendencies, including those who insisted on the central importance of translation. Thus, Moyshe Kulbak became one of his generation's most creative manipulators of folk sources and motifs in a modernist literary framework. None other than Frishman produced during this period a cycle of stories set against the biblical narrative of the Israelites' desert wanderings and the theophany, *Ba-Midbar*; that one of the stories was closely modeled on Anatole France's *Thais*, a work Frishman himself had translated into Hebrew previously, suggests not opposition but complementarity between these imperatives (Jacobson 1987, 83). This interpenetration holds all the more for music and the plastic arts in this period, where the very project of a "Jewish music" or "Jewish art" seemed to imply some kind of fusion between indigenous and pan-European traditions.

Yet in the post-1917 moment, the discourse of deparochialization did in fact find strong echoes (and spurs) in the arts themselves. As Seth Wolitz and other students of Yiddish modernism have shown, if we focus on those who sought self-consciously to be the next wave in Jewish culture (outside the visual arts), we find a broad emphasis on consciously displacing, decentering, and in some cases completely effacing obtrusively "Jewish" elements in their art. In theater, while the Vilna Trupe and Ha-Bimah sought distinctively "Jewish" work,[14] the fledgling theater troupe that would eventually become GOSET initially aspired to a "European" Yiddish theater freed of any "specific repertoire" and sharing the "tasks of world theater," as Aleksandr Granovskii put it in 1919 (Harshav 1992, 147). In the Yiddish literary realm, the Kiev Grupe poets made their mark, as I have said, in good part because of their efforts to craft a lyric persona, voice, and set of themes freed of what Litvakov, one of their champions on this score, called "Jewishy" associations (and especially freed of the indigenous-folkloristic elements so integral to the poetry of many of their predecessors as well as contemporaries). It was no accident that in Markish, Litvakov saw proof that Yiddish literature too was finally on the cusp of being able to express the undetermined, all-embracing, and individual voice that was the supposed seal of modern "universal" literature. This attitude was epitomized for Litvakov in what he saw as Markish's typical phrase: "*stam in velt arayn*" (simply out in the world; out in the world without pretense or identifying mark) (Litvakov 1919a). It resonated in much of Markish's early verse, perhaps most famously in the following 1917 lyric:

> Don't know if I'm at home
> or if I'm afar [*tsi in der fremd*]—
> I'm running! ...
> my shirt's unbuttoned,
> there are no reins on me,
> I'm nobody's, I'm unclaimed [*hefker*, also translatable as wild, licentious],
> without a beginning, without an end ...[15]

More systematically, Markish's older Kiev contemporary Dovid Hofshteyn devoted much of his poetic effort in the 1917–1919 period to developing a lexicon of imagery and poses unfettered by any identifiable Jewish determinants. Speaking, like Markish, in an anti-typological first-person voice, he depicted his poetic self in poem after poem as a lone wanderer on an open road unbound to anything but the beauties of a universal nature (Yosef Tchaikov's cover for Hofshteyn's 1919 book *Ba vegn* depicts this wanderer, dressed as a dandy in cloak and walking stick). At one point, Hofshteyn's poetic self appeared clad in a most un-Jew-

---

14 Thus, Ha-Bimah's Menahem Gnesin justified the choice of Pinski's "Eternal Jew" for a first full-length production with the telling remark that "although it wasn't originally written in Hebrew, it was nevertheless Hebrew through and through and it was deemed very proper for Ha-Bimah to perform it." (Gnesin 1946, 132)
15 The translation is by Chana Kronfeld in collaboration with Bluma Goldstein (Kronfeld 1996, 204) but I have restored Markish's distinctive punctuation (Shmeruk 1964, 375–76).

ish coat of knightly mail: "Today the sun to my new armor/ lent the last golden shine/ and mixed for me of enchanted wine/ a cup of joy." This stood in stark contrast to the strategy of Hofshteyn's best-known prewar poem "In vinter farnakhtn," which still represented a modern Jewish self through a tension between a dreamy Jewish youth and his traditional Jewish home and calendar. Now, no longer bound to any Jewish referent, Hofshteyn's poetic self and his poetry could venture "girded with sunshine ... without fear into all the black caves/ of world and being." (Hofshteyn [1917–1919] 1923)

Having groped for the literary means to depict his own poetic self independently of a reflexively Jewish vocabulary and emancipated from his parental home's all-encompassing Jewishness, Hofshteyn pursued this conscious elision of Jewish elements in a more sophisticated series of poems about children and childhood. In "Vi troyerik-zis iz mentsh tsu zayn" (How sadly sweet it is to be human) he turned to an infant's first moments of self-consciousness, where he could experiment freely with the representation of a completely pre-Jewish self. At the close of the poem, Hofshteyn found a concrete referent for his contemporaries' cherished hope that such a literature of the individual voice could lead alchemically to a "universal" literature:

> ... and suddenly, in the deep of late at night
> to feel a hidden quiver of the soul
> and without moving, suddenly awake
> with every atom sense
> how eternity's wings are moving
> and bitterly to know so little
> yet to know, for instance,
> that the clock now reads two, perhaps three.
> And lying still in the hot glow, in the sweet pain
> with every heart-thread violently yearn
> that every human brother should know this pain
> that every human brother should possess this joy:
> how sadly sweet it is to be human! (Hofshteyn [1917–1919] 1977a)[16]

In a more directly confrontational (and perhaps humorous) move, Hofshteyn's "Vig-lid" (Lullabye) cunningly edited Avrom Goldfaden's pseudo-folk classic "Rozhinkes mit mandlen" to yield a poem that exploited the original's folk rhymes and images but completely denuded them of Jewish figures. As in the contemporaneous prose of Der Nister, the "tsigele" remained (in a direct quote of the Goldfaden original: "a klor vays tsigele"). But Shulamis and the Temple

---

16 Thanks to Marc Caplan for his translation suggestions.

had disappeared; in their place, Hofshteyn offered an unmarked individual lulling his similarly unmarked child: "I rock your cradle/ and sing in your ear/ a little bolt/ has closed a gate there." (Hofshteyn [1917–1919] 1977b)

Of course, as critics recognized to their dismay or delight, Hofshteyn himself was by no means uniformly committed to the complete elision of the Jewish element in modern Jewish poetry (Litvakov 1919a and Reyland 1919 complained; Dobrushin 1919a praised this complexity; cf. Wolitz 1978). In other poems, in fact, he thematized the very demand for the "universal" in Jewish literature as a productive problem, subtly asserting the value and perhaps the inescapability of Jewish associations as one element in any universe of aesthetic expression by a Jewish individual; this was particularly true of a third poem centering around his children, "Nemen." (Moss 2009, 102–4) In this, he was typical. *Mutatis mutandis*, the same respect for the aesthetic value of indigenous sources coupled with an impatient desire to grow beyond them characterized the Kultur Lige's music section that in 1919 declared its commitment to "move beyond the narrow confines of the folk-primitive, build up larger and more complicated forms—to join the modern musical arts in such a way that the national spirit will nevertheless remain whole." (*Kultur-Lige* 1920, 57)

Yet the point remains: by 1917, for growing numbers of artists, the problem of how to move beyond the "narrow confines" of a posited Jewish aesthetics was a motivating, productive artistic problem. It is telling that champions of the *indigenizing* move like Bialik or An-ski themselves clearly felt that this drive to produce a Jewish literature more closely and intimately linked to a posited shared European or universal literature was already ascendant, even a majority commitment. As early as 1897, in a letter to the era's preeminent champion of an anti-parochial stance, Micha Yosef Berdyczewski, Bialik expressed a sour skepticism about what he saw as the increasingly popular notion "that the translation of the poetry of the prophets of the nations will save Israel from all of its sufferings and woes"; An-ski attacked this stance in Yiddish literature in 1908 (Lahover 1956, 247 n10; Moss 2001, 169–70). Bialik's essays of the immediate prewar and wartime period did not present his proposal to build the new Jewish culture from "authentic" Jewish sources as a self-evident starting point for Jewish culture (as is often presumed) but as an explicit *counter* to the "European" drive in a cultural project already well underway, as we have seen.

Finally, we may move from this most hermetic sphere of cultural creativity to the most material: the realm of publishing. I have already alluded to the astonishing resources, effort, and planning that publishers and other cultural institutions invested in translation in the 1917–1919 period. Alongside Stybel's press, the two other leading Hebraist presses of the day also made a place for translation. Moriah sought translations of Homer and Shakespeare from Tshernikhovsky and Grimm's fairytales by Frishman (Y. H. Ravnitsky to Bialik, 20 August 1918, Beit Bialik Correspondence Collection, file *resh*-206). Moscow's Omanut press under the Hebraist-Zionist patrons Hillel Zlatopolski and his daughter Shoshana Persits focused most of its efforts on literary publishing for children. It laid particular emphasis on translations from European children's literature, producing an impressive array of "storybooks and tales for children from the best of world literature." (Tidhar 1947) This emphasis was also evident in the press's 1917 Hebrew journal for young adults, *Shetilim*, which placed work by Hebrew writers like Bialik, Tshernikhovsky, Yaakov Fichman, and Shteynman alongside translations of Wilde, Mickiewicz, Daudet, and even Korean folktales ("Mi-sipurei Korea" 1917). It was paralleled by the program of another Hebrew publishing house founded in Moscow in 1917 in honor of Bialik by Hebraist patron-admirers, the children's book publisher Ahinoar, which planned to publish some 150 children's books drawn mostly from world literature (Ofek 1984, 71).

Litvakov's call for a grand translation program into Yiddish—no doubt inspired in part by the competing Hebraists' leap forward and perhaps by *Vsemirnaia literatura*—came against the backdrop of a similar explosion of translation in the reemerging Yiddish publishing sphere. The Yiddishist-radical Kiever Farlag with which Litvakov was linked made a strong place for translation in its efforts to reshape Yiddish art-literature as a whole, publishing Andersen, Tolstoy, Pushkin, Ivan Franko, Wilde, Longfellow, and Daudet. Other smaller Kiev Yiddishist houses published Andersen (Onhoyb press) and Byron (Dorem-Farlag). The publishing houses Literatur in Odessa and Universal in Warsaw both initiated a "universal-library" series modeled on similar endeavors in other European languages (Dobrushin 1919c). Kharkov Farlag "Idish" planned a "folks-bibliotek" of Yiddish and translated works including Byron, Jack London, and Knut Hamsun (M. D. 1919). The small Moscow publishing house Khaver produced an anthology of European poetry, *Fremds*, as well as translations of Tolstoy, Kuprin, and Maupassant (Tsharni 1943, 227–28; *Shriften* 19[18?]). The most ambitious and well-funded private Yiddishist publishing ventures of the day, Kiev's Folks-Farlag and Kultur-Lige, both made translation from world literature a central aspect of their self-declared (and competing) mission to guide the reemergent Yiddish cultural sphere as a whole (Dinur 1960, 404–5). The Folks-Farlag was founded by Yiddishists more politically and culturally moderate (though no less culturally ambitious) than those of the Kiev-Grupe; among its central figures were moderate socialists like Moyshe Zilberfarb and Folkists like Zeev Latski-Bertoldi, Shtif, and Zelig Kalmanovitsh (the latter two in charge of its translation division). Like Omanut, the Folks-Farlag's division for children's literature emphasized translation of "the classic works of world-literature which usually comprise the reading material for youth." Its division for art-literature aimed to translate "the classic works of the European novel-literature" and "modern lyric poetry" (as well as translations from modern Hebrew literature—a different though no less interesting topic).[17] Ben-Tsion Dinur, who worked for the press, recalls that in its brief existence (founded in late 1918, it dissolved in the drastically altered circumstances of Bolshevik Kiev by 1921), its translation division "prepared translations of the writings of Tolstoy, Chekhov, Byron, Flaubert, Maupassant, and many, many more. And it announced that it planned to translate a selection of the works of Shakespeare, Ibsen, of Goethe and Schiller." (Dinur 1960, 405; *Idisher Folks-farlag* 1920, 8)

By mid-1919, in turn, the more radical wing of Kiev's burgeoning Yiddishist world was poised to pursue a grander publishing program through the richly endowed, commandingly positioned Kultur-Lige publishing house. The Kultur-Lige Farlag declared its intent to focus (besides its educational publishing) on the publication of "classic works, original and translated." (*Kultur Lige* 1919, 41–42) The Yiddishists affiliated with the Kiever Farlag and the Kultur-Lige found themselves catapulted into a position of potential cultural authority with the arrival of Soviet power in Kiev in 1919; by mid-1919, the Jewish Section of the All-Ukrainian Central Publishing House (VseIzdat), charged with publishing "art-literature for adults and children in Yiddish" at the state's expense, came under control of Yiddishists affiliated with the Kultur-Lige like Noyekh Lurie, A. Litvak, and Litvakov himself (Moss 2009, chap. 6). Under their guidance, the Jewish Section did not so much change as expand previous plans: it planned to publish not only original Yiddish works but also translations of European writers, books on "the theory and history of art and literature," and, for children, collections of folktales from around the world and literary translations ("Kunst-khronik" 1919, 86).

Finally, a parallel emphasis on translation from European literature and plans of similar scope characterized the newly emergent Yiddish art-theater sphere as well. By 1920, with new Yiddish art-theater studios and troupes already active in Moscow, Kiev, Warsaw, and beyond, the Folks-Farlag announced that it had a full hundred plays ready to print, "especially European repertoire." (Folks-Farlag announcement, 1920; *Idisher Folks-farlag* 1920, 16) When the Jewish Section of the Soviet All-Ukrainian Theater Committee and the closely linked Kultur Lige Theater Section moved aggressively to create "a modern Yiddish dramatic theater," they commissioned ten translations of European repertoire and spon-

---

[17] On translation *between* Hebrew and Yiddish (and from Russian "Jewish" literature like the *Dybbuk*), which had a completely different ideological meaning (since it was about incorporating "Jewishness," not "foreignness"), see Moss 2003, 217–30.

sored the reediting of existing translations that were, it noted, often "beneath criticism." ("Kunst-khronik" 1919, 90)

When we seek to adduce the ideological motives behind these publishing programs, we face a number of serious challenges. Most of these publishers did not offer (or I have simply not found) the kinds of explicit ideological statements about the meaning of translation that were the stock-in-trade of critics like Litvakov; hence we must reason inductively from the content and practice of these plans, aided by scattered clues to the publishers' own ideologies. Moreover, most of these publishing houses involved congeries of actors with different views and intentions. Furthermore, as Litvakov, Litai, and others complained, some of their publications were not the product of any systematic plan, but rather individual initiatives that had simply come to hand (Litvakov 1919b, 9–10) and which often stemmed at least as much from the individual literary interests of individual author-translators as from any overarching logic of translation on behalf of the literature as a whole. Moreover, there was a significant market for translations, and many of these publishing houses, particularly the Yiddish ones, may have had quite practical reasons for their translations; one report suggests that Warsaw Jewish publishers began to prepare Yiddish translations of European authors during the war with the expectation of strong demand afterward (Goldberg 1919, 19). The sorts of authors selected by some of the smaller publishers like Warsaw's "Universal" or even Moscow's "Khaver"—prose writers like Tolstoy, Kuprin, Hamsun, and Maupassant—were the mainstays of middlebrow literatures across Europe, and were of a piece with the market-driven translation publication evident in prewar Warsaw and New York.

Yet when we consider at least the largest and most significant publishing houses (besides Stybel's)—namely, the Folks-Farlag, Omanut, and the publishing houses of Kiev's Yiddishist radicals—we find clear parallels to the ideas propounded by the champions of translation and good reason to posit a shared set of sensibilities. First, market- and demand-oriented explanations cover scant ground for these presses. Although Hebraist publishing houses like Moriah could, it seems, make a profit even at this juncture (Frishman to Bialik, 11/24 May 1918 in *Keneset* 1940, 34–35), profit was manifestly not the goal of the Omanut or Stybel publishing houses. Although these presses sold their works on the market and clearly hoped that their books would find readers who might not otherwise have put their Hebrew to literary uses, both presses produced physically deluxe works[18] in runs far larger than they could hope to sell and, as contemporaries recognized,

---

18 At least some of Omanut's publications for children were beautiful books with lush color illustrations, in sharp contrast to the chapbook format of the Yiddish children's books produced by Odessa's Farlag Blimelekh or the Kiever Farlag. One observer deemed Stybel's books more beautiful than any contemporaneous Russian efforts (Katz 1927).

they certainly expected substantial loss.[19] There is no reason to assume that translation marked an exception to this more general pattern of what one contemporary called "patronage-national" motives, by contrast with prewar Hebrew publishing ventures that received help from patrons but depended ultimately on market success to sustain themselves (Ben-Yishai 1968, 168). Although there was certainly a greater potential market for Yiddish translations, it was not profit but cultural-ideological vision that shaped the publishing choices of the Yiddishist publishing houses in question. The Folks-Farlag, though a stock company that did aim for profit, subordinated the concerns of its investors to its own sense of Yiddishist mission; deeming one of its tasks the material support of Yiddish writers as such, it apparently offered to pay them as much as they needed (Shtif to Z. Reyzen, 9 August 1920, Yiddish Literature and Language Collection, file 3035). More generally, the Folks-Farlag, the Kiever-Farlag, and many other Yiddishist publishing houses ceded exclusive distribution rights to the Yiddishist Kultur-Lige, which used its near-monopolistic market power not to maximize profits but to achieve Yiddishist goals *against* the natural tendencies of the wartime Ukrainian Yiddish book market itself (Katz 1921, 185; Kalmanovitsh to Vayter, 3 September [1918] in Niger Collection, file 34).[20] Committed to the widest possible distribution of Yiddish books at a moment when "the broad masses" were utterly impoverished, the Kultur-Lige sold its books at close to cost and even sold older stock at its nominal cost despite the staggering inflation of the period (*Kultur Lige* 1919, 39–42). Kultur Lige to the Ministry of Jewish Affairs of Ukrainian People's Republic, undated [probably January 1919], Ministry of Jewish Affairs Collection, file 41). In order to ensure that books in limited supply would reach publicly oriented Yiddishist institutions like libraries and

---

19 Litai referred to Stybel as a publishing house "which is not afraid of material sacrifices, and indeed of the largest [material sacrifices]." (Litai 1919; cf. Ben-Yishai 1968, 172) I have not found primary sources generated by the presses themselves that shed much light on financial and organizational structure, and have rather relied on memoir sources (Ayzenshtadt 1960; Katz 1964, 246–51; Litai 1956; Tverski 1948, 20–21). With regard to Omanut in particular, I have had to rely on general descriptions of its work and the patronage of Persits and Zlatopolski in these memoirs and the unreferenced summation of its work in Shavit (Shavit 1982, 221–22) who notes that it was founded "on a patronage basis." Shavit's statement that the press did not expect profits and that its patrons could cover its losses refers specifically to its activities in Palestine after 1926, but it seems reasonable to infer that the same situation occurred in the even worse economic conditions of revolutionary Russia. On Persits's continued willingness to operate at a loss in the 1930s and beyond, see Pograbinsky (1950–1951, lv).

20 As of early 1919, the publishing houses in question included the Kiever Farlag, Kletskin's Vilna Farlag Ukraine branch, the Folks Farlag, Di Velt, Onhoyb, Der Hamer, and Odessa's Blimelakh (Kultur Lige to the Ministry of Jewish Affairs of Ukrainian People's Republic, undated [probably January 1919], Ministry of Jewish Affairs Collection, file 4).

clubs, it offered such non-profit organizations a set of "the better books" for fifty percent down before making them generally available (*Grunt-oyfgabn* 1918, 32).

Granted that these publishing houses were driven by Yiddishist and Hebraist ideological visions more than material motives, it is more challenging to parse the relationship between reader-oriented educative sensibilities and concerns to shape Jewish literature and culture itself. Some of the Yiddishist and Hebraist publishers evidently did see translation, at least in part, as a direct service to readers. More than Litvakov and other critics, they seem to have cherished the hope that there would be strong popular interest and that these translations would serve to directly reshape the Jewish identity of readers assumed to be less educated and culturally flexible than the intelligentsia itself. The Khaver anthology *Fremds* declared that its goal was "to acquaint the Jewish reader with the best and most important creations of European poetry," which its editor seemed to define as Russian Romanticism, French Symbolism (Baudelaire and Verlaine), and a dash of Decadence (Balmont) (*Fremds* 1918, back cover). Speculatively, we might say that this sort of publication balanced unsteadily between a literary-educative mode and a more subtly market-oriented effort to cater to a prospective middlebrow audience of Jewish readers who, like their prewar Russian counterparts, were increasingly open to once-scandalous Decadence (Wilde, Balmont, Kuprin) and who may have sought a sort of cosmopolitan respectability (Brooks 1978, 112). It may be that Stybel's physically beautiful and anachronistically thick publications—critics were astonished and slightly disgruntled at the 600-plus page length of *Ha-tekufah*—enacted a similar desire for middle-class distinction; Stybel himself was a former clerk of provincial origin only recently made good (Bourdieu 1984).

A more purely ideological, reader-oriented sensibility expressed itself in the substantial concern of the Omanut publishing house, the Folks-Farlag, and the Kiever Farlag with providing literary translations for children and for Yiddish and Hebrew secular schools. Leavening original Jewish works, these translations would forge a harmonious modern (that is, European) Jew—one for whom the pull of Jewish and European identities would not leave the proverbial "tear in the soul" that so many of the translators and teachers themselves carried with them. The rich body of translations offered by Omanut's *Shetilim* speaks to the journal's overarching desire to simultaneously allow its young reader to "find himself in his Hebrew newspaper in his own world and not in a foreign world" while simultaneously bringing him "out of his narrow world." ("Shetilim" 1917; Slutsky 1961, 32–33) According to one account, Omanut's emphasis on translations for children more generally reflected a recognition that Hebrew alone lacked the standard international canon of youth literature "from which all the peoples of Europe drew sustenance." (Pograbinsky 1950–1951, liv) A similar sensibility informed the Kiev Yiddishist children's journal *Shretelekh* (1919), where readers could find Rudyard Kipling and a Japanese fairytale alongside Hofshteyn and Der Nister.

Yet the publishing programs developed by the Folks-Farlag and, apparently, by the more radical Yiddishists around the Kiever Farlag and the Kultur-Lige also seem to have been inspired by the sorts of ideas about reshaping Hebrew and Yiddish literature themselves propounded by Litavkov, Stybel, Shteynman et al. They seem to have aimed for the encompassing, catholic character that was the hallmark of this conception. The Folks-Farlag program described by Dinur speaks for itself. As for its production of numerous theatrical translations, there was no doubt a market in the proliferation of Yiddish theater groups; but it may have also reflected the widely shared desire among Yiddish theater activists, in the words of the Petersburg Jewish Theater Society's literary director M. Rivesman, to "refresh the dirty, moldy Yiddish repertoire and illuminate it with masterful translations" alongside "truly literary, original dramatic works." (Harshav 1992, 145) The culturally and politically radical Yiddishist cultural producers who gathered around the Kiever Farlag and its flagship journal *Bikher-velt* were under Litvakov's strong influence and shared much of his basic vision (Y. Hirshkan to Sh. Niger, 21 October 1917, Niger Collection, file 167). In turn, the Kultur-Lige's vague proposals coupled with the translation plans of its more radical successors suggest a desire to see a body of translated European "classics" serve as no less a fundament of modern Yiddish culture than the Yiddish classics themselves. On the Hebraist side, Persits, the guiding figure of Omanut, seems initially to have envisioned a grand translation program like that the Stybel press would take up; at one point, she invited Bialik himself to serve as the chief editor for a series of "translations from the best of world literature." (Tidhar 1947) She may have dropped it because Stybel himself undertook it in so grand a fashion or because she saw a need to focus on children's books; but the very fact of her commitment to a similar catholic literary vision is significant.

It is difficult to move from these affinities of practice to any more concrete claims about the attitudes of individual actors toward translation in particular and where they fall on the spectrum of attitudes about indigenizing as opposed to universalizing strategies. Persits was evidently committed to endowing Hebrew literature with a "European" profile; this seems to reflect both a notion of national respectability, a concern for *appearances*, and an inner-directed conviction that Jews were Europeans and should shape their culture and psyche accordingly. Yet she also showed a lifelong engagement with traditional Jewish texts and supported An-ski's projected album of Jewish folk art even as she founded Omanut (Pograbinsky 1950–1951, lvi; An-ski Collection, file 8).[21] Her father and partner in Omanut, Hillel Zlatopolski, was the most avid early enthusiast of An-ski's *Dybbuk*; indeed, he worked hard to convince Bialik to translate it for Ha-Bimah (Sh. Tshernovits to Bialik, 3 November (?) 1917, Beit Bialik Correspondence Collection, folder *tet*-92). The Folks-Farlag, the work of many hands, presents a still more complicated picture. At least one of its leading figures, Latski-Bertoldi, sympathized with the more radical Litvakov's call for a deparochialized Jewish culture, even chiding Litvakov for giving too little credit to the ways in which modern *Hebrew* literature—including "Tshernikhovsky's Hellenism and Shneur's simple *goyishkayt*"—had contributed to this process (Latski-Bertoldi, 1919). But Kalmanovitsh and Shtif certainly numbered among those who hoped that modern Jewish culture would build on internal Jewish traditions at least as fully as European *fremds*; the Folks-Farlag in general, evidently under their influence, made a substantial place for translations from the Hebrew, which had the former, altogether different ideological valence.

In short, many of these figures saw great value in the indigenous sources of Jewish culture. Yet in their capacity as activist-publishers, they, like their more radical counterparts Litvakov, Shteynman, or Frishman, also perceived a particularly pressing—perhaps more pressing—need for a massive infusion of non-Jewish culture by 1917.

4 The Sociology of the Deparochializing Imperative

This split between cultural ideology and practice held true, tellingly, even for the most vociferous critic of Europeanism in modern Jewish culture, Haim Nahman Bialik himself. In 1917, laying out his vision for the future of Hebrew culture at the founding conference of the Hebraist Tarbut organization, Bialik grouped "translations of the works of the world geniuses—Shakespeare, Goethe, Heine" among the essential tasks that Hebraists would have to carry out if they had any hopes of transforming East European Jewry (Zerubavel 1917). Bialik had long acknowledged the importance of translation, despite his criticism of excessive Europeanism in Jewish cultural life. He had taken a leading role in the prewar Turgeman publishing imprint for children's book translations (Ofek 1984,

---

[21] The same 1917–1918 subscription list that shows Persits' support for An-ski's project records that Stybel was also a donor, as was one of the founders of the Yiddishist Folks-Farlag (An-ski Collection, file 8).

65–69) and made a place for the world classics in his agenda-setting 1913 disquisition on "The Hebrew Book." Yet he had always—indeed, increasingly—insisted that translation be accorded a strictly subordinate place relative to the indigenous tradition. It is against this backdrop that his speech at the 1917 Tarbut conference is so remarkable, for it did not hedge the call for translation with such critical animadversions. Another remarkable deviation offers an essential clue: Bialik, perhaps the most famous skeptic among his generation of Hebraists about reviving *spoken* Hebrew, embraced even this idea fully in this speech. Both of these (temporary) deviations from his ideological stance resonate with the overriding concern of the speech for "our nationalist youth," who despite their national commitment "do not belong to us in their heart and soul, but to other worlds ... to Tolstoy and to Turgenev and not to Isaiah and Ha-Levi." This concern with a generation slipping away suggests a line of analysis that will help us understand the motives of those writers, critics, and publishers who did not share the radical antagonism to indigenous sources but nevertheless laid heavy emphasis on translation at this moment.

In particular, let us turn our attention back to a hitherto neglected feature of Litai's March 1917 essay on translation. Litai framed his translation program as the only way out of an intolerable choice between "mental abstinence or assimilation." This striking phrase was in fact the title of the article, and was repeated verbatim in his later essay for *Ha-shiloah* on the Stybel press: "The literature of the world ... God Almighty! Is this not the thing longed for by the soul of all those Hebrews who aspire to spiritual wholeness, all those for whom it is hard to bear both intellectual abstinence and the intellectual assimilation which comes through perusal of books written in foreign tongues?" (Litai 1918, 540) Litai's potent rhetoric, like Bialik's turnabout, reflected a third and still more urgent motivation for wholesale translation: not merely to reshape the literature itself or to properly educate Jews as moderns, but to prevent the defection of the Hebraist (and mutatis mutandis, Yiddishist) *intelligentsia* from Jewish cultural engagement.

Concretely, Litai contended that the modern Jewish person, however strong his or her national cultural commitment in general and commitment to Hebrew in particular, could not be expected to confine himself solely to the existing corpus of works in Jewish languages. Yet the obvious recourse to co-territorial non-Jewish languages—particularly Russian—for access to world literature and thought virtually guaranteed linguistic and cultural assimilation. Litai invoked a previous generation's experience as proof and warning: "The maskilim, that is, those who apart from their knowledge of Hebrew attained for themselves general education to a certain degree and mastered one of the culture-languages—

these abandoned Hebrew literature because she could not satisfy their mental and spiritual needs." (Litai 1917)

This argument for translation transposed the issue from one of cultural ideology to one of sociology (and from the needs of literature itself back to the reader, albeit in this case, the intelligentsia reader herself). For Litai, translation had great practical importance for the consolidation of Jewish national culture, not only because it would expand Jewish literature but because it could (he hoped) eliminate this tension. Rather than Judaizing foreign works or seeking to keep them out by cultural *herem*, it would bring them within the linguistic horizons of Jewish national culture as part of a cosmopolitan Hebrew culture.

Litai's anxious argument suggests that we think about the entire emphasis on translation and Europeanization of Jewish culture not merely as reflecting a particular vision of what Jewish culture itself should be but also as a strategic response to an emerging sociological reality. All the actors in question knew from their own experience that the new breed of Jewish readers and *inteligenti* would not and could not limit its own intellectual horizons in the name of Jewishness, and that any version of Jewish national culture that staked its existence on some delimited, "authentic" Jewishness would simply not prove satisfying to people with ever greater unmediated access to the riches of metropolitan cultures unconstrained by such concerns.

Certain aspects of translation practice in this period reflect these concerns. Arguably, the widespread emphasis on translations from European literature for children that I have hitherto treated as a mode of cultural education was also driven by a more anxious recognition that only a Hebrew or Yiddish children's literature which could compete with the attractions and expansiveness of the much more developed Russian (or Polish) children's literature would secure the allegiance of a new generation of Hebrew or Yiddish readers (and writers). One historian of Hebrew publishing suggests that Shoshana Persits's concern for providing Hebrew translations of the standard European youth canon was driven in part by a recognition that Jewish young people sought these works in "foreign languages," that is, Russian (Pograbinsky 1950–1951, liv). More broadly, contemporaries' preoccupation with the fact that the books for children and for adults produced by the Stybel and Omanut presses matched or surpassed the physical beauty of Russian books suggests not only pride but also a deeply felt sense that in the competition for the cultural allegiance of Jewish youth, "Europeanness" even in form was essential (Katz 1927; Shteynman 1919). As one source puts it, Persits felt "the need to publish Hebrew books for students, youth, and the people that could compete from the standpoint of form and content alike—and especially from an aesthetic standpoint quite neglected in Hebrew books—with the best of literature in foreign languages." (Tidhar 1947)

In a different vein, the hitherto-neglected issue of translation of Jewish literature *into* Russian suggests a similar set of concerns. The relatively little translation of this sort that did take place in this period was intended almost exclusively to acquaint Russified Jewish readers with Zionist ideals and, not least, contemporary Hebrew culture. This was an explicit principle for Leyb Jaffe of Moscow's Safrut publishing house, the publisher of almost all such translations at the revolutionary juncture), who declared the Russian-language Jewish book merely a substitute "intended for those circles of readers who lack Hebrew." (Jaffe 1918; Horowitz 1998; Ben-Yishai 1968) In that sense, the ideological valence of translation from Hebrew *into* Russian at this juncture was the diametrical opposite of the translation praxis hitherto examined: translations of Hebrew poetry carried in the press's *Sborniki "Safrut"* or in its 1918 *Evreiskaia Antologiia: Sbornik Molodoi Evreiskoi Poezii* were intended to Judaize the reader rather than Europeanize him further (much less to deparochialize Jewish literature in Russian, a phenomenon that by definition could only be "Jewish" if it was marked by concretely Jewish referents). Yet strikingly, the latter anthology presented a cross-section of contemporary Hebrew poetry that highlighted its most cosmopolitan, unparochial thematics. This was what Gershenzon found in this poetry and stressed in his foreword: whereas the "old Hebrew poetry" (including Bialik) spoke only about "Jewry, like a sick person who speaks without cease about his own sickness," the "young Hebrew poets love like the youth of all countries, and clearly and resoundingly sing out their love; the natural world is open to them, and they depict it lovingly." When they did turn to Jewish matters, they did so as "men, entirely free men." (Gershenzon 1918, vii) An anthology like *Evreiskaia antologiia* could render Hebrew literature respectable to Jews schooled in Russian literature precisely by presenting it as equally expansive.

This strategic calculus no doubt pushed activist-publishers to focus on translation. But it was not merely strategic: it both addressed and bespoke the everdeepening internalization of schemata of appreciation and reception that dictated for the actors in question whether a work of art was experientially compelling (that is, good art) or not. Among the many sources that exemplify this subtle but critically important process are the comments of the journalist Sh. Tshernovits (Sfog) on the newly formed Ha-Bimah theater troupe in 1917. By no means hostile to "indigenizing" sensibilities—Tshernovits played a role in convincing Bialik to translate that most "indigenous" of contemporary works, An-ski's *Dybbuk*, for Ha-Bimah—Tshernovits offered a word of warning to the troupe. Whereas ten years earlier, Hebraists had thrilled to see any sort of Hebrew onstage, now they were familiar with the best of Russian theater and would settle for no less on the Hebrew stage. Ha-Bimah had to

> remember that their audience will not come now to see 'the great wonder' of people performing in Hebrew, but rather to enjoy an artistic performance, and thus it is incumbent upon the managers [of the company] to endeavor both to enrich the content of the plays and to beautify the external aspect, the artistic aspect, of the performers in the plays. (Sfog 1917)

Standards of taste, in other words, were being dictated by growing familiarity with metropolitan, especially Russian, literature. And in order to be compelling, Jewish culture, whatever the content, had to satisfy these metropolitan standards. If any proof was needed, by 1919–1920 these figures could look to the beginnings of the end of what had been a promising synthesis in the Jewish plastic arts between modernism and Jewish folk culture. Even as Abram Efros was hailing the discovery of Jewish "primitive" figures in *pinkasim* and on synagogue walls as an epoch-making event, the most talented practitioners of this synthesis like El Lissitzky were already turning their backs on any such delimitation and moving along lines of aesthetic logic dictated by their allegiance to avant-garde art itself. The same brief flirtation would play itself out a few years later with Polish-Jewish modernists like H. Berlewi (Bowlt 1988, 56; Wolitz 1988, 40 and 1991, 34–36). In the era of the nation-state, museums enshrine these artists as Russian and Polish, respectively.

5 A Different Jewish Cultural Nationalism

The ideal of a "universal," Jewishly unmarked Jewish culture enjoyed an ambiguous fate in the years that followed. Certainly, translation does not seem to have forestalled cultural-linguistic assimilation in any obvious way (though forestalling effects are, of course, hard to measure), at least in Eastern Europe; in the emerging Hebrew-speaking community of Palestine, it may well have had that effect for the younger generation (Amichay-Michlin 2000, 296). As for the idea of a universal Jewish culture itself, its fate differed in accordance with the larger differences in the political and cultural conditions of the various interwar Jewish communities. In the Soviet Union of the 1920s, it gained in force—albeit in tension with acceptably radical and anti-religious versions of folklorism—but it was harnessed ever more tightly to new political demands of the Revolution and thus profoundly distorted. Litvakov and Dobrushin understood deparochialization dialectically in the service of a new, better national culture, but the Bundist turned Bolshevik Moyshe Rafes would have the last word when, in 1919, he warned them that "we Jewish Communists are the great broom which will sweep off the Jewish workers' street all your Mendeles, Peretzs, Sholem Aleichems, your whole petit bourgeois culture." (*Kultur-Lige* 1919, 4; Litvak 1919b) Tellingly, literary translation itself would come to serve in Soviet Yiddish culture less as a culture-building strategy than as a tactic of retreat into a neutral sphere by writers unable to toe the literary-ideological line (Howe and Greenberg, 1977, 14). In freer interwar Poland, the notion of a universal Jewish culture resonated with modernists like the Khalyastre group in the early 1920s (though modernism as such could also valorize indigenous sources) but then arguably fell victim to the more general structural and ideological pressures that, as Seth Wolitz has shown, frustrated any attempt by Jewish national artists to enjoy "personal aesthetic freedom without compromising [their] national identity." (Wolitz 1991, 26) The creative revision of indigenous sources remained (or rebounded as) the organizing principle of many key works of the era, though the anti-parochial commitment remained potent in other loci like the poetics of the American In-zikh group or Meylekh Ravitsh in Poland. Programmatic translation remained a central feature of Hebrew and Yiddish publishing alike in Poland; but with the exception of the Stybel press in the early 1920s—about which one Warsaw writer could enthuse that it had conquered "Japheth in his tent" and created a new "bookshelf" that "Jewish fathers will bequeath to their sons" (Amichay-Michlin 2000, 203)—the grand visions of 1917–1919 found no purchase in Poland. This contrasted notably with the *Yishuv*, where the consolidation of a Hebrew society and state in the making laid the groundwork for the routinization of an open Jewish literature—a notable fact given the current romance in some quarters of the Jewish academy with the ostensible freeing effects of deterritorialized "diaspora culture."

But the explosion of debate and activity around programmatic translation in 1917–1919 is important not only for whatever lasting effects it might have had but as an expression of larger cultural developments in the national intelligentsia's project to create a modern Jewish culture. The intellectuals, writers, and publishers who focused so much effort on systematic, rapid translation in this period sought to create a compensatory literary tradition of universal scope that would reshape the sensibilities and orientations of Jewish writers and thus of Jewish aesthetic culture itself. This was, for many, a means to protect the fledgling modern Jewish culture itself against the far more powerful metropolitan cultures. At the same time, for some it was also an end: the creation of an adequate modern Jewish culture through a programmatic embrace of its stylized opposite, the "European" or "universal."

The historian might protest that the pursuit of so-called Jewish and so-called universal cultural strategies are not inherent opposites but two moments of a single process of cultural creation. Yet contemporaries felt these orientations to be opposed in terms of their practical sense of what Jewish culture as a whole needed most and in which direction it ought to develop. Indeed, we might follow Dan Miron in positing this tension as a generative principle or recurrent structuring tension of the modern Jewish cultural undertaking as a whole. The famous confrontations of the 1890s between the *tseirim* and Ahad Ha'am over the issue of Jewish content and the alien "beauty of Japheth" in Hebrew literary expression, or between Ben-Avigor's Tushiyah publishing house and the Hibat-Tsion Ahiasaf over the place of belletristics and non-Jewish writing on the Hebrew bookshelf, were merely the most public manifestations of an ever-stronger countercurrent within the emerging East European Jewish cultural sphere; this countercurrent is evident too in the recurrent invocations of Hellenism analyzed by Yaacov Shavit, in Yosef Klausner's praise for Peretz's imitative 1894 Hebrew love poetry as a step toward the Europeanization of Jewish literature, and even in Bialik's plaintive private admission in 1892 that much of his poetry was not national (Miron 1987, 35–38; Shmeruk 1971, 7–8; Lahover 1956, 244–45, 247). By 1917, when it seemed both possible and pressing to provide a solid institutional, social, and ideological foundation for the new Jewish culture, a more concrete facet of this tension displayed itself: the very practical question of cultural resources. The Jewish intelligentsia was well aware of the gap between its vision of massive cultural revolution and its own limited cultural and material resources; hence the allocation of these resources to one strategy of culture-building over another assumed a zero-sum logic. Litai's reaction to Bialik's decision to translate An-ski's *Between Two Worlds* is illustrative: he lamented that Hebrew's greatest writer should squander time on this "completely mediocre" play about "'dybbuks'" rather than furthering "the redemption of our language" through translations from world literature like the *Quixote* he had previously begun (Litai 1918, 604).

More broadly, by 1917, this countercurrent had become a flood. The urge to reconcile a commitment to Jewish identity with a universal cultural orientation had become, as opponents and proponents alike recognized, a decisive fact within the national camp itself. In light of this fact, programmatic demands for deparochialization were not peculiar deviations from Jewish nationalism but, firstly, far-seeing efforts to come to grips with real cultural change in ever-broader parts of the Jewish population. Moderate advocates of translation and the champions of a more radical deparochialization alike (Frishman 1932, 57–58) recognized the impossibility of turning these tides back through any sort of willed self-restriction—what Litai called "intellectual abstinence."

More important, we must recognize that such demands were themselves expressions of Jewish nationalism. It is a revealing fact that even the radical universalizers examined here were by no means opposed to the development of specifically Jewish idioms of expression in modern Jewish literature. Indeed, these figures cherished the hope that their engineered deparochialization might lead dialectically to new and distinctly Jewish literary works. Klausner, Shteynman, and many of their contemporaries repeatedly invoked the hope that "the most universal poet" would also give birth to "the most national" poetry (many accorded Tshernikhovsky this laurel); in this, they paralleled a trope common to Russian nationalist literati from Dostoevsky's famed effusions about the uniquely absorptive capacities of Russian genius to Evgeny Anichkov's summation of the Russian Silver Age as a triumphant rechanneling of Western literary trends, though with none of the same confidence about the advantages of cultural underdevelopment (Hoisington 1988; Polonsky 1998). Yiddishists like Dobrushin aspired to see Yiddish poetry rise to the same "national-classical heights" as that attained by Byron, Pushkin, Verlaine, and Bialik, and to "elevat[e] modern Jewishness to an artistic *Weltanschauung*." (Dobrushin 1919a, 94–95) And none other than Litvakov held out the hope that through Europeanization, Jewish literature would "not los[e] but perhaps, on the contrary, [deepen] its uniquely national character." (Litvakov 1919c, 37)[22]

More telling still is the simple fact that even those who most fervently advocated this deparochialization did so explicitly in the name of revitalizing modern Jewish national culture no less than their indigenizing opponents. After all, the point of their undertaking was to strengthen self-sufficient modern Hebrew and Yiddish cultures despite their own sense that these cultures were, as yet, quite inferior to those around them—arguably, the very essence of East European cultural nationalism. Whereas Bialik and others in his camp insisted that Jewish writers and readers compel themselves to work with their own literary "possessions," these figures acted on the view that a modern Jewish national culture could only be truly worthwhile and compelling if it was completely universal in its potentials. Although individual works of such a culture might make use of Jewish realia, symbols, and so forth, there could be no predetermined Jewish limits because that would virtually guarantee stagnation—a stagnation that the radical champions of translation already clearly felt in the Hebrew or Yiddish literature of their own day. Only one limit could not be compromised because it

---

22 Although for some on the left, like Litvakov or Dobrushin, the radicalizing Revolutionary process itself no doubt lent momentum to their emphasis on the universal moment in Jewish culture, it was nevertheless not the determining factor. These figures remained outspokenly committed to a Jewish-national project in their rhetoric well beyond 1919 and, conversely, others in the same left circles like Oyslender pushed the folkloristic line, albeit in secularized fashion. In other words, the Revolution could authorize either move.

was enabling: the limit of language itself. It is no accident that the most radical advocates of deparochialization numbered among the most fervent monolingualist Hebraists and Yiddishists of their day. Though perhaps only the authorizing power of the state could consecrate a piece of art or music as national, the fact of language alone rendered a work of literature or theater part of an ongoing, open-ended national tradition. With a universal fundament gained through translation and sustained by constant interchange with other literatures, a culture might be as wide as humanity but also self-contained and self-sustaining.

Though the efforts of Jewish cultural nationalists to create an encompassing Jewish culture have enjoyed some penetrating scholarly attention, our regnant historical account of Jewish culture and Jewish cultural nationalism remains on the whole resolutely focused on the dynamic of Judaization in its various forms. Yet the will to an unmarked, encompassing Jewish culture must be accorded descriptive and explanatory centrality in our study of Jewish culture and Jewish nationalism both. For it expressed perhaps the most central desire of modern Jewish cultural nationalism: the desire to be both moderns and Jews—to be, as the Yiddishist Latski-Bertoldi put it in a telling recasting of Y. L. Gordon's famous formulation, "honest and whole everywhere, on the street and in *the home*." (Latski-Bertoldi, 1919)

My thanks to Olga Borovaya, Jeff Brooks, Marc Caplan, Marcus Moseley, Anne Eakin Moss, Ben Nathans, Gabriella Safran, and Steven Zipperstein for comments and suggestions. My thanks to University of Pennsylvania Press for permission to republish this piece, which originally appeared (in slightly different form) in Benjamin Nathans and Gabriella Safran, eds., *Culture Front: Representing Jews in Eastern Europe* (Philadelphia, 2008).

Bibliography

Archival Collections

An-ski Collection, Fond 2583, Rossiiskii gosudarstvennyi arkhiv literatury i isskustva (RGALI), Moscow.
Correspondence Collection, Beit Bialik, Tel Aviv.
Ministry of Jewish Affairs of the Ukrainian People's Republic Collection. Record Group 2060.
    Tsentral'nyi derzhavnyi arkhiv vyshchykh orhaniv vlady i upravlinnya (TsDAVO), Kiev.
Niger Collection, Record Group 360, YIVO Institute, New York.
Yiddish Literature and Language Collection, Record Group 3, YIVO Institute, New York.

Published Sources, no author listed

1918. *Di grunt-oyfgabn fun der Kultur-Lige*. Kiev: drukeray fun di yorshim Y. Shenfeld.
1920. Folks-Farlag announcement, *Vilna Leben* (Vilna) 3–4 (June): 53.
1918. "'Hotsaat Stybel' be-arikhat David Frishman." [announcement] *Ha-tekufah* (Moscow) 2 (Nisan-Sivan): back matter.
1920. *Idisher Folks-Farlag*. Kiev: Folks-Farlag.
1917. *Kneset: Divre sifrut*. Odessa: Moriah.
1920. *Kultur Lige: byuleten num. 2*. Kiev: Kultur-Lige.
1919. *Kultur-Lige: a sakh-akl: zamlung*. Kiev: Kultur-Lige.
1919. "Kunst-khronik" *Baginen* (Kiev) 1: 85–96.
1917. "Me-et Tarbut," *Ha-am* (Moscow), 28 April.
1917. "Mi-sipurei Korea," *Shetilim* (Moscow) 3 (2 August): 40–45.
1917. "Shetilim" (advertisement) in *Ha-am* (Moscow), 16 July.
19[18?]. *Shriften: Fremds: Eyropeishe poezye* (Moscow).
1905. *Zamelbukh "Kultur."* Minsk.

Published Authored Sources

Amichay-Michlin, Dania. 2000. *Ahavat I"Sh: Avraham Yosef Stybel*. Jerusalem: Mosad Bialik.
Apter-Gabriel, Ruth, ed. 1988. *Tradition and Revolution: The Jewish Renaissance in Russian Avant- Garde Art, 1912–1928*. Jerusalem: Israel Museum.
Ayzenshtadt, Shmuel. 1960. "Moskvah ha-'ivrit bi-yeme milḥemet ha-'olam ha-rishonah." *Katsir: Kovets le-korot ha-tenu'ah ha-tsionit be-rusiyah*. Tel Aviv: Masadah.
Ben-Avigdor. 1895. "Ha-'ivriut veha-klaliut be-sifrut ha-'ivrit." *Ha-Melits*, 21 April: 2.
Ben-Eliezer, M. 1917. "'Al ha-targumim." *Kneset: Divre sifrut*. Odessa: Moriah.
Ben-Yishai, A. Z. 1968. "Sifrut ve-'itonut 'ivrit be-rusiyah bi-tkufat ha-mahapekhah veaḥarehah." *He- 'Avar* 15: 163–202.
Bialik, H. N. 2000. "Halachah and Aggadah," trans. Leon Simon. In *Revealment and Concealment*, edited by Zali Gurevitch, 45–87. Jerusalem.
Bialik, H. N. [1913a] 1955. "Ha-sefer ha-'ivri." *Kol kitve Ḥ. N. Bialik*. Tel Aviv: Dvir.
Bialik, H. N. [1913b] 1955. "Tse'irut o yaldut?" *Kol kitve Ḥ. N. Bialik*. Tel Aviv: Dvir.
Bialik, H. N. [1916] 1955. "Halakhah ve-aggadah." *Kol kitve Ḥ. N. Bialik*. Tel Aviv: Dvir.
Borovaya, Olga. 2001. "Translation and Westernization: *Gulliver's Travels* in Ladino." *Jewish Social Studies* n.s. 7, no. 2 (Winter): 149–168.
Bourdieu, Pierre. 1984. *Distinction*. Cambridge, MA: Harvard University Press.
Bowlt, John. 1988. "From the Pale of Settlement to the Reconstruction of the World." In *Tradition and Revolution: The Jewish Renaissance in Russian Avant-Garde Art, 1912–1928*, edited by Ruth Apter-Gabriel, 43–60. Jerusalem: Israel Museum.
Brooks, Jeffrey. 1978. "Readers and Reading at the End of the Tsarist Era." In *Literature and Society in Imperial Russia*, edited by William Mills Todd, 97–150. Stanford: Stanford University Press.
Chukovskii, Kornei, and N. Gumilev. 1919. *Printsipy khudozhestvennogo perevoda*. Petrograd: Vsemirnaia Literatura.

Dinur, Ben-Tsion. 1960. *Bi-yeme milḥamah u-mahapekhah: Zikhronot u-reshumot mi-derekh ḥayim.* Jerusalem: Mosad Bialik.
Dobrushin, Yehezkel. 1919a. "Dray dikhter." *Oyfgang* (Kiev): 73–98.
Dobrushin, Yehezkel. 1919b. "Kunst-primitiv un kunst-bukh far kinder." *Bikher-velt* (Kiev) 4–5 (August): 16–23.
Dobrushin, Yehezkel. 1919c. "Universal-bibliotek"; "Literarishe nayes." *Bikher-velt* (Kiev) 1: 39.
Dykman, Aminadav. 1994. "Homeros shel Tshernihovski." In *Shaul Tshernihovski: Ma'amarim u- te'udot,* edited by Boaz Arpali, 447–455. Jerusalem: Mosad Bialik.
Friedberg, Maurice. 1997. *Literary Translation in Russia.* University Park, PA.: Penn State Press.
Frishman, David. 1932. "'Al ha-sifrut ha-yafah." In *Kol kitve David Frishman,* Vol. 8. Warsaw, New York, and Tel Aviv: Lily Frishman Publishing.
Frishman, David. 1940. "Igerot el Ḥ. N. Bialik." *Kneset: divre sofrim le-zekher Ḥ. N. Bialik* 5: 26–36.
Frishman, David. 1922–1923. *Shiv'ah mikhtavim ḥadashim 'al devar ha-sifrut.* Berlin: Dvir.
Gershenzon, M. 1918. "Predislovie." In *Evreiskaia antologiia: sbornik molodoi evreiskoi poezii,* edited by Leib Jaffe, v–viii. Moscow: Safrut.
Gilboa, Yehoshua A. 1974. *Oktobraim ivrim: Toldotehah shel ashlayah.* Tel Aviv: ha-Makhon leḥeḳer ha-tefutsot.
Gnesin, M. 1946. *Darki 'im ha-teatron ha-'ivri.* Tel Aviv: Ha-kibuts ha-me'uḥad.
Goldberg, A. 1919. "Der bikher-mark in Poyln." *Bikher-velt* 2–3 (March): 18–21.
Golubeva, Ol'ga D. 1968. *Gorkii—Izdatel'.* Moscow: "Kniga."
Gomlen, L. 1919. "Kritik un bibliografye: Poezye un beletristik: *Himel un erd.*" *Bikher-velt* 2–3 (March): 42–44.
Greenleaf, Monika, and Stephen Moeller-Sally, eds. 1998. *Russian Subjects.* Evanston: University of Illinois Press.
Grinblat, Natan. 1917–1918. "Reshimot sifrutiyot: 'Olamenu." *Ha-Tekufah* 1 (December–February): 664–675.
Harshav, Benjamin. 1993. *Language in Time of Revolution.* Berkeley: University of California Press.
Harshav, Benjamin, Ed 1992. *Marc Chagall and the Jewish Theater.* New York: Guggenheim Museum.
Hofshteyn, Dovid. 1923. "Di zun hot haynt tsum nayem pantser maynem." *Gezamelte Verk,* Vol. 1, *Lirik.* Kiev: Kooperativer farlag: 41.
Hofshteyn, Dovid. 1977a. "Vi troyerik-zis iz mentsh tsu zayn." *Lider un poemes,* Vol. 1. Tel Aviv: Yisroel-bukh: 57–58.
Hofshteyn, Dovid. 1977b. "Vig-lid." *Lider un poems,* Vol. 1, 59. Tel Aviv: Yisroel-bukh.
Hoisington, Sonia Stephan, ed. 1988. *Russian Views of Pushkin's Eugene Onegin.* Bloomington: Indiana University Press.
Horowitz, Brian, ed. 1998. "Pis'ma L. B. Yaffe k M. Gershenzonu." *Vestnik evreiskogo universiteta* 2 (18): 210–219.
Howe, Irving, and Eliezer Greenberg. 1977. "Introduction: Soviet Yiddish Literature." In *Ashes Out of Hope,* edited by Irving Howe and Eliezer Greenberg, 1–28. New York: Schocken.
Ivanov, Vladislav. 1999. *Russkie sezony: Teatr Gabima.* Moscow: Artist. Rezhisser. Teatr.
Jacobson, David. 1987. *Modern Midrash.* Albany: SUNY Press.

Jaffe, Leyb. 1918. Opening statement, *Sborniki "Safrut"* (Moscow) 1.
Katz, Ben-Tsion. 1927. "Ke-avor tekufah." *Ha-tsefirah* (Warsaw), 4 March.
Katz, Ben-Tsion. 1964. *Zikhronot*. Tel Aviv: N. Tverski.
Katz, Moyshe. 1921. "Di Kultur Lige in Ukrayne." *Di tsukunft* 3 (March): 183–188.
Kazovski, Hillel. 2003. *Khudozhniki Kultur-Ligi/The Artists of the Kultur-Lige*. Moscow: Mosty kul'tury.
Kiel, Mark. 1991. "A Twice Lost Legacy: Ideology, Culture, and the Pursuit of Jewish Folklore in Russian until Stalinization." PhD. diss., Jewish Theological Seminary.
Klausner, Yosef. 1917. "Sifrutenu 4: 'Al Bialik." *Ha-Shiloaḥ* 32, no. 4 (April–June): 452–456.
Klausner, Yosef. 1918a. "Ha-ḥidah 'Tchernihovsky.'" *Ha-Shiloaḥ* 35, no. 2 (August): 104–121.
Klausner, Yosef. 1918b. "Keren-zavit: Nitsaḥon." *Ha-Shiloaḥ* 35, nos. 3–4 (September–October): 343–344.
Korman, Ezra. 1919a. "A. Pushkin. *Poltava*." *Bikher-velt* 4–5 (December): 54–55.
Korman, Ezra. 1919b. *"Fremds." Bikher-velt* 4–5 (December): 56–57.
Kronfeld, Chana. 1996. *On the Margins of Modernism: Decentering Literary Dynamics*. Berkeley: University of California Press.
Kulbak, Moyshe. 1962. "Dos yidishe vort." *Der veker* (Minsk 1918); reprinted in *Di goldene keyt* 43: 238–242.
Lahover, Fishl. 1956. *Bialik: Hayav ve-yetsirotav*. Jerusalem: Mosad Bialik 'al yede Dvir.
Latski-Bertoldi, Z. 1919. "*In Umruh* [review]." *Bikher-velt* 2–3 (March): 29–30.
Litai, A. 1917. "Perishut sikhlit o hitbollelut." *Ha-'Am*, 10 March.
Litai, A. [as A. Ben-Moshe]. 1918. "Sifrut ha-'olam." *Ha-Shiloaḥ* 34, nos. 5–6 (April): 540–546.
Litai, A. [as A.B.M.]. 1919. "*Ha-Tekufah* [review]." *Masuot* 1: 601–616.
Litai, A. 1956. "Ha-'yarid' ha-sifruti-ha-'ivri ha-gadol be-Moskvah." *He-'Avar* 3: 55–59.
Litvak, A. 1919a. "Di farshpreytung fun yidishe bikher in Amerike." *Bikher-velt* 1: 13–15.
Litvak, A. 1919b. "Literatur un lebn." *Baginen* 1 (Kiev): 97–102.
Litvakov, Moyshe [as M. Lit.]. 1919a. "Kritik un bibliografye: *Eygns*." *Bikher-velt* 1 (January): 20–25.
Litvakov, Moyshe 1918. *In Umruh*. Kiev: Kiever farlag.
Litvakov, Moyshe 1919b. "Di sistem fun iberzetsungen I." *Bikher-velt* 1 (January): 9–12.
Litvakov, Moyshe 1919c. "Di sistem fun iberzetsungen II." *Bikher-velt* 4–5 (August): 37–44.
M. D. 1919. "K. Zingman: *Motl der shnayder*." *Bikher-velt* 4–5: 53.
Meitus, Eliyahu. 1917. "Ha-'ahavah' be-shiratenu ha-tse'irah." *Ha-Shiloaḥ* 33, nos. 2–3 (August–September): 255–271.
Miron, Dan. 1987. *Bodedim be-mo'adam*. Tel Aviv: 'Am 'oved.
Moss, Kenneth B. 2001. "Between Renaissance and Decadence: *Literarishe Monatsshriften* and Its Critical Reception." *Jewish Social Studies* 8, no. 1 (Fall): 153–198.
Moss, Kenneth B. 2009. *Jewish Renaissance in the Russian Revolution*. Harvard: Harvard University Press.
Moss, Kenneth B. 2003. "'A Time for Tearing Down and a Time for Building Up': Recasting Jewish Culture in Eastern Europe, 1917–1921." PhD. diss., Stanford University.
Ofek, Uriel. 1984. *Gumot Ḥe"N: Po'alo shel Bialik be-sifrut ha-yeladim*. Tel Aviv: Dvir.
Oyslender, Nokhem. 1919. "Henry V. Longfellow: *Dos gezang fun Hiavata*." *Bikher-velt* 2–3: 41–42.
Parush, Iris. 1992. *Kanon sifruti ve-ideologyah le'umit*. Jerusalem: Mosad Bialik.

Pograbinsky, Yohanan. 1950-1951. "Le-toldot ha-mol'ut." *Jewish Book Annual* 9 (New York): xl–lvii.
Polonsky, Rachel. 1998. *English Literature and the Russian Aesthetic Renaissance*. Cambridge: Cambridge University Press.
Reyland, P. 1919. "Bibliografye: Yung Treyst." *Baginen* 1: 115–117.
Reyzen, Avrom. 1935. *Epizodn fun mayn lebn*. Vilna: Kletskin.
Roskies, David G. 1995. *A Bridge of Longing*. Cambridge, MA: Harvard University Press.
Roskies, David G. 1996. "Rabbis, Rebbes, and Other Humanists: The Search for a Usable Past in Modern Yiddish Literature." In *Studies in Contemporary Jewry 12: Literary Strategies*, edited by Ezra Mendelsohn, 55–77. Bloomington: Indiana University Press.
Rubin, Adam. 2000. "From Torah to Tarbut: Hayim Nahman Bialik and the Nationalization of Judaism." PhD. diss., UCLA.
Shavit, Yaacov. 1997. *Athens in Jerusalem*. London: Littman Library of Jewish Civilization.
Shavit, Zohar. 1982. *Ha-ḥayim ha-sifrutiim be-erets Yisrael, 1910–1933*. Tel Aviv: Ha-kibuts ha- me'uḥad.
Shavit, Zohar, and Yaacov Shavit. 1977. "Lemale' et ha-arets sefarim: Sifrut mekorit le'umat sifrut meturgemet be-tahalikh yetsirato shel ha-merkaz ha-sifruti be-erets yisrael." *Ha-Sifrut* 25: 45–68.
Shmeruk, Chone, et al, eds. 1964. *A shpigl af a shteyn: antologye*. Tel Aviv: Farlag Y. L. Perets.
Shmeruk, Chone. 1983. "Le-toldot sifrut ha-'shund' be-Yidish." *Tarbits* 52, no. 2: 325–354.
Shmeruk, Chone. 1971. *Peretses yiesh-vizye: interpretatsye fun Y. L. Peretses Bay nakht oyfn altn mark un kritishe oysgabe fun der drame*. New York: YIVO.
Shteynman, Eliezer [as Aleph]. 1919a. "Genizah ve-ḥatimah." In "Ma'amarim u-reshimot." In *Erets: Ma'asef le-sifrut yafah ule-vikoret*. Odessa: Erets [Ha-arets?].
Shteynman, Eliezer [as Aleph]. 1919b. "Hotsa'at Stybel." In "Ma'amarim u-reshimot." In *Erets: Ma'asef le-sifrut yafah ule-vikoret*. Odessa: Erets [Ha-arets?].
Shulman, Eliyohu. 1965. "Di tsaytshrift '*Di Yudishe (idishe) velt*.'" *Pinkes far der forshung fun der yidisher literatur un prese* 1 (New York): 122–170.
Sfog [= Sh. Tshernovits]. 1917. "Ha-Bimah." *Ha-Am* 11, 27 January.
Slutsky, Yehudah. 1961. "Ha-pirsumim ha-'ivriyim be-Vrit ha-Mo'atsot ba-shanim 1917–1960." In *Pirsumim yehudiyim be-Vrit ha-Mo'atsot, 1917–1960*, edited by Yitshak Yosef Kohen, 55–131. Jerusalem: ha ḥevrah ha-historit ha-yisra'elit.
Tidhar, David. 1947–1971. *Entsiklopedyah le- ḥalutse ha-yishuv u-vonav*. Tel Aviv: Sifriyat rishonim.
Tsemah, Sh. 1919. "Shaul Tsherniḥovski." *Masuot* 1: 581–598.
Tsharni, Donyel. 1943. *A yortsendlik aza, 1914–1924: Memuarn*. New York: CYCO bikher-farlag.
Tshernikhovsky, Shaul. 1920. *Shirei Anakreon*. Warsaw: Stybel.
Tshernikhovsky, Shaul. 1930. *Sefer Ilias*. Vilna: Stybel.
Tverski, Yohanan. 1948. "Avraham Yosef Stybel." *Ha-tekufah* 32–33 (New York): 14–18.
Ungerfeld, Moshe, ed. 1974. *Bialik ve-sofre doro*. Tel Aviv: 'Am ha-Sefer.
Veidlinger, Jeffrey. 2000. *The Moscow State Yiddish Theater*. Bloomington: Indiana University Press.
Wolitz, Seth. 1991. "Between Folk and Freedom: The Failure of the Yiddishist Modernist Movement in Poland." *Yiddish* 8, no. 1: 26–42.

Wolitz, Seth. 1981. "*Di Khalyastre:* The Yiddish Modernist Movement in Poland: An Overview." *Yiddish* 4, no. 3: 5–19.
Wolitz, Seth. 1988. "The Jewish National Art Renaissance in Russia" In *Tradition and Revolution: The Jewish Renaissance in Russian Avant-Garde Art, 1912–1928*, edited by Ruth Apter-Gabriel, 21–42. Jerusalem.
Wolitz, Seth. 1978. "The Kiev-Grupe (1918–1920) Debate." *Yiddish* 3, no. 3: 97–106.
Zaidman, A. D. 1973. "Literaturnye studii 'Vsemirnoi Literatury' i 'Doma Iskusstv' (1919–1921 gody)." *Russkaia literatura* 16, no. 1: 141–148.
Zerubavel. 1917. "Ha-veidah ha-rishonah." *Ha-am*, 17 April.

Natalia Krynicka
Maneuvering around the "Great Wall of China": Translations of Yiddish Literature into Polish before the First World War

1 Don Quixote Struggling against the Great Wall of China

The history of Yiddish-to-Polish literary translation begins with a publication that immediately became a literary event and found great resonance among critics and readers alike.[1] The person behind it was Klemens Junosza-Szaniawski (1849–1898), an extremely popular writer in his time, author of sketches, short stories, and novels portraying daily life in Warsaw, but also in the countryside and in the Jewish communities. In 1885, he published *Donkiszot żydowski* [*The Jewish Don Quixote*], a Polish adaptation of *Masoes Binyomin Hashlishi*, 1878 [*The Travels of Benjamin the Third*] by Sholem-Yankev Abramovitsh (1836–1917), the founding father of contemporary Yiddish literature who was better known under his nom de plume Mendele Moykher-Sforim (Mendele the Book Peddler). A year later, in 1886, Junosza translated another of Abramovitsh's novels, *Szkapa* (*Di klyatshe*, 1873) [*The Nag*].

Junosza's enterprise had no precedent in the history of translation from Yiddish into Polish or in the history of translation from Yiddish in general. At the time, only the Yiddish-speaking public was familiar with Yiddish literature, while the rest of the society remained largely unaware of its presence. Although several shorter pieces had already been translated into Russian, they were known only to assimilated Jews.

How can this sudden interest in Yiddish literature on the part of a Polish writer and his readership be explained? To be sure, the mood of the era was favorable to such enterprises. The so-called "Jewish question," including the issue of assimilation, poverty of the Jewish masses, "productivization" of Jews, or *cheder* reform, occupied journalists of various political creeds. On the one hand, the anti-Semitic press wrote extensively on the "destructive" role of the Jews in Poland, and strong anti-Jewish attitudes lingered for decades after the

---

[1] The paper is based on one of the chapters of my PhD thesis, which is devoted to Polish-Jewish relations in the light of literary translations (Krynicka 2009).

pogroms of 1881. On the other, Positivist writers, such as Eliza Orzeszkowa, called for tolerance and understanding among the nations. As a result, Junosza's enterprise was greeted with much interest as a new and original "contribution to the Jewish question." This was best reflected in the decision to feature *Donkiszot żydowski* on the front page of a popular daily *Wiek*, which published the novel in installments before it was released as a hardback later in the same year.

This was probably not the only reason for a sudden surge of interest in Yiddish literature. During the second part of the nineteenth century, the "Other" became an object of fascination: as ethnography started developing as a discipline, and travelogues became a popular feature in the press, the number of translations from world literature started to grow rapidly. In the last four decades of the nineteenth century, Jewish protagonists often featured in Polish literature, and numerous works devoted to Jewish life were published. Both familiar and remote, the Jewish world, with its different language, religion, and dress, became increasingly intriguing to readers. Junosza's translations fit in with the trend, which is well illustrated by the fact that *Szkapa* was published in installments in a travel magazine *Wędrowiec*, featured in between travelogues from Asia and America and tableaux depicting rural life.

Although the circumstances were favorable, Junosza's enterprise was so unique that the author felt the need to justify it, especially after the installments of *Donkiszot żydowski* triggered a wide response from readers. The hardback edition was therefore preceded by a long foreword and concluded with an even longer afterword. Junosza begins by explaining that his wish to explore Yiddish literature grew out of a desire to understand the life of his neighbors and his curiosity about the foreign alphabet. To describe the divide between the Christian and Jewish communities, he uses a metaphor of the "Great Wall of China," another expression of the broader cultural fascination with the exotic and unknown:

> We live together on one Earth, and so should know each other, but is it the case? Not in the least. We know the factor, the merchant, the craftsman, and the usurer, but not the Jew. We know nothing about the Jews in their homes, schools, among their fellows, or in the synagogue. Jews come across Christians in the market, at their stands, and only in those places where business is done. Once the transaction has been completed, Jews disappear in their homes, which are separated from the Christian society with the centuries-old Great Wall of China. (Abramowicz 1899, 6)[2]

---

[2] Citations are based on the second edition of the novel, published in the series *Tanie wydawnictwo dzieł Klemensa Junoszy* (1899) [*The Works of Klemens Junosza: An Affordable Edition*]. Unless indicated otherwise, citations from Polish authors have been rendered into English by the translator.

Junosza's statement reflects the Positivist thirst for knowledge and the fascination with Otherness at home. But the author is also quick to signal his mistrust of his Jewish neighbors. His translation, as he suggests in the following passage, is designed to serve as a sort of strategic reconnaissance and help secure a level playing field should any conflict emerge:

> Religion, language, and prejudice drove a wedge in between the two groups of the society in that the Jews had a perfect vantage point from behind the wall on the Christians, their daily life and their strengths and weaknesses, while remaining completely undisclosed to their neighbors. (Abramowicz 1899, 6)

With statements of this kind, Junosza might have been trying to appeal to the anti-Semitic circles that he was affiliated with as a contributor to the *Rola* weekly. Shortly before the publication of *Donkiszot żydowski* in *Wiek*, *Rola* featured a teaser of Junosza's study on jargon literature, so it is probable that the text was initially written as a contribution to *Rola*.[3]

After his translation was met with some criticism, Junosza defended his enterprise as vital to "the Jewish question." Oscillating between two extremes: humanism and military rhetoric, he tried to address both a liberal and anti-Semitic readership.

Junosza's treatment of Mendele Moykher-Sforim's original was a radical one.[4] The title page of the Polish edition does not even feature the name of the author, listing Junosza instead. What is more, the translator not only changed the original title *Masoes Binyomin Hashlishi* [*The Travels of Benjamin the Third*] to *Donkiszot żydowski* [*The Jewish Don Quixote*], but also added a subtitle: "A Sketch from Jewish Jargon Literature." Junosza's rendition therefore is more akin to an essay than a work of fiction. He calls his translation a "synopsis" and intervenes into the text to such an extent that he does not allow the author to speak for himself. The initial chapter contains the author's biography instead of the novel's beginning. Numerous footnotes at the bottom of the page, but also translator's explanations and commentaries in the text disrupt the original flow of the narrative. From time to time, presumably to appeal to the Polish reader, Junosza deprives the author of his voice entirely.

---

[3] In the years that followed, Junosza would drift towards the anti-Semitic camp, while his novels *Pająki: obrazek z życia warszawskiego* (1894) [*Spiders: The Tableau of Warsaw Life*] and *Czarnebłoto: Pająki wiejskie* (1895) [*Black Mud: Rural Spiders*] were highly expressive of anti-Jewish attitudes.

[4] These remarks do not apply to *Szkapa*, which is more in line with the traditional rules of translation.

> I am going to skip the description of the gutters, as I wish to spare some of the displeasing sensations to the reader. For the record, however, I have to add that the description is extremely realistic. I have never come across such a detailed photography of mud before. (Abramowicz 1899, 141)

The reader soon loses track of who is speaking in the text, which is reflected in Maria Konopnicka's review of the novel. This celebrated Polish author erroneously attributes the metaphor of the "Great Wall of China," from behind which the Jews watch the Christians undisclosed, to Abramovitsh himself (Konopnicka 1885).

Mendele Moykher-Sforim's work is, in many ways, lost in translation, as the reader faces difficulty in appreciating its literary qualities and subversive sense of humor. In Junosza's rendering, the novel penned by a Jewish intellectual, and meant as a parody and satire on his contemporaries, morphs into an anti-Semitic caricature.

Junosza's attitude to the Yiddish language and the entire "Jewish question" was a complex and ambivalent one. On the one hand, just like a vast majority of his contemporaries in Poland and worldwide, Junosza considered Yiddish a "linguistic oddity" lacking any grammar, and he often described it as "jargon," which was a generally accepted term at the time (Abramowicz 1899, 4). His agenda was to supplant it with a "civilized" language, that is, the Polish vernacular: "Eradicating the jargon is a beautiful idea," notes Junosza in the introduction (Abramowicz 1899, 4). On the other hand, unlike anti-Semitic circles or the proponents of Jewish assimilation centered around the *Izraelita* weekly (who vehemently opposed any translations from the Yiddish jargon and postulated its full eradication), Junosza believed Yiddish might be useful as a tool of education with the potential to "civilize" and "productivize" the Jewish masses. The very fact that he translated a work of a writer he apparently valued suggests that Junosza also recognized the literary potential of Yiddish.[5] The numerous passages cited directly in Yiddish also give the reader an impression that the language captivated the translator, even if his fascination always verged on derision.

Despite Junosza's dubious motives and his ambivalent attitude to the Yiddish language and Jews in general, his project played a transformative role in shaping the perception of Jewish literature in Poland. Thanks to his translations,

---

[5] It is also evident that Mendele Moykher-Sforim made a significant impact on Junosza as a writer. The latter's works on Jewish subjects prior to and after 1885 differ decidedly. This comes to the fore in the novel *Żywota i spraw imć pana Symchy Borucha Kaltkugla ksiąg pięcioro* (1895) [*The Life and Adventures of Mr Simkha Borukh Kaltkugel in Five Volumes*], which bears an apparent mark of parody and satire characteristic of *The Travels of Benjamin the Third*.

Polish intellectuals and critics discovered Yiddish literature. Because the translator was a highly acclaimed writer himself who published with a popular Warsaw press, his work resonated in significant ways. Bolesław Prus, Maria Konopnicka, and many other eminent Polish authors, reviewed the book with interest. As a writer of considerable standing, Junosza's translations elevated Abramovitsh to prominence; for many years to come, the author was featured in Polish encyclopedias as the only representative of Yiddish literature.

Similarly, Junosza's enterprise resonated very strongly in the Jewish world, both among Polish and Yiddish speakers. The Yiddish-speaking intelligentsia, including Sforim himself, enjoyed the unexpected admiration of Yiddish literature that followed. Junosza's work also strengthened Abramovitsh's position among his contemporaries, blazed the trail for further translations of his works into other languages, and marked an important stage in the difficult process of filtering Yiddish into Polonised Jewish intellectual circles. The fact that it was possible to write literature in this language signaled that Yiddish did not have to be considered a primitive and embarrassing jargon. In the interwar years, some Jewish circles, both Polish- and Yiddish speaking, even idolized Junosza as a herald of Jewish/non-Jewish dialogue.

2 The Meandering Wall

No other Yiddish-to-Polish translator gained as much renown before the First World War as Junosza, although other translation attempts were made in that time. For example, Maksymilian Lewart's (Skwarcz) translation of the novel *Chasyd* [*Hasid*] (*Dos poylishe yingl* [*Polish Boy*], 1869) by Yitzhok-Yoel Linetski (1839– 1915) passed largely unnoticed.[6] From January until August 1888, the translation appeared in installments in the *Gazeta Lubelska* daily, where Junosza published too. Lewart followed closely the example of his predecessor: he used the same subtitle: *Szkic z literatury żargonowej* [*A Sketch from Jargon Literature*], placed his name ahead of Linetski's, provided the text with a foreword, annotated the novel, and quoted numerous words and expressions in Yiddish. Unlike Junosza's translations, however, *Chasyd*—a biting satire on Hasidism and a critique of narrow-mindedness from one of the most prominent writers of the *Haskalah* (Jewish

---

[6] So far, it has been impossible for me to establish whether it was the same Maksymilian Lewart-Skwarcz who, shortly after World War I, published two radically nationalistic pamphlets which criticized the then-Chief of State and later de facto leader of the Second Polish Republic, Józef Piłsudski, among others.

Enlightenment)—remained largely unknown to a wider readership.[7] Both the local character of the publication and the fact that the translator was a little-known figure might have contributed to this outcome.

Despite its very promising beginnings, the Yiddish-to-Polish translation project soon came to a halt. Although Junosza made "jargon" literature available to his compatriots, he failed to change the disdainful attitude towards the language that was still barely recognized as one. Once the effect of its novelty had worn off, the Polish intelligentsia found it difficult to relate to a literature which defied the zeitgeist of the era. The translations were thus soon forgotten.[8]

A language barrier was surely a major obstacle for non-Jewish translators, who showed no interest in translating from Yiddish. The very idea of learning the "jargon," recorded in Hebrew script, was unthinkable for the intellectuals of the time.[9] It is no wonder, then, that such translations in the 1890s were made exclusively by assimilated Jews. This constantly growing group defied Junosza's vision of two communities divided by the "Great of Wall of China." On which side of the Wall should we position the assimilatory weekly *Izraelita* and its readers? Neither *Donkiszot*'s translator nor his followers ever took a stance on that.

The attitude of *Izraelita* towards the Yiddish language and literature underwent a radical change over the years. The magazine's first Editor-in-Chief, Hen-

---

[7] Junosza nonetheless praises the translation in his book *Nasi Żydzi w miasteczkach i na wsiach* [*Our Jews in Towns and Villages*] (Junosza 1889, 47) as a commendable source of information on Jewish religious teaching.

[8] Chone Shmeruk points out that each time subsequent translations from Yiddish literature into Polish were published, the reviewers would be amazed by its existence and express it in their texts (Shmeruk 2000, 103).

[9] Junosza himself probably did not speak Yiddish, even though his translations are full of expressions quoted from the original. In the 1920s, Pinkhes Kon, a researcher of Polish-Jewish relations, provided strong evidence to demonstrate that the Polish writer had intended to learn Yiddish, but that he gave up after two weeks of private tutoring from Yehuda-Leyb Davidsohn, a Jewish student from Belarus, and asked him to provide a working translation of the two novels from Yiddish into Russian, which he would later translate into Polish (Kon 1928, 36–38). The claim that Junosza did not know Yiddish was corroborated by evidence provided by assimilated Jews and the writer's contemporaries (Blumberg 1899, 228). The quotations from the original in the Polish text (which are not accidental: they reveal Junosza's attempts to achieve a comical effect by juxtaposing words from Hebrew, German, and Slavic languages, surprising the reader with a blend of the strange and the familiar) may be explained with a hypothesis whereby Davidsohn provided Junosza with an interpretation of the novel while reading out the excerpts from the original. Similarly, several inaccuracies in the translation of Jewish quotations, as well as several words recorded in Polish and not Lithuanian dialect, the latter used by Davidsohn, may suggest Junosza's personal yet negligible contribution to the translation.

ryk (Samuel Tsvi) Peltyn (1831–1896) was a sworn enemy of the "jargon." In 1885, as soon as first teasers of *Donkiszot*'s publication were featured in *Wiek*, he became one of the fiercest critics of Junosza's enterprise. In 1896, not long before his death, Peltyn's article was featured on the front page of *Izraelita* to protest against the project promoting Yiddish publications in Warsaw (including translations from Jules Verne). He described Yiddish as a "jabber," a foreign element standing in the way of assimilation, and he called for combatting it on all fronts (Peltyn 1896, 35). He would even go as far as to say that Yiddish, as a haphazard and unstructured entity, was the root cause of the alleged Jewish lack of consistency (Peltyn 1896, 36). The tenor of the magazine changed when a Zionist, Nakhum Sokolov (1859–1936), was appointed its Editor-in-Chief. Whereas Peltyn considered Yiddish and education to be mutually exclusive, Sokolov, during his tenure campaigned for more libraries and access to education, specifically including Yiddish learning (A. 1898, 428; Sokołow 1898, 463). This change of attitude was also visible in B. Sofer's 1899 manifesto "Żargon" ["Jargon"], which posits that Yiddish had a number of strengths and that folk literature in Yiddish helped to cultivate readers. The feature was a good example of the shifting approach towards Yiddish in the assimilatory circles: Sofer spoke of "jargon" with visible emotion and claimed that his generation shared a nostalgia for Yiddish (Sofer 1899, 97–98). While Polonization was affecting a growing number of Jews, the assimilatory ideology, programmatically hostile to Yiddish, was losing on significance. Polish-speaking Jewish intellectuals began, increasingly, to revisit their scepticism towards Yiddish, becoming more and more inclined to accept it as the second language of the Jews, after Polish.

At the end of the nineteenth century, *Izraelita* featured a set of articles on the need for ethnographic research among Polish Jews. These essays emphasize the necessity of preserving Yiddish songs and proverbs, following the example of German and Russian researchers (S. R-n 1898, 162). In his article from 1897, Henryk Lew encouraged readers to collect and anthologize depictions of Jewish customs. He asked them to send him materials in the language of their choice, preferably, however, in the "jargon." (Lew 1897, 2) The seminal work in Polish paroemiology, *Przysłowia żydowskie* [*Jewish Proverbs*] (1890) by Samuel Adalberg paved the way for this change of attitude. Adalberg presented Yiddish as both a language in its own right and as a precious source for linguistic research (Adalberg 1890, 2). This advocation of Yiddish in *Izraelita* had a ripple effect: the ethnographic periodicals *Wisła* and *Lud* started publishing texts like Regina Liliental's (1877–1924) studies of Jewish customs, beliefs, and songs, which were based on Yiddish sources.

As Yiddish was slowly accepted as an important source for ethnographic research, it was also, although guardedly at first, recognized as the language of culture by *Izraelita*. From 1888 on, the magazine began to feature translations of Yiddish literature. Opening the series was a short story by Dovid Frishman (1865–1922) *Wspomnienie zmarłych* (*Mazkir neshomes*) [*The Memory of the Dead*]. Translations of Frishman's Hebrew works had already appeared in *Izraelita* in 1884, which probably facilitated the translation of his Yiddish text.

In the 1890s, especially after Peltyn's death, translations of several other Jewish writers, including Yitskhok-Leybush Peretz, Mordkhe Spektor, and Sholem-Aleichem were published. Initially, however, the information on the language of the original was withheld. One of the prominent translators of that time was the previously mentioned critic and Jewish folklore collector Henryk Lew. His translation of Sholem-Aleichem's novel *Stempenyu* (1888), appeared in *Izraelita* from July until December 1898 under the title *Muzykant: romans z życia żydowskiego* [*The Klezmer: A Jewish Romance*]. In 1900, the novel appeared in print at the Hieronim Cohn Publishing House, as the first Yiddish-to-Polish book translation since Junosza's *Donkiszot*. In a review featured in *Izraelita*, the journalist Alfred Lor expressed his hope that *Stempenyu* would mark the "beginning of a translation series" and recommended the publication of an anthology of Yiddish prose that would "provide a brief and general overview of writings that were hitherto unknown to Polish readers." (Lor 1900, 187)

The fact that German and Russian Jews began to take an interest in Yiddish literature at roughly the same time facilitated its acceptance among Polish-speaking Jews too. Another important factor was the ambition, shared by many assimilated Jewish intellectuals, to create a Jewish literature in Polish. As Eugenia Prokop-Janiec notes, such literature was virtually non-existent, a fact that Adolf Jakub Cohn lamented on the pages of *Izraelita* in 1901 (Prokop-Janiec 1992, 17). For the readers of the magazine, which already published numerous translations of Jewish authors writing in German, French, or Russian, translations from Yiddish could fill this gap, providing an insider's perspective on Jewish life in Poland.

Apart from Congress Poland, translations from Yiddish literature into Polish also appeared in Galicia, for example in a Lvov-based Jewish assimilatory magazine *Ojczyzna*. The Agudas Achim Association issued the monthly 1881 to 1892. Although *Ojczyzna* resembled *Izraelita* in that it programmatically opposed Yiddish, it was more open for discussions on its usefulness (Feldstein 1891) and published translations of Yiddish works. They were carried out by Ignacy Suesser (1869–1903), a journalist, critic, and translator of Scandinavian languages. Two consecutive issues from 1891 featured several of his renderings, preceded by an introduction in which the translator framed them as part of a larger whole.[10] In the nineteenth century, when translations from Yiddish mostly concerned prose, Suesser was the first to take interest in Yiddish folk poetry. He believed it expressed the authentic folk inspiration, primitive, but "profoundly original" and "brimming with vital powers." (Suesser 1891, 52) Suesser laid emphasis on the original qualities of these works by resorting to Junosza's metaphor of the "Great Wall of China": "[Yiddish folklore] lives among the Jewish people, protected against daily external influence with the great wall of Jewish difference and preserved in all of its original qualities." (Suesser 1891, 52) While Junosza described the "Great Wall of China" as a frontier separating the Christian world and the Jews, who could watch their neighbors undisclosed, Suesser conceived of it as a two-way barrier. To his mind, however, the wall did not divide the Jewish and the Christian community, but the realm of civilization from the so-called "primitive" world. The latter of which he understood as "a treasure buried away from the sight of the civilized world and waiting for an explorer." (Suesser 1891, 52)

Like Junosza, Suesser highlighted the practical aspect the translations from Yiddish had for researchers of the "Jewish question," and expressed hopes that his initiative would find followers. Among his sources, he named "popular booklets, anonymous anthologies" and itinerant singers. Surprisingly, however, his translations also included a section of *Monish*, an epic poem by Yitskhok-Leybush Peretz (whose name he failed to mention). Peretz' work was originally published in the almanac *Yidishe Folksbibliotek*, edited by Sholem-Aleichem in Kiev (1888). *Monish*, which, in 1891, might have been unknown to Yiddish-speaking Jewish readers outside of Congress Poland,[11] is now considered a foundational text of modern Yiddish poetry. The excerpt featured in *Ojczyzna*, titled *Mój język* [*My Language*], is hard to classify as a piece of folk poetry, though. Peretz, who already made some literary endeavors in Polish and was well-read in European literature, ponders here on the issues of poetic expression in Yiddish, juxtaposing it with other languages that, he believes, are more supple in expressing romantic feelings. The translator might have believed that a text presented as "folk literature" would appeal more to the editors of the magazine. However, it is also possible that, like many of his contemporaries, he considered any text in Yiddish a product of folk literature.

---

10 I have managed to find only one of these translations (Issue 7). The subsequent issue was to feature a continuation titled *Szkice z literatury żargonowej II: pieśni ludowe* [*Essays on Jargon Literature Part Two: Folk Songs*].
11 Although another issue of *Ojczyzna* from the same year featured a review of Peretz' Warsaw-published almanac (Anonymous 1891, 157, 164), the article was likely penned by Wilhelm Feldman.

Wilhelm Feldman, likewise affiliated with *Ojczyzna*, represented a more nuanced approach to Yiddish literature. This eminent literary critic, historian of ideas and the author of the first critical monograph on Young Poland, was born to a poor Hasidic family in Galicia. The year when Suesser's translations were published also saw *Ojczyzna* publish Feldman's pamphlet "On Jewish Jargon." (1891)[12] Fully committed to the Polish national cause and devoted to assimilatory ideas, the author was only twenty-three years old at the time, but he had already published his literary debut, the novel *Żydziak* [*Jew*] (1889) (Mendelsohn 1969). In his pamphlet, Feldman refutes Yiddish as a source of Jewish nationalism and as a tool of Germanization of the Jews in Galicia (Feldman 1891, 16). Feldman's work, however, is full of contradictions, which reflect the tensions between his many personas: that of a researcher, a cultural figure, a politician, a Jew, and a Polish patriot. In some places, he expresses the opinion that Yiddish is a barbaric jargon devoid of grammatical rules and unable to develop; in others, he is concerned that Jewish intelligentsia may enrich and improve it. He envisions that the language of Ashkenazi Jews would disappear on its own, but at the same time suggests drastic measures to prevent its expansion. He begins by calling it a hideous jargon, while a moment later he bemoans that German loan words stifle the authentic Yiddish expression. Finally, he provides an overview of Yiddish literature, press, and theatre plays in the Russian Empire, citing amply from the *Yidishe Folksbibliotek* almanac. Although he considers the bulk of Yiddish literary production to be of mediocre quality and denies Yiddish literature the right to exist, he also concedes that some works are on a par with European literature (Feldman 1891, 25). He also lists particularly talented Yiddish writers, including Peretz, Abramowitsh and Linetski, whom he even compares to Dickens (27).

Feldman seems to be well read in Yiddish literature, and his quotations from Yiddish also include translations from world literature and academic papers for the general public. His bibliography, likewise, features many Yiddish-language works. All this suggests a vibrant Yiddish publishing activity. Yet in his concluding remarks, Feldman acknowledges Yiddish merely as a fascinating object of academic scrutiny for linguists, historians, ethnographers, sociologists, or those who wish to learn more about Jewish life (49–50). Despite his bias, though, Feldman's pioneering overview of Yiddish literature is a relatively relia-

---

[12] It was hardly the first contribution from Feldman on Yiddish matters. In 1886, *Ojczyzna* featured his critical review of *Donkiszot*'s translation, in which he accused Junosza of an arbitrary approach to the original and conflated the author's voice with his own (Feldman 1886, 6).

ble source of information and remained for years to come the only Polish-language study of this kind.

3 Trenches along the Wall

Eighteen years after *Donkiszot żydowski* appeared, another Yiddish-to-Polish translator, Jerzy Ohr, followed in the footsteps of Junosza, editing an anthology of Jewish prose titled *Miliony!* [*Millions!*]. Ohr, who contributed all the translations, was a controversial figure whose complicated biography reflects the predicament of the society divided by the "Great Wall of China." Born in 1871 to a Jewish family, he spoke fluent Polish and Yiddish and made his first literary endeavors in both languages. He published in *Yidishe Bibliotek*, a Warsaw-based literary almanac run by Yitskhok-Leybush Peretz, and *Izraelita*, where he was a columnist. In the 1890s, the magazine also featured his short stories and translations from Yiddish. He seemed like a perfect intermediary between the two sides of the wall. However, after an argument with *Izrealita*'s Editor-in-Chief Nakhum Sokolov, he began contributing to the *Niwa Polska* magazine, where, as an "expert on Jewish matters," he published anti-Semitic texts. He subsequently converted to Catholicism and changed his name from Ohrenstein to Ohr, and later to Oreński (Lew 1898, 517–18; anonymous 1926; Rejzen 1928, 171–72). In interwar Poland, he served as Officer on Jewish Matters at the Ministry of Home Affairs and continued his collaboration with the anti-Semitic press. Shortly after the release of *Miliony!* in 1905, he published a pseudo-scientific pamphlet on Polish loan words in Yiddish, *Polszczyzna w żargonie żydowskim* [*Polish Words in Jewish Jargon*]. The text listed approximately two thousand such borrowings, quoted, however, not in their authentic Yiddish usage but in the "pure" form. Based on this research, Ohr developed a theory that Jews used two jargons: a German-(Yiddish) and a Polish-based one, the latter being the subject of his research. Ohr's biography reflects the predicament of many Jews who, attracted by assimilatory ideas, found no other way of leaving their native environment than actively combatting it. Straddling the two worlds, they were truly accepted by neither.

The anthology of Yiddish and Hebrew prose *Miliony!* was published at the time when Ohr was already considered an "expert on Jewish matters." The book was circulated 1903 as part of a popular publishing series devoted to Polish and world classics and distributed in affordable editions with a weekly circulation of approximately twenty thousand copies. It featured contributions from major figures of Jewish literature, including Sholem-Aleichem's *Miliony!: powieść giełdowa w liścikach* [*Millions!: A Stock-Exchange Novel in Letters*] and

Matuzalem [*Matusalem*], as well as Peretz' *Dusza* [*Soul*]. It also included Izaak Wiernikowski's short story *Subiekt łódzki* [*A Shop Assistant from Łódź*], translated from Hebrew. The title of the anthology referenced a chapter from Sholem-Aleichem's epistolary novel *The Adventures of Menakhem-Mendl* about a broker at the Kiev stock exchange. Peretz's story had been previously published by Ohr in *Izraelita* in 1895, where the author added a brief section at the end that is nowhere to be found in the Yiddish original. In his introduction, Ohr quotes Junosza on the "Great Wall of China" dividing the two nations. He was selective, however, in referring to his predecessor. Ohr left out all of Junosza's conciliatory remarks in the Positivist spirit and concentrated instead on the passages that stress the necessity to know one's enemy. Additionally, Ohr tended to be inaccurate in his quotations. Where Junosza says: "Knowing, knowing thoroughly thy enemy, his strengths and his strategies (though, admittedly, I am far from calling the Jews an enemy) is half the battle," (Abramowicz 1899, 227) Ohr provides the following rendition: "Knowing, knowing thoroughly thy 'opponent' (so to speak) is half the battle." (Ohr, 1903, 6) This small change, which takes Junosza's reasoning a step further, well reflects the ambiguous nature of Ohr's translation. On one level, his anthology is a call for understanding between the two nations; on closer scrutiny, however, it is more of a gesture towards those who would consider Jews their enemies.

Ohr's attitude toward Yiddish literature is ambivalent. He builds on Junosza's enterprise, bringing two great literary classics to the Polish readers, but his motivations have more to do with practical gains from field reconnaissance than the literary qualities of the works. Ohr's foreword also exposes his ambiguous position as a translator. Although he has already left his native Jewish setting, he is not yet at home in the Christian environment, which still considers him a stranger. Instead of speaking with his own voice, therefore, he hides behind the words of the celebrated author Junosza. Framing his project as a continuation of these earlier efforts, he adds prestige to his translation project and clearly opts for one side of the wall.

While Ohr only alludes to this ambivalence, the anonymous author of the introduction to Sholem Asch's *Miasteczko* [*A shtetl*] (1904) was explicit in his language. Chone Shmeruk identified him as the Polish writer Zdzisław Dębicki (Shmeruk 2000, 102), the literary editor of the *Biblioteka Dzieł Wyborowych* series, which published the translation of Asch's novel in 1910.[13] A celebrated au-

---

13 *Miasteczko* was published undated: the National Library of Poland's catalogue indicated 1910 as the year of its publication, whereas Monika Adamczyk-Garbowska suggests that it was at the turn of 1910 and 1911 (Asz 2003, 227).

thor in Polish and foreign Yiddish literary circles, Asch had enjoyed great popularity among German and Russian readers for a few years already at the time, and was also endorsed by the Polish intelligentsia, including eminent writers such as Stanisław Witkiewicz and Stefan Żeromski (Jankowski 1959). In the years 1905–1906, some of his plays were staged in Polish theatres. Several of Asch's stories had already been translated into Polish and featured in *Izraelita*. Some of them were later reprinted in his collection *Nowele* [*Short Stories*], issued in 1906 by the Księgarnia Powszechna publishing house with a dedication to Stanisław Witkiewicz. The book edition fails, however, to provide the identity of the translators, whereas the stories featured in *Izraelita* name Zygmunt Majerczyk and Moshe Shpira. Asch's wife, Matylda, was also said to have contributed to the translation (Prokop-Janiec 1992, 1254).

The introduction to *Miasteczko*, again, makes a reference to the metaphor of the "Great Wall of China." Whereas for Junosza, the wall separated Jews and Christians, in this iteration the dividing line runs between Jews and Poles. What is more, the translator of *Miasteczko* blames the cleavage between the two communities on Yiddish. He presents the language of Ashkenazi Jews not so much in terms of a clumsy jargon, bound to vanish when exposed to the salubrious effect of education, but as a premeditated barrier or a strategic ruse, intended to keep the Polish neighbors in the dark:

> Jargon literature is a fact. It has emerged and been developing, gaining ever wider readership among the Jewish masses. Humble in its beginnings, it is now gaining artistic import, ranging from translations and adaptations to original creations. Yet, born in Poland, it separates itself from the Polish society with an impenetrable wall of the foreign tongue, which we cannot speak and will never be able to. (Asz 1910, 1:5)

Asch's translator may have been motivated by a desire to know the Other. But the Other is now no longer an object of impartial ethnographic research, or a "savage" that needs to be civilized to become a rightful member of the body politic. Instead, the Other morphs into a political and ideological opponent and military rhetoric is deployed to frame the encounter in terms of *Kulturkampf*:

> Little do we know not only about what happens abroad, but also in our own backyard and our own society, where Jews form a significant group and are increasingly opposing our national goals and vital interests.
>
> We have recently taken up their gauntlet and entered the era of culture struggle, whose ultimate outcomes are still unpredictable. These days, a thorough reconnaissance of the enemy's forces is not only a need, but a duty.
>
> This is why we are now publishing this work of Jewish jargon in Polish translation. (Asz 1910, 1:6)

The introduction to Asch's *Miasteczko* is striking because of its radical formulations on the hermetic nature and the inaccessibility of Yiddish. It is hard to imagine similar statements on any other language. After all, why should it be reprehensible that the literature of a foreign language can be accessed only through translation? No Polish critic would ever bemoan the fact that Hungarian is a language "we cannot speak and will never be able to"; neither would he or she complain about the inaccessibility of Hungarian literature.

The use of first person plural in the sentence suggests that the author is constructing a sense of collective identity that excludes the Other. The very existence of a foreign literature on the national territory is presented as a source of frustration, and even anxiety. This attitude is reflected in the next part of the preface, where the author repeats that "no one reads works written in jargon," (Asz 1910, 1:6) from which it is clear that he is not interested in the literature itself (even if he credits it with a certain maturity), but rather he is interested in the texts merely insofar as they serve as a reflection of the political beliefs of the community from which they derive.

There is a question that is left unanswered both on the title page of *Miasteczko* and in the foreword: If *we* "cannot and will never be able to speak" Yiddish, who has translated the book?[14] The author of the introduction also never mentions other translations created by assimilated Jews, or the fact that the bilingual Polish-Jewish community could deliver many more such translators. All the facts that do not fit the dichotomy "us–them" sustained here are simply omitted.

Another paradox of this translation is that, of all Yiddish writers, it was Sholem Asch, generally known as a strong advocate of Jewish-Christian rapprochement, that the militant editors chose for the purpose of presenting evidence of the hostile scheming of the enemy camp. His idealized image of a shtetl where Jews and non-Jews live in peaceful cohabitation, using different prayers to address the same God, is actually the best reflection of Asch's conciliatory tendencies. The translator of *Miasteczko*, however, seems to be unaware of the disparity between Asch's message and his own text. What he chooses to emphasize is, instead, the fact that Asch is an influential figure, enjoying a global renown both in Jewish and non-Jewish circles. The translator also notes with appreciation that Asch is a Polish Jew through and through:

---

14 Monika Adamczyk-Garbowska, who edited the second edition of *Miasteczko*, published in 2003 by the Towarzystwo Przyjaciół Janowca nad Wisłą, after a thorough comparison of the translation with the original suggests that the former was based on the German translation of 1909 (Asz 2003, 227–31). Eugenia Prokop-Janiec in turn indicates it was Moshe Shapiro (Shpira) who translated several other works of Asch from the original (Prokop-Janiec 1992, 1254).

Asch is a Jew born and raised in Poland, so he thinks and feels the way a significant part of Polish Jewry does—that is, those not yet infected by the Litvak influence, or led astray by the radicalism of Jewish nationalism or Social Democracy. (Asz 1910, 7)

The gradation of otherness is evident here: a Polish Jew is still more acceptable than a foreign one. The unmistakable rhetoric of the National Democratic camp, however, is as evident here as anti-Semitism that was gaining momentum at the time.

4 Bridges over the wall

At the same time, large scale Yiddish-to-Polish translation projects were underway in Zionist, or, more broadly, Jewish national circles. Several such translations were featured in the anthology *Safrus: książka zbiorowa poświęcona sprawom żydostwa* [*Safrus: A Collected Volume Devoted to Jewish Matters*], published in 1905. Over three hundred pages in length, this carefully edited volume, richly illustrated by the Lvov-based painter Wilhelm Wachtel (1875–1942), was meant to present the Jewish national ideas and contemporary Jewish culture to a wide audience. The collection contains literary works, both poetry and prose, as well as articles on Zionism, history, literature, art, and Jewish folklore. The volume was edited by Jan Kirszrot (1879–1912), one of the founders of the Zionist movement in Congress Poland and an advocate of Jewish arts and crafts. A circle of academic youth *Safrus* (Hebrew: literature) that he belonged to, gathered prominent Zionists, such as Izaak Gruenbaum or Apolinary Hartglas, and accepted members of other Jewish organizations, including the Bund.[15]

In the book's introduction, Kirszrot provides an overview of the Jewish assimilation project in Poland, which he considered to be a failure. He believed that the majority of the Jews attracted to assimilatory ideology had reached a dead end, and they remained stranded between the Jewish community they lost touch with and Polish society, which had not accepted them as rightful members. Such Jews were the primary target group of the *Safrus* anthology, which aimed to introduce them to the Jewish cultural legacy through translated writings.

A sizeable portion of the collection consists of translations from Hebrew (Bialik, Tchernichovsky, Feuerberg) and Yiddish (Avrom Reyzen, Yitskhok-Leybush Peretz, Sholem Asch, Hersh-Dovid Nomberg). It also includes an essay

---

[15] Yitskhok-Leybush Peretz was also affiliated with *Safrus* (see: Schiper, Tartakower, and Hafftka 1932, 1:528).

on Yiddish literature by the influential critic Isidor Elyashev (better known under his nom de plume Bal-Makhshoves). While Yiddish took on a somewhat ambivalent standing in the assimilatory *Izraelita*, *Safrus* was the first publication of this kind to regard all three languages—Polish, Yiddish, and Hebrew—in equal measure as vehicles of Jewish culture. Translations from Yiddish, therefore, play here an instrumental role in the process of dissimilation, a term coined by Milton Yinger to define a backlash to acculturation and the return to the culture of origin (Yinger 1981). Shulamit Volkov applied the term to describe the identification processes of German Jews in the post-assimilation period (Volkov 1992). The "return to grassroots" was initiated several years earlier by an entire generation of Jewish intellectuals in Germany and Austria, under the spiritual leadership of Martin Buber, the founder of cultural Zionism (his paper on Jewish art was also featured in *Safrus*).[16]

While the majority of authors in *Safrus* were represented with one text only, the editor made an exception to Moris Rozenfeld (1862–1923), a Polish-born Jewish poet who emigrated to the United States as a young man and whose works enjoyed great popularity among Jewish readers in the United States and elsewhere. His three poems featured in the volume depicted the hardships of the Jewish people expelled from Zion and the poverty of immigrant workers in America. They were translated into English in 1898 by Leo Wiener, one of the pioneers of Yiddish scholarship in the United States, and later into German by the Jewish intellectual Berthold Feiwel, who was affiliated with Buber. The German edition of his poetry, *The Songs of the Ghetto*, with beautiful illustrations by Ephraim-Moshe Lilien, was reprinted several times, reaching the circulation of many thousands of copies. Rozenfeld also gained popularity among Polish speakers. Apart from the *Safrus* anthology, in the years from 1903 to 1908, three other volumes of Rozenfeld's poetry were published in Polish translation. They attracted great interest not only by virtue of their content, but also because of particular melodious qualities of his poems, many of which became adapted into popular songs. Rozenfeld was in fact the first Yiddish poet in Polish translation to be published in a book format.[17]

Apart from *Izraelita*, which continued to publish translations of Yiddish authors until its last issue in 1912, the Zionist weekly *Głos Żydowski*, founded in

---

[16] As pointed out many years earlier by Samuel Hirszhorn, the Polish critic and writer Andrzej Niemojewski (who was not yet affiliated with the anti-Semitic far right at the time) reviewed the anthology with much interest and hailed it as a new phenomenon in Polish literature (Hirszhorn 1930, 3).

[17] His translators, Israel Waldman (1881–1940), Samuel Hirszhorn (1876–1942) and Alfred Tom (1879–1944) were all adherents of the Zionist movement.

Warsaw in 1906 and soon renamed into *Życie Żydowskie* (1906–1907 and 1916–1919), also joined the effort. Just like the *Safrus* anthology, the magazine conceived of Yiddish literature as an element of Jewish national heritage that should be made available also to those Jews who do not speak the language. The team of translators including Ewelina Lindowska, Jakub Lewkowicz, and Zygmunt Majerczyk (affiliated with *Izraelita*) rendered the texts by Sholem-Aleichem, Dovid Frishman, Yitskhok-Leybush Peretz, and others.

The Yiddish-to-Polish translation project evolved since its inception in two directions. On the one hand, non-Jewish editors, inspired by Junosza, harnessed translation into the service of nationalist rhetoric, as a tool of "discovering the Other" in the new political atmosphere that discouraged intercultural rapprochement. On the other hand, Polonized Jews who shunned Yiddish for a long time started to embrace Yiddish translations in Polish as a means of affirming their Jewish identity. This tendency continued in the interwar years and led to a boom of translations from Yiddish. A number of Polish-language Jewish dailies such as the Warsaw-based *Nasz Przegląd*, Lvov-based *Chwila*, or Kraków-based *Nasz Dziennik*, as well as many magazines (for example, *Opinia, Ster, Miesięcznik Żydowski, Nowe Życie*, or *Ewa*) began to feature regular translations from Yiddish (and occasionally Hebrew) literature. They also provided regular information on current events in Yiddish culture, published reviews of Yiddish books and theater plays, and featured interviews with Yiddish writers. Translations by Saul Wagman, Jakub and Paulina Appenszlak, Samuel Hirszhorn, Rachela Auerbach, and Maurycy Szymel, to name but a few, were published in installments and later often reprinted as books. About forty translations from Yiddish were published at the time, mostly prose, including classics and contemporary authors, as well as volumes of poetry, plays, and youth literature. Some of them were issued by Yiddish publishing houses, such as Brzoza, Gitlin, and Levin-Epshtayn, as well as in specialized publishing series devoted to translations.[18] One may venture to say that, in this time, a sufficient number of bridges were thrown over the divide separating the Yiddish-speaking Jewish community from the Polonized Jews, for those willing to navigate between the two worlds.

Although Jewish readers were a primary target group for the translations of Yiddish literature, Polish readers also constituted an important audience. Many

---

18 One such series, *Biblioteka Pisarzy Żydowskich* was established by Safrus Publishing House (1924–1929), affiliated with *Nowy Przegląd* and specializing in novels, whose name was inspired by the 1905 anthology. The other was a series specialized in affordable paperback editions for adults and youth, *Biblioteczka Pisarzy i Klasyków Żydowskich* [Jewish Writers and Classics' Library] (1925–1926) by the Orient Publishing House, which also issued translations from Polish into Yiddish.

translators, hoping to combat anti-Semitic stereotypes in the Polish society, directly addressed non-Jewish readers by encouraging them to engage with the wealth of Jewish literature. Hopes for cultural understanding through literature failed, however, and the Polish-language Jewish press often bemoaned the lack of interest for Yiddish literature in translation among the Polish readers. Reviewers only rarely noticed such translations, and knowledge of Yiddish literature among Polish writers and critics was very limited.[19] The only Yiddish authors who found greater resonance were those published in the 1930s by the Polish publishing house Rój, but they were already writers of international renown, such as Sholem Asch or Israel Joshua Singer (I.B. Singer's elder brother). These translations were even reviewed by the leading Polish literary magazine *Wiadomości Literackie*, which usually showed little interest in Yiddish literature. Still, such works were often translated via German without the original language of the publication being even mentioned.

To be sure, with time, Yiddish literature received some recognition among Polish readers. It also started featuring in Polish literary encyclopedias, such as *Wielka Literatura Powszechna* [*Great World Literature*]. Some prominent Polish literati, like Leopold Staff, Stanisław Przybyszewski, or Stanisław Ignacy Witkiewicz spoke of it with appreciation (Jankowski 1959; Staff 1926; Arnsztejn 1927; Przybyszewski 1925). Yet, despite all that, the "Great Wall of China" envisioned by Junosza was far from crumbling.

translated from Polish by Bartosz Sowiński

Bibliography

Anonymous. 1885. "Don Kiszot żydowski, p. Klemens Junosza, Izraelita oraz nasze uwagi." *Przegląd Tygodniowy* 34: 441–442.

Anonymous. 1886. "Wrażenia literackie: K. Junosza, Donkiszot żydowski..." *Ateneum* 1, no. 41: 358–359.

Anonymous. 1891. "Z dziedziny żargonu: J.L. Perec: Di jidisze bibljotek." *Ojczyzna* 20: 157, 164.

Anonymous. 1926. "[notka o Jerzym Ohrze]." *Nasz Przegląd* 249: 15.

A. 1898. "Odgłosy, Bibljoteczki ludowe." *Izraelita* 44: 428.

Abramowicz, Sz.-J., and K. Junosza-Szaniawski. 1885a. "Donkiszot żydowski: szkic z literatury żargonowej żydowskiej." *Wiek*: 139–173.

---

[19] This is demonstrated by a survey titled "Luminarze literatury i nauki polskiej o kwestii żydowskiej," [Eminent Polish Scholarly and Literary Figures on the Jewish Question] published in first annual issues of *Nasz Przegląd* in 1924 and 1925.

Abramowicz, Sz.-J., and K. Junosza-Szaniawski. 1885b. *Donkiszot żydowski: szkic z literatury żargonowej żydowskiej*, Warszawa: T[eodor] Paprocki i Sp. druk. Wieku.
Abramowicz, Sz.-J. 1886a. "Szkapa (Die Kliatsche)." *Wędrowiec:* 13–32.
Abramowicz, Sz.-J. 1886b. *Szkapa (Die Kliatsche).* Warszawa: Księgarnia A. Gruszeckiego.
Adalberg, S. 1890. *Przysłowia żydowskie.* Warszawa: J. Jeżyński.
Adamczyk-Garbowska, M. 2004. *Odcienie tożsamości: Literatura żydowska jako zjawisko wielojęzyczne.* Lublin: UMCS.
Arnsztejn, M. 1927. "Der apostol fun libe." *Literarishe bleter* 48: 932–933.
Asz, Sz. 1910. *Miasteczko*, vol. 1–2. Warszawa: Biblioteka Dzieł Wyborowych.
Asz, Sz. 2003. *Miasteczko.* With afterword by M. Adamczyk-Garbowska. Janowiec: Towarzystwo Przyjaciół Janowca nad Wisłą.
Asz, Sz. 1906. *Nowele.* Warszawa: Księgarnia Powszechna.
Bechtel, D. 2002. *La Renaissance Culturelle Juive en Europe Centrale et Orientale 1897–1930: Langue, Littérature et Construction Nationale.* Paris: Belin.
Biegeleisen, H. 1886. "Przeglądy literackie, K. Junosza, Don Kiszot Żydowski, szkic z literatury żargonowej żydowskiej." *Przegląd Tygodniowy* 2: 24.
Blumberg, M. 1899. "Klemens Junosza jako żydoznawca." *Izraelita* 21: 228.
Borkowska, G., and M. Rudkowska, eds. 2004. *Kwestia żydowska w XIX wieku: Spory o tożsamość Polaków.* Warszawa: Cyklady.
Brzezina, M. 1986. *Polszczyzna Żydów.* Warszawa: PWN.
Datner, H. 2007. *Ta i tamta strona: Żydowska inteligencja Warszawy drugiej połowy XIX wieku.* Warszawa: Żydowski Instytut Historyczny.
Feldman, W. 1893. *Asymilatorzy, syonisci i Polacy: Z powodu przełomu w stosunkach żydowskich w Galicyi.* Kraków: Księgarnia St. Baranskiego.
Feldman, W. 1891. *O żargonie żydowskim, studium publicystyczne.* Lwów: Redakcja Ojczyzny.
Feldman, W. 1886. "Przegląd literacki: Donkiszot żydowski, szkic z literatury żargonowej żydowskiej, przez Klemensa Junoszę, W-wa 1885." *Ojczyzna* 2: 6.
Feldstein, H. 1891. "Żargon żydowski jako cel i jako środek." *Ojczyzna* 4: 26–28, 16: 123–125.
Friszman, D. 1888. "Wspomnienie zmarłych." *Izraelita:* 36–38.
Hirszhorn, S. 1930. "Źródło i rozmiary bojkotu literackiego." *Nasz Przegląd* 12: 3.
Jankowski, E. 1959. "O 'polskim' epizodzie Szaloma Asza." *Przegląd Humanistyczny* 3: 165–170.
Jeske-Choiński, T. 1886. "Przegląd literacki, K. Junosza, Donkiszot żydowski..." *Niwa* 267: 216.
Junosza-Szaniawski, K. 1889. *Nasi Żydzi w miasteczkach i na wsiach.* Warszawa: Niwa.
Kaszewski, K. 1886. "Drobna beletrystyka, K. Junosza, Don kiszot żydowski..." *Kłosy* 1081: 173.
Kirszrot, J., ed. 1905. *Safrus: Książka zbiorowa poświęcona sprawom żydostwa.* Warszawa: Safrus.
Kon, P. 1928. "Vi azoy hot Junosza ibergezetst Mendelen in poylish?" *Bikher-velt* 7: 36–38.
Konopnicka, M. 1885. "Nowe książki: K. Junosza, Donkiszot żydowski." *Świt* 21 (87): 167.
Krynicka, N. 2009. "Les rapports culturels entre Juifs et Polonais à la lumière des traductions littéraires, 1885–1939." PhD diss., Paris 4.
Lew, H. 1898. "O godność prasy." *Izraelia* 49: 517–518.
Lew, H. 1897. "W kwestji ludoznastwa żydowskiego." *Izraelita* 1: 2.

Linecki, J. J. 1888. "Chasyd (Dus polische Jüngel), szkic z literatury żargonowej żydowskiej przez Maksyma Lewarta." *Gazeta Lubelska*: 1–121.

Litvine, M. 1991. *Translations into and from Yiddish*. Oxford: Oxford Centre for Postgraduate Hebrew Studies.

Lor, A. 1900. "Szalum-Alechem: Muzykant..." *Izraelita* 16: 186–187.

Mendelsohn, E. 1969. "Jewish Assimilation in Lvov: The Case of Wilhelm Feldman." *The Slavic Review* 28: 577–590.

Ochwat, A. 2004. "'Świat nowy, zupełnie nam nieznany': Rola żydowskiej literatury żargonowej w twórczości Klemensa Junoszy-Szaniawskiego." In *Kwestia żydowska w XIX wieku: Spory o tożsamość Polaków*, edited by Grażyna Borkowska and Magdalena Rudkowska, 201–219. Warszawa: Cyklady.

Ohr, J., ed. 1903. *Miliony! Przekłady z pisarzy żydowskich*. Warszawa: Biblioteka Dzieł Wyborowych.

Ohr, J. 1905. *Polszczyzna w żargonie żydowskim*. Warszawa: L. Straszewicz.

Orzeszkowa, E. 1882. *O Żydach i kwestii żydowskiej*. Wilno: Wydawnictwo E. Orzeszkowej i s-ki.

Peltyn, S. C. 1885. "Coś o żargonie żydowskim." *Izraelita* 28: 221–222.

Peltyn, S. C. 1896. "Żargon i jego literatura." *Izraelita* 5: 35.

Perec, J.-L. 1895. "Dusza." *Izraelita*: 25–28.

Prokop-Janiec, E. 1992. *Międzywojenna literatura polsko-żydowska jako zjawisko kulturowe i artystyczne*. Kraków: Universitas.

Prokop-Janiec, E. 1992. "Recepcja żydowskiej literatury." In *Słownik literatury polskiej XX wieku*, 1252–1259. Wrocław: Zakład Narodowy im. Ossolińskich.

Prus, B. 1885. "Kronika tygodniowa: Żywy obraz pt. Żydowski Don Kiszot." *Kurier Warszawski* 183: 2.

Przybyszewski, S. 1925. "Pisarze i uczeni polscy o kwestji żydowskiej: Stanisław Przybyszewski." *Nasz Przegląd* 1: 5.

Reyzen, Zalman. 1928. *Leksikon fun der yidisher literatur, prese un filologie*, 1st ed., s.v. "Orensztejn, J. L.", 171–172. Vilne: B. Kletskin.

Rozenfeld, M. 1903. *Wiązanka*. Warszawa: Księgarnia E. Weidenfelda i Brata.

Rozenfeld, M. 1906. *Pieśni pracy*. Warszawa.

Rozenfeld, M. 1908. *Pieśni z ghetta: Pieśni narodu: Pieśni życia*. Warszawa: H. J. Rudno.

S., R-n. 1898. *Odgłosy: "Z dziedziny folkoru żydowskiego."* *Izraelita* 15: 162.

Schiper, I., A. Tartakower, and A. Hafftka, eds. 1932. *Żydzi w Polsce odrodzonej: Działalność społeczna, gospodarcza, kulturalna*, Vol. 1. Warszawa: Żydzi w Polsce Odrodzonej.

Shmeruk, Ch. 1989. "Hebrew-Yiddish-Polish: A Trilingual Jewish Culture." In *The Jews of Poland Between Two World Wars*, edited by Y. Gutman, E. Mendelsohn, and J. Reinharz, 285–311. Hanover: University Press of New England.

Shmeruk, Ch. 2000. *Legenda o Esterce w literaturze jidysz i polskiej: Studium z dziedziny wzajemnych stosunków dwóch kultur i tradycji*, trans. M. Adamczyk-Garbowska. Warszawa: Oficyna Naukowa.

Sofer, B. 1899. "Żargon." *Izraelita* 10: 97–98.

Sokołów, N. 1898. "Drogi oddziaływania." *Izraelita* 48: 463–464.

Staff, L. 1926. "Leopold Staff o sprawie żydowskiej, wywiad z prezesem Związku Literatów i Dziennikarzy Polskich." *Nasz Przegląd* 76: 4.

Steffen, K. 2004. *Jüdische Polonität: Ethnizität und Nation im Spiegel der polnischsprachigen jüdischen Presse, 1918–1939*. Göttingen: Vandenhoeck & Ruprecht.
Szolem-Alejchem. 1898. *Muzykant: romans z życia żydowskiego*. Warszawa: Hieronim Cohn.
Suesser, I. 1891. "Z żydowskiej poezji żargonowej." *Ojczyzna* 7: 52–53.
Volkov, Sh. 1992. *Die Erfindung einer Tradition: Zur Entstehung des modernen Judentums in Deutschland*. Vol. 29, *Schriften des historischen Kollegs*. München: Stiftung Historisches Kolleg.
Viltshinski, Y. 1928a. " Yidish-poylishe iberzetsungen." *Bikher-velt* 4: 8–16, 6: 24–34.
Viltshinski, Y. 1928b. *Yidishe tipn in der poylisher literatur*. Varshe: Kultur-Lige.
Yinger, M. J. 1981. "Toward a Theory of Assimilation and Dissimilation." *Ethnic and Racial Studies* 3: 249–264.
Zieliński, W.K. 1886. "Przeglądy literackie, S. Abramowicz, Szkapa (Die klatsche)." *Przegląd Tygodniowy* 50: 5.

Marek Tuszewicki
Non-Jewish Languages of Jewish Magic: On Homeliness, Otherness, and Translation

Although both Judaism and Christianity imposed a number of limitations on magical practices because of the belief that witchcraft was an insult to God, folklorists made continuous efforts to negotiate exceptions from religious rule. Healing practices based on magical incantations such as healing spells, enchantments, and verbal acts of averting the "evil eye" became popular among Christian and Jewish communities in the Polish-Lithuanian Commonwealth. It is far from true to say that magic shaped folk healing practices, which were incredibly syncretic in nature. Natural means (for example herbal medicine) or methods used by other systems of medicine (like blood letting) played an important role in folk medicine, too. It is certain, however, that at least until the beginning of the twentieth century, folk medicine grew in importance in areas where it was difficult to find formally trained medical practitioners.

Among Central and Eastern European Jewry, the magical healing practices that emerged out of written religious and kabbalistic traditions took on new form because of illiteracy. Both the Ashkenazi community and the local people (Polish and Ruthenian peasants, etc.) developed their own elaborate cultural systems, which remained impermeable to outside influences in some areas, but fluid and malleable in others. In folk culture, otherness constituted an ambiguous category. From the traditional ethnocentric perspective, difference was derided and ridiculed as negative. That said, Ludwik Stomma points out that "unintelligible and mysterious speech would also become ... magical speech." (2000, 21)[1] In principle, each member of the outgroup, even a neighbor, could be ascribed the status of a witch doctor. This was even more likely if they used a different language, a strange alphabet, or objects associated with witchcraft, such as books (Libera 2003, 98–105; 1995, 253). This preconception can be found also in the beliefs of Polish Jewry. In many regions, on seeing a Catholic or Orthodox priest, Jews would resort to a number of practices traditionally applied against evil charms or witches, using the *figa* gesture (Yid. *fayg*),[2] casting a pin, or saying a magical incantation, etc. (Fayvushinski 1958, 200; Lilientalowa 1898,

---

[1] Unless indicated otherwise, citations from Polish authors have been rendered into English by the translator.
[2] Translator's note: A gesture of showing a thumb thrust between the curled index finger and the middle one.

279; 1900, 640).³ Folk tales from eastern Galicia feature a landowner turned wizard who morphed into a black cat to abduct little babies from Jewish homes after dark (Benczer 1893, 120–21). It was also a widespread belief that pregnant Jewish women, who were particularly vulnerable to magic, should not pay any visits to Christian homes (An-ski 1914, 22).

Apart from the capacity to inflict harm, the Other was also believed to possess healing powers. Historical sources provide evidence that Jewish communities transformed objects formerly used in Christian worship into magical accessories, for example amulets that protected against fever with the name of Jesus or pendants featuring depictions of the Blessed Virgin Mary (Weissenberg 1897, 367–69; 1907, 357; Grunwald 1900, 75). The Mława Yizkor Book, for example, features an account about an old Jewish woman who fainted on her way to the morning prayer, or *selichot*.⁴ When a large crucifix was found on her neck, she responded that "since so many people believe in this, it might be a god of some sort." (Yunis 1950, 72) Similarly, many Jews believed that household items took on magical properties when exposed to something ritually unclean. People treating a sore throat by swaddling their necks in a stocking were advised to rub the stocking in with non-kosher soap, since "kosher soap does not warm up as much." (N.N. 1962, 63) It is also significant that Jewish communities adopted an array of terms from Slavic languages to describe informal practitioners of medicine. Words such as *znakher*, *toter*, or *ovtshazh* (Polish: *owczarz*, literally "shepherd") primarily denoted non-Jewish folk healers and, only secondarily, practitioners of folk medicine—regardless of their origin. Similarly, *baba*, or a woman practicing folk medicine, was referred to using the same terminology as in Slavic communities (*bobe*, *viedme*, and *koldunye*).

Relative isolation prevented Jews of the Ashkenazi diaspora—who did not know the Latin alphabet (Yid. *galkhes*, or "priestly script")—from absorbing magical practices through written channels. Neither Hebrew nor Yiddish sources mention a transfer of such knowledge via non-Jewish texts. If Jewish readers reached for books or pamphlets in the vernacular, they did so in the hope of obtaining information on natural medicine approved by formally qualified medical experts. However, it can be said with much certainty that Jews adopted the customs and beliefs of their Christian neighbors through oral channels. As a result, Jewish folklore absorbed regionally specific magical practices.

---

3 Slavic peasants resorted to similar practices in the belief that Catholic or Orthodox priests were always followed by evil (see Moszyński 1934, 290).
4 Penitential prayers during the Jewish High Holidays.

Magical healing practices permeated Jewish culture as part of an interaction between Jews and their non-Jewish setting, the intensity of which grew in relative proportion to the distance from urban centers. With only sparse information on the subject, it is impossible to draw a detailed map of their points of contact. The presence of Christian servants at Jewish homes and the activities of itinerant merchants fostered the exchange of these beliefs between the two communities (Weinreich 2008, 537). The Jewish historian Nakhmen Blumental mentions that the local washerwoman Pavlyukha was a regular guest at his family home in Borszczów (today's Borshchiv, in western Ukraine). Not only did she provide medical care by setting dislocated fingers, for instance, or making the sign of the cross on the affected cheek as a spell to cure mumps, but she also shared her knowledge on mystical ways to fight physical ailments (Blumental 1973, 169–77). Similarly, neighborly relations between the two groups promoted an exchange of such wisdom, which was less common in cities or towns, but almost universal in rural areas (Goldberg-Mulkiewicz 2003, 92; Banasiewicz-Ossowska 2007, 109–39).[5] These interactions may have evolved out of centuries-old feudal structures in these areas. Jewish innkeepers, for example, played an important role as intermediaries between healers and their patients. Since "old wives are easy to come by at the bar," (Lew 1896, 306) inns and taverns served as important information hubs and meeting places with witch doctors especially as they provided amenities to aid in the treatment process, such as warm rooms, warm water, meals, hot tea, and herbal infusions.

1 Incantations in *loshn-koydesh* (Hebrew) and *mame-loshn* (Yiddish)

The ethnographers who took part in a research expedition to Volhynia (1912–1914) pointed out that local Jewish female healers would cast spells in Yiddish, Ukrainian, or a formula combining both. Hebrew spells, in contrast, belonged to the domain of men (Rechtman 1958, 300). According to Salomon An-ski, spells intended to avert the "evil eye" (in contrast to healing spells) belonged in the realm of the sacred. Such incantations were reported to resemble prayers, and

---

5 See also Słomka 1983, 95: "Rural Jews and Christian peasants lived in particular harmony, Jewish children growing up among their peasant peers, which often ended up in baptism. It was usually young Jewish women who accepted christening to marry farmhands or farmers' sons."

the ritual itself was more akin to that of religious devotion (An-ski 1925, 164).⁶ An overview of ethnographic sources reveals the basis for An-ski's conclusions. In fact, an exceedingly large number of Hebrew spells believed to avert the "evil eye" was derived from biblical passages and kabbalistic motifs. Evil charms were dispelled not only by folk healers from the uneducated strata of Jewish society, but also by *soferim*—who made a living by writing and correcting sacred scriptures—and by Hasidic leaders.

Jewish communities were barely familiar with *loshn-koydesh*, especially in rural areas, which led to the split between elite and popular Jewish healing magic. In other words, Jews living outside of urban centers could resort to Jewish magic on their own only in limited ways, as they failed to understand the language. That said, Hebrew and Aramaic content was quite prominent in folk healing practices too. Given the role of script as a medium of magic, the two languages played a fundamental role in linking the rituals to the realm of the sacred. This last fact was noted by ethnographer Regina Lilienthal, who has suggested that evil charms were mainly dispelled by pious and learned men (2007, 52). Since it was not always possible or advisable to contact the learned, practitioners would adopt selected Hebrew content by translating it into the vernacular. One of the most popular incantations of this kind, the treatise on three women, is worth a closer scrutiny. Its central motif, present in all of its existing variants, are three women sitting (standing) "on a large stone" or "on top of a rock." Although it is difficult to trace the origins of the image, which brings to mind the dialogues of Saint Sophie's or Saint Ottilie's daughters (Biegeleisen 1929, 243), the motif appeared in the practical kabbalistic texts and was transferred from there into folk healing practices:

Hebrew variant:

Shalosh nashim yoshvot al shen sela.
Akhat omeret khole ani
Ve-akhat omeret eyni khole
Ve-akhat omeret eyni khole ve-lo yihie khole

Keshem she-eyn le-yam derekh le-dagim eyn lahem bliya,
Kakh lo yihie le-Pb"P mamash shum ayn ha-ra.

Yiddish variant:

Tfuy, tfuy tfuy!

Pb"P hot a ayn-hore tsu felen
Pb"P hot a ayn-hore tsu felen
Pb"P hot a ayn-hore gefelt.

Dray vayber zitsen oyf a shteyn,
Eyne zogt: Pb"P hot a ayn-hore
Di tsveyte zogt: neyn

---

6 Benjamin Wolf Segel, too, pointed out that illiterate people treated written amulets as rituals, since—in contrast to learned Kabbalists—they found it impossible to understand their meaning (Segel 1897, 59).

Ben porat Yosef ben porat glei-ayn banot tsaada alei-shur
Va-yemararuhu va-robu va-yistemuhu baalei khitsim
Va-teshev beytan kashto va-yafozu zeroei yadav m-idei avir Yaakov mi-sham roe even Yisrael (Gen 49:22 – 24).

Az yashir Yisrael et-ha-shira ha-zot ali beer enu-la
Beer hafarua sharim karua nedivei ha-am bi-mekhokek be-mishanotam u-mi-midbar Mata-na
U-mi-Matana Nakhaliel u-mi-Nakhaliel Bamot U-mi-Bamot Hagay asher bi-sade Moav rosh ha-pisga ve-nishkafa al-pnei ha-yeshimon (Num 21:17 – 20).

Keshem she-nitkhazek ve-nitrape melekh Yehu-da Khizkyahu me-khalav
Hitkhazek ve-hitrape Pb"P mi-shum ayn ha-ra

Ba-shem A"G"L"A. (An-ski 1909, 76)

Di drite zogt: fun vanen zi iz gekumen ahin zol zi avekgeyn.

Oyf ale puste felder oyf ale viste velder
Vu keyn mentshn geyen nit, vu keyn fis tretn nit
Vu keyn broyt vakst nit, vu vilde khayes firn zikh.
Dortn zol zi farblaybn un Pb"P optretn un Pb"Ps ru nit shtern.

In a guter mazldiker sho hobn mir dir opgesh-prokhn.

(Genezt) Ha-a!... Ha-a!... Ha-a. (Lilientalowa 2007,55)

English translation of the Hebrew variant:

Three women are sitting on top of a rock:
First woman says "I'm ill"
Second woman says "I'm not"
Third woman says "I'm not and won't [?] be"

As the sea is uncharted and the fish know no disease,
N., the son of N., will be touched by no evil.

Joseph is a fruitful bough, even a fruitful bough by a well, whose branches run over the wall.
The archers have sorely grieved him, and shot at him, and hated him.
But his bow abodes in strength, and the arms of his hands were made strong by the hands of the mighty God of Jacob, from thence is the Shepherd, the Stone of Israel,

English translation of the Yiddish variant:

Hoick! Hoick! Hoick!

N., the son of N., is under a spell, is under a spell, is under a spell.

Three women are sitting on a rock:
First woman says "he's under a spell,"
Second woman says "no, he isn't,"
Third woman says "he'd better go back where he comes from."

In all deserted fields, in all deserted woods,
Where people never go, [where human feet won't tread],
[Where grain never grows], where only wild animals dwell,
The evil must remain and leave N., the son of N., and his peace should not disturb.

Then Israel sang this song: "Spring up, O well!
Sing ye unto it!
The princes dug the well; the nobles of the people dug it by the direction of the lawgiver, with their staves!" And from the wilderness they went to Mattanah,
and from Mattanah to Nahaliel, and from Nahaliel to Bamoth,
and from Bamoth in the valley that is in the country of Moab to the top of Pisgah, which looketh toward Jeshimon.

As Khizkyas, the King of Judah, was fortified and recovered from disease,
You, too, fortify and protect N., the son of N., from evil spells

With the name of A.G.L.A.[7]

We have put a spell on you in the right hour.

Ha-a! ha-a! ha-a! (the person casting a spell yawns)

Even a passing glance at these texts reveals that the Hebrew variant is not only more complex in structure, but also makes more references to Jewish scriptures. Apart from the passage about the three women, it features two extended excerpts from the Torah: on Joseph (Gen 49:22) and the wandering in the desert (Num 21:17–20).[8] It was the former that inspired a belief (expressly stated in the Talmud) that Joseph and his progeny are immune to the "evil eye."[9] The latter, in turn, should be interpreted with the help of the legend of Miriam's well, which followed the people of God and whose waters had magical properties (see Schwartz 2004, 387). The passage on fish, depicted as immune to the evil charm, was directly related to both. The closing lines of the undoing charm also make a reference to biblical history (Exod 20:7); they manifest prayer-like qualities and conclude with the holy name of God. Other Hebrew variants, and less frequently also Yiddish variants, typically feature the following concluding formulas: *amen, sela, netsakh va-ed* (amen, forever, for ages, for eternity). Created with kabbalistic combinations, the name of God and the names of angels are featured alongside, or instead of, these formulas. In this particular case it is:

---

[7] Unless indicated otherwise, translations from the Hebrew and Yiddish into Polish were provided by the author. Translations into English were provided by the translator.
[8] All quotations from the Bible provided according to the Twenty-first Century King James Version.
[9] According to rabbinical interpretations (Berachot, 20a), the phrase should not be read "by a well" but "dispelling the evil eye."

A.G.L.A.: *Ata gibor le-olam Adonai*, "Thou, O God, for ever and powerful" (see Rozenberg 1907, 105; Sperling 1957, 564; Lilientalowa 2007, 55–56; Ochana 1987, 62b–63b; *Segulot u-refuot* 1913, 15).

Apart from the actual spell averting the "evil eye," the Yiddish variant also includes information on accompanying performative practices, such as spitting and yawning. It also contains the introductory ("N., the son of N., was touched by evil...") and closing formulas ("In the right hour..."). The core of the charm is constituted by the utterance of the three women, which is only slightly altered from the Hebrew variant. Some sources limited the whole ritual only to this key passage, which may point to a pattern in such folk translations from the sacred language into the vernacular (see Robinsohn 1894, 20). The absence of biblical citations or the names of God was a characteristic feature of most Yiddish renditions of this incantation. That said, some of the versions featured the citation about Joseph (*Segulot u-refuot* ca. 1800, 6a–6b), but it was usually supplanted by the following characteristic formula: "Just as the evil eye had no power over Joseph, let it have no power on N., the son (or daughter) of N." (Segel 1897, 59)

The translation recorded by An-ski also featured a motif known as "casting off the evil eye," an enormously popular theme that was used on its own. Jewish sources quote it in Yiddish and Slavic versions, which we will come back to in the next section of this chapter. The presence of this motif in the Yiddish version points to an attempt to incorporate translated incantations into a magical tradition based on folk mythology based on other than biblical sources.

2 Slavic Incantations

Direct borrowings from Slavic magical incantations were rarely recorded in printed sources. They are, however, far more frequent in Jewish manuscripts. Textual material of this kind is to be found in almost every part of Central-Eastern Europe. With much certainty, they were already recorded in Hebrew at the time of the Polish-Lithuanian Commonwealth. At the beginning of the 1920s, historians discovered an eighteenth-century medical manuscript that recorded Belarusian healing spells in Jewish script (Biadula 1921, 33–35). Similar texts based on Ukrainian originals can be found in a manuscript dating to the same period, titled: *Sefer ha-Kheshek* (Petrovsky-Shtern 2011, 23). Finally, a healing spell against "rose" (red rash or spots on the skin) which begins with the (distorted) words *"Szedł Pan przez rzekę Cedrową"* ("The Lord God crossed the Cedron River") was recorded in a manuscript from the early twentieth century, originating from the Russian partition of Poland (*Segulot u-refuot* 1913, 10; see also: Wereńko

1896, 196). Such borrowings had a local character, and could be limited to a specific area or, in some cases, even a single household. However, if a given practice gained recognition among its new users, it would be recorded in diaries and transferred to other households through this channel.

It is worth noting that Central and Eastern European Jews would be most familiar with local languages if they lived in the countryside. Such *dorfsyidn*, or rural Jews, would share a number of unique characteristics with their Slavic neighbors. The areas they inhabited were often located far away from their places of worship, and they rarely participated in religious rituals; since they worked hard, they were also unable to study the Talmud. They fell behind the rabbinical ideal, and their language filled with words and collocations characteristic of the local Slavic vernacular. The presence of such Jewish cultural idiosyncrasies is reflected in a collection of household advice recorded in the second half of the nineteenth century in Lithuania. Apart from several entries in Hebrew and Yiddish, the book also features a Belarusian healing spell against fever whose main protagonist is *svyatoy Abram* (Shimon ben Abraham of Dzieweniszki/Dieveniškės in today's Lithuania, 1876, 21).

Some of the Slavic strategies of disease prevention were adopted by Jewish communities through contact with non-Jewish healing practices. A good example is a short incantation to undo an evil charm, recorded from a Ukrainian Jewish girl: *Naha za nahoy, vsya zle lykha za taboy* ("Step by step, all evil charms will [follow] you") (Yoffie 1925, 377), or a healing charm against warts used in Belarusian shtetls: *Myesyats molodoi, iak budyesh za lysom, zabyere moyi vysym* ("Young moon, as you disappear behind the woods, take my eight [warts with you]") (A.W. 1962, 62). Unfortunately, such fragments say little about the process of adaptation that they underwent. Two instances of an extremely popular healing incantation against toothache warrant closer scrutiny. One variant comes from the collection of An-ski and was originally published in Cyrillic transcription:

Maladzyk tchy buv ty na tym svyetu? – Buv. – Tchy vydau ty tam mertvych? – Vydau. – Tchy bolyts u mertvych zuby? – Nyet, nye bolyt. – Iak u mertvych zuby nye bolyt tak tchtoby nye bolylyi zuby u vek vetchnyi Plony El. (An-ski 1925, 165; Wereńko 1896, 157; Talko-Hryncewicz 1893, 358–64)

Young man, have you been to the other world?—Yes, I have.—Have you seen the dead?—Yes, I have.—Do they have toothache?—No, they never do.—Since the dead never have toothache, may N., the son/daughter of N., never have toothache, either.

The incantation is clearly a Belarusian healing spell that features a single Jewish element: the name of the person affected by the toothache. The traces of adaptation are more visible in the other variant, which was recorded in Hebrew script:

> *Myasets, Myasets molodoi, roh zolotoi tobye naprybutek a mynye nazdruvyi. Myasents, Myasents tsybalyts myertvym zubyi nybalyts. Ve-ha-khole iashiv be-ze ha-lashon Nyechai ymynye nybolyts. Ken iomar g"p.* (Maggid 1910, 587–88)
>
> Moon, young Moon, a horn of plenty to you in wealth, and to me in health.—Moon, Moon, do the dead have toothache?—No, they never do. Let the sick answer by saying: May I never have toothache, either. Repeat t[hree] t[imes].

Strikingly, this extended passage was written in Hebrew script. Transcription is, however, not the only trace of Jewish adaptation. The excerpt also features detailed instructions on how to perform the ritual. The corrupted rendering of the Ruthenian original, which nonetheless does not significantly distort the text, can be blamed on the process of notation (from hearing). Most likely, the first passage is devoid of similar errors because it was "corrected" by the collector, who provided it to the ethnographer. In any case, neither of the incantations betray any traces of manipulation with its original meaning. Presumably, they were used in a community that was familiar with the local vernacular and less likely to transform the texts.

We can gain more insight into the ways in which foreign magical incantations were adapted into Jewish culture, by analyzing another, highly popular Slavic healing spell: "Go to the mountains, to the woods, to arid roots, where no man and no living creature can reach." (see Kotula 1976) Not surprisingly, Jewish ethnographic sources contain analogous texts. The widespread popularity of such spells was based, on the one hand, on the belief in the real performative agency of the word and, on the other, on the commonality of motifs related to the fact that folk topography positioned mountains, forests, and deserts beyond the human realm.[10] One good example of this kind is a healing spell recorded in Lida (today's Belarus): *Oyf puste felder un velder, in alde drerdn, in farlozene krenitses...* ("To deserted woods and fields, to the ends of the earth, to arid wells") (Ganuzovitsh 1970, 219). It would be difficult to demonstrate that the passage is a borrowing, let alone its direction. But even if it makes little sense to speculate about when this shared Jewish-Slavic pattern emerged, it is worth examining its different variants, as they clearly support the hypothesis of borrowing. Evi-

---

10 One interpretation (Sperling 1909, 11) has it that the Hebrew word *shed* ("demon") denoted a creature living in the fields (Hebr. *sade*). Accordingly, those who had to spend the night in the fields were advised to hang a garlic bulb around their necks (Segel 1894, 323).

dence provided by Jewish ethnography furnishes numerous examples of Slavic incantations against evil demons that were adopted by Jews without major alterations. Even if Yiddish influence is detectable, it is impossible to establish whether or not it was added by ethnographers during notation. Two such popular examples, frequently cited in literature, come from the East Slavic territory: *Ny hory, ny hory, ny buri, ny kory* (Brav 1992, 53; Rechtman 1958, 297) and *Ny hory, ny bory, ny denbyny kory* (Robinsohn 1894, 20).

These widely circulating popular incantations against evil demons were, however, incorporated into Jewish healing spells in a manner that highlighted their foreign origin. The following two examples demonstrate how such Slavic passages feature in Yiddish healing spells, playing the function of magical elements. Their foreignness was a desired feature, which is why they would not undergo translation, but merely interpretation. One such incantation in an undoing spell is cited by Regina Liliental:

> *Orene, vorene, dembene, korene, veytsene klayen*
> *Biz morgn zol dos gut oyg nisht dayen.*
> *Un azoy vi afn balkn kon keyn korn nisht gerotn*
> *Azoy zol Pb"P dos gut oyg nisht shotn* (Lilientalowa 1924, 268).
>
> *Orene, vorene,* oak, rye, wheat bran,
> Let the "good eye" vanish by dawn.
> And if no grain sprouts off the ceiling
> May the "good eye" do no harm to N, the son of N.

A shorter variant of the same healing spell can be found in an autobiographical novel by Yitzhok Yoel Linetski (1839–1915), where it was featured as an apotropaic incantation against an evil demon: *Orine borine, dembene korine, veytsene klayen—glaykh oyfn beys-hakhayim* ("...straight to the graveyard") (Linetski 1921, 38; see Ehrlich 1919, 59). The other example, which makes a more straightforward reference to the *ny hory ny bory* variant, comes from the collection of the New-York-based ethnographer Yehudah Leyb Kahan:

> *Nie hore, nie more, nit veyts un nit klayen,*
> *Sorele zol mer nit veynen un shrayen.*
> *Ven es vet oyf der stelie korn gerotn,*
> *Demolt zol mayn kind a gut oyg shotn* (Kahan 1952, 277).
>
> *Nie hore, nie more,* neither wheat nor bran,
> May Sorele stop crying and screaming,
> So long as rye ripens at the ceiling,
> My child will be hurt by the "good" eye.

In both cases, the opening passage of the healing spell comes from a Slavic incantation. This is demonstrated at a number of levels, both through similarities in tone and rhythm. Liliental was the first to suggest that these passages must have been borrowed. It seems that Slavic "arid roots" (*korene*) produced a sonic connotation with the Yiddish adjective "rye." This guided further transformations that the text was exposed to in the process of adapting it to Jewish practice. A simple rhyme deriving from Slavic folklore became the root of a new Jewish incantation.

3 Translation or Lack Thereof

There are more examples of Yiddish healing practices and incantations that have their equivalents in Slavic folklore. We can therefore risk a hypothesis that, to some degree, the Yiddish versions are faithful renderings of local healing spells. This is corroborated by Slavic mythology. A handbook titled *Raphael ha-malakh* advised its readers to stop hemorrhage with the following spell: *Untern a shvartsn yam ligt a vayser shteyn. Untern shteyn rinen* ("A white rock lies under the black sea. Underneath the stone they flow") (Rozenberg 1907, 104). The passages feature a motif of white rock or rock immersed in the sea (usually livid, black, or white), which enjoyed much popularity in Slavic healing magic and was interpreted by ethnographers as a metaphor of the center of universe (cf. Bartmiński 1996, 381–82; Brzozowska 1993, 31–33). The motif has reached the Jewish tradition in its original form, which is demonstrated by a Russian healing spell against hemorrhage recorded in the Jewish periodical *Yevreyskaya Starina*: "In the livid sea lies a rock, on the rock sits an old wife, an old wife sits on the rock…" (Maggid 1910, 587). Most likely, the Yiddish version was shortened as it was adapted to a new language system, but it retained—as in the case of the treatise on three women—the core element that secured the magical properties of the text.

Conclusions about the origin of various magical incantations in the Jewish tradition have to be made with caution, though. Popular among Eastern European Jewry, the habit of throwing a milk tooth into a stove, followed by the incantation *Mayzele, mayzele, na dir a beynernem tson un gib mir an ayzernem* ("Mouse, mouse, take this tooth of bone and give me one of iron") (Sosnovik 1924, 168), was likewise widely known in the Slavic communities. However, it was also found in the German-speaking lands, for example in Styria and Bavaria (see Wereńko 1896, 133; Udziela 1891, 275; Hovorka and Kornfeld 1908, 827–30).

What is more, Jewish communities used a certain number of healing spells derived from, or influenced by, Latin. Liliental quotes the incantation *Ora fora vermi korsaka, vermi, vermi*, to be uttered while pouring hot lead into "silent water," which was believed to be an effective remedy against vermin (Lilientalowa 2007, 59). The words are featured in a variety of Hebrew and Yiddish handwritten and printed sources, in a number of different variations. By the beginning of the twentieth century, however, they were traced back to a Latin text (Maggid 1910, 582). Another example of this kind is a healing spell against "rose," composed of strings of words: *Palis tupkilut baritse partum ... rakulis tamilis daritsu paylus* (*Segulot u-refuot* 1913, 6, 10).[11] The incantation was not only said aloud but also written down, alongside with some drawings, to be used to dress the spot affected by the disease. The foreign sound of these healing spells resembles magical incantations against "rose" that were widespread in Central and Eastern Europe. In this case, however, they originate from corrupted Latin texts.

Jewish sources provide several different versions of incantations that resemble the textual material recorded by Slavic authors, for example *Resi, Pete, Teti, Espesiesie* or *Pila Rosa Afpa Possa* (Segel 1894, 55; Lilientalowa 1905, 172; Rosenzweig-Blander 1974, 155).[12] Just as in the case of healing spells, the process of recording the text in a different alphabet would often lead to distortions. In some cases, however, Jews would refrain from such transcription and use the incantations in the Cyrillic alphabet instead; an example of such practice is given by An-ski, who recorded a recommendation to feed a person bitten by a rabid dog with a piece of bread with the Cyrillic inscription: *Aron li Aron, viarize, berize, delef, davir* (An-ski 1925, 166).[13]

4 Conclusions

Based on these few examples, we can conclude that various health-related beliefs travelled quite freely between the two communities. Jews used the counsel of non-Jewish folk healers, which is evidenced by countless ethnographic, historic, and literary sources. Even the Hebrew encyclopedia *Maase Tuviya*, whose first edition was published in Venice in 1706/1707, mentions a remedy against Polish plait, which was recorded by the author's father from one old village housewife

---

[11] She probably recorded a similar remedy for "rose" in an interview with a Jewish immigrant to Saint Louis (see Yoffie 1925, 382).
[12] See: Biegeleisen 1929, 40, 130–137 (*Rosa passor syx pilla, Róża patl pili pazur, Rosa filia pastoralix, Rosa filius pastoralis, Róża pilla pastor bonus*); Talko-Hryncewicz 1893, 310 (*Palap Asor Rosapap Ailag*).
[13] See: Wereńko 1896, 188–89. *Aron + Aaron ... + Braza + Brazeyda + Delfin + Dedelfin ....*

(Kohn 1907/1908, 99b). More than two hundred years later, the Jewish writer Yisroel Yehoshua Trunk recalled in his memoirs how, in his infancy, a herdsman (*shof-pastukh*) soothed his crying with a pair of shears (Trunk 1946, 14). Many more examples of this kind can be provided. Magical incantations borrowed from local culture were typically purged of Christian references (though not always successfully).[14] They still contained, however, other motifs reflecting the characteristic traits of Slavic folklore. Based on written sources exclusively, it is impossible to reconstruct the afterlife of non-Jewish incantations within the Jewish communities. Print, and to a lesser degree also manuscripts, render them in variants already adapted to the norms and standards of Jewish culture. They feature Talmudic formulas *Ploni ben Plonit*,[15] which stood for the anonymous patient, Old Testament heroes, or concluding formulas such as *amen sela*. Some variants of the healing spells that are more deeply ingrained in Jewish practice exist in Yiddish translation. The renderings tend to reduce the content of the original to a relatively short opening phrase. A similar phenomenon can be observed in the process of transferring magical incantations from *loshn-koydesh* to *mame-loshn*. It must be pointed out, however, that some of the parallels between Jewish and Slavic folklore reveal shared roots rather than mutual influences (for example with regard to humorism or links to classical astrology). Last but not least, from the perspective of participants in magical practices, translation was also not always desirable, as foreign-sounding incantations had their important function.

translated from Polish by Bartosz Sowiński

Bibliography

[A.W.] 1962. "Gleybenishn: Zgules kegn brodavkes." *Yidisher Folklor* 3: 62–63.
Adamczyk-Garbowska, M., A. Trzciński, and A. Kopciowski, eds. 2009. *Tam był kiedyś mój dom... Księgi pamięci gmin żydowskich*. Lublin: Wydawnictwo UMCS.
An-ski, Salomon. 1909. "Zagavori ot durnogo glaza, bolyazney i nieschastnyh sluchayev (Obsprecheniss, Verreidung) sriedi Yevreyev syaviero-zapadnago kraya." *Yevreyskaya Starina* 1: 72–80.
An-ski, Salomon. 1914. *Dos yidishe etnografishe program*. Petrogrod: Yidisher Historish-Etnografisher Gezelshaft.

---

14 Some rabbis found it acceptable to resort to incantations featuring the names of Jesus and the saints by arguing that the religious message is irrelevant; what really counted was the sound of the words that was intended to bring relief to the patient (see Zimmels 1952, 140–41).
15 The name of the patient was always provided with that of their mother.

An-ski, Salomon. 1925. "Opshprekhenishn un farreydung bay di litvish-raysishe Yidn." In Vol. XV *Gezamlte shriftn*, edited by Salomon An-ski, 153–167. Wilno, Warszawa and New York: Sh. Shreberk.

Banasiewicz-Ossowska, E. 2007. *Między dwoma światami: Żydzi w polskiej kulturze ludowej.* Wrocław: Wydawnictwo Atut.

Bartmiński, J., ed. 1996. *Słownik stereotypów i symboli ludowych*, Vol. 1. Lublin: Wydawnictwo UMCS.

Benczer, B. 1893. "Jüdische Volksmedizin in Ostgalizien." *Am Ur-quell* 4: 120–121.

Biadula, Ż. 1921. "Rukapis czernakniżnika XVIII wieku (Bahatyja matariały pa biełaruskaj etnagrafii)." *Wolny Sciah* 5: 33–35.

Biegeleisen, H. 1929. *Lecznictwo ludu polskiego*. Kraków: Polska Akademia Umiejętności.

Belova, O. 2007. "Narodnaia magiia v regionakh etnokulturnykh kontaktav slavian i evreev." In *Narodnaia meditsina i magiia*, edited by O. Belova et al., 110–136. Moskva: Sefer.

Blumental, N. 1973. *Tsurikblikn*, Vol. 1. Tel Aviv: Ha-Menora.

Brav, A. 1992. "The Evil Eye Among the Hebrews." In *The Evil Eye: Casebook*, edited by A. Dundes, 44–54. Madison: The University of Wisconsin Press.

Brzozowska, M. 1993. "*Motyw białego kamienia w polskiej kulturze ludowej.*" *Twórczość Ludowa* 1–2 (23): 31–33.

Ehrlich, H. 1919. "Abzähl- und andere Kinderreime sowie Tänze aus Lemberg." *Mitteilungen zur Jüdischen Volkskunde* 2: 58–61.

Fayvushinski, A. 1958. "*Pruzhener folklor.*" In *Pinkes Pruzhene, Bereze, Maltsh, Shershev, Selts: Zeyer oyfkum, geshikhte un umkum*, edited by M. W. Bernstein and D. Farer, 199–205. Buenos Aires: Landslayt-Fareyn fun Pruzhene, Bereze, Maltsh, Shershev un Umgegnt in Argentine.

Ganuzovitsh (Ganuz), J. 1970. "Emtsaim we-segulot le-girush pakhad ve-le-bitul ayn ha-ra." In *Sefer Lida*, edited by E. Damashek, 219. Tel Aviv: Irgun Yocei Lida be-Yisrael.

Goldberg-Mulkiewicz, O. 2003. *Stara i nowa ojczyzna: Ślady kultury Żydów polskich*. Łódź: Polskie Towarzystwo Ludoznawcze.

Grunwald, M. 1900. "Aus Hausapotheke und Hexenküche." *Mitteilungen der Gesellschaft für Jüdische Volkskunde* 1: 1–87.

Hovorka, O., and A. Kronfeld, eds. 1908. *Vergleichende Volksmedizin*, Vol. 2. Stuttgart: Strecker&Schröder.

Yunis, Z. 1950. "*Di alte heym.*" In *Pinkes Mlave*, edited by Y. Shatski, 27–130. New York: Welt-Farband-Mlawer-Jidn.

Kahan, Y. L. 1952. "Paraleln tsu yidishe minhogim un zgules." In *Shtudies vegn yidisher folksshafung*, edited by Y. Kahan, 275–278. New York: YIVO.

Kohn, T. 1907/1908. *Maase Tuviya*. Kraków-Podgórze: Moyshe Sternberg.

Kotula, F. 1976. *Znaki przeszłości: Odchodzące ślady zatrzymać w pamięci*. Warszawa: Ludowa Spółdzielnia Wydawnicza.

Lew, H. 1896. "O lecznictwie i przesądach leczniczych ludu żydowskiego." *Izraelita* 36: 306–307.

Libera, Z. 1995. *Medycyna ludowa: Chłopski rozsądek czy gminna fantazja?* Wrocław: Wydawnictwo Uniwersytetu Wrocławskiego.

Libera, Z. 2003. *Znachor w tradycjach ludowych i popularnych*. Wrocław: Towarzystwo Przyjaciół Ossolineum.

Lilientalowa, R. 1898. "Przesądy żydowskie." *Wisła* 11: 277–284.

Lilientalowa, R. 1900. "Przesądy żydowskie." *Wisła* 14: 369–644.
Lilientalowa, R. 1905. "Wierzenia, przesądy i praktyki ludu żydowskiego." *Wisła* 19: 148–176.
Lilientalowa, R. 1924. "Ayn-hore." translated by N. Epshteyn, *Yidishe Filologie* 4–6: 245–271.
Lilientalowa, R. 2007. *Dziecko żydowskie*. Warszawa: Midrasz.
Linetski, Y. Y. 1921. *Dos poylishe yingl*. Wien: Der Kval.
Maggid, D. 1910. "Inoyazichniye zagavori u ruskikh yevreyev v XVIII i nachale XIX v." *Yevreyskaya Starina* 3: 580–591.
Moszyński K. 1934. *Kultura ludowa Słowian: Cz. II. Kultura duchowa*. Kraków: Polska Akademia Umiejętności.
N. N. 1962. "A bintl gleybenishn fun Zhitomir." *Yidisher Folklor* 3: 63.
Ochana, R. 1987. *Mare ha-yeladim*. Jerusalem: Ateret.
Pertovsky-Shtern, Y. 2011. "'You Will Find It in the Pharmacy': Practical Kabbalah and Natural Medicine in the Polish-Lithuanian Commonwealth, 1690–1750." In *Holy Dissent*, edited by G. Dynner, 13–54. Detroit: Wayne State University Press.
Rechtman, A. 1958. *Yidishe etnografye un folklor*. Buenos Aires: JIWO.
Robinsohn, J. 1894."An ajen-hore oder Güt Aeug." *Am Ur-Quell* 5: 20–21.
Rozenberg, J. J. 1907. *Raphael ha-malakh*. Piotrków: self-published.
Rosenzweig-Blander, D. 1974. "Shteyger, minhogim, zgules." In *Shidlovtser izker-bukh*, edited by B. Kahan, 154–157. New York: Shidlovtser Landsmanshaft in Nyu-York.
Schwartz, H. 2004. *Tree of Souls: The Mythology of Judaism*. New York: Oxford University Press.
Segel, B. W. 1894. "Materyały do etnografii Żydów wschodnio-galicyjskich." *Zbiór Wiadomości do Antropologii Krajowej* 17: 261–332.
Segel, B. W. 1897. "Wierzenia i lecznictwo ludowe Żydów." *Lud* 3: 49–61.
Słomka, J. 1983. *Pamiętniki włościanina: Od pańszczyzny do dni dzisiejszych*. Warszawa: Ludowa Spółdzielnia Wydawnicza.
Sosnovik, E. 1924. "Materialn tsu der yidisher folksmeditsin in Waysrusland." *Yidishe Filologie* 2–3: 160–168.
Sperling, A. I. 1957. *Taamei ha-minhagim*. Jerozolima: Eszkol.
Sperling, A. I. 1909. *Taamei ha-minhagim oyf ivre-taytsh*, II. Lemberg: self-published.
Stomma, L. 2000. *Antropologia kultury wsi polskiej XIX w*. Gdańsk: Tower Press.
Talko-Hryncewicz, J. 1893. *Zarys lecznictwa ludowego na Rusi Południowej*. Kraków: Akademia Umiejętności.
Trunk, Y. Y. 1946. *Poyln: Zikhroynes un bilder*, Vol. 2. New York: Unzer Tsayt.
Udziela, M. 1891. *Medycyna i przesądy lecznicze ludu polskiego*. Warszawa: M. Arct.
Weinreich, M. 2008. *History of the Yiddish Language*, translated by Shlomo Noble. New York: YIVO Institute for Jewish Research.
Weissenberg, Samuel. 1897. "Südrussische Amulette." *Verhandlungen der Berliner Gesellschaft für Anthropologie, Ethnologie und Urgeschichte* 29: 367–369.
Weissenberg, Samuel. 1907. "Krankheit und Tod bei den südrussischen Juden." *Globus* 91: 357–363.
Wereńko, F. 1896. "Przyczynek do lecznictwa ludowego." *Materyały Antropologiczno-Archeologiczne i Etnograficzne* 1: 99–228.
Yoffie, L. R. 1925. "Popular Beliefs and Customs among the Yiddish-Speaking Jews of St. Louis, Mo." *The Journal of American Folklore* 38: 375–399.

Zimmels, H. J. 1952. *Magicians, Theologians and Doctors: Studies in Folk-Medicine and Folk-Lore as Reflected in the Rabbinical Responsa 12th-19th Centuries.* London: Edward Goldston.

Archival Materials

ben Abraham from Dziewieniszki, Szymon. 1876. Manuscript from the Collection of the Jewish Historical Institute in Warsaw. Signature: rkps. 771.

Segulot u-refuot. 1913. London, Microfilm from the Collection of the Library of the Jewish Theological Seminary. Signature: MIC. #9862.

Segulot u-refuot. c. 1800. Manuscript from the Collection of Bibliotheca Rosenthaliana. Signature: HS. ROSS. 444, pp. 6a–6b.

Migrations and Inspirations

Joachim Schlör
"Da wär's halt gut, wenn man Englisch könnt!" Robert Gilbert, Hermann Leopoldi and the Role of Languages between Exile and Return

1 Introduction

This chapter emerged out of two different areas of research. The first is my own interest in Robert Gilbert's work and in the different cultural milieus where his lyrics and songs have been written: late Weimar Berlin as a center of avant-garde popular culture, Vienna before the *Anschluss* of 1938, Paris as a place of temporary refuge in 1938–1939, New York as a place of exile after 1939, and finally Munich and Zurich as places of remigration (see Schlör 2012). The second research area has been developed by members of the Parkes Institute for the Study of Jewish/non-Jewish relations at the University of Southampton within a project under the working title "Jewish Places as Arenas for Translation and Transfer in Jewish/non-Jewish Relations," which tries to connect notions of "place" with the idea of "translation" and transfer in order to combine elements of the "spatial turn" and the "translational turn" in search for answers to two questions: What *makes* a place? How does place-making work through language and translation? More precisely, the project asks: How have "Jewish" places been constructed and negotiated, and what was the role of languages and of translations in these processes?[1] David Roskies has described the relationship between Jews and non-Jews as a "market place of voices." (2004, 270) Trying to make sense of the discourses acted out in such places, the project aims to demonstrate the strategic importance of translation and transfer in Jewish/non-Jewish relations across the ages; consider the significance of "place" in such relations from a geographical, historical, and cultural point of view; address questions of authenticity and appropriation in acts of cultural transfer and translation; describe how the various places can be understood as places of translation and transfer.

---

[1] The project application has been led by my colleague Dr Andrea Reiter at Southampton. For a discussion of the "turns" in the Humanities, see Bachmann-Medick 2006, and recently *American Historical Review*, Forum titled "Historiographic 'Turns' in Critical Perspective."

Research into migration and displacement, that is, the study of migration experiences which contain both the memory of a lost home and the need—and ability—to (re)construct new centers of creativity, cannot be separated from research into integration and place-identity, i.e., the study of the relationship between different Jewish communities and the place(s) relevant to them. Studying translation as a form of exchange and of "co-construction" (Biale 1994) can provide us with the opportunity to link these areas. Translation is a method of crossing boundaries. The translation and transfer (of languages but also of values, beliefs, histories and narratives from past to present; of ideas from one culture into another, or from one medium into another) can be regarded as a central link between the experiences of displacement and the adventure of integration and settlement. Translation provides actors with a chance to re-invent themselves; it is relational, interactive and process-oriented, to use notions developed by proponents of a *histoire croisée* (Werner and Zimmerman 2006). Translation has a potential for "performing" identity, which has allowed Jews to exist in bi- or even multicultural communities of discourse and often bestowed on them the function of bridge-building. Translation and transfer as cultural practices are of specific importance in places of emigration, where the experience of rupture and interruption requires new forms of interaction and communication.

Such places—Berlin shortly before the Nazi's rise to power, Vienna between 1933 and 1938, Paris before the outbreak of World War II, New York during the war years, but also the cities of post-war Europe—can be regarded as very specific *arenas*, or locales where boundaries are challenged and crossed, where a link can be made between agents and processes of translation and transfer.

2 "Berlin ade"[2]

The first task of this text will be to make readers familiar with some people whose names might mean nothing to them, although many will surely be able to sing or hum some of the songs they wrote. Werner Richard Heymann, the composer who cooperated with Robert Gilbert on many occasions both before and after the war, put that very fittingly into words which can be found today on a commemoration plaque on his former house (built by Erich Mendelsohn) on Karolinger Platz 5 in Berlin-Westend: "You might not know me, but you have

---

[2] This is the title of Gilbert's 1933 poem in which he reflects about his own emigration from Berlin and Germany. The poem juxtaposes the titles and themes of German popular songs with the new reality the emigrant faces: not being part of this culture anymore and yet being challenged to keep this tradition among the cultural baggage he takes into exile.

heard a lot from me." [*Sie kennen mich nicht, aber Sie haben schon viel von mir gehört.*] The very fact that their names are forgotten is due to the political circumstances: the Nazis' rise to power in Germany, the persecution of Jews and political opponents after March 1933—and their emigration from Germany. In some ways, one could say, this emigration is not yet over, and although both Heymann and Gilbert (and Leopoldi) did indeed come back to Europe in the early 1950s, it is safe to say that none of them did really "settle" or "make their home" here anymore. Instead they lived, to use a notion that has become very popular in recent years, transnational and transcontinental lives.

Robert David Winterfeld was born in the poor eastern part of Berlin (Warschauer Strasse, "above the horse stables") in 1899 (Gilbert R. 1972, 103). He was the son of Max Winterfeld, a circus orchestra conductor and composer, who already had changed his name to Jean Gilbert, in a city that aspired to become a European metropolis and, in those years, saw Paris as its role model. With one successful operetta (*Die keusche Susanne*, 1912), containing the *Schlager* "Puppchen, Du bist mein Augenstern," Jean Gilbert managed to fulfil the "Berlin dream" of moving westward into a villa on the Wannsee Lake shore. Today the place belongs to a divers club, after having hosted an Institute for Silviculture under the Nazis and well into the post-war period, thus no traces of its former owner can be found. After fighting in World War I, Robert returned a pacifist and a socialist. He had inherited his father's musical talent and hoped to put it to use supporting the political left in Weimar Germany. His song "Stempellied," composed by Hanns Eisler and interpreted by Ernst Busch, the "Barrikaden-Tauber," was an indictment of the capitalist system, and of "those above" ("*die da oben*") for sending the unemployed masses into misery and despair; it became an icon for Germany's worker's movement.[3] Gilbert collaborated with Hanns Eisler and performed at festivals for "New Music," for example in Baden-Baden 1927. During these years he also established a life-long friendship with the philosopher Heinrich Blücher. When he married and felt the need to earn serious money, Gilbert started to work for movie and operetta productions; within a very short time, he became Germany's most prolific and highest-earning songwriter.[4] With Werner Richard Heymann (1896–1961), Gilbert wrote the songs

---

[3] Stempellied (Lied der Arbeitslosen), Text: David Weber (= Robert Gilbert), Musik: Hanns Eisler. See Erinnerungsort.de – Materialien zur Kulturgeschichte, http://erinnerungsort.de/stempellied-28lied-der-arbeitslosen-29-_171.html (accessed August 5, 2013).

[4] This is documented in a file archived at the State Reparation Office (Landesamt für Entschädigung) in Berlin; Gilbert's application for material compensation of losses suffered on the grounds of Nazi persecution has been successful. Landesamt für Entschädigung Berlin, Akte Robert Gilbert, 50836, M5.

for *Die drei von der Tankstelle* ("Ein Freund, ein guter Freund" and "Liebling, mein Herz lässt Dich grüßen"),[5] for *Der Kongreß tanzt* ("Das gibt's nur einmal" and "Das muß ein Stück vom Himmel sein");[6] for Ralph Benatzky's operetta *Im weißen Rössl*[7] he wrote the songs that made the play so successful: "Im weißen Rössel am Wolfgangsee," "Im Salzkammergut, da kammer gut lustig sein" and "Was kann der Sigismund dafür, dass er so schön ist." In the period that ended abruptly in 1933, Gilbert was a major actor in, and contributor to, Germany's popular music industry.

Hermann Leopoldi, whose life and work has been researched by Georg Traska and Christoph Lind (2012), was born as Hersch Kohn on August 15, 1888, in Gaudenzdorf, Meidling, which is today a part of the city of Vienna. His father Leopold Kohn—who changed the family name to Leopoldi in 1911—was a musician and taught his sons to play the piano. In 1904, at the age of sixteen, Hermann got his first job as a piano accompanist; in 1916 he had his first solo appearance in the Viennese establishment Ronacher. After the war, together with his brother Ferdinand and Fritz Wiesenthal, Leopoldi founded a cabaret called "L.W." in Vienna's first district. Among the artists who performed there were Charlotte Waldow, Franzi Ressel, Armin Berg, Hans Moser, Szöke Szakall, Max Hansen, Fritz Grünbaum, Karl Valentin, Raoul Aslan, and Otto Tressler. Some of them stayed behind in Vienna after 1938, others met again in different circumstances during their emigration to the Americas. The cabaret was closed in 1925, but by then Leopoldi had acquired fame as one of the most popular composers and presenters of Austrian, and especially Viennese, folklore—if that is the right word. The "Wienerlied" is a very specific, very urban, cultural genre, part of Vienna's popular culture in the same way as the coffeehouse or the "Heuriger." Leopoldi called himself a "Klavierkünstler." More than a pianist, he was a storyteller, a comedian, a coiner of words and phrases. He travelled all over Europe and performed, often together with Betja Milskaja, in Berlin, Paris, Prague, or Budapest.

In the spring of 1933, under the new rulings set by the Reich Chamber of Culture, most—though indeed not all—of the German artists connected to the movies and shows quoted above emigrated, initially (with a hope of return) to neighboring countries (Dahm 1986). Vienna provided Robert Gilbert and other expellees with venues for performances and with colleagues—such as Hermann

---

[5] Germany 1930, Director Wilhelm Thiele. See: "Die Drei von der Tankstelle." *Ufa-Magazin* 9 (Berlin: Deutsches Historisches Museum 1992).

[6] Germany 1931, Director Erik Charell. See: Reichow 1993.

[7] Premiered on 8 November 1930 in Berlin's Großes Schauspielhaus, directed by Erik Charell, starring Max Hansen and Camilla Spira. See Peter and Clarke 2007; Tadday 2006.

Leopoldi and Rudolf Weys (1898–1978)—to collaborate with, as well as a related language for the writing of songs. This period between 1933 and 1938—when, according to Karl Kraus, "the rats were entering the sinking ship" (in Spiel 1994, 233)—was marked by fruitful collaborations and successful performances, but the lyrics of the songs, and the poems Gilbert wrote, were clearly influenced and overshadowed by what was to come: the civil war and Hitler's entry into Austria. The lighter muse of the Berlin years made place for sarcasm and dark humor; at the same time, it is fascinating to see how Gilbert picked up the Viennese dialect—a first lesson, one might say, in cultural transfer. While Gilbert, whose *Fremdenpolizei* file shows more than thirty different addresses during these five years, managed to escape and reunite with his wife and daughter in Paris, Leopoldi was refused entrance to Czechoslovakia, sent back to Vienna, arrested on April 26, 1938, and brought to a concentration camp, first to Dachau and later, in September of the same year, to Buchenwald. There he wrote the music for the *Buchenwald-Lied*, with lyrics by Fritz Löhner-Beda (who, hoping in vain for an intervention by his friend Franz Lehár, was murdered in the camp). Leopoldi's wife and parents, who had already emigrated to the United States, secured an affidavit and thus managed to organize his release. Via Hamburg he came to New York where his family and journalists waited for him—the picture of Leopoldi kissing the American ground in New York's harbor has become famous. To quote Einzi Stolz, Leopoldi "was for all of us like a creature from another planet: thanks to a rescue campaign that bordered on a miracle, he survived the horror of the camps in Buchenwald and Dachau. He has always kept the faith in the good in humans and remained an optimist, sharing his courage and confidence in those hard times." (Leopoldi and Möslein 1992) The awareness of the new European reality, with the occupation of neighboring (once so familiar) countries and the persecution of Jews and political opponents, brought the emigrants in New York closer together.

Among the people Leopoldi met there was Robert Gilbert. In Paris Gilbert, who had reunited with his wife Elke and daughter Marianne, met up with Heinrich Blücher (and his new partner, Hannah Arendt) again, and managed to gather all the documents needed to board the ship "Aquitania" on March 25, 1939, from Cherbourg to New York. The family settled in the Bronx and for the next twelve years, 51 West 236th Street in Riverdale became a home away from home. While his daughter's memoirs—published in English as *Memoirs of a Mischling: Becoming an American* (2002) and translated into German under the title *Das gab's nur einmal: Verloren zwischen New York und Berlin* (2007)—give the impression that only she, Marianne (Gilbert Finnegan), managed to "become an American" whereas her parents, especially her father, remained stuck in exile circles, Robert Gilbert's letters to Rudolf Weys and papers documenting the collaboration with Hermann Leopoldi in New York tell a slightly different story. But before we get there, one more development needs to be mentioned.

Recent research has shown that a musical dialogue and exchange between Europe and the United States, which had taken place in the early decades of the twentieth century, partly replaced Berlin's love-affair with Paris and everything Parisian. While shows and plays on Broadway had drawn from the European (especially Austrian) operetta, the new American musical innovations in turn influenced and inspired this short-lived but intense heyday of ambitious and sophisticated German popular and entertaining culture. A two-way traffic of transatlantic contact and exchange had already been open. Erik Charell, the director of *Im weißen Rössl*, had visited the United States in the 1920s, where he saw the "Ziegfeld Follies" on Broadway and imported the ideas of big revues, chorus lines, and dancing troops back to Germany (Clarke 2007).[8] As Francois Genton remarked, "[a]round 1930, a popular culture emerged in Germany which was modern, part of the avant-garde, but at the same time conscious of tradition, and leading the field in Europe. Many of the protagonists of this culture were educated and qualified German Jews." (2012, 325) It is hard to say, in hindsight, if this engagement with the lighter muses conflicted with Gilbert's left-wing political attitudes. In any case, Gilbert managed to add a number of provocative and ironic elements to Benatzky's show, for example, the competition between a Jewish and a non-Jewish producer (of male undergarments) who both spend their holidays in Kaiser Franz Josef's Austria.

The experience of emigration in the year following Austria's 1938 *Anschluss* was marked by the searching for jobs and accommodation, applying for visa and affidavits, and the loss of German citizenship. Transitioning one's career to another country, across the Atlantic, was a task fraught with challenges. "It's a damn tough country," Gilbert writes to Rudolf Weys on June 24, 1939 (Gilbert R. 1939). Some of his former colleagues, among them the emigrated members of "Die Leute vom Naschmarkt," a Viennese musical comedy ensemble founded by Weys in 1933, seemed to have some success—he adds with a skeptical tone—by performing their old sketches in English. But this success, he felt, would not last. European topics, and European rhythms, had become either suspicious or at least removed from the taste of the American public. The need to learn the new language was as obvious as the need to develop new topics and adopt a new style in the writing of songs and of music.

---

8 For Charell's American experience with the Ziegfeld shows see http://www.ralph-benatzky.de/main.php?cat=6&sub_cat=16&task=3&art_id=000330 (accessed August 28, 2013).

3 "*Refugee heißt Nebbich*": Robert Gilbert and Hermann Leopoldi Exiled in New York

The second task of this chapter is to reconstruct the cultural situation of those emigrants living in New York in 1939. In some ways, the ground for their cultural activities had already been prepared because New York had emerged as a cultural center for newly-arrived immigrants. The *landsmanshaftn,* associations for the mutual support of immigrants who came from the same cities, or regions, had already provided millions of Jews from Eastern Europe with the opportunity to start their American lives, supported by a familiar environment (Soyer 2001). But in Robert Gilbert's case, the circumstances were not as convenient. The flat the family could afford was far up north in Riverdale, and Gilbert's wife, Elke, earned the money they needed as a beautician and dressmaker in Lower Manhattan. Robert was often alone at home, trying to write lyrics and music, and the old piano wore the many cigarette burns as a symbol of little success. This is, at least, how his daughter, Marianne, remembers the story. The crucial problem for the writer was the language. Marianne acquired American English easily ("*Marianne spricht schon Englisch wie ein altes Mayflower-Girl*" [Gilbert R. 1939]) and began to forget her German. Gilbert later recollected: "I have lived in America for ten years, it was, for me, a very, very good time. I came with three hundred dollars, lent from somebody, and landed in a horrible apartment under awful circumstances trying to earn a living. How could I do that? My English was not as good as that of somebody who had grown up on these streets. I grew up on the streets of Berlin, my knowledge of Shakespeare hasn't helped me here at all. I had to learn the slang." (Gilbert R. 1939)

The Gilberts received US citizenship in 1944 and, from the few letters of the period that I could find, I have got the impression that they intended to stay rather than return to Europe. The problem they faced was how to make a living. Gilbert's letters to Weys, as well as later letters to Blücher, in which he recalls the time in New York, are full of projects and dreams, many of which were never realized. But most of them deal with the topic of language—and of translation. Gilbert wrote poetry in German and performed, sometimes for a public of two- or three hundred fellow émigrés who were able to understand him. He also worked for small fees as an accompanist for other artists: "I would recite my Berlin poems to those who could understand them and accompanied European artists: the fees were minimal." (Pacher 1979, 10) The only publication of the period is *Meine Reime, Deine Reime,* which appeared in a German publishing house based in New York and for which Hannah Arendt, in her *Menschen in finsteren Zeiten*, called Gilbert "the successor [Heinrich] Heine never had." (Arendt

1989, 291) But he also tried to translate his own—as well as other authors'—texts into English.

Leopoldi seems to have been more successful at the start, since he did not hesitate to use the existing network of Austrian and Austrian-Jewish immigrants. He soon started to perform in "Eberhardt's Café Grinzing" in Manhattan, where he also met his partner (for the stage and for life), Helly Möslein. Kurt Robitschek, Arthur Berger, Armin and Jimmy Berg, and Helly herself helped him to adapt his repertoire to the English language. They created a new—urban—form of play, the "Short Operetta," they set up an authentic Grinzing wine bar and served "liver soup, schnitzel with a salad, plum dumplings and coffee with whipped cream" together with their music (Klösch, Thumser, 2002, 34). With songs such as "I am a quiet Drinker" or "A Little Café Down the Street" they celebrated their arrival in *Exilcafés*, for example the "Old Vienna" or the "Viennese Lantern."[9] Songs about wine and coffeehouses or about the beautiful girls of Vienna seemed to touch the heart of the American public, whereas the harder, more serious, more political traditions that "Berlin" brought to New York remained within the circle of German-Jewish immigrants—or travelled further on to Los Angeles, where Werner Richard Heymann was quite successfully writing music for movies, such as *To Be Or Not To Be* directed by Ernst Lubitsch. I do not know, and I have not found any hint in the correspondence, even between Heymann and Gilbert, as to why Gilbert never made his way to Hollywood. He sat in New York, complained about the summer heat, wrote poems and satirical texts for the German language émigré paper *Aufbau*, participated in a competition for the best German-language exile song—and won it, with a political song, with Paul Dessau's music, that had the very symbolic title "Höre uns, Deutschland!" He also participated in the Austrian cultural programs, for example in a (re)-staging of *Das weiße Rössel am Central Park*, where he collaborated with Robert Stolz, one of the very few non-Jewish artists who decided to leave their native Austria. He also participated in tributes to European artists—among them Robert's father, Jean Gilbert, who had become the conductor of a radio orchestra in Buenos Aires and died there in 1942, a fact Robert only learned from newspapers.

Most importantly, however, he began to work with Hermann Leopoldi. The song "Da wär's halt gut, wenn man Englisch könnt" (It would be good if one spoke English), which Gilbert and Leopoldi wrote together in 1942/43, captures everyday situations, such as meeting people, dating a girl, or trying to find a

---

[9] It would be interesting to discuss at some point *why* the Austrian popular culture, especially the "Wiener Lied," found access to the American—and British, if we think of Richard Tauber—public much more easily than the musical and lyrical tradition from Berlin, Robert Gilbert's home and place of reference.

job, in which it would be good to know the English language. The lyrics are basically German, but in this song, and in many others that followed, English idioms and phrases find their way into the text—as they did into the lives of these émigrés.

This is the point—in time and space—where all the threads and topics I have mentioned so far come together. The best decision the artist can take is to make the very problem he faces—the lack of fluency in the new language—the main topic of his work. Given that his English is not good enough to write poetry or lyrics for music, he writes a song about his English not being good enough. For the researcher of such stories, it is fascinating to "see" artists at work. Gilbert writes the lyrics; his attention is on the words. He sends them to Leopoldi, whose focus is on the music. Leopoldi alters not words or phrases, but rhythm; he is looking for dramatic moments in the text so that he will be able to perform it. And he sends the whole thing back to Gilbert, who adds a line, or a rhyme, to accommodate Leopoldi's wishes. Georg Traska and Christoph Lind in Vienna have found a file containing some eighty pages documenting this collaboration. Poems, short dialogues and whole scenes for a play, "Heimat im Koffer," that was never to be written or performed; drafts, written over, amended, typed up again, set to music, rejected, finally accepted and—at least in some cases—also performed and published.

> Die Sprache, die ich früher sprach, die konnt ich fließend sprechen
> doch English language, Schreck loss noch, do hob i holt no Schwächen.
> Mit evening school, do fing es an, ich nahm a English lesson
> Doch hab ich, was ich evening's kann, beim breakfast schon vergessen
> Man merkt mir an am Dialekt,—wann ich Amerika entdeckt.
> Jo do wärs halt guat, wenn ma Englisch kennt, a bissl mehr als nur how do you do
> Doch so long ma nur sogt: I can't understand, do ghört man net really dazua.
> Und solang ma ned waß, dass a brush is a Bürstl,
> A dog is a Hund, und d'Hot dog san d'Würstl
> So long bleibt ma das, wos ma greenhorn nennt
> Jo do wär's halt guad, wenn ma Englisch könnt. (Leopoldi H. 2011)[10]

As Europe became more and more cut-off from America during the war, Gilbert strove to make the United States his new home. His unpublished poems and songs show an effort to integrate American culture, and to "become an American." In Gilbert's own view, this attempt has worked quite well; in a February 1951 letter he writes: "I have been living in New York since 1939, and I became

---

10 See also the CD *Hermann Leopoldi im Amerika* which, for some reason, does not contain this crucial song.

a permanent resident here after I had turned, as I like to say, not just into an American but almost an (American) Indian." (Gilbert R. 1951) Based on the few letters and documents kept today at Berlin's Academy of the Arts, Gilbert's feeling of having "arrived" reflects his personal and family situation much more than his professional career. He did not, in fact, manage to integrate into the American musical industry. Europe under Nazi occupation, on the other hand, seemed very far away in these years. It was nearly impossible to receive news from friends or relatives, as the whole continent had turned into a black hole that had destroyed the flourishing culture of the past, unless it had, in tiny trickles, escaped to so many places of exile.

4 Bridge-Builder and Border-Crosser

Gilbert made the journey back across the Atlantic, mainly for financial reasons, only four years after the end of World War II. He left the United States in 1949, at first only with the intention to find work in Europe *and* to remain a US citizen and a resident of New York. In his letters to Rudolf Weys he presents himself as a kind of American uncle who sends parcels to friends and inquires about the situation "over there." Between the lines, though, the urgent need to reconnect can be felt. Whereas Hermann Leopoldi returned to Vienna and was celebrated there (although the story of his persecution was rarely mentioned), Gilbert kept his distance. He stayed first in Munich, writing lyrics and poetry for Erich Kästner's cabaret *Kleine Freiheit*, and slowly built up new networks of contact and collaboration both in the theater and in the emerging post-war German film industry. Towards the end of the 1950s, a new area of work opened up quite unexpectedly. Frederic Loewe, formerly Friedrich Löwe, (1901–1988), the author of the musical *My Fair Lady*, asked Gilbert to produce a German translation of the play's libretto (Loewe 1958a). Finally, the songwriter's transnational and translational experience started to pay off: the English language that he never mastered well enough to write became a tool of transmission and bridge-building. In the years that followed, Gilbert—now based in Minusio, Ticino (Switzerland) and very decidedly not in Germany again—translated around twenty popular American musical comedies into German. With his moderation of a dialogue between the English and German languages, in plays such as *Annie Get Your Gun*, *Oklahoma*, and especially *Cabaret*, his last translation (in 1970), Gilbert helped to bring American popular culture (back) to Europe and to make it accessible to an audience he once knew—and did not know anymore (and was quite doubtful about), at the same time.

A file of letters, kept today in the archive of Berlin's Academy of Arts, containing the correspondence between Frederic Loewe and Robert Gilbert, documents—quite similarly to Gilbert's and Leopoldi's collaboration in New York—the ongoing dialogue between the creator of the play and the words Alan J. Lerner made so famous, on the one hand, and Gilbert, who was tasked with translating into German famous lines like: "The rain in Spain stays mainly in the plain." On November 20, 1958, Frederick Loewe (Lerner & Loewe, 120 East 56th Street, New York, NY) wrote a letter to Robert Gilbert, Villa La Mirandola, Minusio bei Locarno, Switzerland.

> My dear Robert,
> I am sorry not to have written to you before. Number one, this work is not of immediate pressure. Number two, I have been too busy with other things and number three, I don't know exactly what to tell you.
> WITH A LITTLE BIT OF LUCK (Mit 'nem Fingerhut voll Glück), I like the best of the three so far. I COULD HAVE DANCED ALL NIGHT (Haett' gern die Nacht durchtanzt), still hasn't found my full enthusiasm. I suppose it has to do with the weakness of the first line of the refrain [gap]. Now, the second version of it, I like, of course, much better, with the exception of the first line, which again is very weak (Ich hätt' am liebsten heut'). ON THE STREET WHERE YOU LIVE is, of course, very nice but again fails to excite me. It is unnecessary at this point to tell you they are all excellent lyrics and my admiration for you remains undiminished. It just isn't quite right for MY FAIR LADY. ...
>
> Dear Robert, I know that this is going to be tough work but we must not forget that it is MY FAIR LADY, which means it must be perfect and that there is no time limit on this. Please be not disappointed and keep on trying.
> As to your question about which dialect to use in German—I would suggest that you look up and see what they did in the German 'Pygmalion' versions previously, for as you know it was done in German (Vienna).
> Much love,
> [handwritten] Fritz (Loewe 1958b)

Two Germans communicating in English (and how German this English is!) give us an amazing insight into their workshop. Today we know, because we have heard it and seen it on the stage so often, that it reads "Mit 'nem klein' bißchen Glück" and "Ich hätt' getanzt heut Nacht," and somehow we see the translator sweating at his desk. On 21 January, 1959, Gilbert sent a letter to Heinrich Blücher: "Workwise, I spend a lot of time in Munich. Or Vienna, as it comes. Now I am translating *My Fair Lady* into German—a tough cookie since it is so matted, or felted [*verfilzt*] with the English language and purely English associations [*Bezüglichkeiten*]." (Gilbert R. 1959) Fritz, the old friend, is quite demanding, and the famous wording "Es grünt so grün" had not at all been there from the start, but had been worked out, sentence by sentence, verse by verse. It had not even been clear from the start that the German play would use the Berlin dialect. There is a Viennese version as well, in fact, there are dozens of versions in so many languages, but for us, I would maintain, Eliza Dolittle could only "berlinern": "Nur een Ssimmerchen irjendwo." How else should that sound? But it has not fallen from the skies, it has been compiled and developed and discussed between 56th Street in New York and Villa La Mirandola in Minusio.

Recent research in Translation Studies has developed new questions in the context of *cultural translation*. As the organizers of a recent conference at the University of Graz in Austria postulated, these new approaches

> abolish the dichotomist or binary conceptions that are still omnipresent even in the research on cultural transfer (for example by means of the more or less implicit normative notions, such as source culture or target culture). The attention now turns to places of contact and fault lines, zones of transition, displacements, and forms of intermediation in the processes of cultural exchange, but also to those differences that evade translatability or are indeed not translatable. (Steiner 2010)

That might be a little too sophisticated for *My Fair Lady*, but Robert Gilbert, in his own—and much more beautiful—language puts it quite similarly. Transition, displacement, intermediation, and exchange form important elements in a life trajectory characterized by ruptures, wanderings, and relations between different worlds. It is the notion, and the practice of translation, which brings these elements together. This is how he expresses it himself:

> Between two languages, there are delicate and fragile bridges—above an abyss of misunderstandings. Should it happen that one of them (be it idiom or dialect, slang, jargon, lingo, literary or spoken language) wants to get to the other and that they meet on this eternally swaying surface and exchange a greeting, then we can never be sure if they both mean the same, even with the simplest "How do you do" or *"Guten Morgen."* Often therefore they pass each other silently, or even worse: they talk at cross purposes. (Gilbert R. 1951–1961)[11]

This is Robert Gilbert speaking, in a text that I first discovered in the archive but then also found printed in a paperback edition of *My Fair Lady*. The difficult

---

11 In the German original: "Zwischen zwei Sprachen gibt es zierliche, zerbrechliche Brücken – über einem Abgrund von Mißverständnissen. Will die eine zur anderen, und kommt es zufällig vor, daß die beiden – jeweils Idiom, Mundart, Dialekt, Slang, Jargon, Lingo, Schrift- oder Umgangssprache genannt – auf ewig schwankender Unterlage einander begegnen und einen Gruß austauschen, dann kann man nie ganz sicher sein, ob sie auch beide dasselbe meinen, und sei es nur mit dem simpelsten ‚How do you do' oder ‚Guten Morgen'. Oft gehen sie deshalb stumm aneinander vorbei. Oder noch schlimmer: Sie reden aneinander vorbei." (trans. J.S.)

business obviously has challenged him to try and write down his thoughts about the newly acquired, or required, form of art:

> And then there comes the adventurous border crosser, also known as a translator, who tries to create a connection, between those two conflicting tongues—a reasonably sustainable connection—which means he endeavors, honestly and literally in the sweat of his brow to make a halfway meeting possible and to prevent, on the one hand, the emergence of a space of banality within which the simplest 'Yes' or '*Ja*' will be rolled out into platitude, and, on the other hand, to prevent them from landing in the abyss of misunderstandings—from where no bridge-wanderer will ever return. (Gilbert R. 1951–1961)[12]

A bridge wanderer, a border crosser—these seem to be apt descriptions for the role of a translator. Like others before him, Gilbert also uses an image which makes sense only in German. The "*Übersetzer*" has the task of "ferrying over," ("*über zu setzen*") like an old ferryman. He walks between the colors of the rainbow, thinking in terms of siltation or dilution, of ballast and babble, or splashing, of maelstrom and recess, and he names the two claims made on him from the left and from the right: fidelity, where the foreign original is concerned, and loyalty in regard of "his own tribe," namely the German language. He sees himself swinging to and fro, like the pendulum of a grandfather clock, or balancing on the very thin thread of synonyms, juggling seventeen dictionaries on the tip of his nose. "Only the self-evident becomes evident to others" would be the fitting motto for him who calls himself a mere "echo," a mediator or middleman with only one hope: that he will be perceived of as close as possible to the homely and neighborly voice from next door: "*wahrgenommen beinahe für die allen so traute und nachbarliche Stimme von nebenan.*"

So many of these notions seem to deserve elaboration and discussion—but surely "homely," *traut*, and "neighborly," *nachbarlich*, immediately remind us of their contrary, the experience of being made "foreign" by the power of Nazi law. *Cabaret*, more than any other play, brings this experience back to Gilbert's mind—the play is set in Berlin, and its plot unfolds against the background of the Nazis' rise to power. In a letter to Friedrich Torberg, Gilbert confirms that

---

[12] In the German original: "Da erscheint dann gewöhnlich ein abenteuernder Grenzgänger, gemeinhin Übersetzer genannt, der die Verbindung zwischen den zwiespältigen Zungen herzustellen versucht – eine halbwegs haltbare Verbindung –, das heißt, er bemüht sich im redlichen, ja buchstäblichen Schweiß seines Angesichts darum, daß die beiden sich möglichst auf halbem Wege treffen und letzten Endes nur ja nicht auf einem Gemeinplatz landen, auf dem selbst ein lapidares ‚Ja' oder ‚Yes' zu einer asthmatischen Plattitüde ausgewalzt wird – und andererseits nur ja nicht dort, wovon kein Brückenwanderer je verlautbar wiederkehrt, nämlich im besagten Abgrund der Mißverständnisse." (trans. J.S.).

his own experience, the fact that he had been an eye-witness, qualified him for the translation of *Cabaret:* "I lived there. I know the time, the language, the silence. Who is going to tell me what and how used to be said and sung there?" (Gilbert R: 1969) The authenticity of his translation has been emphasized by Tatyana Shestakov in her analysis of *Cabaret:*

> A Musical like *Cabaret*, with its linguistic and cultural duality, which seems logical considering the history of the play and the genre, requires a translator who would to some extent have the same 'split personality,' or rather 'split nationality' that the original play has. Robert Gilbert was the perfect interpreter who, as a German and a man of the theatre, operetta, cabaret, and himself the author of cabaret texts as well as soldier of the First World War, could become Christopher Isherword's and Joe Masteroff's German-language voice. (2003)

The quality of the translation, she continues, can be seen in the fact that "no recent re-translations of *Cabaret* have been needed." Only Gilbert had "the profound knowledge of the political, social and historical aspects of the source and target societies, as well as that of the world of theatre." (Shestakov 2003)

5 Conclusion

In recent years, some authors in the areas of Cultural Studies, Diaspora Studies, or post-Colonial Studies have celebrated, if this is the right word, (symbolic) "homelessness" and cosmopolitanism as the only possible form of existence in modern times.[13] With this case-study in mind, I cannot agree. Gilbert's life and work in translation may reflect, in some ways, a general experience of mankind in the twentieth century, but it is also a very specific experience, and a very specific *Jewish* experience, which cannot easily be translated into a kind of role model for other migrant groups or indeed for the exiled situation of modern man (and woman) today. Two important contexts need to be made visible: first, the emergence of a cultural exchange between, for example, Berlin, New York, Los Angeles, and Munich, that began long before the Nazis' rise to power in Germany, and continued after the liberation in 1945; second, the transnational network created, out of sheer necessity and despair, by those German and Austrian Jews who emigrated from Nazi Germany after 1933. American musicians and composers visited Europe and the centers of musical activity, such as Vienna,

---

13 For a critical assessment see Sznajder 2008, 2011. See also Cathy Gelbin's and Sander Gilman's AHRC-funded research project "Cosmopolitanism and the Jews": http://personalpages.manchester.ac.uk/staff/Cathy.Gelbin/Cosmopolitanism_and_the_Jews.html (accessed February 15, 2014).

Berlin, Paris, London, and many other places, already during the second half of the nineteenth century, but more and more during the *fin-de-siècle* and the interwar years. From there they brought to the United States ideas, melodies, stage design, and many more aspects of the European opera, operetta, and other genres. European musicians, composers, directors, and performing artists—at the very same time—visited the Americas and brought experiences from there back home. It is therefore impossible to say that one area "influenced" or "guided" the other. Rather, we have to imagine a constant dialogue and exchange, a kind of cultural third space (Bhabha 1995), which is neither "European" nor "American," but which is constructed through exchange: through visits, travels, performances, discussions, reviews, letters, and—in many cases—even musical cooperation. While much of this exchange has taken place in relatively quiet years and voluntarily, one very important period has been marked by the experience and the consequence of forced emigration—when European artists, mainly but not exclusively Jews, had to leave Germany and later Austria, Czechoslovakia, Poland, and other countries under Nazi domination or occupation, and most of them, after shorter stays in European places of exile, arrived in the Americas, in Buenos Aires, in Mexico City, in New York, or in Los Angeles. Partly they could build up contacts through an already existing network.

From 1933 on, under the growing pressure of anti-Semitism in Nazi Germany, German Jews saw themselves confronted with the need to leave Germany—the country that had been their *Heimat* for centuries. One half of Germany's Jews, approximately 280,000 out of 500,000, emigrated to various destinations around the world, at first to neighboring countries (Czechoslovakia, France, the Netherlands, Great Britain), later to places as far away as Argentina, China, or Australia. The two major countries of immigration—each one of them a possible new *Heimat*—were the United States and Palestine, then under British administration. While the (cultural) history of these emigrants can be studied in the larger context of Jewish migrations from Eastern and Central Europe after 1880–1881, it is important to note that many of these German-Jewish emigrants, wherever they went, retained some aspects of their German identity and culture, their language, their love for books and education, for music and many other aspects of their former life, which they did not want to be taken away by the Nazis. What has initially been described as a failure—in Israel, to fulfil completely all Zionist requirements of equality and a break with Diaspora traditions; or in the United States, to assimilate completely with American culture—can now be regarded as quite a successful story of integration without complete assimilation.

Finding a job, mastering a new language, adjusting to the climate, thinking about Germany and the loss of friends and family—these were universal experiences made by German Jews all over the world. But in order to find out *how* they coped with these challenges and to learn which strategies they developed—including the one our protagonists chose: a return to Europe and, partly, even to Germany—we need to look at the individual experiences. While the cultural history of this migratory experience and the emerging transnational network of contact and communication has been partly written (see Krohn et al. 1998), creating an overview, a "map" of this global but very individual narrative will be hard, maybe even impossible. It might be more important to collect and study individual life stories—such as the one presented here.

Heinrich Blücher writes a wonderful letter in 1960 (which might never have been sent): "I try to imitate you. I try to use German as a literary language in such a way that it is determined by an inner Berliner diction." Gilbert's poems, Blücher says, have managed this challenge. The German language, he says, has been too complacent, even submissive, to the Nazi conquest. If there is resistance, if there is love and "real nourishment," it needs to be re-discovered in the language of the city.

> Ich schrieb Dir vor Jahren meinen Wunsch, mich philosophisch auf Berlinisch ausdruecken zu koennen. Das habe ich gemeint und versuche es. Obgleich ich mich bemuehe, die englische Sprache besser und reiner zu sprechen, glauben doch viele meiner besseren Studenten und ein paar mir nahestehende Kollegen, etwas Berlinisches, Pariserisches oder New Yorkerisches herauszuhoeren: eine Art Rhythmus einer anderen Realität, der sie manchmal fuehlen macht, sie seien nicht im Klassenzimmer, sondern auf der Strasse, bei dem Eckensteher. (Blücher 1960)[14]

I find it very difficult to translate this passage, and a discussion of this declaration of love to urban culture and the language of the street might lead us too far away from the topic of translation. Still, we can say that the (lost) arena of Berlin has been the foundation of something to which the newly acquired (but never completely inhabited) arena of New York, even under the circumstances of emigration and exile, has added another something. What this "something" might be—especially in the context of translation—seems quite hard to define. I can only advise the German speakers among the readers to have a look at Robert Gilbert's "Leierkastenodyssee," which, in Hannah Arendt's words, has given Berlin, and Berlin's "Mund- und Denkart"—vernacular *and* mind-set—a place in world

---

[14] "I wrote to you many years ago about my dream to be able to express myself philosophically in the Berlin dialect. I meant it and I am trying to achieve it. No matter how hard I try to speak English in a better and more perfect way, many of my best students and close colleagues believe to hear something Berlin-ish, Parisian, or New-York-ish: a rhythm of another reality transports them out of the classroom into a street full of loafers." (trans. J.S.)

poetry. While the vernacular faced problems in exile and partly got lost, the mind-set survived.

Det Jeschäft is' richtig—"that's a good deal," to offer something approaching a translation—was one of the key sentences in *Im weißen Rössel*, regularly uttered by one of its protagonists, fashion manufacturer Wilhelm Giesecke, the typical "Berliner" out of his place in Austria. And "det Jeschäft is' richtig" writes Gilbert in a letter from 21 January, 1962, to Blücher in New York: about *My Fair Lady* which runs successfully in Berlin, "no street girl ever had such a run." (Gilbert R. 1962) Here he indeed meets himself (or rather his former self), on a wobbly bridge, and they both have changed. Remaining in close touch with his friends who decided to stay in the United States, especially Hannah Arendt and Heinrich Blücher, he led a life of cultural in-between-ness and constant translation. The former arenas where his poetical and musical talent had developed, Berlin in those fruitful and dangerous years before 1933, Vienna as a first place of exile and later Paris and New York, have indeed provided him with the opportunity to acquire enough of the new language to be able to participate actively in the transfer of American post-war popular culture to Europe, and to contribute to the return of modern, avant-garde culture once driven out, together with him, from Germany.

Bibliography

Arendt, H. 1989. *Menschen in finsteren Zeiten*. München: Piper.
ARH Forum. 2012. Historiographic 'Turns' in Critical Perspective." *American Historical Review* 117, no. 3: xiii–xv.
Bachmann-Medick, D. 2012. *Cultural Turns: Neuorientierungen in den Kulturwissenschaften*. Reinbek bei Hamburg: Rowohlt.
Bhabha, H. 1995. *The Location of Culture*. London: Routledge.
Biale, D. 1994. "Confessions of an Historian of Jewish Culture." *Jewish Social Studies*, New Series 1, no. 1: 40–51.
Blücher, H. 1960 (29 September). "Letter to Robert Gilbert from 29 September 1960, Library of Congress, Manuscript Division."
    http://memory.loc.gov/mss/mharendt/01/010640/00033d.gif (accessed 10 May 2011).
Clarke, K. 2007. "Im Rausch der Genüsse: Erik Charell und die entfesselte Revueoperette im Berlin der 1920er Jahre." In *Glitter and Be Gay: Die authentische Operette und ihre schwulen Verehrer*, edited by Kevin Clarke, 108–139. Hamburg: Männerschwarm.
Dahlke, G.K., and Karl G., eds. 1988. *Deutsche Spielfilme von den Anfängen bis 1933: Ein Filmführer*. Berlin: Henschel Verlag.
Dahm, V. 1986. "Anfänge und Ideologie der Reichskulturkammer. Die 'Berufsgemeinschaft' als Instrument kulturpolitischer Steuerung und sozialer Reglementierung." *Vierteljahrshefte für Zeitgeschichte* 34, no. 1: 53–84.
Die Drei von der Tankstelle. 1930. dir. W. Thiele, Germany.

Der Kongreß tanzt. 1931. dir. E. Charell, Germany.

Genton, F. 2012. "'Ein Freund, ein guter Freund...' oder: Freundschaft in Krisenzeiten: Zur Geschichte eines Motivs in der Unterhaltungskultur Deutschlands, Frankreichs und Nordamerikas (1930–1938)." In *Lied und populäre Kultur: Jahrbuch des Deutschen Volksliedarchivs Freiburg*, edited by M. Fischer and F. Horner, 311–325. Münster and New York: Waxmann.

Gilbert, R. n.d. Bestand Robert Gilbert, Nr 117, Briefe von und an Friedrich Loewe. Archiv Darstellende Kunst, Akademie der Künste Berlin.

Gilbert, R. 1929. *Stempellied (Lied der Arbeitslosen)*, Erinnerungsort.de – Materialien zur Kulturgeschichte, http://erinnerungsort.de/lied/stempellied-lied-der-arbeitslosen/ (accessed August 5, 2013).

Gilbert, R. 1939 (19 August). Letter to Rudolf Weys, Nachlass Rudolf Weys, Rathausbibliothek Vienna.

Gilbert, R. 1951 (19 February). Letter to Franz Arnold, Archiv der Akademie der Künste Berlin (AdK), Robert-Gilbert-Archiv, Nr 117, Briefe an und von Franz Arnold.

Gilbert, R. 1951–1961. Über das Übersetzen. Manuscript, Archiv der AdK, Robert-Gilbert-Archiv, Arbeitsnotizen, lfd. Nr 243, Werkbücher 1951–1961.

Gilbert, R. 1959 (29 January). Letter to Heinrich Blücher. Library of Congress, Manuscript Division, http://memory.loc.gov/mss/mharendt/01/010640/00019d.gif (accessed May 10, 2011).

Gilbert, R. 1960 (29 September). Letter to Heinrich Blücher. Library of Congress, Manuscript Division, http://memory.loc.gov/mss/mharendt/01/010640/00033d.gif (accessed May 10, 2011).

Gilbert, R. 1962 (21 January). Letter to Heinrich Blücher. The Hannah Arendt Papers at the Library of Congress: Blücher, Heinrich—Correspondence—Gilbert, Robert—1961–1969 (Series: Family Papers, 1898–1975, n.d.), http://memory.loc.gov/cgi-bin/query/P?mharendt:2:./temp/~ammem_FhN7 (accessed March 15, 2010).

Gilbert, R. 1969 (05 July). Letter to Friedrich Torberg. Rathausbibliothek Vienna, Nachlass Friedrich Torberg.

Gilbert, R. 1972. "Leierkastenodyssee." In *Mich hat kein Esel im Galopp verloren: Gedichte aus Zeit und Unzeit. Mit einem Nachwort von Hannah Arendt*, edited by Robert Gilbert, 101–132. München: R. Piper & Co.

Gilbert, Finnegan M. 2007. *Das gab's nur einmal: Verloren zwischen New York und Berlin*. Zürich: Diogenes.

Grosch, N, and W. Jansen, eds. 2012. *Zwischen den Stühlen: Remigration und unterhaltendes Musiktheater in den 1950er Jahren*. Vol. 4, *Populäre Kultur und Musik*, 87–114. Münster: Waxmann.

Klösch, Ch., and R. Thumser. 2002. *From Vienna: Exilkabarett in New York 1938 bis 1950*. Wien: Picus Verlag.

Krohn, C.-D. et al. 1998. *Handbuch der deutschsprachigen Emigration 1933–1945*. Darmstadt: Wissenschaftliche Buchgesellschaft.

Leopoldi, H., and H. Möslein. 1992. *In einem kleinen Café in Hernals...* Wien: Verlag Orac.

Leopoldi, R., ed. 2011. *Leopoldiana: Gesammelte Werke von Hermann Leopoldi und 11 Lieder von Ferdinand Leopoldi in zwei Bänden*. Wien: Doblinger.

Loewe, F. 1958a (12 February). Letter to Robert Gilbert, Briefe von und an Friedrich Loewe, Akademie der Künste Berlin, Archiv Darstellende Kunst, Bestand Robert Gilbert, Nr. 117.

Loewe, F. 1958b (20 November). Letter to Robert Gilbert, Briefe von und an Friedrich Loewe, Akademie der Künste Berlin, Archiv Darstellende Kunst, Bestand Robert Gilbert, Nr. 117.

Logemann, J. 2013. *Migrants as 'Translators:' Mediating External Influences on Post World War II Western Europe, 1945–1973*, http://www.transatlanticperspectives.org/article.php?rec=32 (accessed November 1, 2013).

Pacher, M. 1979. "Der gespaltene Dichter." *et cetera* 10 (December): 3–12.

Peter, H., and K. Clarke. 2007. *Im weißen Rössl: Auf den Spuren eines Welterfolgs*. St. Wolfgang: Verlag Weisses Rössl GmbH.

Reichow, J. 1993. "Der Kongreß tanzt." In *Deutsche Spielfilme von den Anfängen bis 1933: Ein Filmführer*, edited by G. Dahlke and G. Karl, 270–272. Berlin: Henschel Verlag.

Roskies, D. 2004. "The Task of the Jewish Translator: A Valedictory Address." *Prooftexts* 24, no. 3: 263–272.

Schlör, J. 2012. "Leerstelle Berlin 1951: Robert Gilbert und die Folgen dieser heillosen Jahre." In *Zwischen den Stühlen: Remigration und unterhaltendes Musiktheater in den 1950er Jahren*. Vol. 4, *Populäre Kultur und Musik*, edited by N. Grosch and W. Jansen, 87–114. Münster: Waxmann.

Shestakov, T. 2003. "The History of the English-German Translation of the Musical Cabaret: Breaking the Stereotypes of Foreignisation and Domestication in Translation." *Orées* 4, no. 3: http://orees.concordia.ca/numero4/essai/shestakov.shtml (accessed February 15, 2014).

Soyer, D. 2001. *Jewish Immigrant Associations and American Identity in New York, 1880–1939*. Detroit: Wayne State University Press.

Spiel, H. 1994. *Glanz und Untergang: Wien 1866 bis 1938*. Munich: dtv.

Steiner, J. 2010. Call for Papers of the conference: "trans-lation, trans-nation, trans-formation", 16–18.6.2010, http://hsozkult.geschichte.hu-berlin.de/termine/id=14067 (accessed May 10, 2011).

Sznajder, N. 2008. *Gedächtnisraum Europa: Die Visionen des europäischen Kosmopolitismus. Eine jüdische Perspektive*. Bielefeld: Transcript Verlag.

Sznajder, N. 2011. *Jewish Memory and the Cosmopolitan Order*. Cambridge: Polity Press.

Tadday, U., ed. 2006. *Im weißen Rössl: Zwischen Kunst und Kommerz*. Vol. 133/134, *Musik-Konzepte*. München: Edition Text & Kritik.

Traska, G., and C. Lind. 2012. *Hermann Leopoldi, Hersch Kohn: Eine Biographie*. Wien: Mandelbaum Verlag.

Werner, M., and B. Zimmermann. 2006. "Beyond Comparison: Histoire Croisée and the Challenge of Reflexivity." *History and Theory* 45: 30–50.

Na'ama Sheffi
The Politics of Translation: The German-Hebrew Case

The fall from the Garden of Eden and the construction of the Tower of Babylon not only posed linguistic barriers, but also made translation an utterly unachievable task. "It is from this point on that translation will become an inevitable, but also impossible—that is, never perfectly achievable—condition of human existence," notes Samuel Weber (2005, 71). George Steiner (2004, 1) develops this idea further, maintaining that translation is a *condition humana*, or as he puts it: "Every language act is a translation." In translating the Bible from Latin into German, Martin Luther sought to break a fundamental barrier by allowing everyone to understand and interpret the text. At the same time, his work also instigated the modern conception of translation as means for the construction of social-national consolidation (Gilmont 2003, 213–37). With the expansion of literacy and the birth of bestsellers, translation became a tool for the distribution of belles-lettres and scientific writings. According to the classic definition introduced by Walter Benjamin ([1923] 2000, 75–83) almost a century ago, a good translation is dependent not only on the translatability of a word, but also on the possibility of finding a suitable replacement, and not necessarily an identical one, in the receiving language. Today, with the advent of Google Translate, a machine that is the realization of *Star Trek*'s "Universal Translator," Benjamin seems outdated; the fantasy has materialized and the conquest of the Tower of Babylon has been accomplished (Lezra, 2012). However, as approachable as foreign languages have become, the act of translation remains influenced by socio-political contexts.

This chapter will analyze the cultural forces that have shaped the selection of books translated from German into Hebrew. This endeavor began in the late eighteenth century with the translation of Moses Mendelssohn's *Phädon* in 1787, which was intended for a limited public of Hebrew readers, most of which were already familiar with the German original. The fact that Jewish intellectuals have invested such great financial resources and scholarly efforts in an apparently pointless endeavor, targeted at a very narrow audience that was perfectly capable of reading the German originals, is a paradox that calls for further explanation. The enterprise can be explained by two factors: the high esteem of German culture in the eyes of Jewish intellectuals who lived in the German *Kulturgebiet* or who were educated according to German standards; and the rise of Jewish national revival as an answer to growing European nationalism, particularly following the French Revolution. From the late eighteenth century until the early twenty-first century, more than two thousand books have been translated in a variety of genres. This project can be viewed as part of the revival of Hebrew as a modern, secular, and colloquial language. It also reflects modern German-Jewish relations, from the epoch of Jewish emancipation to its brutal demise under the Third Reich. Although we might expect that this translation project came to a halt during the National Socialist period, the publication of German writings in Hebrew, in fact, flourished during these years. This time, however, it was German Jews who, for the first time, constituted the majority among translated authors. In the following years, after World War II and the establishment of the state of Israel, the enterprise declined for a few decades, and then from the 1970s on, it gained a new momentum (Sheffi 2011; Sheffi 2015, 143–59).

In this chapter, I wish to probe phenomena related to the German-to-Hebrew translation project from its early days to the present. An analysis of this long and complex period can illuminate the process of transformation from the fruitful German-Jewish contact, as discussed by Peter Gay (1993, 93–168), to what Dan Diner defined as post-war "negative symbiosis." (1986, 9) First, I discuss the reasons behind the initial attempts to translate works aimed at an audience that was fluent in German. In the following sections of the essay, I go on to illuminate the dynamics behind the fluctuations, the changes of pattern in the selection of particular genres, and the targeted age groups. An important variable is also the presence of Jewish authors in the developing repertoire in different periods. Explaining this variance has special importance as it relates to the intensification of the translation project during the Nazi era and the following decline in translations after 1945.

The history of German-to-Hebrew translation enterprise could be divided into six periods:
- The initial years (1780–1880) focused on translating the classics, children's and youth literature, as well as books devoted to natural history and medicine;
- The expansion years (1881–1932) included, in order of importance, translations of prose, poetry, plays, and non-fiction, with children literature making up as much as one-third of all translations;
- The period of resistance to National Socialism (1933–1947) was characterized by an extraordinary investment in translating German-Jewish writings and works by authors who were considered anti-Nazi. This period had its beginning as early as the 1920s, and extends past 1945—both because of the political uncertainty in Germany and the persisting ideological emphasis on pre-state Israel;

- The transformation years (1948–1969), which marked the new Israeli statehood and the reexamination of the Hebrew-German cultural connections;
- The reestablishment of significant literary contacts (1970–1989), which stimulated the translation of a mixture of highbrow and lowbrow literature with an emphasis on themes related to the Nazi era;
- The years since the reunification of Germany in 1990, which seem to present a standard mixed repertoire with special attention to books for children and youth and novels that touch upon the fall of the Weimar Republic and the Nazi regime.

Throughout the years, the center of the Hebrew translation project fluctuated between different locations. Initially, it was based mostly in Eastern Europe, in the areas that comprise today's Lithuania, Ukraine, and Poland. Following the wave of pogroms in the Russian Empire at the turn of the twentieth century, which resulted in the deliberate destruction of Hebrew publishing houses, translation activity moved westward to Warsaw and to regions influenced by the German culture—Kraków, Lvov/Lemberg and Piotrków—and then to Berlin, and, to some degree, England and the United States. During the 1920s, Hebrew publishing relocated its center of activities to the *Yishuv* (the Jewish settlement in Palestine), but in part remained in Western Europe and the United States. With the establishment of the state of Israel, the Hebrew literary center settled in Israel permanently (Shavit 1994, 422–77).

Beginning in the late eighteenth century, and throughout the nineteenth century, only a handful of books were translated from German into Hebrew each year. Most of them fall into three major categories: classics, books for children and youth, and books on natural science. The classics comprised works by Johann Gottfried Herder, Heinrich von Kleist, Karl Gutzkow, Johann Wolfgang von Goethe, Friedrich Schiller, and Immanuel Kant. The selections for children and youth included stories and legends from Jewish history, and the discoveries and adventures of New World pioneers by Joachim Heinrich Campe. The translated works devoted to natural history and medicine included books by the physicians Christoph Girtanner and Christoph Wilhelm Hufeland, natural historian Harald Othmar Lenz, and the Jewish reformist and autodidact Aaron Bernstein. Interestingly, there was no practical demand for these translations because many of the potential readers lived either in the *deutsche Kulturgebiet* or in the East European regions, where Jews spoke German and attended German-language schools (Amburger 1984, 16–18).

It seems, therefore, that the objective of the German-to-Hebrew translation project was different—namely, that of nurturing the revival of Hebrew and its transformation from a language that had been limited almost entirely to religious rituals and writings, into a secular, spoken vernacular. According to Benjamin ([1923] 2000, 76), translation is situated in the present evolving mother tongue of the translator, while the original is inscribed in the language of a past culture. However, in the case of early translations into Hebrew, where the target language was not a mother tongue, but a revived, invented secular language, one must question what the process was and what it served. The necessity to create proper colloquial terms for words that had never existed in Hebrew has forced translators to either borrow biblical structures or to conjugate Latin or common verbs from other languages into Hebrew-sounding words (Fischler 1990, 6–35).

Thus, the project of translation from German into Hebrew played a role in the Jewish-Hebrew national awakening by helping to transform the ancient language into a modern one. The transfer of ideas from one language to another also facilitated the import of the post-1848 discourses of nationalism from Europe, especially the unifying German lands. Focusing on the particularities of this translation project can therefore help us understand better the complex process of nation-building (Hobsbawm 1992, 1–14).

In his distinction between national and natural languages, Samuel Weber (2005, 66) maintains that Portuguese, for instance, is more of a national language than English, French, German or Spanish, each serving several nations. Hebrew can be therefore construed as having a higher status as a language bounded, in many ways, by the borders of a single nation. Nitsa Ben-Ari (1999, 293) probes the translation process into Hebrew from a different angle. She argues that the unique development of Modern Hebrew, embraced by the Jewish Enlightenment (*Haskalah*), enabled a literary language on such a high level of sophistication, that it caused a belated advent of spoken language into the literature. This assertion is consistent with Lawrence Venuti's argument, that

> Nationalist translation agendas have often been initiated by cultural elites who aim to impose their linguistic and literary values on an entire population. The success of these agendas shows, however, that nationalisms cannot be viewed simply as forms of class dominance: translations must be accepted by a mass audience to be effective in constructing national languages, cultures, identities. (Venuti 2005, 178)

In other words, the success of Hebrew-speaking elite in promoting literary translations into Hebrew was only the first step in the long process of negotiating a true Israeli vernacular.

In the eyes of those Hebrew publishers, editors, and translators who have been brought up in the spirit of the German *Bildung*, the translated classics provided a model of cultural life. Educating the youth with stories based on Jewish history and novels that praised the pioneering spirit of the New World dovetailed into an emerging interest in Hebrew national identity, as well as its pioneering values. The translation of books in the field of natural sciences, in turn, opened up a path for Jewish intellectuals to gain acceptance in the society at large. Being barred from vocations associated with land ownership, Jews often pursued and excelled in knowledge-based occupations. Again, one must bear in mind that although these translations were technically not necessary because the originals were equally accessible to Jewish scholars, they did play a significant role in the creation of a Modern Hebrew scientific vocabulary.

After centuries in which the Hebrew language was confined to mostly liturgical usage (with the exception of Jewish poetry during the Jewish Golden Age in Spain), it was Moses Mendelssohn who paved the way for a change. His writings —*Phädon* (1787) and *Briefe* (1794)—were the first to be translated from German into Hebrew in the modern era. *Nathan der Weise* by his German intellectual counterpart, Gotthold Ephraim Lessing, was translated in 1856. Both scholars challenged the place of Jews in society in general and in the German-speaking world specifically. While Mendelssohn demanded that Jews choose a national affiliation—either German or Jewish, and avoid using the hybrid Yiddish language —Lessing called for a tolerant society that accepts all beliefs and ethnic identities. Thus, the discourse over the place of the Jewish nation had been interwoven into the translation project since its inception (Gay 1979, 108–9; Feiner 1995, 133–67; Wollgast 2004).

Mendelssohn's plea was rooted in the understanding that German, more than any other European language, was the *lingua franca* of the European Jewish settlements (Toury 1982, 77). What is more, German gained prominence in the wake of the *numerus clausus* policy in East European institutions of higher learning and the discriminating examinations imposed on Jews. As a result, Jewish youth became more motivated to become fluent in German in order to pursue their studies in German-speaking academic institutions instead. The return of these young German-educated Jewish intellectuals home contributed to the growing familiarity with German-language culture among the East European Jewish elite. Ever since the beginning of organized *Aliyah* (immigration of Jews to their homeland) and the rise of the Zionist movement in the late nineteenth century, the place of German as a Jewish *lingua franca* was secured. Indeed, it even featured, along with Hebrew, as the official language of the Zionist congresses.

The Jewish national revival influenced the project of German-to-Hebrew translation as well. The shift from theoretical discussions to active settlement in the ancient homeland intensified the debate regarding the strategy to be used: should the Jews revive their culture prior to inhabiting the land of their ancestors, or vice versa? How could they best legitimize their state—through diplomatic negotiation or *fait accompli* in the form of existing settlements? The solution that eventually emerged was synthetic Zionism that combined diplomacy with the policy of creating settlements. Although the Zionists disagreed on the use of specific strategies, they were unanimous on the question of the revival of Hebrew as a spoken, living language. This context explains the choices made by publishers and translators in this period. From 1881—the beginning of *Aliyah*—until the late 1920s, seven to eight books were translated from German to Hebrew every year; of these, one third were intended for children and youth. Tales by the Brothers Grimm were particularly popular. Another important section consisted of Jewish fables and legends by Meir Marcus Lehmann, along with Jewish historical stories by Phoebus Philippsohn and Ludwig Philippsohn (Ben-Ari 2006). While the latter set of authors could be related to promoting a Jewish national awareness, the inclusion of the German literary heritage represented by the Brothers Grimm might seem rather peculiar in this context. Yet it can also be argued that this translation strategy aimed to train young readers in speaking Hebrew, as it was expected that the next generation would conduct its daily life in the nation's ancestral language. The popularity of the Grimm Brothers and the lack of German children books by Jewish authors justified this choice.

The same rationale stood behind the concurrent expansion of the corpus for adult readers. From the 1880s on, translators often selected plays and non-fiction books. This shift is surprising. Hebrew-speaking theaters were not yet founded, and it is doubtful whether readers of Hebrew were also able to understand spoken language and dialogue. Furthermore, Jewish students conducted their studies at European, mostly German-language, universities. It is therefore clear that such translations did not respond to a practical demand. Rather, they anticipated the future as described by the utopian writings of early Zionism, which envisioned a Jewish state with a complete cultural infrastructure, comprising theaters and institutions for higher learning (Herzl [1902] 1921; Lewinsky 1892). The same period had also seen the publication of dictionaries, such as Mosche Schulbaum's (1904) *Hebrew-German/German-Hebrew Dictionary*, which originated from a project he had already launched in 1871, while translating *Die Räuber* by Friedrich Schiller into Hebrew (Waldman 1989, 226). The appearance of dictionaries further facilitated the process in which Hebrew was slowly assuming the role of a colloquial, spoken language.

Beginning in the 1930s and spanning the establishment of the state of Israel in 1948, a significant increase in German-to-Hebrew translations took place. Between seventeen and twenty translations were published annually, with peaks of thirty books per year. On the one hand, this growth can be attributed to the rising number of Hebrew readers, and on the other, to major political transformations— such as the gradual demographic and geographical expansion of the *Yishuv* and the diplomatic pressures for the establishment of a Jewish state. This last objective, which was part of the Zionist endeavor, became crucial as the anti-Semitic attacks in Europe intensified, reaching a peak with the rise of National Socialism in Germany.

During those years, Jewish writers constituted the majority of translated authors for the first time. As they became targets for National Socialist propaganda, with their works removed from public libraries and subject to public burning, most famously in the Opera (Bebel) Square in Berlin on May 10, 1933, the *Yishuv* publishers decided to rescue these endangered works by translating them. Works of Lion Feuchtwanger, Stefan Zweig, Franz Werfel, Jakob Wassermann and Vicky Baum were now, often hastily, being translated into Hebrew. Their standing in the literary world and the fact that their books became bestsellers in the original also played a role (Vogt-Praclick 1987, 63–64, 69, 85, 152–53). The recovery and preservation of the texts through acts of translation was communicated in the *Yishuv* society as an ideological gesture of anti-Nazi resistance, but it was a small comfort in an otherwise grim situation in which Zionist leaders had little influence on international affairs.

The attitude of Hebrew publishers toward non-Jewish German writers followed a simple rule: those among them who became—or who were embraced by—the Nazis fell out of favor. The 1912 Literature Nobel Prize laureate, Gerhart Hauptmann, had been the darling of the Hebrew publishing circle, and several of his plays and stories were included in anthologies or printed as separate volumes from the late nineteenth century until the early 1930s. Even as late as November 1932, a Hebrew newspaper critic praised the "depth and human sensitivity" of his works (Calvary 1932, 5). However, after having been embraced by the Nazi regime, Hauptmann lost this status (Ben-Chorin 1945, 59). Thomas Mann, the 1929 Nobel Prize Laureate, whose nationalistic views were well known, was another prominent example.

Mann's popularity in the *Yishuv* followed a complicated trajectory. Although he gave an anti-Nazi speech in the wake of the NSDAP electoral success in the late 1920s, his poignant speech on the fiftieth anniversary of Wagner's death in early 1933, right after the Nazis' rise to power, painted him once again in clearly nationalistic colors. His praise of Richard Wagner, and of the powerful tribal-national Siegfried motif (from *The Ring*), was likewise noted in the *Yishuv* press (Benjamin 1929, 1–2). In 1936, just before his German citizenship was revoked, a *Yishuv* magazine criticized Mann for letting himself be exploited as a façade, a fig leaf covering up the true nature of the Nazi regime (Alschech 1936a, 24; Alschech 1936b, 14). At the same time, Mann's open letter to the Swiss essayist and critic Eduard Korrodi, published in *Neue Zürcher Zeitung* on February 3, 1936, indicated his wish to identify with all exiled literary circles regardless of their nationality (German, Swiss, Austrian, and Czech) or faith. Mann also maintained that, despite living in exile, he had stuck to the spirit of Europeanism and Germanism (Carlsson and Michels 1986, 205–9). This brought one critic to conclude that "[a]fter 1933 Mann's political pendulum continued to swing to the left" (Ziolkowsky 1986, xviii). Indeed, already in July 31, 1933, in a letter to Hermann Hesse, Mann noted:

> Day after day the news from Germany, the deceit, the violence, the ridiculous show of "historical grandeur," the sheer cruelty, fill me with horror, contempt, and revulsion. I am no longer moved by the "blue-eyed enthusiasm" you speak of. (Carlsson and Michels 1986, 24)

Finally, the ban on Mann's publications in the Third Reich and his public anti-Nazi speeches turned him into a favorite of *Yishuv* intellectuals (Mann 1939, 9). To a society with meager resources and no political or military international influence, the literary realm offered a unique platform for political debates and some degree of symbolic leverage.

In various ways, Jewish-Hebrew intellectuals continued to be receptive to German culture and politics in the late 1920s and early 1930s. One such practice was the prompt translation of highly popular German authors addressing ethical issues, consistent with *Yishuv* ideals and political outlooks. Jakob Wassermann's *Der Fall Maurizius*, a study of the legal struggle against injustice, which shed light on the moral transformation of the early twentieth century German society, is a case in point. The book sold 25,000 copies within four weeks, and 112,000 before the fall of the Weimar Republic. This success was in part due to Wassermann's reputation in the German literary world: he was the editor of *Simplicissimus*, and socialized with renowned authors such as Thomas Mann, Rainer Maria Rilke, Arthur Schnitzler and Hugo von Hofmannsthal. Moreover, the publication of such sensitive material at a time of severe political unrest probably contributed to the widespread interest in his novel. The Hebrew translation appeared in 1933, just five years after its original publication, which indicates how much cultural debates in Germany resonated among the *Yishuv* intellectuals.

Another case in point was *Im Westen nichts Neues* by Erich Maria Remarque (published 1928), which sold 30,000 copies within a month (Vogt-Praclick 1987, 37, 49–53). Its first Hebrew translation, by Jakob Horowitz, was published just a year later, followed by Shraga Jemueli's (Pinchas Milakowski's) version in 1930. Critic Jacob Sandbank (1929, 14) extolled Remarque as an "outstandingly gifted poet" who impressively delivered the story of a whole generation. In his review of *Im Westen nichts Neues*, Sandbank notes that Remarque speaks of life during the war on the Franco-German front, with all its horrors, through the words of a serviceman, an anonymous soldier who speaks in the name of the tens of thousands of youngsters who went straight from school to the battlefield, to the front.

Sandbank, of course, commended the first translation of the novel. Yet despite his success, Remarque polarized his Hebrew-reading critics. David Marani (Spiegel) (1930, 113–14) offered an alternative reading of the book, when he wrote:

> In Germany, where rigid military tradition is still extremely pervasive, Remarque's book might induce in many young readers an excitement and enthusiasm for warfare and all of its powerful and compelling experiences.

This level of attentiveness to German cultural life and its political context continued despite the financial and technical obstacles that Hebrew publishers faced during World War II, such as shortages of paper and zinc printing plates. For example, Zweig's passionate autobiography, *Die Welt von Gestern*, was published in Hebrew only two years after its original publication, in 1944, at a time in which maritime transportation to Palestine was virtually paralyzed, making printing materials scarce.

It would be reasonable to expect that the revelations about the mass extermination of the Jews during the Holocaust that were reaching the *Yishuv*, the arrival of survivors, and the resulting rejection of the German language, would bring the translation project to a halt, or at least dramatically reduce the output of German-to-Hebrew translations. Such a trend would be consistent with Israel's effort to develop a comprehensive Zionist educational framework that addressed the challenges posed by the Holocaust and its aftermath (Zertal 2010; Arad-Ne'eman 2003, 5–26; Feldman 2010). Clearly, the country's needs and priorities lay elsewhere. Educating the tens of thousands of new immigrants in the young state claimed resources and energy. In the first decade of Israel's existence, the population more than tripled from 650,000 to over two million inhabitants. Native Hebrew-speaking authors responded to the demand for new, original literature (Weitz 1996, 179–91). And yet, despite all this, from 1948 to the present, more than 1,400 books have been translated from German into Hebrew, including reprints and new translations of previously translated books. Interestingly, the 1950s and the 1960s saw only a small portion of these translations, less than three hundred books, but the numbers have risen in the 1970s, in which another three hundred translations appeared.

The first two decades of statehood were formative for Israeli society and its culture. Suffering from a shortage of resources and struggling to maintain its fragile borders, Israel remained steeped in its earlier *Yishuv* culture. An initial examination of the translated corpus of the 1948–1967 period reveals a decline to an average of fourteen books per year. A number of factors may explain this development. A group of young native writers began to attract the attention of Israeli publishers (Shapira 2000, 622–34). At the same time, as the integration of new immigrants became an urgent priority, the newly established Ministry of Education directed publishers to meet specific curricular demands. It is also plausible that the heightened sensitivity to German culture and language drove publishers to reduce their involvement in German-to-Hebrew translations.

Most of the books translated from German into Hebrew in the first two decades of statehood consisted of reprints, new translations of old titles, books by Jewish authors, and texts by writers who were believed to be opponents of National Socialism. The complex cases of Thomas Mann and Erich Kästner, whose contacts with the Nazis were at the time still unknown, point to the fact that these assumptions were not always correct. Among the classics of the period were Goethe, Heinrich Heine, the Brothers Grimm, Heinrich von Kleist, and Hermann Hesse. The favorite German-language Jewish authors included Stefan Zweig, Arthur Schnitzler, Franz Kafka, Franz Werfel, Lion Feuchtwanger and Vicki Baum. A number of authors, such as Thomas Mann, Erich Maria Remarque, Erich Kästner, Bertolt Brecht, as well as Hitler's beloved Karl May, and other, lesser known writers were published either because of their political involvement against National Socialists or the popularity of their literary subjects.

The coming to power of National Socialists increased the attention of Jewish intellectuals in the *Yishuv* for the works of their brethren in Germany. But interest in translating books authored by Jews into Hebrew had characterized the German-to-Hebrew translation project since the times of Mendelssohn. During the time of the Third Reich, translators selected works out of a determination to salvage banned Jewish works. Following World War II, there were fewer Jewish authors writing in German. Post-Holocaust Germany—especially in the first decades—held little attraction for Jewish intellectuals. The cases of Jean Améry (Hans Chaim Mayer), who deserted German culture for the French one after the war, or Stefan Heym (Helmut Flieg), whose earlier work was, for ideological reasons, written in English, are illustrative of this trend. Thus translated authors included mostly writers who were active before the war.

Some of the translations of German-Jewish authors were commissioned because of the impact they exerted on the literary world. The numerous reprints of *Der Prozess* and *Die Verwandlung* by Kafka were related to the fact that these books were included on the Israeli high school curricula.[1] It is therefore difficult

---

[1] This information is based on elementary and secondary school curricula, collected in the Archive of Jewish Education in Israel and the Diaspora, Tel Aviv University.

to tell whether the translations of Kafka were inspired by Max Brod's efforts to save his writings from oblivion or whether Kafka attracted attention as a unique literary voice. The same is true for the later translation of Heym's *Ahasver, Der König David Bericht, Kreuzfahrer von heute*, and *Collin*; Heym's inclusion into the Hebrew canon was most probably related more to his critique of Germany and the high quality of his writing than to his Jewish origin alone.

After the Holocaust, when the majority of non-Israeli Jewish writers lived in the United States and not in the German-speaking countries, the interest of Israeli intellectuals in German culture also expanded to encompass non-Jewish writers.[2] The translations of Karl May and Erich Kästner from the 1950s and 1960s deserve closer attention in this respect. May's Wild West stories had already been translated during the *Yishuv* period, and many of them were reprinted or retranslated in the first two decades of statehood. Although May himself was neither a racist nor was he involved in politics, his continued popularity in Israel is peculiar in the light of Hitler's known predilection for his work (Von Feilitzsch 1993, 173–89; Ziegler 1999, 111–21). In a literary circle that rejected Hauptmann for the way he was embraced by the Nazi regime, the uncritical adoption of this author of children's literature does seem like a concession made for the sake of a diverse repertoire. It could also be the case that children's literature was deemed more harmless, unlike novels for adults that would be read by a more knowledgeable and critical audience.

The translations of Erich Kästner, who was politically engaged and critical of the Nazis, fit the paradigm better. Although Kästner cooperated in the production of the Nazi film *Der ewige Jude*, directed by Fritz Hippler to celebrate the twenty-fifth anniversary of German cinematography, this single event did not stain the author with the mark of a collaborator. Given that Kästner's diary of the war years was originally published in German only in 1961 and under an obscure title of *Notabene 45* (a second edition, titled *Das Blaue Buch*, was published in 2006), it is possible that this scandalous fact was known only to a narrow literary circle in Israel. A serious debate on Kästner's past took place in Israel only in the year 2000, when his children's classics were revived by a new Hebrew translation (Mank 1981; Melamed 2013). However, it may also well be that Kästner's literary accomplishments and popularity convinced publishers to turn a blind eye to his murky past.

---

[2] With the current mounting interest of young Israelis in German culture and the growing numbers of Israelis immigrating to Germany, this trend may be reversed. The Israeli expats and the Russian-Jewish community in Germany may spawn the next generation of German-Jewish authors (Wogenstein 2013, 106–8).

Numerous retranslation projects from the 1950s and 1960s attest to the enduring importance of German culture in the eyes of Jewish intellectuals. New versions of previously translated titles also reveal the development of the Hebrew language over the two centuries of its revival as a modern and secular language with a growing number of speakers. Some of the translations—commissioned both in the first two decades of statehood and today—illustrate Benjamin's idea of translation as an interpretation in the receiving language (Benjamin [1923] 2000; Mirski 1978, 306–11). Since Modern Hebrew was still only being developed, new translations were constantly needed to keep up with the rapid changes in the receiving language.

Significant examples are the frequent retranslations of Brecht's plays from German or from mediating languages. There were three translations of *Die Dreigroschenoper* and *Mutter Courage und ihre Kinder* respectively, and two translations of *Der Kaukasische Kreidekreis* and *Der unaufhaltsame Aufstieg des Arturo Ui*.[3] Likewise, Thomas Mann's *Buddenbrooks* was translated twice, and so was his *Der Tod in Venedig*.[4] The many retranslations not only meet the aesthetic and linguistic standards that Benjamin postulated, but are also good examples for the "fidelity" of the translator, who is expected to be "*faithful* to the source." (Steiner 2004, 8) In a society that had revived its ancient language and then established a state in its ancient homeland, the continuous evolution of the language is more than a philological phenomenon. It attests to the fact that the ossified language became alive; the many retranslations of this period are therefore evidence of the infiltration of spoken language into the literary scene, and indicate the embrace of the language by the growing Israeli population. Given this specific situation, the phenomenon of continuous retranslations becomes symptomatic of wider socio-political developments.

The 1970s marked another significant shift. Translations from German came to include two popular genres—romance novels and suspense books. The decade also saw an inundation of artistic titles by young and critical German authors: Max Frisch, whose renowned *Homo Faber* had been translated already in 1963, Siegfried Lenz, whose play *Die Zeit der Schuldlosen* had been translated as

---

[3] Translations of *Die Dreigroschenoper* were authored by Avraham Shlonsky (1955), Shimon Sandbank (1960), and Ehud Manor (stage adaptation, 1982). *Mutter Courage und ihre Kinder* appeared in the translation of Raphael Eliaz (1970), Shimon Sandbank (1982), and Anat Gov (stage adaptation, 2002). *Der Kaukasische Kreidekreis* was translated by Mordechai Tel-Tzur (1960), and Nathan Zach (1963, 1983) and *Der unaufhaltsame Aufstieg des Arturo Ui* by David Avidan (1980), and Avraham Oz (1998).

[4] *Buddenbrooks* was translated by Mordechai Temkin (1930), and Nili Mirski (1985). *Der Tod in Venedig* by Rina Lotan (1965), and Nili Mirski (1988).

early as 1962, only a year after its original production, as well as Heinrich Böll, Günter Grass, and Peter Weiss.

This polarization of the repertoire is perhaps the clearest indication of the political implications of the Israeli translation policy, which by now refrains from a downright rejection of Germany as the source of the extreme anti-Semitism that led to the worst catastrophe in Jewish history. Until the 1970s, the early statehood period saw mostly the renewed translations of German classics, the writings of German Jews, and a few works by Germans who were critical of their own society—be it the Third Reich or post-war West Germany. In the twenty to thirty years that followed World War II, Israeli publishers selected mostly books that they thought would be palatable to local readers. However, in the 1970s, this approach was changing to a more diversified selection of works for translation. The choice to translate popular literature suggests a certain normalization, both in the repertoire of the German literary canon, and of Israeli-German relations in general. The choice to translate works by significant critics of National Socialism and of West Germany reflects a political agenda that called for a renewal of cultural relations after the break forced by the Nazi racist laws and the Holocaust. What has already been achieved through diplomacy and reinforced by the first Israeli Prime Minister David Ben Gurion's pragmatic approach to what he conveniently termed "the other Germany"—the reparations agreement, and the establishment of full diplomatic relations—was now echoed in the literary repertoire. It is important to note that the diversification of the German-to-Hebrew translations took place at the time when musicians such as Richard Wagner, Richard Strauss, Carl Orff and Franz Lehar—all considered to be influential under the Nazi regime—were still banned in Israel (Sheffi 2013, 106–10).

By the 2010s, the German repertoire in Hebrew included eighteen titles by Böll, thirteen by Grass and Lenz respectively, and five titles by their ideological successor, Bernhard Schlink. The Israeli interest in these authors is triggered, to a large degree, by their willingness to cope with the dark German past and even to confess their personal complicity. The specific relationship between these authors and their readers attests to Levy and Sznaider's (2006, 13) thesis that Germans still view themselves as perpetrators while Israelis identify themselves as victims. I would suggest that the translation of Böll, Grass, Lenz and Schlink reflects the incorporation of the self-critical German narrative into the Israeli literary repertoire. In fact, Israeli literary critics were quick to point out the connection between socio-political events and the literary world. In 1975, one of them noted:

> When Eichmann was caught, a photo of him during a physician's examination in the prison cell was printed in the newspaper ... Psychologists noted that this kind of photo softens the monstrous image we wish to preserve in children's eyes ... I mention this in order to demonstrate the contradiction in *The Tin Drum* ... The reader's feelings toward the private character—Oskar the dwarf—are transferred to the symbolized—defective Germany—and vice versa. (Orian Ben-Herzl 1975, 33)

By emphasizing the idea of "softening the monstrous image," the critic suggests that Israelis made efforts to face their traumatic past. Moreover, she links this effort with the translation of an especially difficult story, suggesting that literature is one of the tools through which Israelis have been processing their collective past, as well as confronting the narrative of the German historical experience.

In 1999, when Schlink's first novel *Der Vorleser* was translated into Hebrew (four years after its original publication), the US-based Israeli historian Omer Bartov spoke of the contradiction between the decrease in the number of survivor testimonies and the growing interest in the Holocaust. He also pointed out that the focus on the sorrows of the novel's main protagonist, Michael, who identifies with the perpetrator, is a mirror image of Israelis' identification with Holocaust survivors, suggesting that identification may be determined by national affiliation no less than it is by universal moral values (Bartov 1999, 1; Bartov 2000, 29–40).

The latest development in the repertoire of German literature in Hebrew translation occurred at the turn of the twenty-first century, when children's literature started to comprise the bulk of the translations. Between 1991 and 2012, 225 out of 523 books translated from German (forty-three percent) were works for children and youth. In the last five years of this period, the ratio rose to sixty percent. Most of them were small-sized books for which royalties were low, and which rarely required extensive investments in graphic design.

Israeli publishers and editors name several interconnected reasons for the high proportion of translations for children and youth: a growing shortage in translators from German into Hebrew, the difficulty in finding a German repertoire compatible with the Hebrew readers' taste, and a relatively abundant and attractive supply of books for children and youth in German.[5] Importantly, the scarcity of German-to-Hebrew translators that is evident with regard to novels for adult readers does not apply to books for children and youth, as many inexperienced translators take their first steps in translating such short German texts.

---

[5] I wish to thank the editors and publishers who shared their knowledge and experience with me: Rachella Sandbank, Shimon Riklin, and Yaron Sadan.

This situation marks a generational change. The nineteenth century's translators lived in a German-speaking society, while conducting at least part of their private lives in Hebrew. Few translators meeting that demographic profile have continued to work in the twentieth century, and they were joined by younger translators who were native Hebrew speakers from German-speaking homes. In the last couple of decades another profile has emerged—that of scholars with an academic or personal interest in German.

Children's and youth literature comprised an important segment of German-Hebrew translations even at the turn of the twentieth century, when the Jewish youth in Palestine were expected to be the first generation to conduct their life in Hebrew. The abundance of German-to-Hebrew translations for children and youth at the turn of the twenty-first century may appear less obvious. It is perhaps motivated by the hope to provide the young generation with a rich literary repertoire as an alternative to cyberspace. Here, once again, the German-Hebrew cultural transfer addresses a certain demand in the Hebrew-speaking society. That is to say, in the case of children's and youth literature, the translation project reflects not only high esteem for the source culture, but also the needs of the target society.

Conclusion

The attitude of Hebrew readers to German-language literature, initially characterized by great interest and admiration, has always been contingent on the sociopolitical context. Translations from German have had a unique status because they related to the most traumatic chapter of Jewish history. Assuming the validity of Levy and Sznaider's (2006) thesis about the internalization of the perpetrator and victim status by Germans and Israelis respectively, it seems that the attitude of Hebrew readers towards German writers is likely to remain tense for years to come.

A singular case of translation from German into Hebrew in the early twenty-first century is Hans Fallada's *Jeder stirbt für sich allein*, originally published in 1947. The story explores the underground activity of a Berlin couple whose son fell on the French front during World War II. Via postcards they spread around the capital city, they call for civil disobedience. Translated into Hebrew following the success of its renewed translation into English and American English, it sold 120,000 copies in Israel within eighteen months, in part due to intensive marketing and special sales. In a population of eight million, one third of whom are native Russian- or Arabic-speakers—not to mention the ultra-Orthodox readership that constitutes circa ten percent of the population and is mostly interested in religious writings—it was a remarkable marketing achievement. It seems that despite the many years that have passed since World War II, Israelis are still fascinated by the troubled history of Germans and Jews.

This lasting fascination and mutual curiosity is reflected also in contemporary Hebrew literature. Nathan Shaham's (born 1925) latest novel *Dormant Account* (2013) tells the complex story of an Israeli publisher who continues the task of his own grandfather, a German-to-Hebrew translator. The trans-generational story reveals moral tensions and recurring dilemmas. In the novel, Shaham addresses such questions as cultural boycott and social reconciliation, suggesting that both of these strategies are actually driven by the same fundamental sense of indignation, and an eternal moral debt that the Germans, according to the Jews, will never be able to repay. Both also function as power mechanisms. The book also touches upon the theme of younger Germans who may refuse to continue to pay the price for their forefathers' sins.

As I have been trying to show, the attitude of Jewish, and later Israeli, intellectuals towards the German literary canon and its translation has shifted considerably over time. In its early days, it reflected high esteem, even admiration for German literature. Translation from German into Hebrew had the initial aim of expanding the predominantly liturgical, ossified language, shaping it into a modern and secular one, as well as providing Hebrew speakers with a universal education. Jewish intellectuals of the nineteenth century, who had served the Zionist endeavor in Central Europe and took part in the translation project in the early years of Israeli statehood, considered German literature as a necessary part of *Bildung* and a valid alternative to traditional Jewish education (Volkov 2001, 165–83). They were also the last generation who, even if they came from Eastern Europe, were still socialized in the tradition of the *Deutsche Kulturgebiet*. In the 1930s, this admiration gave way to political criticism. The public book burnings in German town squares impelled publishers and translators to try and salvage those banned works by giving them a Hebrew version. Thus the repertoire in the first two decades of statehood had been limited to works by authors who could be accepted by the Israeli public—the classics, and works by German-Jews and Germans opposing the National Socialist regime. While the 1970s saw the inclusion of popular literature into the translation repertoire, a further shift in the 1990s brought children's and youth titles back to the fore of German-to-Hebrew translations.

Throughout the years, German literature has occupied a central position in the eyes of Jewish and Israeli intellectuals. It has been admired passionately and criticized with the same zeal; embraced with appreciation and rejected with indignation. Hebrew-German relations have never been a merely intellectual matter, but a deeply emotional one as well.

Bibliography

Alschech, (Yaacov Cahan). 1936. "Thomas Mann's Clarification," (in Hebrew). *Hapoel Hatzair:* February 28, 1936, 14.
Alschech, (Yaacov Cahan). 1936. "Thomas Mann's Citizenship was Annulled As Well," (in Hebrew). *Hapoel Hatzair:* December 24, 1936, 24.
Amburger, Erik. 1984. "Die deutschen Schulen in Russland mit besonderer Berücksichtigung St. Petersburgs." *Studien zum Deutschtum im Osten [Deutscher Einfluss auf Bildung und Wissenschaft im Östlichen Europa]* 18: 1–26.
Arad-Ne'eman, Gulie. 2003. "Israel and the Shoah: A Tale of Multifarious Taboo." *New German Critique* 90: 5–26.
Bartov, Omer. 1999. "Germany as Victim," (in Hebrew). *Haaretz* Literary Supplement: April 28, 1999, 1.
Bartov, Omer. 2000. "Germany as Victim." *New German Critique* 80: 29–40.
Ben-Ari, Nitsa. 2006. *Romanze mit der Vergangenheit: Der deutsch-jüdische historische Roman des 19. Jahrhunderts und seine Bedeutung für die Entstehung einer jüdischen Nationalliteratur*, translated by Dafna Mach. Tübingen: Max Niemeyer Verlag.
Ben-Chorin, Shalom. 1945. "Literature and Art in the World: Thomas Mann," (in Hebrew). *Gasit* 8 (2–3): 59.
Benjamin, Walter. [1923] 2000. "The Task of the Translator." In *The Translation Reader*, edited by Lawrence Venuti, 75–83. London and New York: Routledge.
Brod, Max. 1942. "The Death of Stefan Zweig," (in Hebrew). *Hapoel Hatzair:* March 4, 1942, 5.
Calvary, Moshe. 1932. "Gerhard Hauptmann: On his Seventieth Birthday," (in Hebrew). *Moznayim* 23: 5.
Carlsson, Anni, and Volker Michels. 1986. *The Hesse/Mann Letters: The Correspondence of Hermann Hesse and Thomas Mann, 1910–1955*, translated by Wolfgang Sauerlander. London: Arena.
Diner, Dan. 1986. "Deutsche und Juden nach Auschwitz: Negative Symbiose." *Babylon* 1: 9–20.
Feilitzsch, Heribert von. 1993. "Karl May: The *Wild West* as Seen in Germany." *Journal of Popular Culture* 27, no. 3: 173–189.
Feiner, Shmuel. 1995. "Mendelssohn and Mendelssohn's Disciples: A Reexamination." *Leo Baeck Institute Yearbook* 40: 133–167.
Feldman, Jackie. [2008] 2010. *Between the Death Pits and the Flag: Youth Voyages to Holocaust Poland and the Performance of Israeli National Identity*. New York and Oxford: Berghahn Books.
Fischler, Bracha. 1990. "The Trajectories of Names: On the Development of the Terminology of Bird Names (1866–1972)," (in Hebrew). *Language & Hebrew* 4: 6–35.
Gay, Peter. 1979. *Freud, Jews and Other Germans*. Oxford: Oxford University Press.
Gilmont, Jean-Francois. 2003. "Protestant Reformation and Reading." In *A History of Reading in the West*, edited by Guglielmo Cavallo and Roger Chartier, 213–237. Cambridge: Polity Press.
Herzl, Theodor. [1902] 1921. *Altneuland: Roman*. Berlin: B. Harz.

Hobsbawm, Eric. 1992. "Introduction: Inventing Traditions." In *The Invention of Tradition*, edited by Eric Hobsbawm and Terence Ranger, 1–14. Cambridge: Cambridge University Press.

Jakobson, Roman. [1959] 2000. "On Linguistic Aspects of Translation." In *The Translation Studies Reader*, edited by Lawrence Venuti, 113–118. London and New York: Routledge.

Levy, Daniel, and Natan Sznaider. 2006. *The Holocaust and Memory in the Global Age*. Philadelphia: Temple University Press.

Lewinsky, Elchanan Leib. 1892. *A Journey to Eretz-Israel in the Year 2040*, (in Hebrew). Odessa: Hatechiya.

Lezra, Jacque. 2012. "Translation." *Political Concepts: A Critical Lexicon*. http://www.politicalconcepts.org/translation-jacques-lezra/ (accessed April 10, 2013).

Mank, Dieter. 1981. *Erich Kästner im nationalsozialistischen Deutschland: 1933–1945: Zeit ohne Werk?* Frankfurt am Main: Verlag Peter Lang.

Mann, Thomas. 1939. "The Urgency of Politics," (in Hebrew). *Hapoel Hatzair*: September 13, 1939, 9.

Marani (Spiegel), David. 1930. "The War in the German Novel," (in Hebrew). *Achdut*: July 1930, 113–114.

Melamed, Ariana. 2000. "The Bad Years of Erich Kästner," (in Hebrew). http://www.ynet.co.il/articles/1,7340,L-32059,00.html (accessed July 23, 2013).

Mirski, Nili. 1978. "The Third Territory: Unacademic Reflections on the Problems of Literary Translation," (in Hebrew). *Siman Kria* 8: 306–311.

Orian Ben-Herzl, Yehudith. 1975. "The German Tin Drum," (in Hebrew). *Maariv*: September 12, 1975, 33.

Rabbi Benjamin (Joshua Radler-Feldmann). 1972/73. "Thomas Mann—Where Did He Come From?" (in Hebrew). *Moznayim* 36: 1–2.

Sandbank, Jakob. 1929. "The Cry of a Generation," (in Hebrew). *Hapoel Hatzair*: April 5, 1929, 14.

Schulbaum, Mosche. 1904. *Neues, vollständiges deutsch-hebräisches Handwörterbuch*. Lemberg: H. Schlag.

Shapira, Anita. 2000. "From the Palmach Generation to the Candle Children: Changing Patterns in Israeli Identity." *Partisan Review* 67: 622–634.

Shavit, Zohar. 1994. "The Rise and Fall of the Hebrew Literary Centers 1918–1933," (in Hebrew). *Iyunim Bitkumat Israel* 4: 422–477.

Sheffi, Na'ama. 2011. *Vom Deutschen ins Hebräische: Übersetzungen aus dem Deutschen im jüdischen Palästina 1882–1948*. Göttingen: Vandenhoeck and Ruprecht.

Sheffi, Na'ama. 2013. *The Ring of Myths: The Israelis, Wagner and the Nazis*. Brighton, Chicago and Toronto: Sussex Academic Press.

Sheffi, Na'ama. 2015. "Aus dem Deutschen ins Hebräische: Übersetzungsgeschichte als politische Kulturgeschichte." In *Sprache, Erkenntnis und Bedeutung—Deutsch in der jüdischen Wissenskultur*, edited by Arndt Engelhardt and Susanne Zepp, 143–159. Leipzig: Leipziger Universitätsverlag.

Steiner, Gorge. 2004. "Anthropological Foundation, Cultural Contexts and Forms of Translation." In *Übersetzung / Translation / Traduction*, edited by Harald Kittel, Armin Paul Frank, Norbert Greiner, Theo Hermans, Werner Koller, José Lambert, and Fritz Paul, vol. 1, 1–10. Berlin: Walter de Gruyter.

Toury, Jacob. 1982. "Die Sprache als Problem der jüdischen Einordnung im deutschen Kulturraum." *Jahrbuch des Instituts für deutsche Geschichte* 4: 75–96.
Venuti, Lawrence. 2005. "Local Contingencies: Translation and National Identities." In *Nation, Language, and Ethics of Translation*, edited by Sandra Bermann and Michael Wood, 177–202. Princeton and Oxford: Princeton University Press.
Vogt-Praclick, Kornelia. 1987. *Bestseller in der Weimarer Republik, 1925–1930*. Herzberg: Traugott Bautz.
Volkov, Shulamit. 2001. "Die Ambivalenz der Bildung. Juden im deutschen Kulturbereich." In *Das jüdische Projekt der Moderne*, edited by Shulamit Volkov, 165–183. München: Verlag C. H. Beck.
Waldman, Nahum M. 1989. *The Recent Study of Hebrew: A Survey of the Literature with Selected Bibliography*. Cincinnati, OH: Hebrew Union College-Jewish Institute of Religion.
Weber, Samuel. 2005. "A Touch of Translation: On Walter Benjamin's *Task of the Translator*." In *Nation, Language, and Ethics of Translation*, edited by Sandra Bermann and Michael Wood, 65–78. Princeton and Oxford: Princeton University Press.
Weitz, Yechiam. 1996. "The Debate Concerning the Role of Culture in the State's First Years." *The Journal of Israeli History* 17, no. 2: 179–191.
Wogenstein, Sebastian. 2013. "Israel, Germany and Austria in Contemporary Germanophone Literature." *Prooftext* 33, no. 1: 105–132.
Wollgast, Siegfried. 2004. *Moses Mendelssohn und die Toleranz zu seiner Zeit*. Dessau: Moses Mendelssohn Gesellschaft.
Zertal, Idit. 2010. *Israelis' Holocaust and the Politics of Nationhood*. Cambridge: Cambridge University Press.
Ziegler, Harry. 1999. "History and Popular Fiction: Two Worlds Collide. A Reply to Feilitzsch's Article on Karl May." *Journal of Popular Culture* 33, no. 2: 111–121.
Ziolkowsky, Theodor. 1986. "Introduction." In *The Hesse/Mann Letters: The Correspondence of Hermann Hesse and Thomas Mann, 1910–1955*, edited by Anni Carlsson and Volker Michels, translated by Wolfgang Sauerlander, xvii–xviii. London: Arena.

Mahmoud Kayyal
Hegemony and Ideology in the Translations between Arabic and Hebrew Literatures in Modern Times

Foreword

Questions about the relationships between hegemony, ideology, and translation arise repeatedly and from a range of perspectives in Translation Studies. Scholars representing the cultural-historical perspective believe that extra-literary influences affect translation. Therefore, it is possible to say that the production of translations is part of the "vagaries and vicissitudes of the exercise of power in a society." (Bassnett and Lefevere 1990, 5) Postcolonial scholars reject the traditional view of translation as an approach to understanding the Other. Rather, they perceive translation to be first and foremost a matter of aggressive contact, whereby the translated texts function to enforce hegemonic cultural values on dominated peoples and to conceal colonial violence (Calzada-Pérez 2003, 4–5). Other functionally-orientated scholars have agreed that all translations are ideological. Hence, in their view, social agents' interests, goals, and objectives determine the choice of the source text and the purpose at which it is aimed (Schäffner 2003, 23).

1 Arabic-Hebrew-Arabic Translations

The broad issue of modern intercultural contacts between the Arabic and the Hebrew cultures cannot be detached from the political conflict that exists in the Middle East and ideological discourses that accompany it. Therefore, the current study argues that a relationship of coercion exists between the two cultures, stemming, on the one hand, from the Arab view of Hebrew culture as a part of the Western neo-colonial culture and, on the other, from the majority-minority relations between Jews and Arabs in Israel.

These political and ideological sensitivities evolved into conflicting interests and perspectives on the issue of Arabic-Hebrew and Hebrew-Arabic translation. Some view these translations as important tools in deepening their knowledge and familiarity with the hostile Other's culture. Other circles contend that translations can promote understanding and coexistence between Arabs and Israeli

Jews. Some still argue that translated texts could provide an alternative narrative to present to the Other's readership.

Therefore, the translations in question, conducted in the shadow of political, ideological and nationalist tensions between the two cultures, were dominated by political and ideological considerations. Actually, those involved in translation were obliged to follow specific ideological guidelines as to the selection of works to be translated, the translation policy, the dissemination of the translations, and their reception. In fact, we can distinguish between the following three ideologies that dominated the development of this translation activity and dictated various translation paradigms:

A. The Zionist ideology led to three central approaches to translation: the romantic-Zionist model in Hebrew-Arabic translations, which was designed to promote the love of the Land of Israel, the revival of the Hebrew language, and the consolidation of Jewish national consciousness; the Orientalist paradigm in Arabic-Hebrew translations, which aimed to help recognize and understand the hostility of the Arab world while assuming a patronizing attitude towards Arabic culture; the Israeli establishmentarian mode in Hebrew-Arabic translations, which promoted identification with the national collective, the pioneering ideal, the symbols and values of the young state, and most of the Zionist premises.

B. The anti-Zionist ideology spurred two main translation paradigms: the postcolonial orientation in Hebrew-Arabic translations in the Arab world, which accompanied the intensifying process of "cultural de-colonization," especially after the defeat of 1967; and the postcolonial approach in Arabic-Hebrew translations in Israel, which attributed great importance to undermining the Zionist narrative and to presenting an alternative Palestinian-Arab one.

C. The hybrid ideology evolved into two dominant methods of translation: the Israeli-Arab approach to Hebrew-Arabic translations, which resulted in translations that maintained and strengthened the cultural hegemony of the majority; and the Arab-Jewish paradigm in Arabic-Hebrew translations, which was mindful of the original cultural identity of the Sephardic Jewish translators but was simultaneously influenced by the Zionist narrative, especially in matters relating to the Arab-Israeli conflict.

2 The Zionist Ideology

With the rise in power of the Zionist movement, which encouraged Jews around the world to immigrate to the Holy Land, great political tension emerged between Jews and Arabs in the Arab world, especially in Mandatory Palestine. Gradually, Zionist ideologies became central to intercultural dialogue by promoting particular strategies of translation between Hebrew and Arabic.

The establishment of the State of Israel, which constituted the fulfillment of the Zionist vision, marked the strengthening of the Zionist ideology and the translation practices that accompanied it. Out of a drive to suppress the national aspirations of the Palestinians remaining within the borders of the country and sever the Arab-Jews from their cultural heritage, the Israeli state adopted a translation policy that suited its needs.

2.1 The Romantic-Zionist Paradigm in Hebrew-Arabic Translations

Alongside the growth of Zionist activity and the accelerated revival of the Hebrew language in the late nineteenth and early twentieth centuries emerged a desire among Jewish intellectuals to translate secular Zionist texts. Hence, Jewish translators like Nissīm Mallūl (1892–1959), who supported the Zionist activities, joined forces with authors and publishers to translate works and texts that openly promoted Zionist interests.

The romantic Zionist approach to translation that characterized the period between the end of the nineteenth century and 1948 attempted to promote a love of the Land of Israel, the revival of the Hebrew language, and the consolidation of Jewish national consciousness. An outstanding translator who championed this paradigm was Salīm al-Dāwūdī (1870–1952), whose personal perceptions, public activity, and translation policy emphasized his commitment to this cause.[1]

al-Dāwūdī understood his translation of the Hebrew novel *Ahavat Tzion* (Love of Zion) (1853) by Abraham Mapu (1808–1867) as an important step in elevating the status of the Hebrew language. This translation, in his view, demonstrated to the Jewish people—especially the younger generation—that Hebrew

---

[1] Salīm al-Dāwūdī was born in Safed, Palestine, in 1870. He was the son of Rabbi Makhlūf al-Dāwūdī, who was appointed *Ḥakham Bashi* (Chief Rabbi) of the community of Akko and its surroundings, and later of Haifa. Salīm learned Torah from his father and Sephardic scholars in Safed and Arabic language and literature at the school of Rabbi Zaki Cohen in Beirut. He worked as a teacher in the *Alliance Israélite Universelle* schools in Tiberias and Jerusalem, after which he became a teacher in Egypt. In Cairo, he served as Secretary of the Rabbinical Court. Afterwards, he returned to Israel and taught in the general education network of schools (See Tidhar 1947, 123–24, 207; Ben-Dor 1981).

was a living language of literary prose, and Hebrew literature had the status of any other foreign writing translated into Arabic (Ben-Dor 1981, 26). His translated novel *Maḥabat Ṣihyūn* appeared in Cairo in two editions (in 1899 and 1921–22). Notably, the translator's veneration of the original text, whose poetic and biblical language he regarded as a masterpiece, inspired him to use elegant language in the target literature, as well as to provide a translation that would faithfully reflect the spirit and content of the original text. This context explains his inclination to preserve the Jewish aspects of the work (Kayyal 2008, 72–73).

2.2 The Orientalist Paradigm in Arabic-Hebrew Translations

Following the establishment of the State of Israel, Zionist Orientalists, who were active since the late nineteenth century, devoted special attention to translating Arabic literary works into Hebrew. In their view, the need for these translations did not stem from the literary quality of the original works, but rather from the capacity of these works to reflect the cultural and social reality in the region. In other words, they were to serve as important learning materials about their Arab surroundings. Hannah Amit-Kochavi notes that the translation of these works was founded on academic knowledge. Outstanding texts were translated verbatim and supplied with footnotes, while experts in Arab language and literature wrote reviews on them (Amit-Kochavi 1999, 35–36). Among the renowned Orientalists to be noted are Menahem Kapeliuk (1900–1988) and Joseph Joel Rivlin (1889–1971), who translated the Qur'an and *Arabian Nights*.

Kapeliuk was one of the Zionist Orientalists who selected noteworthy Arabic texts to be translated into Hebrew.[2] His ideological proximity to the Zionist movement fueled his determination to become acquainted with the Arab milieu.[3] However, Kapeliuk's arrogant Orientalist approach to Arabic culture and literature marred his translation efforts. He considered translation as an act of broad-

---

[2] These translations include works such as the autobiographical novel *al-Ayyām* (The Days, 1929; in Hebrew: *Yamim*, 1932) by Ṭaha Ḥusayn (1889 1973); the famous novel *Yawmiyyāt Nā'ib fī al-Ariyāf* (Diary of a Village Prosecutor, 1937; in Hebrew: *Yomanu shel Toveʿ be-Kfari Metzraiym*, 1945) by Tawfīq al-Ḥakīm (1898–1987); and the famous novel *al-Liṣṣ wal-Kilāb* (The Thief and the Dogs, 1961; in Hebrew: *ha-Gannav ve-ha-Klavim*, 1970) by Najīb Maḥfūẓ (1911–2006).
[3] Kapeliuk was born in Russia in 1900. He received a traditional education at the Hebrew school founded by the local Zionists and was a member of the Zionist pioneering movement "he-Ḥalutz." He immigrated to Palestine in 1922 and proceeded to study Arabic and Islam at the Hebrew University of Jerusalem. In 1927, he began to write for the local newspapers, in particular for *Davar*, where he was responsible for the Arab section (Tidhar, 1961, 3812–13).

ening the Hebrew reader's knowledge of Arab society. Hence, he selected works that would expand such knowledge while marginalizing their literary worth, even in the case of works of literature considered masterpieces in their source culture. Indeed, it is doubtful whether Kapeliuk's main purpose was to enrich the target reader's literature with Arabic masterpieces. His translations were literal, and he added many footnotes, especially to the sections that could contribute to expanding knowledge about Arab society. He also ignored the artistic and stylistic uniqueness of the translated works subverting them in compliance with the linguistic and stylistic norms that he patronizingly considered to be superior. In this way, his literary translations do not differ from translations of theoretical texts dealing with Arab society.

In his translation of *The Days* by Ṭaha Ḥusayn, for example, Kapeliuk decided that this autobiographical work should be narrated in the first person and not the third person, as the author did. In making this change, he intervened substantially with the style and uniqueness of this work—a work whose outstanding feature is the imagination aroused by the use of the third person in an autobiographical story (Allen 1982, 36). It is no wonder, then, that Arab intellectuals consider the Hebrew translations carried out by Arabists and Orientalists affiliated with the Israeli authorities not only to have contributed to the critical reception of Arab literature in the Hebrew culture but also, paradoxically, to have caused considerable distortion to the image of Arabic literature in the eyes of the Hebrew reader (Khīr 1993, 4–5).

2.3 The Israeli Establishmentarian Paradigm in Hebrew-Arabic Translations

In the early years following Israel's founding and in an attempt to promote several fundamental ideological principles central to the new state, the establishment tried to control both the Arabic and the Hebrew cultures and the contacts between them. An examination of the translations made in the establishment context, especially during the period 1948–1967, shows that Israeli officials hoped to present the Arab reader with a translated text that would correspond to the ideological expectations of the Israeli-Zionist mainstream. Despite the crisis in the value system related to the Zionist principles that struck Israeli society in the 1950s, Zionist establishment ideology continued to exert a strong influence over the Jewish community in Palestine and post-state Israeli society (Eisenstadt 1973, 327; Adler and Kahana 1975, 188). Two basic concepts characterized this approach to translation:

1. The demand to "identify with the national collective, with the pioneering ideal and with most of the Zionist conventions" (Weissbrod 1989, 43) was reflected in the tendency to idealize the Zionist society and enterprise.
2. The belief that the state is a melting pot of cultures and ethnic identities within it, so as to emphasize the common and unifying elements rather than the different and divisive ones.

The works selected for translation reflected the establishment's ideological mindset, and many translators, among them Eliyahu Aggasi (1909–1991), Meir Ḥaddād (1914–1983), Tuvia Shamosh (1914–1982), Zakkay Aharon (b. 1927), and others, were at the same time key national activists. Moreover, their translation corpus also often included commentary that directly expressed the viewpoints of members of the establishment. Most of these translations were published in the establishment newspapers like *al-Yawm* (the day) and by the establishment publisher *Dār al-Nashr al-'Arabī*.[4]

One such prominent establishmentarian translator was 'Ezra Ḥaddād (1900–1972).[5] Ḥaddād, who immigrated to Israel in 1951, immediately joined in the political and cultural activities of the ruling party. In his translation activity, he not only chose works in tune with the establishmentarian ideology, but also adopted strategies that sharpened their message in the target language. Therefore, he attempted in his work as a translator to idealize Israeli society and to emphasize its shared and unifying values. He also made efforts to conserve in translation the cultural specificity of the Zionist-Israeli way of life. He attributed great importance to the assimilation of the unique fundamentals of Israeli social and political life in order to provide a response to the Arab Palestinian narrative and to strengthen the creation of a national identity.

In his translation of the Hebrew novel *Neftuli Adam* (*Human Meanders*, 1929; in Arabic: *Ṣirā' Insān*, 1955) by the establishmentarian author Yehuda Burla,

---

4 This publisher circulated, for example, all the anthologies of stories translated from Hebrew into Arabic in the 1960s: *'Aīn al-Riḍā* (Fully Satisfied) by Yehuda Burla (1887–1969) (1965); *Ṣabāḥ Nahār Jadīd wa-Qiṣaṣ 'Ukhrā* (Morning of a New Day and other Stories) by various authors (1966); *Yamīn al-Ikhlāṣ* (Oath of Allegiance) by Shmuel Yosef Agnon (1887–1970) (1968).

5 'Ezra Ḥaddād, author, scholar, and translator, was a renowned public figure in Iraq. Born in Baghdad in 1900 into a traditional family, he worked as a teacher and school principal. Like many educated Jews in Iraq, he was bi-lingual, able to express himself in both Hebrew and Arabic alike. From 1924, he began publishing articles in two Jewish-owned Arabic journals *al-Miṣbāḥ* (The Lamp) (1924–1929) and *al-Ḥāṣid* (The Reaper) (1929–1938). He also wrote didactic books in Hebrew for the Iraqi Jewish community. After immigrating to Israel, he continued devoting much of his time to the history of Babylonian Jewry and its folklore (Ḥaddād 1973, 20–21).

Ḥaddād added, for example, a sentence that has no parallel in the Hebrew text: *Min a'māl bāhira fī arḍ al-Ābā' wal-ajdād* (of the magnificent work in the land of our fathers and ancestors) (Burla 1929, 12; Burla 1955, 107–8). This addition was probably ideologically motivated, aiming to enhance the Zionist pioneering enterprise while emphasizing the historical connection between Jews and the Land of Israel.

3 The anti-Zionist Ideology

As is typical in violent national conflicts, an antagonistic polemic discourse tinged with stereotypes and prejudice overtook the Arab world regarding all matters concerning the Israeli Other. Israel and its culture were often presented as part of a neo-colonial incursion, foreign to the region and framed as a new Crusader-like entity. Many Arabs denied the existence of a Hebrew language, literature, and culture, justifying this view by arguing that Judaism is a religion and not a nation and that the Jews are a mélange of people with nothing much in common (Ḥijāzī, 1995).

Lack of knowledge about Jewish culture occasionally also led Arabs to rely on stereotypes that prevailed in Europe, including those that surface in anti-Semitic literature. Hence, a tendency emerged in Arabic writing—particularly in popular literature—to stereotype and demonize the Israeli-Zionist-Jew (Somekh 1996, 240–41). Arab scholars did not challenge this cliché because, in their opinion, Arabic literature largely ignored the Jewish character or treated it more humanely (or at least no worse) than Western European literature did. Hence, some argued that these negative depictions were, in fact, based on the psychology and personality of the Jew (Idrīs 1993, 113–26, 184–85).

At the same time, it is important to note that the establishment of the State of Israel symbolized a new era for Palestinian Arabs who remained in the territory of the new state. They not only faced a national tragedy as they lost their homeland (*Nakba*) and became refugees in their own country, but they also had to struggle for physical survival in the state that took their lands.[6] As this generation was slowly recovering from the trauma of the *Nakba* and launching a fight for their civil and national rights, they began adopting a national anti-establishment discourse.

---

[6] Rabinowitz and Abu Bakir (2002, 29, 35–36) have labeled "survivors" the generation born before 1948, which experienced in their youth the traumatic loss of homeland, displacement, and the need to flee.

3.1 The Postcolonial Paradigm in Hebrew-Arabic Translations in the Arab World

In the 1950s and 1960s, Arab intellectuals attached no importance whatsoever to the recognition of Israel and its culture. The Arab world took interest in Israeli culture from a military intelligence, rather than from a literary perspective. Government officials and various research institutions in the Arab world mainly concentrated on Israel's social, economic, military, and political situation but, translations and analyses in these fields remained, for the most part, classified as security information (al-Baḥrāwī 1977, 11).

The intensifying process of "cultural de-colonization" in the Arab world, especially after the defeat of 1967, resulted in attempts on the part of the Arab society to recover from the colonial experience and to examine and confront the perspective of the Other in order to redefine one's own cultural and national identity (Jacquemond 1992, 146). The Israeli Other, which had wrought that defeat and caused the process that followed in its aftermath, thus began to attract academic and public interest after a long period of avoidance and denial.

In accordance with this postcolonial translation paradigm, works of Modern Hebrew literature selected for translation into Arabic reflected a hostile and condescending attitude towards Arabs and Islam, emphasized social and political tensions within Israeli society, or revealed the propagandist nature of the Hebrew literature (al-Shāmī 1988, 12–13).

In 1979, for example, the Iraqi journal *al-Aqlām* (Pens) published a special issue on "Zionist Literature." The editors of the issue emphasized their wish to expose the racist nature of these texts and the ways in which they contributed to the Zionist-imperialist "cultural invasion." (al-Kabīsī 1979, 3–6) Given this premise, it is not surprising that the Iraqi author Badīʿa Amīn related to Hebrew literature and the translations in this special issue of *al-Aqlām* as the product of Zionist ideology and therefore schematic, stereotypical, racist, and stripped of artistic value (Amīn 1979, 111).

The most relevant translations were principally carried out by two groups of translators. The first consisted of journalists and intellectuals interested in Hebrew literature—even though some of them were unfamiliar with the Hebrew language. Renowned Palestinian authors Ghassān Kanafānī (1936–1972) and Muʿīn Bsīsū (1927–1984), the Egyptian columnist ʿAbd al-Munʿim Salīm (1929–2004), the Jordanian author Ghālib Halsa (1932–1989), and others belonged to that group. The second pool of translators consisted mainly of scholars from the Hebrew departments of Egyptian universities, like Nāzik ʿAbd al-Fattāḥ, Rashād al-Shāmī (1943–2006), and Aḥmad Ḥammād, among others.

The strategies of these translators were marked by the addition of preambles, epilogues and explanations that were supposed to simultaneously justify the translation and help the reader understand the political, social, cultural, and literary background of the text. Translations were also characterized by adherence to the original text, while preserving Jewish and Israeli cultural distinctiveness. This policy led occasionally to semantic deviations that arose from a lack of direct contact with Israeli culture and the spoken Hebrew language.

One of the most important scholars and translators of modern Hebrew literature in the Arab world is Ibrāhīm al-Baḥrāwī (b. 1944), who published widely on Israeli-Hebrew culture and literature and the Arab-Israeli conflict.[7] In his translations, al-Baḥrāwī tended to adhere to the original text, which he perceived as a foundation for learning about Jewish culture and society. He even adopted terms and words from the Israeli-Hebrew narrative, explaining these alongside the text with footnotes. But the lack of familiarity with Israeli experience also led him to significantly deviate from the source text at the same time, reinforcing some prejudices about Israeli society.

In 1972 al-Baḥrāwī translated a short story that featured a lengthy dialogue between two Israeli soldiers sitting beside the Suez Canal during the War of Attrition in 1970. Explaining what motivated him to translate the text, he said in 2010 that the story was to regenerate the Egyptian national pride by means of revealing the state of mind of Israeli soldiers under the military pressure exerted by the Egyptian army (al-Baḥrāwī, 2010).

This motivation suggests that the translation of Israeli-Hebrew literature in the Arab world was to serve a redefinition of the Arab cultural and national identity—which was an important objective in the process of cultural decolonization.

3.2 The Postcolonial Paradigm in Arabic-Hebrew Translations in Israel

The repression of the Palestinian *Nakba* narrative in Israeli culture, the sense of deprivation and exclusion of Palestinian citizens in Israel, and the colonial reality that prevails there has had consequences. Following the conquest of the Pal-

---

[7] Ibrāhīm al-Baḥrāwī was born in Port Said, Egypt, in 1944. He studied Hebrew language and literature at Ain-Shams University and attained his doctorate in that field in 1972. He lectured in Hebrew literature at Ain-Shams and other Arab universities in Egypt and elsewhere. He maintained a regular column in several Egyptian newspapers and was involved in a number of political moves connected to the Arab-Israel conflict. For a complete list of the author's books and essays, see the author's website, www.bahrawy.com, (accessed November 27, 2016).

estinian population of the West Bank and Gaza Strip in 1967, educated Palestinians in Israel began undermining the Zionist narrative and presenting an alternative Palestinian postcolonial discourse in its place.

This postcolonial shift in Israel was reflected in translations of texts that destabilized the Zionist narrative and undermined the foundations of Israeli political discourse. This approach has been adopted by publishing houses, such as Mefras and Andalus, and by translators, like Anton Shammas (b. 1950), Muḥammad Ḥamza Ghanāyim (1957–2004), and Naʿīm ʿArāyidī (1948–2015). Their objective was to enable the acceptance of the translated works in the target culture, hence translations emerging out of this context tended to lean towards equivalence rather than literal translation and sought Hebrew alternatives to Arabic concepts and unique linguistic and stylistic characteristics of the source texts.

Anton Shammas,[8] for example, focused on translating works by Palestinian authors from Arabic to Hebrew as well as those related to the division and dispersal of the Palestinian people. His remarks and the type of works he translated indicate that he sought to give presence to the repressed and marginalized narrative of the Palestinian minority. By translating it into the language of the majority Jewish culture, he wished to undermine the foundations of the Zionist political discourse in Israeli society (Kayyal 2011, 88).

Shammas translated into Hebrew three novels by the Palestinian author Imīl Ḥabībī (1922–1996 al-Waqāiʿ al-Gharība fī Ikhtifāʾ Saʿīd Abī al-Naḥs al-Mutashāʾil (The Strange Events in the Disappearance of Saʿīd the Unlucky, the Pessoptimist, 1974; in Hebrew: ha-Opsimist: ha-Khronikah ha-Moflaʾah be-Hiʿalmoto Shel Saʿīd Abū al-Naḥs al-Mutashāʾil, 1984, 1995); Ikhṭayyi (What a Pity, 1985; in Hebrew: Ekhtayyeh, 1988); and Khurāfiyyat Sarāyā Bint al-Ghūl (Fairy Tale of Saraya the Ogre's Daughter, 1991; in Hebrew: Saraya, Bat ha-Shed ha-Raaʿ: Khurāfiyya, 1993). The three novels deal with various aspects of the Palestinian tragedy—especially with the complex reality that the Palestinians who remained in Israel found themselves in. Shammas' selection of these novels and the special linguistic characteristics of his translations stimulated discussion and debate among the Hebrew critics. They regarded these translations as attempts to break through the "bounds of the Hebrew canon by the rejected fringe of the Arab national mi-

---

[8] Anton Shammas was born in 1950 in the Arab village of Fassuta (Fassūṭa) in the Galilee. He earned his BA degree at the Hebrew University of Jerusalem and was one of the founders and editors of an Arabic literary journal, al-Sharq. As of 1975, he produced TV programs and pursued a career in the Hebrew press, where he published numerous commentaries, some of which provoked heated debate regarding Israel's identity and democratic character. In 1987, he decided to distance himself from Hebrew culture and now serves as a Lecturer at the University of Michigan, USA (For a detailed biography, see Kayyal 2009).

nority culture and penetrate the territory of the authoritative majority culture." (Hever 1989, 186–87)

4 The Hybrid Ideology

An ideologically hybridized group is, generally speaking, "one whose behavior and ideological discourse display influences of more than one type of ideal rationale in near equal measure."[9] Two groups of Israeli citizens find themselves, in a particular way, exposed to conflicting identities and ideologies: Palestinian citizens of Israel, and the Jews of Arab origin. In terms of translation, both of these groups developed a hybrid ideology that was a compromise between competing narratives.

Thousands of Jews from Arab countries immigrated to Israel, particularly from Iraq and Morocco. Their transition was shaped by many difficulties, including the living conditions in the transit camps and the challenges of adjusting to a new culture. They also struggled with the fact that their new society displayed contempt towards their cultural heritage. Given the Zionists' principle to "negate the Diaspora," traditions brought from the exile in the Diaspora were only very selectively accepted in the process of nation-building (Lissak 1996, 78–79).

Israel's Arab citizens belong to the Palestinian people and the Arab majority that surrounds Israel, while at the same time constituting an ethnic minority that seeks to integrate with Israeli society. Opposing trends of alienation and integration affect the Arab population, faced with the uneasy coexistence of their civic (Israeli) and national identity (Arab/Palestinian). Demotion of the Palestinian population to the margins of society and the growing nationalist tendencies increased Palestinians' alienation vis-à-vis the Israeli state, while the economic situation and the failure of national emancipation led to a greater integration of this disenfranchised group (Landau 1993, 119–23; al-Ḥaj 1996, 90–91).

4.1 The Israeli-Arab Paradigm in Hebrew-Arabic Translations

Cultural and linguistic phenomena that are characteristic of ethnic minorities appear among Palestinians in Israel. Such typical phenomena include increased

---

[9] Thomas Hegghammer, "The Ideological Hybridization of Jihadi Groups," *Current Trends in Islamist Ideology*, Hudson Institute, November 18, 2009, http://www.hudson.org/research/9866-the-ideological-hybridization-of-jihadi-groups (accessed November 27, 2016).

linguistic interference of Hebrew in colloquial Arabic and the rising number of bilingual authors. These occurrences typify situations in which a subjugated minority culture is forced to conserve and strengthen the hegemony of the dominant culture, thereby exacerbating the predicament of the marginalized group.

This trend was also reflected in the work of Palestinian translators, citizens of Israel who were translating Hebrew literature into Arabic, like Maḥmūd Bayādsī (b. 1932), Maḥmūd ʿAbbāsī (b. 1935), Anton Shammas, and Muḥammad Ḥamza Ghanāyim. They could be described as "enslaved intermediaries,"[10] not only because they related to the Hebrew culture as a hegemonic one, but also because this attitude permitted the penetration of foreign cultural and linguistic elements into their dominated culture, thereby intensifying the challenge to their cultural identity.

Anton Shammas' Hebrew-Arabic translations of the 1970s were published in semi-establishment platforms, like the literary journal *al-Sharq* (The East), the publisher *al-Mashriq*, and the Institute for Translation of Hebrew Literature.[11] His approach to these translations was characterized by the interference of linguistic and cultural elements from the source language within the translated text, and by many deviations from the linguistic, stylistic, and ethically accepted norms in the target culture.[12] In fact, the linguistic interference of Hebrew, present in the vernacular of the Arab population in Israel, finds its clearest expression in various strategies of translation: a disregard for the lexicographic rules of Arabic; a maintenance of the syntactical structures of Hebrew; a translation of borrowed semantics and linguistic innovations; a use of Hebrew words transli-

---

10 Richard Jacquemond believes that in colonial times, in translating from the language of a hegemonic culture to language of a dominated culture, translators seemed to take on the role of a trusted intermediary, through whom the dominated culture loses its identity while simultaneously adapting and permitting the hegemonic linguistic cultural base to be accepted by the dominated culture (1992, 155–156).

11 These translations include: an anthology of children's poems and stories *ha-Masaʿ El ha-Ey Ulay* (The Journey to Island Maybe, 1944; in Arabic: *al-Safra ilā Jazīrat Yumkin*, 1972) by Miriam Yalan-Stekelis (1900–1984); a special issue of the journal *al-Sharq* (1973); a bilingual Arabic-Hebrew anthology *bi-Ṣawt Muzdawaj/ be-Shni Kolot* (Two Voices, 1974); a novel about the Holocaust *Kokhav ha-Efer* (Star of Ashes, 1966; in Arabic: *Kawkab al-Ramād*, 1975) by the Holocaust survivor Yehiel Dinur (Ka-Tzetnik) (1909–2001); an anthology of poems *me-Kaytz le-Kaytz* (From Summer to Summer, 1964; in Arabic: *Min Ṣayf ilā Ṣayf*, 1977) by David Rokeah (1916–1985); and others. (For more details about Shammas' Hebrew-Arabic translations, see Kayyal 2011, 78–81).

12 Coarse expressions, curses, intimate body descriptions, and descriptions of sexual acts that exist in the original Hebrew texts have been preserved in their Arabic translations, although the Arab audience is mostly traditional and conservative.

terated into Arabic; and a use of words that sound phonetically close to the original expression.

Thus, for example, Jewish or Israeli culture-specific items that have been transliterated into Arabic can be found in Shammas' translation, like *Bārtīzānīm* in Arabic for Hebrew *Partyzanim* (the partisans), *Ṣihyūn* for *Tzion* (Zion), *Maʿ-barāh* for *Maʿbarah* (transit camp) and *al-Shīkūnāt* for *Shikounim* (housing projects) (Kaniuk 1974). However, Shammas also introduces words borrowed from Hebrew that are not necessarily related to Israeli or Jewish life and certainly do have Arabic equivalents. For example, the word *Mukarzal* (curly) is borrowed from Hebrew, although it is neither connected to the Jewish and/or Israeli experience nor does it lack an Arabic equivalent (Kaniuk 1974, 238; Kaniuk 1979, 13).[13]

Anton Shammas himself expressed his dissatisfaction with his translations from Hebrew to Arabic describing them as "Inverted Slides." (Shammas 1985, 19) Shammas apparently refers to this metaphor to indicate that the translations both appear to be exact copies of the original and unacceptable to the readership. This, in his opinion, results from the distancing between the two cultures and languages, as Hebrew has, in his view, lost its Semitic attribution under the influence of European and American culture. Shammas' metaphor seems pertinent to most of the translations between the two literatures, Hebrew and Arabic, not only because of the closeness of Hebrew to Western cultures and its distance from its Semitic sources, but mainly due to the involvement of non-literary ideological considerations, which make these translations unacceptable to the readership even if, as I have tried to show, they are faithful renderings.

4.2 The Arab-Jewish Paradigm in Arabic-Hebrew Translations

Educated Jews from Arab countries (especially Iraq), who saw themselves as Jews belonging to Arab society (Arab-Jews), were subjected to the melting pot policy of the Israeli governments, which demanded that they renounce and shake off their cultural heritage in order to integrate in Israeli society. All the while, many of them, like Sami Michael (b. 1926), Shimon Ballas (b. 1930), and Sasson Somekh (b. 1933), continued to write in Arabic and to maintain contacts with Arab culture. In this way, a complex and multifaceted cultural environment emerged, drawing on both Arabic and Islamic cultures, and Western Is-

---

[13] This strategy could be attributed either to the bilingualism of the translator or to the foreignization trend in Translation Studies, which can be explained as a conscious strategy of exposing the new reader to the language and culture of the source text.

raeli culture. Translations of Arabic literature stemming from this milieu acquired a political character because they were seen as encouraging Jewish-Arab co-existence and seeking peace between Israel and its Arab neighbors.

Intellectuals of Arab-Jewish heritage regarded Arabic culture as the mother culture in which Arabs and Jews grew up together in the countries of their origin. The translational paradigm they represented sought to preserve the original cultural identity of Oriental Jews. Translation was a way of expressing nostalgia and love of Arabic culture. In conjunction, the Zionist narrative influenced their work, especially in matters pertaining to the Arab-Israeli conflict.

Shimon Ballas,[14] for example, was subject to contradicting political and cultural influences in his work as a translator, especially of Palestinian literature. On the one hand, his desire to preserve his Jewish-Arabic cultural identity and his personal identification with the Palestinian nation, given his closeness to communist circles in Israel, contributed to his desire to give expression to the Palestinian narrative by translating works of Palestinian literature (Snir 1998, 178). On the other, the dominant Zionist narrative that had taken possession of Israeli society urged him to renounce the Palestinian narrative and even the very existence of such a nation.

His most important translation is of the anthology of Palestinian fiction *Sipurim Falastiniyim* (Palestinian Stories), published in 1970. As a pioneering act of translation of Palestinian literature into Hebrew, the importance of this collection derived not only from the way it served to introduce the Palestinian voice to the Hebrew readership, but also the way it explicitly celebrated the existence of a Palestinian literature at a time when Palestinian national identity was denied in the Israeli political discourse (Amit-Kochavi 1999, 72).

However, careful examination of the works chosen for the anthology shows that Ballas selected writings that fortified his views regarding the Palestinian tragedy and the nature of Palestinian literature. Thus, he translated many works that depicted the "mass flight" of Palestinians from their homeland and the erosion of their trust in the Palestinian leadership and the Arab countries.

---

14 Shimon Ballas was born in Baghdad in 1930. After graduating from high school in Baghdad, he studied journalism and published stories, review columns, and articles in Arabic. He immigrated to Israel in 1951 and spent over a year in a transit camp. He worked as the Arab Affairs correspondent at the communist daily *Kol ha-'Am* (The People's Voice) from 1956 to 1961. In 1970, he enrolled in a PhD program in Paris, where he wrote his dissertation on the reflection of the Israeli-Arab conflict in Arabic literature. On his return to Israel in 1974, he was appointed as a lecturer for Arabic literature at the University of Haifa. After his retirement, he devoted his time to writing. See the website of the Institute for the Translation of Hebrew Literature (ITHL): http://www.ithl.org.il/page_13692 (accessed November 27, 2016).

Indeed, he even included in his anthology a story called *al-Yahūdī wa-Zujājat al-Kūnyāk* (The Jew and a Glass of Cognac) by ʿAwaḍ Shaʿbān (b. 1934), which was structured to reflect the apparent anti-Semitic tone of Palestinian literature—although the author is not Palestinian but rather Lebanese.[15] Ballas adopted a patronizing attitude in translation, demonstrated in numerous deletions and linguistic and stylistic elevations, while making attempts to preserve some of the unique linguistic and stylistic characteristics of the source text (Kayyal 2011–2012, 249–50). His work reflects the contradiction inherent in the policy of considering not only the literary value of the works selected for translation, but also the extent to which they represent political and ideological narratives.

5 Conclusions

The Arabic-Hebrew-Arabic translations of literary works have been conducted in the shadow of a prolonged, bloody national conflict. Therefore, those involved had diverse interests and conflicting ideologies, and they steered their approaches to translation in directions that matched their ideological orientation. Political considerations were central determinants both in terms of the purpose of the translations and their linguistic and stylistic characteristics. As a result, three rivaling policies have emerged.

The Zionist ideology influenced three major translation paradigms: the romantic-Zionist approach, the Orientalist, and the Israeli establishmentarian approaches. From the late nineteenth century until 1948, Hebrew-Arabic translation was dominated by the romantic-Zionist trend, which aimed to consolidate Jewish national consciousness. This paradigm was characterized, on the one hand, by careful rhetorical and stylistic choices, based on the use of linguistic structures that are common in classic Arabic literature, and on the other, by the inclination to preserve unique Jewish cultural elements.

The Orientalist-Zionist mode expressed interest in the Arab region, while displaying a condescending and dismissive attitude towards the Arabs and their culture. The associated Arabic-Hebrew translation paradigm stressed the informational value of the works translated from Arabic literature, minimizing their artistic worth, and even significantly deviating from their original artistic structure. From 1948 to 1967, Hebrew-Arabic translation in Israel was dominated by the Israeli establishmentarian paradigm, which aimed to consolidate the nation-

---

[15] See the website of the author, ʿAwaḍ Shaʿbān: http://www.awadshaaban.com (accessed November 27, 2016).

al collective, disseminating the values of the young state. This approach to translation was intended to introduce the reader to translated texts that corresponded with the Israeli-Zionist ideology and adopted the Israeli linguistic and cultural discourse.

The anti-Zionist ideology, which accompanied the process of "cultural decolonization," especially after the defeat of 1967, inspired new postcolonial translation strategies both in the Arab world and in Israel. After 1967, the postcolonial approach dominated the Arab world, urging to examine the self from the perspective of the Other and, at the same time, to undermine the Zionist narrative and present it as a racist neo-colonial one. The Hebrew-Arabic translation paradigm rooted in this approach was characterized by a choice of works that reflected the social and political tensions in Israeli society or portrayed the Arabs with arrogance and racism. Alongside these particular selection criteria, introductions and explanatory notes were being added to the text. Moreover, translators tended to adhere to the original text even when that involved objective difficulties that arose from the ignorance of the Israeli way of life and colloquial Hebrew. They also preserved dimensions of Jewish and Israeli culture, commenting these in the footnotes.

The postcolonial turn in Israel attached a great importance to undermining the Zionist narrative and presenting an alternative Palestinian Arab one. The Arabic-Hebrew translations it spawned constituted an attempt to embed Arabic literature into Hebrew culture and to create an opportunity for the alternative Palestinian narrative to infiltrate the Israeli public awareness. Postcolonial translators were trying to achieve this goal by means of highlighting the artistic value of the works and emphasizing their stylistic uniqueness.

Finally, the hybrid approach to translation was triggered by Palestinian authors from Israel and the Jews of Arab origin. Such translations by Israelis with Palestinian heritage contributed to preserving and reinforcing the cultural hegemony of the majority and even to the interference of linguistic and cultural elements from the dominant culture into that of the minority. Some of these translations lacked linguistic and stylistic uniformity; their quality suffered from the interference of cultural and linguistic elements from the source language and many deviations from the accepted linguistic, stylistic, and ethical norms of the target culture. The Arab Jewish translators, in turn, attributed great importance to maintaining the cultural identity of the Oriental/Mizrahi Jews. Their translation projects were to express nostalgia and love of Arabic culture, without completely discarding the Zionist narrative and the atmosphere of hostility that existed between Israel and its Arab neighbors.

Translations between the Hebrew and Arabic literatures have become part of the political vortex between the Zionist and the Palestinian national movement.

Even if they are motivated by aesthetic and literary merits of a given text, they remain political. A change to this status quo could only be achieved by a relaxation of political tensions. A truly fruitful cultural and literary dialogue will only be enabled once the target audience can finally focus on the literary quality of the translations and not judge them based on prejudices and stereotyping.

Bibliography

Adler, Haim, and Reuven Kahana, eds. 1975. ʿArakhim, Dat ve-Tarbut [Values, Religion and Culture]. Jerusalem: Akademon, Hebrew University. [Hebrew]
Allen, Roger. 1982. *The Arabic novel: An historical and critical introduction*. Syracuse, NY: Syracuse University Press.
Amīn, Badīʿa. 1979. "Qirāʾa fī ʿAdad 'al-Aqlām' al-Khāṣṣ bil-Adab al-Ṣihyūnī" [Reading in the Special Issue of 'al-Aqlam' about the Zionist Literature]. *al-Aqlām* 14 (12): 106–117. [Arabic]
Amit-Kochavi, Hannah. 1999. "Tergomi Sifrut ʿAravit le-ʿEvrit: ha-Rikaʿ ha-Histuri-Tarbuti Shelahem, Meafinihem u-Maʿmadam be-Tarbut ha-Matarah." [Translations of Arabic Literature into Hebrew: Their Historical and Cultural Background and Their Reception by the Target Culture] Ph.D. diss., Tel-Aviv University. [Hebrew]
al-Baḥrāwī, Ibrāhīm. 1977. *al-Adab al-Ṣihyūnī bayna Ḥarbīn: Ḥuzayrān 1967 wa-Tishrīn 1973* [Zionist Literature between two Wars: June 1967 and October 1973]. Beirut: al-Muʾassasa al-ʿArabiyya lil-Dirāsāt wal-Nashr. [Arabic]
al-Baḥrāwī, Ibrāhīm. 2010. "Ḥiwār Jundiyyayn Isrāʾīliyyayn Taḥt al-Qaṣf al-Miṣrī 1970" [Dialogue of Two Israeli Soldiers in 1970 under the Egyptian Bombing]. *al-Miṣrī al-Yawm* 2249, no. 10 (August). [Arabic]: http://today.almasryalyoum.com/article2.aspx?ArticleID=265462&IssueID=1858 (accessed November 1, 2016).
Bassnett, Susan, and André Lefevere. 1990. *Translation, History and Culture*. London and New York: Pinter Publishers.
Ben Dor, Yisrael. 1981. "Tergom ʿAhavat Tzion' le-ʿAravit le-Rabbi Salīm al-Dāwūdī Zʾʾl be-Sof ha-Meʾah ha-Kodemet" [The Translation of "The Love of Zion" into Arabic by Rabbi Salim al-Dawudi, of Blessed Memory, at the End of the Last Century]. *Ba-maʿrakhah* 21 (250): 26–27. [Hebrew]
Burla, Yehuda. 1929. *Neftuli Adam* [In Darkness Striving]. Jerusalem: Metzpe. [Hebrew]
Burla, Yehuda. 1955. *Ṣirāʿ Insān* [Human Conflict] (trans. ʿEzra Ḥaddād). Tel Aviv: Ṣundūq al-Kitāb al-ʿArabī. [Arabic]
Calzada-Pérez, Maria. 2003. "Introduction." In *Apropos of Ideology: Translation Studies on Ideology—Ideologies in Translation Studies*, edited by Maria Calzada-Pérez, 1–22. Manchester, UK: St. Jerome Pub.
Eisenstadt, Shmuel Noah. 1973. *Ha-Ḥevrah ha-Yisraelit: Rekaʿ, Hetpatḥut o-Baʿaiot* [Israeli Society: Background, development and problems]. Jerusalem: Magnes. [Hebrew]
Ḥaddād, ʿEzra. 1973. *Sofer u-Meḥanekh me-Bavel: Dapi Zikaron le-ʿEzra Ḥaddād zʾʾl* [Author and Educator from Babylon: Memory Pages for ʿEzra Ḥaddād of Blessed Memory]. Merhavia: ha-Merkaz le-Tarbot ve-le-Ḥinokh, Histadrut. [Hebrew]

al-Ḥaj, Majid. 1996. "ha-Hetaargenot ha-Politit shel ha-Okhlosiah ha-'Aravit be-Yisrael: Hetpthot Merkaz be-Tokh Sholaiym" [Political Organization of the Arab Population in Israel: Development of Center in Marginal]. In *Yisrael Lekrat Shnot ha-Alpaiym, Ḥevrah, Politikah, ve-Tarbot* [Israel towards the New Millennium, Society, Politics and Culture], edited by Moshe Lissak and Baruch Knei-Paz, 90–102. Jerusalem: Hebrew University, Magnes and Machon Eshkol. [Hebrew]

Hever, Hannan. 1989. "Le-Hakot be-'Akevo Shel Achilles" [Striking on Achilles' Heel]. *Alpayim*, 1: 186–193. [Hebrew]

Ḥijāzī, Aḥmad 'Abd al-Mu'tī. 1995. "Thaqāfat Umma ... Am Thaqāfat Afrād?" [Culture of Nation... or Culture of Individuals?]. *Ibdā'* 12, no. 1 (January): 4–5. [Arabic]

Idrīs, Muḥammad Jalā'. 1993. *Al-Shakhṣiyya al-Yahūdiyya: Dirāsa Adabiyya Muqārina bayna Riwāyatayy Ivanhoe li-Scott wa-Aḥmad wa-Dawūd li-Fatḥī Ghānim* [The Character of the Jew, a Comparative Literary Study of Scott's Ivanhoe and Fathi Ghanim's Aḥmad and Dawud]. Cairo: 'Aīn lil-Dirāsāt wal-Buḥūth al-Insāniyya wal-Ijtimā'iyya. [Arabic]

Jacquemond, Richard. 1992. "Translation and cultural hegemony: The case of French–Arabic translation." In *Rethinking Translation: Discourse, Subjectivity, Ideology*, edited by Lawrence Venuti, 139–158. London and New York: Routledge.

al-Kabīsī, Ṭarrād. 1979. "Hadhā al-'Adad ... Limādhā?" [This Issue... Why?]. *al-Aqlām* 14 (9): 3–6. [Arabic]

Kaniuk, Yoram. 1974. "Ḥayāt Klārā Shiyāṭū al-Ḥilwa" [The Beautiful Life of Clara Shiato] (trans. Anton Shammas). In *bi-Ṣawt Muzdawaj / be-Shni Kolot* [Two Voices], edited by Anton Shammas, 234–252. Haifa: Beit Hagefen, Jerusalem: Martin Buber's Center. [Arabic]

Kaniuk, Yoram. 1979. "Ha-Ḥaiym ha-Yafim Shel Clara Shiato" [The Beautiful Life of Clara Shiato]. In: Yoram Kaniuk. *Lailah 'al ha-Ḥof 'em Transistor* [A Night on the Beach with Transistor], 7–29. Tel-Aviv: Ha-Kibbutz ha-Me'uḥad. [Hebrew]

Kayyal, Mahmoud. 2008. "Salim al-Dawudi and the Beginnings of the Arabic Translation of Modern Hebrew Literature." *Target* 20 (1): 52–78.

Kayyal, Mahmoud. 2009. "Anton Shammas." In *20th Century Arab Writers*. Vol. 346, *Dictionary of Literary Biography* [DLB], edited by Majd Al-Mallah and Coeli Fitzpatrick, 238–243. Detroit and New York: Gale Cengage Learning.

Kayyal, Mahmoud. 2011. "From Left to Right and From Right to Left: Anton Shammas's Translations from Hebrew into Arabic and Vice Versa." *Babel* (Revue internationale de la traduction / International Journal of Translation) 57 (1): 76–98.

Kayyal, Mahmoud. 2011–12. "Shimon Ballas Mutarjim(an) lil-Adab al-Filasṭīnī" [Shimon Ballas as a Translator of Palestinian Literature]. *al-Karmil* 32–33: 236–261. [Arabic]

Khīr, Nazīh, ed. 1993. *Liqā' wa-Muwājaha fī al-Adab al-'Ibrī wal-'Arabī/ Mefgash ve-'Emut ba-Yitzirah ha-'Aravit ve-ha-'Evrit* [Meeting and Confrontation in Hebrew and Arabic Literature]. Haifa: al-Karma. [Arabic/ Hebrew]

Landau, Yaakov. 1993. *Ha-Mi'ut ha-'Aravi be-Yisrael 1967–1991, Hibitim Pulitiym* [The Arabic Minority in Israel 1967–1991, Political Aspects]. Tel-Aviv: Am Oved. [Hebrew]

Lissak, Moshe. 1996. "'Edah ve-'Adatiot be-Yisrael be-Prespektivah Historit" [Ethnic Community and Ethnicity in Israel from Historical Perspective]. In *Yisrael Lekrat Shnot ha-Alpaiym, Ḥevrah, Politikah, ve-Tarbot* [Israel towards the New Millennium, Society, Politics and Culture], edited by Moshe Lissak and Baruch Knei-Paz, 74–89. Jerusalem: Hebrew University, Magnes and Machon Eshkol. [Hebrew]

Rabinowitz, Dan, and Khawla Abu Bakir. 2002. *Ha-Dor ha-Zakuf* [The Upright Generation]. Tel Aviv: Keter. [Hebrew]
Schäffner, Christina. 2003. "Third Ways and New Centres: Ideological Unity or Difference?" In *Apropos of Ideology: Translation Studies on Ideology—Ideologies in Translation Studies*, edited by Maria Calzada-Pérez, 23–42. Manchester, UK: St. Jerome Pub.
al-Shāmī, Rashād. 1988. *al-Filasṭīniūn wal-Iḥsās al-Zā'if bil-Dhanb fī al-Adab al-Isrā'īlī* [The Palestinians and the False Sense of Guilt in Israeli literature]. Cairo: Dār al-Mustaqbal al-Arabī. [Arabic]
Shammas, Anton. 1985. "'Al yamin vesmoul batergom" [About Right and Left in Translation]. *'Iton 77*, no. 64–65: 18–19. [Hebrew]
Shenhav, Yehuda, ed. 2004. *Kolonialiot ve-ha-Matzav ha-Postkoloniali* [Coloniality and the Postcolonial Condition]. Jerusalem: Van Leer Institute and Ha-Kibbutz ha-Me'uḥad. [Hebrew]
Snir, Reuven. 1998. "Ma'galim Neḥtakhim Bein ha-Sifrut ha-'Evrit le-Bein ha-Sifrut ha-'Aravit" (Intersecting Circles between Hebrew and Arabic Literature]. In *Bein 'Ever le-'Arav: ha-Maga'im Bein ha-Sifrut ha-'Aravit le-Bein ha-Sifrut ha-Yehudit bi-Yme ha-Benayim uba-Zman ha-Ḥadash* [Between Hebrew and Arabic: Contacts between Arabic Literature and Jewish Literature in the Middle Ages and Modern Times], edited by Yosef Tobi, 177–210. Tel-Aviv: Afikim. [Hebrew]
Somekh, Sasson. 1996. "Dmoyot Yehudim ba-Sifrut ha-'Aravit shel Yamino" [Jewish Characters in the Contemporary Arabic Literature]. In *Sofrim Moslemim 'al Yehudim ve-Yahdut* [Muslim Writers on Jews and Judaism], edited by Hava Lazarus-Yafeh, 235–245. Jerusalem: Merkaz Zalman Shazar le-Toldot Yisrael. [Hebrew]
Tidhar, David. 1947. *Encyclopedia le-Ḥalutzi ha-Yishuv u-Bonav: Dmoyot ve-Tmonut* [Encyclopedia of the Pioneers and Builders of the *Yishuv*: Images and Photos]. Vol. 1. Tel Aviv: Sefriyat Reshonim. [Hebrew]
Tidhar, David. 1961. *Encyclopedia le-Ḥalutzi ha-Yishuv u-Bonav: Dmoyot ve-Tmonut* [Encyclopedia of the Pioneers and Builders of the *Yishuv*: Images and Photos]. Vol. 11. Tel Aviv: Sefriyat Reshonim. [Hebrew]
Weissbrod, Rachel. 1989. "Magamot be-Tirgom Sipuret me-Anglit le-'Evrit, 1958–1980" [Trends in the translation of English fiction into Hebrew, 1958–1980]. Ph.D. diss. Tel-Aviv University.

Agnieszka Podpora
The Saint of Socialist Palestine: Yosef Haim Brenner in Polish Translation

1 The Broken Heart of a Jewish Intellectual

In 1925, a Warsaw-based publishing house Orient issued in print a Polish translation of the short story *Ha-motsa: Ha-reshimah min ha-ʿavar hakhi ḳarov* [*The Way Out: Sketch from the Immediate Past*] by Yosef Ḥaim Brenner, a Hebrew author murdered four years earlier during the Arab riots in Jaffa, Palestine. The Polish text in Józef Szofman's translation was given the title *Wyjście: Epizod palestyński wojny światowej* [*The Way Out: A Palestine Episode of the Great War*] and was released as a paperback, in a series that published a regular spate of small and affordable volumes of Jewish literature in Polish translation. In the interwar years, the formula, which was also adopted by the rival publishing house Safrus, served as a way of introducing Jewish writings into Polish culture, especially Yiddish-language authors such as Yosef Opatoshu, Sholem Aleichem, Yitskhok-Leybush Peretz, and Sholem Asch (Prokop-Janiec 1991). In the two-volume anthology featuring the reprints of all the issues in the Orient library, Brenner's story stands out as the only translation from Hebrew in the entire series (Holcblat et al. 1928).

Hebrew literature was present in interwar Poland both in the original and in translation. Publishing houses such as Shtibel, periodicals like *Ha-Teḳufah*, Polish-language Zionist dailies (*Chwila*, *Nasz Przegląd*, and *Nowy Dziennik*), cultural and literary magazines (for example *Nowe Życie*), and Zionist periodicals run by student fraternities and youth organizations all provided a forum for such texts.

Unlike the work of some eminent and highly popular Hebrew poets such as Ḥaim Naḥman Bialik and Saul Tchernichovsky, Yosef Ḥaim Brenner's oeuvre was rarely published or reviewed in Polish. The author thus remained largely unknown in Poland until his tragic death, which resonated very strongly among the Jewish intelligentsia well beyond Palestine.

"Brenner has fallen," read the telegram that allegedly arrived at the editor's office of *Chwila*, the Lvov-based Jewish daily that reported in detail on the "Jaffa affair"—the Arab riots near Tel Aviv in May 1921. An obituary of "one of the tow-

---

The article was written in the framework of a project funded by the National Science Centre (NCN), following the decision No. DEC-2012/07/N/HS2/00968.

https://doi.org/10.1515/9783110550788-010

ering figures of Hebrew letters" was immediately circulated alongside with a short biographical note (Anon 1921).[1] Interestingly, the article, which did not seriously engage with any of Brenner's texts, perpetuated some of the critical clichés about his work. His writing was reported to "push the outer form and artistic quality to the background and bring to the fore the psychological depth, collective and individual soul-searching, and poignant examination of human misery that the artist himself experienced in a variety of forms."[2]

Brenner's innovative style, as demonstrated in his famous essay *Ha-genre ha-erets-iśraeli ye-avizarehu* [*The Eretz-Israeli Genre and Its Attributes*] (Brenner 1910),[3] went against the grain of the classical conventions defined by the previous generation of Hebrew writers. Often criticized in his lifetime for lack of refinement,[4] Brenner's "non-literary" writing eventually came to be interpreted as a perfect realization of the idea of realism understood as a medium of truth. Surely, the momentum of the Jewish settlement project in Palestine and the circumstances of Brenner's tragic death in an Arab riot of previously unprecedented magnitude contributed to this change in reception.

---

[1] A word of thanks goes to Maria Antosik-Piela and Marta Drażyńska for their assistance in finding articles on Brenner in *Chwila*.

[2] Unless annotated otherwise, all the translations into Polish were provided by the author. All the translations from Polish into English were provided by the translator. All the titles in Polish were provided in original spelling. For the English translation of Brenner's *Ha-motsa*, see Brenner 1975.

[3] Brenner's essay is one of the pivotal critical pieces in the history of Hebrew literature and lays out the fundamental tenets of his understanding of prose, especially that written in and about Eretz Israel. The author criticizes local literary figures such as Meir Wilkanski and Shlomo Tsemaḥ, who in his opinion provided false depictions of Palestine as a small Jewish state that concentrates all that is beautiful in the old continent while compensating for the hardships of the Jewish life in Europe. In Brenner's view, the reality of the *Yishuv* was much more difficult and hard to bear. According to Brenner, the truth of literature, while based on the experience of reality, is nonetheless not derived from a simple *mimesis*, but through a confrontation with the truth of life to be revealed in the text.

[4] Brenner came under harsh criticism from several authors, including Bialik who in the years 1904–1905, as the literary editor at the high-brow literary magazine *Ha-Shiloaḥ*, happened to review and edit texts submitted by the young author, then aspiring to the Hebrew literary elite. Although Brenner was only seven years his junior, Bialik, who already enjoyed the standing of a renowned and respected writer, accused Brenner of stylistic negligence and incompetence as an artist. At the same time, as his correspondence shows, he valued Brenner for a fresh perspective and his artistic sensibility (Shapira 2008, 69–71). The reception of Brenner's oeuvre in the literary circles of the era and the nature of his relationship with some of its representatives has attracted research and heated debate to date (Avneri 2009; Beer 1992).

Thus, both in the *Yishuv*[5] and in the Diaspora, posthumous depictions of Brenner presented the author as a lay prophet of Jewish Palestine, a writer who described the land "as it was." For many readers, his individual experience gave him the unique perspective to penetrate the collective Jewish psyche in the newly reborn homeland.[6] Such tenor, which became increasingly idealistic over time, characterized the majority of the references to Brenner's writings that were featured in the Polish-language Jewish press after his death. Despite the poor informative value of these short obituaries, these texts significantly contributed to Brenner's image as an "outstanding laborer of the pen" and a towering figure of Hebrew literature who was instrumental in the process of forging a Jewish identity and rebuilding the nation. This perspective was shared by Józef Szofman, who, writing under a nom de plume, called Brenner in *Nasz Przegląd* "an outstanding figure of the new Hebrew literature" and placed him in the pantheon of Jewish Palestine, next to Yosef Trumpeldor or A.D. Gordon (Ben-Szalom 1923).[7]

In contrast to other authors writing on Brenner in Poland in the 1920s, Józef Szofman spoke Hebrew. The translator, who could read Brenner's works in the original, was aware of the significance of the author within the working milieus in Palestine. Szofman himself adhered to left-wing Zionism when he was young, and only later, in the 1930s, shifted towards Revisionist Zionism. He attended the Hinukh gymnasium in Warsaw, where Polish was the main language of instruction, but extended Hebrew courses were also offered. In 1923, as a law student at the University of Warsaw, Szofman became an active member of Jewish student fraternities of Zionist orientation, including the "Jardenia" Academic Zionist Organization and the "Zelotia-Kanaim" Zionist Academic Fraternity. In the years

---

5 The term refers to the Jewish community in Palestine prior to the foundation of the state of Israel.

6 The early readers of Brenner's oeuvre, both in his lifetime and after his death, well until the 1950s, treated his works as either "less than" or "more than" literature. The documentary, autobiographical, and fragmentary qualities of his prose were interpreted either in a critical light, as shortcomings of technical and imaginative abilities, or in a positive light, as attempts at breaking the mold of literary convention in quest for the "truth" and "proximity to life." It was not until the subsequent generations of critics that Brenner's approach was appreciated as a full-fledged system of literary devices and an element of a refined, real-time game played with readers and critics alike, which Menakhem Brinker called the "rhetoric of honesty." (Brinker 1990, 11–26)

7 Yosef Trumpeldor was a Zionist activist and a World War I veteran; he served in the British-allied Jewish Legion and supported Jewish immigration to Palestine. Following his death during the desperate defense of Tel Hai settlement against Arab intruders in 1920, he was hailed as a national hero and the central figure of Zionist national mythology. Aharon David Gordon was a thinker and a left-wing Zionist ideologue, the founder of the Ha-Poel ha-Tsa'ir movement, as well as the spiritual guide to second and third 'Aliyah pioneers.

1925–1926, when his collaboration with *Nasz Przegląd* was most intense, he worked as Head of the Press and Propaganda Department of the Jewish National Fund (Ķeren Ķayemet le-Iśrael) in Poland (Tidhar 1947, 1037).

Apart from Brenner's *Ha-motsa*, Szofman also translated into Polish a selection of writings by Ahad Ha-'am, one of the leading ideologues of Zionism, the leader and founder of cultural Zionism. The "Zelotia-Kanaim" Fraternity published them in paperback in 1928, as Issue No. 1 in their series "Bibljoteka Sjonistyczna" [Zionist Library]. The editors of the series intended to "address a comprehensive set of issues that emerged in the tremendous work of reviving the People of Israel in the restored Land of Israel." (Ahad Ha-Am 1928, 4) The introduction to the book, most probably written by Szofman himself, reads:

> The Jewish community of Poland, especially young people, seem to display a sad ignorance of *the real state of the restoration of Palestine*. All they know about the idea of Zionism and the accomplishments of this greatest Jewish movement is based on loose, irregular, fragmentary, and what is worse, inaccurate information from daily press. This gap is particularly felt in people who, for one reason or another, cannot access Hebrew or, at least, Jewish sources. (Ahad Ha-Am 1928, 3; emphasis mine)

"Filling the gap of ignorance on Jewish matters among our [Polish-Jewish] intelligentsia" was the primary goal of the Bibljoteka Sjonistyczna founders, and an objective that Szofman also pursued in his early years as journalist and translator. For him, the fundamental problem of Jewish intelligentsia in Poland was a detachment from Hebrew sources, which, to his mind, represented both a centuries-long tradition and the cultural values underpinning the Jewish national revival. In his article celebrating the opening of the Hebrew University in Jerusalem, Szofman offered the following diagnosis on Polish and, more broadly, European Jews: "we have no cultural background, ... despite growing national awareness among the Jewry, we tend to assimilate ourselves culturally even more." (Szofman 1925e) In Szofman's understanding, the separation from the fabric of the new Hebrew culture revived in Palestine was the major tragedy of the nationally-aware members of the European Jewish intelligentsia at the beginning of the twentieth century. In his journalistic writings Szofman often used the metaphor of a "heart rent asunder"[8] to illustrate this inner drama of a person

---

[8] Through this metaphor, Szofman makes a reference to a widely publicized polemic between the Hebrew writer Mikhah Yosef Berdyczewski and Aḥad Ha'am in the closing years of the nineteenth century. Berdyczewski rebelled against the limited space that Aḥad Ha'am accorded to belles-lettres in his vision of new Hebrew culture. The former particularly opposed the latter's suggestion that Hebrew readers should satisfy their aesthetic needs with European literatures in the vernacular as better developed and richer than Hebrew letters. According to Berdyczewski,

torn between the vision of a new, remote homeland and the quotidian deeply immersed in a reality far removed from the national community developing in Jewish Palestine. Hence, Szofman's contributions to *Nasz Przegląd* were aimed mainly at showcasing new Hebrew writings to wider readership (by means of reviews of translations and literary criticism) and describing current developments in the *Yishuv*. He was also bent on demythologizing immigration to Eretz Israel, which is why he devoted much of his writings as a journalist to the practical and political aspects of the *'aliyah*,[9] the ultimate destiny, in his view, of each and every European Jew.

2 The Bard of the Revolution

According to Józef Szofman, the tear in the hearts of the diasporic Jewish intelligentsia could only be healed with knowledge of the "true" Palestinian reality, made accessible through Hebrew sources, especially literature. This sheds some light on Szofman's mission to familiarize the Polish readership with the figure of Yosef Ḥaim Brenner, whom he considered an outstanding realist and eyewitness to the major watershed in Jewish history, "surrounded with a sacred halo by the working class of Palestine." (Ben-Szalom 1923) "It is sad news," wrote Szofman "that his name does not resonate with all Jews, and that some heard it for the first time only on the occasion of his heroic death." While making Brenner accessible to Polish readers, Szofman depicted the author as a prophet of the new homeland who debunked the biased and distorted representations of Jewish life in Palestine: "His vision was always clear. Nothing could escape his attention. He saw through the weaknesses of the Jewish Diaspora and Jewish socialists; neither was he oblivious to the shortcomings of Palestine." (Ben-Szalom 1923)

However, despite the fact that in his work as a journalist and translator Szofman strove to explore the complexity of Palestinian reality, which he believed was best captured by Brenner, he was far from objective in his mission as an in-

---

it would leave the readers with "hearts rent asunder." (Holtzman 2011, 107–11) Szofman's recourse to Berdyczewski's metaphor demonstrates his excellent knowledge of the developments in the debate on the Jewish national revival in Palestine.

9 *'Aliyah* (Hebrew: "ascent") refers to the general Zionist ideal and the actual practice of immigration of Jews from the Diaspora to Palestine, and later to the state of Israel. The term is also used to describe the subsequent waves of migration to Palestine.

termediary.[10] As a Zionist and a socialist in the 1920s, he believed that the only obvious way of "solving the Jewish question" in Europe was through working-class Palestine, developed from its foundations by Jewish pioneers (Hebrew: *ḥalutsim*). In Szofman's columns in *Nasz Przegląd*, the new Jewish homeland, "where new homes, factories, and settlements spring up on a daily basis," (Szofman 1925a) appears as the only chance for modernization and improvement of Jewish life, reduced by the long exile. Characteristic of Zionist discourse, the quintessentially revolutionary rhetoric of building a "new world" in Palestine entailed hope for a national and moral revival that was not only territorial, but also qualitative—that is, social. Such a change was expected to occur through the radical transformation of social relations and the individual metamorphosis of all Jews through constructive work. Szofman wanted to see Yosef Ḥaim Brenner as the bard of a new community defined in such terms:

> He knew that a new world was emerging; he knew that the courageous architects were in for a daunting task of laying the foundations for everything: Jewish labor, Jewish grammar schools, and Hebrew as a living national language. He was a staunch believer in the victory of the Idea and the Absolute; he believed that a new society in the ancient Palestine would constitute a great leap forward on the way to reviving the humanity. (Ben-Szalom 1923)

In his columns, Szofman supported this quintessentially ideological and mystical vision of Brenner as a prophet of the Jewish revolution. For example, he quoted his own translation of the writer's relatively early text (Brenner 1905), published during Brenner's stay in London, first in the Jewish newspaper *Ha-Yehudi* (December 1905), and later in the magazine *Ha-Meorer* [*The Awakener*][11] (June 1906), which the author founded himself. Although the original text was written under completely different historical circumstances—in the wake of the Russian

---

[10] He expressed his commitment in an explicit way by frequently contributing heated polemics against current Polish Jewish journalism on Palestine. In one of his pieces, he took issue with the author of a travelogue who in her description of Palestine compared Tel Aviv, the city symbolizing the endeavors of the architects of the new Jewish homeland, to an "only child of a wealthy banker, who had his side locks cut off, and dressed in a white sailor's suit was sent to the beach with an English tutor." (Szofman 1925a) In his polemic with journalists skeptical about immigration to Palestine, written on the occasion of the Warsaw Palestine Exhibition of 1925, Szofman argued: "Let us imagine for a while that the Palestine Exhibition were held in 1910 or 1920. Which exhibits would we put on display? The sand dunes of what is now the city of Tel Aviv? Or the marshes of the Jezreel Valley, where new Jewish settlements flourish on the lands belonging to the Jewish National Fund? Or the rocks from the arid lands of Judea and Samaria?" (Szofman 1925c)

[11] The title of the periodical, which was probably inspired by the text in question, was derived from a Russian revolutionary lexicon (Shapira 2008, 83).

Revolution of 1905 and the ensuing pogroms of Russian Jews—its revolutionary message resonated with the leaders of the Yishuv, who used its fragments out of context and turned them into an unofficial creed of the Jewish pioneers in Palestine. Józef Szofman translated passages of this text to paint a mystical aura around Brenner:

> To awake you I came, my brother, to awake you: seek, oh man, the ways of the world, ask the way, ask "hither"? ... Listen, son of Israel, listen, young man, raise your head, raise your head high, and the gates of the world shall open. Without respite, without fear! With no trace of lie, no trace of weakness! Away with the clouds, leave your tenebrous cavern. Rid the fetters of violence! Enter the garden, look into the face of Being, comprehend it, become pure and sacred![12] (Szofman 1925d)

Brenner the Awakener emerges here as a spiritual "guide for the perplexed," embodying the prime ideals of the socialist pioneers' movement, such as the revival of the Hebrew language, a return to roots, the building of the new homeland with manual labor, and the shaping of the new man and the new world. In his articles, Szofman tapped into the mood prevalent in Palestine after Brenner's death, when the enthusiastic pioneers of the Second Aliyah embraced him as a hero. After all, Brenner not only promoted Zionist ideals, but also attested to them with his own life, almost like a Christian saint. This secular "canonization" of Brenner responded to the demand, widespread among the Jewish pioneers in Palestine at that time, for moral and ideological role models that could galvanize the entire community and legitimize its existence. This meant that Brenner's work and his biography needed to undergo a re-interpretation in line with Zionist principles. For Szofman and the Zionist circles, Brenner came to epitomize an intellectual who did not alienate himself from the working class, an active socialist who worked hand in hand with the ḥalutsim, and thereby fulfilled the Zionist ideal not only in theory, but also in practice.

After Brenner's death, his myth only gained in popularity, spreading into the Diaspora. Yet the image of his life and work emerging from this idealized vision had little do with his actual biography or the complexity of his literary oeuvre. Born in 1881 in the Russian Empire to a traditional and modest Jewish family, Yosef Ḥaim Brenner experienced firsthand the new winds blowing through Europe at the turn of the twentieth century. In his youth, he abandoned traditional religious education and left his family home in search of secular scholarship and

---

[12] Although little is known about whether Szofman had access to the entire original or only the excerpts, he captures the reader's attention with a canny compilation of the fragments and by bringing out its original revolutionary rhetoric in elevated Polish.

literature. Harsh living conditions in the Russian Empire and the mandatory conscription to the Imperial Russian Army motivated him to leave the country for London and Lemberg [today's Lviv, Ukraine]. Wherever he went, he joined the local milieus of exiled Jewish intellectuals in their attempts to revive Jewish cultural life. These endeavors found expression, among others, in the Hebrew-language magazine *Ha-Me'orer* [The Awakener] that he set up in England at a time when major Jewish newspapers and magazines were clamped down on in the Russian Empire.

Contrary to the legend that emerged after his death, Brenner did not initially dream of immigration to Eretz Israel, and when he did arrive there in 1909, it was for reasons other than sheer ideology (Shapira 2008, 164–66). In his biography, Anita Shapira makes clear that, although, at a young age, he became involved in the labor movement, including its more revolutionary branches, Brenner never crossed the line to become a doctrinaire or a blind follower of ideology (2008, 27–43). What is more, he had a fundamentally pessimistic attitude to life in general, and, more specifically, to the prospects of a Jewish national revival in Palestine, or elsewhere. This stance originated in his melancholy disposition, intellectual formation based on Nietzsche's philosophy and Dostoevsky's novels, as well as his personal experiences of exile. When Brenner finally decided to leave Europe for Palestine, he dragged the last remains of his youthful revolutionary enthusiasm to pin hopes on the project of building a new and better Jewish world. However, his life and creative pursuits in Eretz Israel were to be marked with disenchantment.

Upon his arrival, Brenner decided that he would like to commit to the project of building a new national abode through physical labor. To his great disappointment, however, he soon realized that he was not cut out for manual work. Since he commanded much respect as an emerging literary figure among the Jewish intelligentsia, he soon became involved in initiatives aimed at building a Hebrew literary center in Palestine, which also allowed him to continue his individual creative pursuits. However, Brenner would never come to terms with this arrangement. His personal failure in fulfilling the Zionist ideal of turning into a working intellectual cooled his enthusiasm for the project of transforming Jewish society (Govrin 1989, 109–10). Observing life in the Jewish settlements and in the newly constructed city of Tel Aviv, he came to the disheartening conclusion that Palestine was far from witnessing any social revolution; to the contrary, it only perpetuated the same bad habits, vice, and power relations that he saw in the Diaspora. Brenner expressed this view multiple times in his works written after he settled in Eretz Israel, especially in *Shkhol ye-kishalon* [*Bereavement and Failure*, 1920], his last novel, full of bitter satire on the Second Aliyah.

Such thinking was fundamentally at odds with the basic tenets of Zionism that Józef Szofman adhered to as he began to promote Brenner's oeuvre in his journalistic writings. This dissonance failed, however, to keep him from perpetuating the myth of Brenner as the patron of the Zionist revolution. It took deep root in the interwar Polish-Jewish milieus and prevailed long after Szofman himself turned towards Revisionism and gave up journalism altogether. In anniversary articles appearing in 1931, the idealized image of Brenner is not only adopted by the successors of Szofman, but often also radicalized, verging on the grotesque, for example: "He was an ordinary worker, and for a long time he worked hand in hand with the ḥalutsim, who fertilised the sun-scorched earth with their blood and toil, turning the malaria-infested marshes into the orchards of paradise. ... He was the reviving spirit to our workers, someone who tirelessly exhorted them to have a pure, healthy, and creative life." (Tomer 1931a)

This and similar articles—published in the Polish-language Jewish press of the 1930s to encourage teenagers active in the Zionist youth organizations— clearly drew on the image of Brenner the Awakener. Thus, exhorting the youth to "raise their heads and leave the tenebrous cavern," these texts presented Brenner as the "apostle" of the Jewish revival, "proudly holding the Jewish national banner." (Tomer 1931b) Focused on the messianic theme and extolling Brenner's personal virtues, they often misrepresented facts. A case in point is the article *Poeta chaluc [A Ḥaluts Poet]* (Adler 1931), which was intended to present Brenner's life and evolution as an artist. Apart from basic factual inaccuracies, the author of the text modified the writer's biography entirely by adding episodes of physical labor, for example, as a woodcutter and harbor porter, as if his original biography was not sufficiently proletarian.

Józef Szofman, who fundamentally opposed idealized depictions of life in Palestine, never resorted to such blatant manipulations. There is no doubt, however, that he himself was responsible for disseminating the myth of Brenner in Poland, not least, with the help of his translation of Brenner's *Ha-motsa*. The Polish translation of the short story is clearly marked by the tension between Szofman's intent to render Brenner's powerful expression of "truth," which he admired, and the translator's belief in the didactic role of literature in conveying this truth.

3 *The Way Out*

The story entitled *Ha-motsa* [*The Way Out*] is a unique item in Yosef Haim Brenner's oeuvre for a number of reasons. It was probably written in 1918 as one of the sketches that the writer gradually collected to publish, presumably as a volume of short stories from the life of the *Yishuv* (Shapira 2008, 352). The text was first issued in print in 1919 in the magazine *Ha-Arets ye-ha-'Avodah* [*The Land and the Work*] and was a part of seven short "tableaux" of wartime incidents in Palestine (Abramson 2003, 73). Additionally, the story took on a mythological aura because the copies of some of the short pieces were discovered after Brenner's death among the papers he had left in his flat in Tel Aviv, as well as in the house on the outskirts of Jaffa where he stayed during the Arab riots. Saved from the looted building, they belonged to the few surviving pieces of Brenner's late legacy. The writer was reported to have taken the originals with him during evacuation; as he previously lost some of his manuscripts, he always carried them at his side in a leather bag. Yet, the bodies discovered in the vicinity of the Jaffa house, including Brenner's, were stripped of virtually everything, and the bag was never to be found (Shapira 2008, 349).

The seven pieces, including *Ha-motsa*, which was the longest and most fully developed in the series, constitute one of the few immediate literary Jewish responses not only to the Great War in Palestine, but also to World War I in general (Abramson 2003, 73). The story is set against the backdrop of wartime Palestine, where the Jews, displaced from Tel Aviv and Jaffa by the Turks, wander aimlessly as General Allenby approaches from the south. Deprived of their homes overnight, the refugees roam to the north of the country, where they expect to find temporary shelter among the Jewish communities in the areas removed from the front. The story begins when a group of refugees arrives at the gates of one such Jewish settlement. The protagonist, an old proletarian teacher and a local farm resident, notices the crowd of scruffy, starving, and ill people, whom he decides to help, first on his own by sharing bread collected among his neighbors, and later by interceding for them at the local *moshavah* council.[13] Sadly, one of the refugees' children dies because of the tardiness and cold-heartedness of the *moshavah* residents and their leaders, who are determined to keep the refugees away from the settlement. The old teacher feels a moral obligation to bury the body of the starved infant, and a Turkish soldier comes to his assistance. However, the protagonist's foot is injured during burial, which makes it impossible for him to continue his mission. The story concludes with a meaningful scene in which the limping old man is lost in thought about a newly arrived transport of refugees while soaking his swollen toe in cold water.

Ha-motsa is based on the author's personal experience. Brenner, his wife, and their young son lived in Tel Aviv during General Allenby's offensive. The

---

[13] *Moshavah* is a form of rural Jewish settlement in Palestine, and later in Israel, operating according to cooperative principles.

Brenner family also became refugees after October 1917, when they had to flee the city to roam from one settlement to another. Initially, their situation was relatively comfortable, mainly due to Brenner's tenure as a teacher in the Herzliya gymnasium,[14] which, also evacuated, was able to secure decent living conditions for their teaching staff. However, after he lost his job, Brenner had to move to Hadera, a settlement in the north, which must have served as a model for the story's setting. Brenner, who agreed to pay an inordinate amount of money to rent a room at a local farmer's, saw the crowd of refugees camping out daily on the outskirts of the *moshavah*. They lived in terrible conditions, on bare ground, and without access to clean, potable water. The local council of Hadera refused to have any contact with the refugees because of the threat of a typhus epidemic. The writer witnessed a child die in the arms of an emaciated mother. He buried the child, assisted by a Sephardic worker (Shapira 2008, 293–94).

As Glenda Abramson notes, Brenner was a writer whose oeuvre developed, to a large extent, in response to the social and political situation of his time and his own experiences (2003). Brenner's late pieces can be therefore regarded as yet another product of his signature realist workshop which was aimed at capturing "the 'truth' in which the war is less an event than an abstract trigger for his subjective consideration of Jewish response." (Abramson 2003, 74) The reality of World War I in *Ha-motsa*, or rather single snapshots of the wartime panorama, are rendered by means of naturalistic, austere, and poignant descriptions of dirt, illness, death, decomposing bodies, and fear. It is not so much the decline of universal moral principles or pioneer ideals that Brenner decries here, but the fact that they have been betrayed by those who swore to follow them. Brenner's wartime miniatures reveal a fundamentally critical perspective on the new Jewish world, whose image is exposed in crisis as a mirror reflection of the Diaspora.

We can ponder on why it was this particular story, so far removed from the Zionist myth, that Szofman decided to translate into Polish. Following Brenner's death, his closest friends and confidants in Palestine took on a mission to collect his full legacy and protect the copyrights to secure a future income for his son, Uri Nissan. The Shtibel publishing house was entrusted with Brenner's collected works in the original (in 1924, the first four volumes were already available in Warsaw, which Szofman obviously noticed), but the rights to publish particular

---

[14] Set up in 1905, the Herzliya gymnasium was the first secondary school in Jaffa; five years later it was transferred to Ahuzat Bayit, one of the earliest residential areas in Tel Aviv. From its foundation, the gymnasium enjoyed an excellent reputation, with many celebrated artists and public figures among its alumni. Brenner worked there as a literature and language teacher from 1915 to 1917.

works, both in the original and in translation, were managed very carefully (Shapira 2008, 352). In order to commemorate the author, circles closely affiliated with Brenner in Palestine chose to publish his works in their magazines, a posthumous tribute of sorts. This is why the first issue of the People's Library series run by the *Ha-Po'el ha-Tsa'ir* newspaper featured *Ha-motsa*, which found considerable resonance both in Eretz Israel and in the Diaspora as one of the final pieces in Brenner's oeuvre.

Szofman, who at the time worked as Head of the Press and Propaganda Department at the *Histadrut* [General Organization of Workers] in Poland, probably knew about the publication (it is quite likely that he first read the story in the issue) and could make an enquiry about the copyrights. That said, his choice to focus his attention on the story, apart from pragmatic reasons, also had deep ideological underpinnings. Since the main protagonist of *Ha-motsa* was identified with the author, the piece was immediately incorporated into the canon of Brenner's posthumous cult. Although the figure of the old teacher as depicted by Brenner was not unambiguous, the character's actions almost universally inspired ethical exegesis in terms of quintessentially moral deeds of the last remaining righteous deeply moved by the suffering of other human beings. Józef Szofman is likely to have interpreted the story along those lines, too. In his introduction to the Polish translation of the story, Szofman returned to his vision of Brenner as a ruthless realist, who best captured the wound in the Jewish heart, because he felt it himself. Although the Polish translator framed Brenner's work as strongly autobiographical (Szofman 1925b, 8), he also considered it as representative of the universal Jewish experience. The constant tension between the individual and the community, literary pursuits and history, creativity and "truth," and between a human of flesh and blood and a symbol, defined the essence of Brenner's legend. Both the Polish translation of *Ha-motsa* and Szofman's introduction blur the distinction between the author, the narrator, and the protagonist (both individual and collective).

In the introduction to *Ha-motsa* Szofman presents Brenner as a social activist who, although not a Jewish nationalist himself, "could have easily said: 'I do not need to incite nationalism or preach national unity: my daily life is purely national.'" (Szofman 1925b, 10) This way Szofman, aware of Brenner's reservations towards Zionism and ideology in general, tried to frame the author's attitude in a way that allowed him to position Brenner's story within a wider Zionist narrative. The same motivation might have prompted his statement that "Brenner's major objectives were the Hebrew language, Palestine, and social justice." He also attributed to Brenner the conviction that only those who came to Palestine "for the sake of the nation" could feel disappointment at what they found there. Those who came with a true spiritual calling—never would. (Szofman

1925b, 10) This rhetoric resonated profoundly with the readers of *The Way Out* in Polish. The articles on Brenner published in the Polish-language Jewish press in the 1930s likewise interpreted the story in purely autobiographical terms: "The earthly life of Brenner was one of hardship. He would roam the rocky roads barefoot and hungry. However, all this could hardly break the poet's spirit, who, despite all this, came to the successful aid of the refugees and the homeless driven away from their abodes by the Turks." (Tomer 1931a)

Szofman uses a similar strategy to take the bite of Brenner's ruthless diagnosis of the *Yishuv* conveyed in *Ha-motsa*'s powerful images of decay. The translator's foreword is fashioned in such a way that the narrative on the life and works of Brenner pivots around the war, presented as a turning point for his life and worldview. Szofman thus suggests that World War I and the third wave of Jewish migration to Palestine triggered an "inner metamorphosis" in Brenner that "strengthened his belief in victory." (Szofman 1925b, 12) What logically follows is that the author's biting critique of the *Yishuv* concerned the time prior to World War I, and that the pessimism of Brenner's works, as Szofman ascertains, ultimately led to the "affirmation of life" and prompted a "creative impulse spurring to action." (Szofman 1925b, 11) In this light, it is of little surprise that Szofman considered *The Way Out* to be "unquestionably the best work" (Szofman 1925b, 7) of Brenner to be published after the war.

4 The Translator and the Truth of Literature

The analysis of the Polish translation of Brenner's *Ha-motsa* must necessarily begin with an acknowledgment of its linguistic quality, accuracy, and attention to verbal expression. Szofman's command of both Hebrew and Polish is remarkable. This is particularly visible in the way he rendered Brenner's naturalistic depictions of the refugees and their appalling living conditions. In the original (Brenner 1918), these passages combine the roughness of colloquial Hebrew with pathos. They sound equally poignant in Józef Szofman's rendition:

> Cienie ludzi. Staruchy leżą obok rozrzuconych paczek. Kobiety w rozdartych koszulach, z nagą piersią. Twarze dziewcząt dawno niemyte, dawne widmo młodzieńczości spełzło z ich twarzy. Siedem – osiem sierot więdnących. [The shadows of people. Old people lying around scattered bags. Women in tattered shifts, with bare breast. Girls' faces long unwashed, the appearance of youth long gone from their faces. Seven or eight withering orphans.] (Brenner 1925, 19)

The translation also reflects the psychological depth of the protagonist, conveyed by means of auctorial narration. For the Polish reader, the text offers insight into the moral dilemmas of the old teacher through lexically rich prose. Szofman also masterfully renders some challenging Hebrew syntax.

> Co będzie? Co będzie? Wszyscy załamani, przygnębieni, głodni, nadzy, zakażeni chorobami zakaźnemi, przybędą, *wypadną* [yupletu] z kolei i usiądą tu pod niebem; *będą żarci przez upał* [maakhal le-ḥorev ha-shemesh] za dnia, a chłód i rosę w nocy, *nękani febrą, zieloną febrą miejscową* [maakhal le-ḳadaḥat ha-makom, ha-ḳadaḥat ha-yeruḳah]. Skorupki gliniane nie mogące ruszyć się z miejsca, niezdolne zrobić cośkolwiek dla siebie … Kto ich nakarmi? Kto ich napoi? Kto wyleczy? Co będzie?
>
> [What is going to happen? What is going to happen? Depressed, dejected, hungry, naked and infected with contagious disease, they shall come, *fall out* [yupletu: literally "shall be discharged"] from the train and sit here under the sky; *they shall be stung with* heat by daylight [maakhal le-ḥorev ha-shemesh], and cold and dew by night; *they shall be pestered by fever, the local green fever* [maakhal le-ḳadaḥat ha-makom, ha-ḳadaḥat ha-yeruḳah]. Broken clay shells, they cannot move forward, unable to do anything for their own sake… Who's going to feed them? Who's going to give them drink? Who's going to heal them? What is going to happen?] (Brenner 1925, 17; highlighted by the author, explications in brackets by the author)

Szofman's work contains only few factual inaccuracies. In one instance, he interprets the phrase *kadur ha-tsofim* as a chain-fixed machine gun [*kulomiot przytwierdzony łańcuchami*] (Brenner 1925, 17), but the expression actually denotes a balloon demarcating the front line (Shapira 2008, 293). The confusion was probably due to a peculiar notation of the word "balloon," which in its dictionary form, even in a pocket Hebrew-Polish dictionary from the time (Nussbaum 1920), reads *kadur poreaḥ* [literally: blooming sphere].

To render the setting of Brenner's story, Szofman mobilized a whole repository of Zionist vocabulary developed over the years, among others, by the Polish Zionist press. The two major points of reference in the represented world are a pioneers' cooperative, or *moshavah*—a major Jewish settlement and seat of the local authorities—and a nearby farm, or *ḥavah*, where the main protagonist lives.[15] Szofman renders the two terms in Polish as *kolonia* and *ferma*, respectively. The former denoted a settlement of Jewish pioneers on the land purchased by the Jewish National Fund (Ḳeren Ḳayemet le-Iśrael). In the Zionist idiolect, the word connoted both the "great Jewish colonization work" in Palestine and, more broadly, the act of taming the land and gaining dominion over it. The adherents to the Jewish colonization of Palestine considered Jewish settlements to

---

[15] In harsh wartime conditions, foreign aid failed to reach the shores of Eretz Israel, and both citrus fruit and wine exports, as well as the imports of necessary supplies, became limited. The *moshavot* and their affiliated farms, which could provide sustenance with agricultural produce, fared much better than the cities.

be the very heart of the Zionist movement and the core of Zionist practice. They were the backdrop of the Zionist revolution that was to transform Jewish society.[16] The proletarianization of the intelligentsia, which aimed at transforming the "sickly professor" into a "swarthy pioneer," was expected to begin at the farms, that is, agricultural training facilities established both in the Diaspora and in Palestine since the beginning of the Jewish colonization process.[17] The represented world in *The Way Out* is thus composed of the elements that are central to the Zionist vision, while the Polish translation gains an additional tinge of the Diaspora-based revolutionary rhetoric of the ʻaliyah.

Brenner seems to have been aware of the fact that the idiolect of the European ḥalutsim, which they brought with them from Europe, would fade in the Hebrew text. In an attempt to preserve it, he included some words, like ḳolonyah, in dialogues instead of the Hebrew equivalent *moshavah*. On closer scrutiny, the original also reveals that Brenner was sensitive to a variety of discourses, rhetorical devices, and linguistic manipulations, and he skillfully applied them in his literary work. In *Ha-motsa*, the Jewish authorities and residents of the colonies dehumanize the refugees in order to bypass the moral imperative to save human life, which is deeply ingrained in Judaism. Right from the very beginning, this process of dehumanization is reflected in the story's language. In the passage depicting the transport[18] of the refugees on a freight train normally used for shipping wood, human beings are juxtaposed with logged trees—puny, sickly, or dead. Later in the story, members of the emigration council deploy sanitary and epidemiological rhetoric and, in another passage, people are compared to pigs in a vulgar joke. The Polish translation, however, fails to convey this crucial aspect of Brenner's prose, rendering only the most obvious cases that are either explicit or difficult to omit. Szofman's interpretation of the text suggests that he wanted to take the sting out of these passages. For example, in a line uttered by one of the residents of the village about the newly arrived refugees, the Hebrew stem *r-ḥ-sh*, which usually refers to insects and means "to crawl, to swarm, to

---

[16] In his travelogue from Palestine, Jakub Appenszlak, writer, translator and a contributor to *Nasz Przegląd*, wrote about Jewish colonies that the land, once rid of rocks and sand, would become a fecund oasis in which "grapevines crawl down the slopes and the divans of greenery unfold." (Appenszlak 1925)

[17] One such farm, for example, was established 1919 in the then village of Grochów on the outskirts of Warsaw (today's Ostrobramska residential estate area) by young people from the He-Ḥaluts youth organization. At the turn of the nineteenth century, a similar farm, Ḥayat Kinneret, was set up in Palestine by Artur Rupin.

[18] In the original, the expression is provided in Hebrew transcription, which only adds to the dehumanized image of the refugees.

creep," is used to describe people camping out on bare ground among the trunks of logged trees. Szofman, however, renders the verb neutrally as *poruszać się* [Polish: to move] (Brenner 1925, 18).

The translation also neutralizes the inner tensions of the *Yishuv*, reflected in the very language that refers to the refugees. The protagonist initially calls them "exiles" (*golim*: stemming from *galut*, which is a negative term for the Diaspora) or simply "souls" (*nefashot*). As the story develops, he begins to use the word "newcomers" (*ha-baim*), which is neutral, but obscures the situation, until finally, in a conversation with the *moshavah* council, he conforms to their language of discrimination and contempt. This shift is particularly visible in one of the lines uttered by the old teacher, who informs the local council about the newly arrived exiles: "forty-two new souls ... immigrants ... have come" [*arba'im u-shtayim nefashot ... mehagrim ... bau*]. The local authorities deploy the contemptuous term "immigrants" [*ha-mehagrim*], as if the refugees were not Jews, sometimes longtime residents in Palestine, but strangers alien to the community of Eretz Israel. Szofman's translation reads only: "forty-two ... refugees ... have come" [*czterdziestu dwóch ... uciekinierów ... przybyło*]. (Brenner 1925, 23)

If it was not for the fact that such passages contributed to the negative portrayal of the *Yishuv*, we could ascribe this imprecise rendering to a lapse in attention on the part of the translator, or to his insufficient understanding of the text. However, an analysis of Szofman's choice of words, omissions, and paraphrases seems to support the hypothesis that the translator introduced them on purpose.

Brenner's original represents the *Yishuv* as a diverse community of people who do not always conform to the Zionist ideal of Hebrew speaking, secularized ḥalutsim, following exclusively the "religion of labor" [*dat ha-'avodah*][19] and tilling the land. Among the refugees, we also encounter a wealthy man, travelling with loads of baggage and, unlike all the others who sleep on bare ground, living in a tent and able to pay any price for accommodation. Although he is arrogant, quarrelsome, and indifferent to the hardships of his companions, his money gives him a chance to enter the colony. The Polish translation, perhaps as the exception proving the rule, renders the character with the original's intensity. However, a yeshivah student [Hebrew: *avrekh*] is rendered simply as a "young man."

Several passages in the story suggest that the characters speak languages other than Hebrew. This is a signature mark of Brenner, whose artistic strategy

---

[19] The term was frequently (though erroneously) attributed to A.D. Gordon, a thinker pivotal for the ḥalutzim of the Second and Third 'Aliyot, who made the notion of work, both in its physical and creative aspects, the central points of his ethics (Silberscheid 1992, 108–9). Gordon's teachings were similar to Brenner's oeuvre in that they were exposed to arbitrary interpretations already in the author's lifetime and even more so after his death.

was to portray the emerging spoken Hebrew in its birth pangs. While striving to adopt the forefathers' tongue, Brenner's characters often fail to express themselves, or confuse languages, and often resort to Yiddish. Although *Ha-motsa* is not the most characteristic text in this respect, it features some Yiddish interjections or calques that sound foreign in Hebrew. One of the refugees, for example, addresses the old teacher with the phrase *rav yehudi*, which is a direct calque of the Yiddish *reb yid*. These subtle devices are lost in the Polish translation. Szofman, who considered Brenner "one of the greatest figures of Hebrew letters," would have him speak and write only Hebrew. His own condescending attitude to Yiddish is apparent in the introduction, where he puts the following statement, attributing it to Brenner:

> We, who were revived by the Hebrew language and whose souls were enriched by it; for whom it is the only life-giving spring and the inalienable part of our being, which we adhered to entirely; we refuse to accept it (Yiddish)[20] and we will never come to terms with it. (Szofman 1925b, 10)

Although Brenner was attached to Hebrew as a means of artistic expression, he was, in fact, well versed in Yiddish and Russian, his formative languages, and did not shy away from publishing in Yiddish either, especially in the early period. At one point, he put it bluntly in a letter to a friend: "I can write well in Yiddish and I have sworn no oath. I do not care about the aura of sacredness [around Hebrew] either." (Shapira 2008, 110)[21] Hence, Brenner did not feel obliged to use exclusively Hebrew and he never diminished the role of Yiddish.

Szofman gives a similar treatment to the references to the Jewish religious tradition present in the original text of *Ha-motsa*. Although Brenner was spiritually removed from it, religion, as a deeply ingrained childhood experience, was a reservoir of inspiration for him. On the one hand, the Polish translation skillfully emphasizes the references to the story of Exodus. This key narrative of Jewish collective memory reverberates in the story's title, which also references the Jewish exodus from Europe. On the other hand, the translator completely ignores Brenner's cryptoquotations from the Talmud, as well as the vocabulary derived from the discourse of rabbinical exegesis. It seems as if Szofman brought out Brenner's references to Jewish tradition only in the passages underpinned with irony. A good example is the faithfully translated discussion between the helpless old teacher and the officials, who resort to mercantile arguments. To counter

---

20 The newspaper article that featured this passage before Szofman incorporated it into his foreword figured the phrase "we do not want Yiddish." (Szofman 1925d)

21 Translated into Polish by the author. Translated into English by the translator.

their reasoning in this confrontation, the protagonist deploys his entire rhetorical repertory, quoting biblical passages and using rabbinical formulas (Brenner 1925, 24–25). At the same time, the translation omits Brenner's references to traditional religious upbringing shared by many residents of the *Yishuv*, who, just like the author, abandoned religion later in life.[22]

The Polish translation of *Ha-motsa* also neutralizes some negative characteristics that Brenner ascribed to the refugees, such as stupidity, pettiness, passivity and a sense of entitlement. Szofman also resorts to a number of devices intended to dampen the writer's subtle yet poignant social critique. Below, I juxtapose Szofman's translation with my own, which follows Brenner's original as closely as possible (Brenner 1925, 16):

> nic nie robili, cała bowiem ich praca polegała na przysłuchiwaniu się strzałom, dysputowaniu na różne tematy strategiczne oraz jękach i skargach [they were doing nothing, all their work was listening to shooting, discussing various strategic topics, as well as moaning and grumbling].

vs.

> nic nie robili, *nie kiwnęli palcem, by poprawić swoją sytuację,* a cała ich praca polegała na przysłuchiwaniu się strzałom, dysputowaniu na różne tematy strategiczne oraz jękach i skargach [they were doing nothing, *they did not move a finger to improve their situation,* all their work was listening to shooting, discussing various strategic topics, as well as moaning and grumbling].[23]

Omitting the marked phrase utterly changes the meaning of the original. The Polish translator did not hesitate to modify the text also in other cases, and to a much larger extent. The most striking example of omission is a lengthy passage in the last section of the story, in which the *moshavah* council refuses to bury a dead infant, while the mother of the child, Ḥayah (literally: alive), pushing away the little corpse, implores them to bring her the daily ration of bread, because she is hungry.

Like many of Brenner's other works, *The Way Out* challenges the Zionist dogma of radical social change in the "new" Jewish world. This is evident not only in the passages describing the social makeup of the refugees and their be-

---

[22] Szofman followed a similar procedure in his translation of the quotes from Brenner's article featured in *Ha-meʿorer*, which abounds in references of this kind.

[23] An alternative translation into Polish provided by the author. The Polish translation rendered into English by the translator. In order to facilitate the comparison, the alternative translations are as close to Szofman's version as possible.

havior, but also in the ruthless critique of the *Yishuv*'s establishment, driven by the capitalist power relations. Particularly symptomatic in this context is a scene at the seat of the immigration council, which made a decision about the future of the refugees. When the main protagonist comes to alarm the council about the stranded people who are in desperate need of help, he can find neither the chairman nor other members, who are all asleep. When they are finally available, they justify their continued refusal to help with the sanitary hazard that the refugees pose, the inflated prices for bread and transportation, and the accommodation that local farmers demand. Witnessing this cynicism and heartlessness of the councilors, the old teacher exclaims: "Murderers!" [*Rotsḥey nefashot!*], which in the Polish translation becomes: "Thieves!" [*Złodzieje!*] (Brenner 1925, 22) In the subsequent section, when the room begins to fill with profiteers and grain dealers, it soon turns out, amidst jostling and haggling, that the chairman of the *moshavah* council is an illegal flour dealer who profits from the hardship of the refugees. This key piece of information is missing from Szofman's translation, and the entire scene is rendered in such a way that it takes the sting out of the criticism and the satire of the original.

The same happens to the complexity of the central protagonist, who Brenner's contemporaries, and Shofman himself, considered to be an alter ego of the author. In the original, the old proletarian teacher from the *moshavah* is torn by contradictions. Although he feels a moral obligation to aid the refugees and tries to come to their rescue, there are also moments when he shirks this responsibility. Brenner brings the helplessness of the protagonist—his incapacity to drive any significant change—to the fore, which can be interpreted as a reflection of his own personal failure to transform into a working intellectual.

Regrettably, the Polish translation eradicates this ambiguity of the original that prevents the readers from passing a definitive moral judgment on the motivations of the protagonist. Szofman emphasizes the heroic deeds of the teacher, such as bringing aid to the refugees or heeding the moral obligation to bury the infant's body. At the same time, he neutralizes the passages that portray the protagonist's helplessness vis-à-vis the power structures of the *moshavah*, or suggest that his motivations are not exactly morally impeccable. In the finale of the story, as the teacher dislocates his toe on the way to the graveyard, Brenner ironically speaks of *petsʻa enosh*, which literally means a "deadly wound." Szofman renders it in Polish as "he sustained a painful wound" [*zranił się bardzo boleśnie*]. This minor injury becomes a pretext for the protagonist to abandon any activity, a convenient and morally justified "way out" of the situation. Brenner puts it across as: "He put his toe into the cold water; it was so swollen that he could barely move, even to meet the needs of his own. And so he felt discharged from meeting the needs of others. Utterly discharged. Relief descended upon him." [*Hu śam et ha-etsbʿa ba-mayim ha-ḳarim, ye-zo tsavta, ʿad shelo hayah ya-khol aḥar kakh lazuz mimekomo gam le-tsarkhav. Paṭur hayah, apo, mikhol tsar-khey aḥerim. Paṭur legamrey. Baah ha-haḳalah.*] The Polish translation, in turn, reads: "He put his toe into the cold water; it was so swollen that he could barely move, even to meet the needs of his own. He felt free." [*Włożył palec do zimnej wody, taki był spuchnięty, że nie mógł potem ruszyć się z miejsca, nawet dla swoich potrzeb. Wolny był teraz.*] (Brenner 1925, 32)

Szofman omits entire phrases, even paragraphs, of the original text that could frame the protagonist in an ambivalent light, such as the scene of digging the grave alongside a Turkish soldier. He also reduces the ambiguity of Brenner's prose, opting for just one of the possible interpretations. The procedure is clearly visible in the final section of the story. Brenner's image of the hungry protagonist, who is groping for a single slice of bread hidden among the books, was to a large extent edited out in the Polish translation (interestingly, Szofman makes no mention of a library in the teacher's house either). The thoughts of the protagonist, as he finally discovers the bone dry piece of bread, read, in the Polish translation: "What a shame, he thought, when a piece of bread goes to waste now ..." [*Szkoda – myślał, szkoda teraz każdej kromki chleba...*] (Brenner 1925, 32). The original actually leaves more space for interpretation: "What a shame, he thought, each piece of bread now..." [*Ḥaval, ḥaval... – ḥashav – kol prusat leḥem ʿatah...*]. This grey area of ambiguity extends to the whole story, which can also be read as a universal parable of internal affairs of the *Yishuv*. The Polish translation rules such a possibility out right from the start. The choices of the translator, as well as his (partly justifiable) decision to change the subtitle of the story from *A Sketch from an Immediate Past* to *A Palestine Episode of the Great War*, reflect a certain interpretive framework.

Despite its brevity, *Ha-motsa* is a well-developed and subtle literary work, which might be perceived as representative of Yosef Haim Brenner's entire oeuvre. As such, it poses a daunting challenge to any translator. The work of Józef Szofman, who was a contemporary of the author and witnessed the momentous changes that transformed the European Jewry, was clearly influenced by his own subject position. The Polish translation of *The Way Out* thus responds to the demands of the historical moment it was created in. Szofman's intentions as a translator were most probably in line with his own interpretation of Brenner's realism:

> In his struggle against all forms of self-deception and the deception of others, Brenner found it redundant to excessively polish the content and form of his literary works. That is why, the plot of his novels is usually simple and unadorned, narrated in a realistic manner and far from the spectacular or the sensational; his style is heavy, as heavy as a ham-

mer, which only testifies to the magnitude of his talent and moral power that enabled him to express so much with such modest means of expression. (Ben-Szalom 1923)

However, in the heat of his own struggle against "self-deception and the deception of others" as to the prospects of a Jewish future in Europe, Józef Szofman reduced the depth and complexity of Brenner's story, which only ostensibly seems simple, rough, and devoid of artistic qualities. By skewing the text to conform with the myth of the new Jewish world and Brenner as its "patron saint," the Polish translator betrayed what he himself felt lay at the heart of Brenner's writing and what the author considered the quintessential truth of literature.

Translated from Polish by Bartosz Sowiński

Bibliography

Abramson, G. 2003. "No Way out: Brenner and the War." *AJS Review* 27, no. 1: 73–87.
Adler, A. 1931. "Poeta chaluc." *Chwila* 4340: 9.
Ahad, Ha-Am. 1928. *O sjonizmie duchowym*. Warszawa: Akademicka Korporacja Sjonistyczna Zelotia.
Anon. 1921. "Józef Chaim Brenner." *Chwila* 831: 2–3.
Appenszlak, J. 1925. "Dziennik podróży do Palestyny." *Nasz Przegląd* 102: 4–5.
Avneri, S. 2009. "Ha-omnam hit'alel Bialik be-Brenner? [Did Bialik Really Bully Brenner?]." *Ha-Arec*, http://www.haaretz.co.il/literature/1.1238827 (accessed 26 February 2014).
Beer, Ch. 1992. *Gam ahavatam, gam śinatam: Bialik, Brenner, Agnon. Ma'arakhot yaḥasim* [Love and Hate: Bialik, Brenner, Agnon]. Tel Aviv: Am Oved.
Ben-Szalom, J. 1923. "W rocznicę śmierci Brennera." *Nasz Przegląd* 40: 3.
Brenner, Y.H. 1905. *'Al ha-derekh* [On the Road]. http://benyehuda.org/brenner/al_haderex.html (accessed 26 February 2014).
Brenner, Y.H. 1910. *Ha-genre ha-erets-iśraeli ye-avizarehu* [The Eretz-Israeli Genre and Its Attributes]. http://benyehuda.org/brenner/baaretz_071.html (accessed 26 February 2014).
Brenner, Y.H. 1918. *Ha-motsa* [The Way Out], http://benyehuda.org/brenner/motsa.html (accessed: 26 February 2014).
Brenner, Y.H. 1925. *Wyjście (epizod palestyński wojny światowej)*. Warszawa: Orient.
Brenner, Y.H. 1975. "The Way Out." In *Modern Hebrew Literature*, edited by Robert Alter, translated by Yosef Schacter, 139–157. New York: Behrman House.
Brinker, M. 1990. *'Ad ha-simṭah ha-ṭveryanit: maamar al sipur u-maḥshavah be-yetsirat Brenner* [The Narrative and Thought in the Work of Y. H. Brenner]. Tel Aviv: Am Oved.
Govrin, N. 1989. *Alienation and Regeneration*. Tel Aviv: MOD Books.
Holcblat, M. et al. 1928. *Życie nieznane*. Warszawa: Orient.
Holtzman, A. 2011. *Mikhah Yosef Berdyczewski*. Jerusalem: Zalman Shazar Centre.
Nussbaum, J. 1920. *Kieszonkowy słownik polsko-hebrajski*. Kraków: J. Nussbaum.

Prokop-Janiec, E. 1991. "Biblioteka Pisarzy Żydowskich – po raz trzeci." *Dekada Literacka* 27, http://dekadaliteracka.pl/index.php?id=993 (accessed 26 February 2014).

Shapira, A. 2008. *Brenner: Sipur ḥaim* [Brenner: A Biography]. Tel Aviv: Am Oved.

Silberscheid, U. 1992. "Ha-metaḥ beyn aśiyah li-yetsirah be-torato shel A.D. Gordon [The Tension between Labor and Creativity in the Works of A. D. Gordon]." *Katedra* 65: 100–116.

Szofman, J. 1925a. "Jak ja to widzę (Co przed rokiem pani Moszyńska widziała w Palestynie)." *Nasz Przegląd* 95: 6.

Szofman, J. 1925b. "Józef Chaim Brenner." In *Wyjście: (epizod palestyński wojny światowej)*. Biblioteczka Pisarzy i Klasyków Żydowskich, Warszawa: Orient.

Szofman, J. 1925c. "Trzeba umieć patrzeć (Na marginesie wystawy palestyńskiej)." *Nasz Przegląd* 342: 6.

Szofman, J. 1925d. "Twórczość Brennera." *Nasz Przegląd* 102: 5.

Szofman, J. 1925e. "Zadania wszechnicy hebrajskiej." *Nasz Przegląd* 92: 4.

Tidhar, D., ed. 1947. "Yosef Shofman." In *Entsiḳlopediah le-ḥalutsey ha-Yishuv u-vonay* [The Encyclopaedia of the Pioneers and Architects of the Yishuv], Vol. 2, 1037.

Tomer, C. 1931a. "Józef Chaim Brenner." *Chwila* 4351: 7–8.

Tomer, C. 1931b. "Józef Chaim Brenner." *Chwila* 4337: 7–8.

Z.T. 1926. "Józef Chaim Brenner (W piątą rocznicę śmierci)." *Chwila* 2657: 8.

Translation after the Shoah

Dorota Glowacka
The Tower of Babel: Holocaust Testimonials and the Ethics of Translation

> What remains? The language remains.
> —Hannah Arendt, *Essays in Understanding*

> To truly bear witness to it, one must make language anxious.
> —Jean-François Lyotard, "The Survivor"

1 Homeless in the House of Language

In his essay "Language in Exile," Imre Kertész explains that he writes exclusively about the Holocaust because it "does not have and cannot have its own language." (2004, 194)[1] No particular language could possibly contain the experience of the Holocaust. If there were such a language, notes Kertész, it would be so full of violence and grief that it would destroy those who used it (185). Holocaust testimonies cannot be written except in "an accidental language," and they will never belong to a native tongue (196). To the extent that one must express oneself in one of the national languages, the Holocaust remains homeless in the house of language. Kertész writes, "Europeans who survived the Holocaust can tell the story of the suffering in one of the European languages; but none of these languages is their own, and neither is the tongue of the nation which the author has borrowed to write his tale." (194) In his view, this "homelessness" also affects the accounts written in the survivor's mother tongue. Hence the experience of the Holocaust is "unspeakable" not because it falls outside human linguistic competence conceived in universal terms. Rather, what happened cannot be properly articulated since no national language has been able to absorb it or to coin words and expressions capable of conveying its catastrophic dimension. As a result, the survivor does not know "in what language she should tell her story," to quote Izolda Regensberg, the protagonist of one of Hanna Krall's (2006, 16) biographical reportages. Literary critic Alan Rosen (2005) states that "*every* language is going to be unfaithful to the camp experience, taking what existed only in fragments and rendering it in a medium that is intact.

---

[1] A version of this chapter appeared in Dorota Glowacka, *Disappearing Traces: Holocaust Testimonials, Ethics and Aesthetics* (University of Washington Press, 2012). The translations of passages from Kertész' *Język na wygnaniu* are mine, based on the Polish version of the book.

What one sees (or reads) then is the Holocaust filtered through civilized discourse, the Holocaust as it were, according to the coherence of a single cultured tongue." (6)

In this chapter, I will consider Holocaust testimonies in relation to the question of translation, understood here as both exchanges between languages within a text and renditions of the text into another language. As implied in Kertész's remarks, a Holocaust testimony is always a translation into another language. Moreover, it is often a translation without the original, even in the case of writers such as Kertész or Primo Levi, who returned to their hometowns after the war and penned their memoirs in their mother tongue (Hungarian and Italian, respectively).

In his study of the role of the English language in the transmission of Holocaust testimony, Alan Rosen (2005) notes that Jews of Eastern Europe (the population most directly targeted for extermination) were distinguished by their multilingualism. On the eve of World War II, their ability to speak several languages stood in contrast with nationalist strategies of their respective countries of residence, which promoted homogenous linguistic cultures (2). As the Holocaust unfolded, the mélange of languages was reflected in diaries and chronicles written by the victims. Rosen shows that in the ghettos, the choice of a native tongue for everyday communication, as well as for writing down a record of events, reflected the language users' particular circumstances. For instance, the deliberate use of Yiddish instead of Polish in the Warsaw ghetto became an expression of Jewish solidarity, and it signaled increasingly tense relations with former Polish neighbors and a growing sense of Jews' isolation from the national community. In turn, switching from Yiddish to Hebrew (as was the case of diarist Abraham Levin or poet Yitzak Katznelson, after the wave of deportations from the Warsaw ghetto in 1942) was an expression of Zionist hope and Jewish pride in leaving what the writers knew would be a posthumous record. Because those choices were by no means arbitrary, Rosen argues that we also need to consider the choice of language in testimonies written *after* the war, by survivors who, for the most part, found themselves displaced from their former linguistic communities. After the Holocaust, that choice had a profound impact on the survivors' strategies of self-identification and their ability to heal, thus determining how they remembered the events and even the very content of that memory.

According to Israel Knox, the editor of the first *Anthology of Holocaust Literature* (1960), the most "crystallized" expression of Eastern European Jewry's war experiences were memoirs written in Yiddish. For Knox, these memoirs bore witness to the atrocities perpetrated on "the essence of [Eastern European Jewish] civilization." (quoted in Rosen 2005, 9) Yet what exactly did these memoirs express and to whom were they addressed? As Annette Wieviorka (2006) points out, unlike pre-war chronicles of particular communities, these individual memoirs, as well as collective *Yizker-bikher* (memory books) commemorating the genocide, arrived into a complete void, bereft of a community of speakers that would provide a context for memorialization and meaningful interpretation of events (27). Deprived of an audience, confronted with a wall of incomprehension, and impossible to publish, these harrowing testimonials in Yiddish bore witness to the disappearance of the very world in which they would have been read and understood. For Wieviorka, the homelessness of Yiddish after the war resulted in an effective silencing of witnesses. She mentions, for instance, that Yiddish-language poet Abraham Sutzkever from Vilna was not allowed to give a deposition in Yiddish at the Nuremberg trials, and his account was limited to a brief testimony in Russian.

To expose the rupture in the language of testimony wrought by linguistic displacement and the disappearance of the Yiddish-speaking community, Wieviorka discusses Elie Wiesel's *Night*, which was first written in Yiddish, printed in a small edition in Brazil in 1956, and then published in French in 1958. Drawing on Naomi Seidman's meticulous comparison of the Yiddish and French versions of the text, Wieviorka notes a fundamental shift in narrative focus between the two versions. The longer one, *Un di Velthot geshvign* (*And the World was Silent*), expressed sentiments typical for survivor accounts that emerged immediately after the war, such as the desire to overcome death and exert vengeance on the perpetrator. By contrast, in the abridged version in French, which was revised under the mentorship of the Christian writer François Mauriac, the survivor's experiences acquired a more universal dimension and became an existential reflection on the human condition. The act of translation from Yiddish to French enabled Wiesel to embark on a lifetime journey of speaking for those who could not testify for themselves. Wieviorka's analysis implies, however, that this translatory gesture was ambivalent because, by universalizing the survivor's ordeal, the French version obliterated the unique experiences of Eastern European Jewry and the Yiddish world of Wiesel's childhood.

Following the war, different national governments implemented the politics of assimilation and forgetting, either forcefully (in the countries under the communist rule) or covertly (in Western Europe, Israel, and the United States). Paradoxically, these trends compounded the annihilation of *Yiddishkeit* perpetrated by the Nazis. In this context, Rosen's and Wieviorka's reflections on the fate of Yiddish during the Holocaust suggest that, just as "complete witnesses" to the Holocaust were those who "drowned" and can therefore no longer testify for themselves, in Primo Levi's memorable words, complete testimony would have been possible only in a language few could speak after the war.²

In her study of Holocaust memoirs written in English, Susan Robin Suleiman notes that a significant number of Holocaust memoirs were written in the language of the survivors' adopted countries. A number of survivors report that a neutral language (such as English), free from the inscription of violence, first made it possible for them to "speak," to put the trauma into words. Since the "truth" of the experience was so strongly associated with their native tongues, a neutral, distant language helped them surmount debilitating traumatic associations and "attenuate slightly the fiery pain." (Yaffa Eliach quoted in Rosen 2005, 11) In those cases, the distance afforded by another language was the enabling factor in telling the story. Not quite naming what the survivor was trying to articulate, foreign words acted as a protective shield that allowed the storytellers to harness traumatic memories and translate them into a narrative.

Considering Kertész's assertion that there is no national language in which the Holocaust story can truly be told, can we then speak of a translinguistic horizon that structures Holocaust testimony? I will explore this question in the context of Emmanuel Levinas's ethical philosophy, drawing on his articulation of the ethical essence of language as Saying. I will also turn to Walter Benjamin's reflection on translation, in his seminal essay "The Task of the Translator," and consider the task of the translator as an ethical task. The lives of both Levinas and Benjamin were deeply affected by the events of the Holocaust. Benjamin, a German Jew, took his life in 1941 on the Franco-Spanish border when he was trying to flee from the Nazis. Levinas's entire family was murdered, while he himself was imprisoned in Nazi labor camps. Both Levinas and Benjamin worked as translators at some point in their lives, although in very different circumstances. Benjamin was a well-known translator of French literature, lauded for his rendition into German of Charles Baudelaire's *Tableaux parisiens*, while Levinas was enlisted in the French army as a translator from Russian and German, which most likely spared him the fate of being sent to a death camp. Necessarily, then, the matter of translation suffuses the work of both thinkers, and in the case of Levinas is inseparable from the testimonial impetus that animates his philosophical texts.

The question that emerges through my analysis of their work is about what it would mean to consider translation as an act of bearing witness in its own right.

---

2 See Levi 1988, 84.

2 Language in Exile

In his short poetic prose *Conversation in the Mountains*, Paul Célan (2001) describes two Jewish wanderers, the inhabitants of the land, who gaze from the top of a hill upon the fertile, green valley beneath and muse about the language that belongs to that place:

> That's the kind of speech that counts here, the green with the white in it, a language not for you and not for me—because I am asking, who is it meant for then, the earth, it's not meant for you, I am saying, and not for me—, well, then, a language with no I and no Thou, pure He, pure It, d'you see, pure They and nothing but that. (398)

This conviction that the language of the country in which they live has never truly belonged to them, common among diasporic Jews, permeates all of Kertész's writings. After the Holocaust, the survivors' sense of being disowned by their language became much more acute because "Auschwitz" had rendered that linguistic exile permanent and irreparable. For Kertész (2004), the language of exclusion, which designates those who are never quite welcome at the hearth in the house of language, not only sentenced them to death in the camps but also marked them as perennial strangers after the war (177). If the Holocaust bequeathed traumatic memory upon the Jews, says Kertész, it also took away from them the language in which to speak about it (175). For Kertész, the survivor's "borrowed" existence after Auschwitz is then inseparable from an essential homelessness of the language in which he tries to speak about his experiences.[3]

After the war, Kertész returned to Budapest to live and write amid his former community of speakers. Insofar as he remained a foreigner within his native Hungarian, however, he had never truly "returned home." Yet he also found a strange consolation in this privation. He writes, "[t]he more I am a stranger in my language, the more I am credible to myself, the more credible what I write seems to be. I like writing in Hungarian, because [paraphrasing Kafka], the better I feel the impossibility to write." (183) For Kertész, alienation from his native tongue becomes a necessary condition for writing, since it allows him to perceive a rupture of language "after Auschwitz" and to articulate this traumatic split. The national language in which Kertész writes his literary testimony is both the language of his childhood and the language in which he experienced displacement,

---

[3] In his acclaimed memoir *Fateless* (1975; retranslated as *Fatelessness* in 2004), as well as in *Kaddish for a Child Not Born* (1990), Kertész repeatedly refers to his life after the Holocaust as "borrowed," as existence that did not properly belong to him.

deportation, and near-death in the camps. Before he eventually wrote *Fateless*, however, Kertész made a living as a translator from German, the language he had learned in the camps. It is possible then that, for years, his Auschwitz story, which waited for so long to be told, was displaced by the writer's activity as a translator from German.

Like Kertész, Jean Améry (Hans Mayer), an Austrian Jew, continued to write in his native German, although at the time of the publication of *At the Mind's Limit* (*Jenseits von Schuld und Sühne*, 1966) he had been living in Belgium for two decades. In the chapter "How Much Home Does a Person Need?" Améry reflects on the status of "expellees" from the Third Reich (57). For Améry, those who were forced from their communities lost not only all of their possessions but also a sense of belonging to a "people." As their neighbors became "informers or bullies, at best, embarrassed opportunists," the exiles were robbed of their origin, as if their entire past had been "confiscated." (42, 58) Améry grieves the loss of his native language, even though he continues to write in German. For him, a local dialect from the place of one's birth and childhood determines one's sense of self and a person's location within a network of human relations. Once an individual is removed from his "immediate place of origin," (43) his identity unravels and he no longer knows who he is. Moreover, the loss forces him to realize that, as in Célan's parable about the two Jews on a hill, the place and language he loved as a child were never truly his, as if he had "appropriated [them] illegally." (51) Améry recalls that he first became aware of this dispossession when, in a chance encounter with an SS officer during his resistance activities in Belgium, he heard him speak in the dialect from Améry's native region in Austria. The uncanny mixture of emotions brought on by the contrast between the language that he associated with home and the uniform marking the speaker as a deadly foe "sent here from the hostile homeland to wipe me out" (50) caused Améry to conceal his origin and to answer the officer in French. As a result, he later assumed a French-sounding pen name, since he could no longer recognize himself in the "plain German name." When even his proper name, which his friends used to call him, is, as he feels, taken away from him, even the memories of his friends cease to exist (44). His entire past falls away, as does the history of the country he used to call his own, its landscapes now marred by a recollection of swastikas hanging out of farmers' windows on the day of the *Anschluss*. Thus, unlike those who, by virtue of possessing religion, have created for themselves "a portable home," Améry finds himself "completely uprooted." (45) Yet he cannot make himself comfortable in his new language either because, as an émigré, he can only "parrot [it] poorly." A foreign language will never become "a real friend": "*La table* will never be the table: at best one can eat one's fill at it." (52) At the same time, Améry's German is gradually "crumbling away" and atrophying, devoid of the nourishing force of life experience (the only "life experience" German brought him was the threat of death). He bemoans the expropriation of his mother tongue and fears that, as a man deprived of his proper language, he will be forever estranged from his community and even from himself.

3 *Traduttore Traditore*, or the Translatory Impasse

The languages in which Holocaust memoirs were first published after the war—or into which they were translated—often reflected the dominant national politics of memory. Władysław Szpilman's diary, for instance, which inspired Roman Polański's acclaimed film *The Pianist* (2002), first appeared in a heavily censored form 1946, and it remained virtually unknown in Poland until 2001, when it was reissued to coincide with the release of the film in that country as *Pianista: Warszawskie wspomnienia 1939–1945*, on the initiative of Szpilman's son. The new Polish edition, however, was preceded by a 1999 translation into English. Similar tribulations befell Ida Fink's semi-autobiographical novel *The Journey* and her short stories, which were written in Polish and published, for the most part, outside Poland, although they first received critical recognition only after their translation into English.[4] The publication of Fink's short stories and of her novel in Poland (in 2003 and 2004, respectively) was accompanied by the author's celebratory tour of the country, from which she had been expelled in 1957. After decades of exile from the country in which they could find a community of speakers, these Holocaust testimonials returned home, to their mother tongue. However, this homecoming was mediated by another language, in this case, English, into which they had been translated in the meantime and in which they had received acclaim. Yet the language community and the political reality of the country to which Szpilman's and Fink's texts returned many years later were not the same, and the reception of the works in Poland had been influenced by their former success in English.

---

4 The English translation of Fink's short stories, *A Scrap of Time and Other Stories*, appeared in 1989; the translation of her novel *The Journey* in 1992; the volume *Traces*, containing stories and short plays in English translation appeared in 1997. Fink's stories were included in the first anthology of women's Holocaust writings about the Holocaust, entitled *Different Voices* (edited by Carol Rittner and John K. Roth, St. Paul: Paragon House, 1998).

In the decades after the war, English became the dominant language in which many of the Holocaust memoirs were written or into which they were translated; only in English were they celebrated, or even published at all, even though very few of their authors initially wrote in that language. As mentioned above, for many survivors, the relative neutrality of English with regard to the Holocaust and its marginality with respect to languages such as Yiddish, Hebrew, Polish, Ukrainian, German, and others in which the events of the Holocaust were experienced, served as a buffer against the rawness of pain and thus facilitated transmission. English was an "amnesiac language," a lens through which the fragmented, uncontainable experience was refracted and homogenized.

One of the most striking examples of the tension between linguistic appropriation and the palliative effect of giving testimony in English is the story of Isabella Leitner's rewritings of her Holocaust memoir.[5] In her last revision, *Isabella: From Auschwitz to Freedom* (1994), Leitner seeks to gather together all of her previous accounts, to sum up a decades-long labor of remembering and, presumably, to achieve a sense of closure. At the opening of the book, Leitner reminisces about the moment when she reached for the box containing the scraps on which she first wrote her memories in Hungarian "and began to translate them." (16) From the outset, the process of narrativizing her inchoate memories is thus enabled by translation. The language of Leitner's first retelling in English, *Fragments of Isabella*, largely preserved the rawness and intensity of the author's wartime experience, even if it was already blanketed by English and by her husband's editorial assistance. Throughout subsequent rewritings of her story, Leitner's writing style reflects not only her growing maturity but also her increased linguistic competence in the language of her adopted country, while the "foreignness" of her idiom becomes increasingly less noticeable.

Significantly, English is the native tongue of Leitner's husband, to whom the author dedicates her book and expresses gratitude: "This book belongs to him." Leitner's last account is followed by an epilogue written by Irving Leitner, in which he acknowledges a profound debt to his wife for her continuous acts of love that have allowed him to maintain hope. Clasped between the dedication

---

[5] Isabella Leitner (1924–2009) was deported to Auschwitz from her native Hungary in May, 1944. She scribbled the first version of her memoir on scraps of paper in her native Hungarian, immediately after the liberation. It was not until 1978, however, that she published *Fragments of Isabella*, in which, with the help of her American husband, Irving Leitner, she translated her notes into English. Later, Leitner revised her initial text several times, adding, rearranging, and editing her "fragments." *Saving the Fragments: From Auschwitz to New York* (1985) and *Isabella: From Auschwitz to Freedom* (1994) appeared as co-authored with her husband.

to her English-speaking husband and the epilogue, Leitner's narrative betrays the "husbandry" of her story performed by the English language. Insofar as her (unpublishable) fragments, initially written in Hungarian, were expropriated into the language in which she could (and was allowed to) bear witness, Leitner's book truly "belongs" to her husband. Yet, interestingly enough, the epilogue is not the last word in the book: it is followed, somewhat inconsequentially, by a coda titled "*Lager* Language," in which Leitner, with some help from Ruth Zerner, a professor at Lehman College, reflects on the mongrel *Lager* language that she and her fellow inmates used in the camp. The appendix is preceded by an explanation that Leitner first recorded these comments "in my native Hungarian tongue almost immediately after I arrived in this country in 1945. What I did—and after so many years—I am glad I did." Leitner writes:

> There is an English language, there is French. There is Russian, also Spanish. There is Hungarian, there is Chinese. According to the Bible, God punished humanity in Babel with a madness of languages, but there is one language even God cannot understand—only we do, those of us who were prisoners in the shadow of the crematorium. I call it *Lager* language, and each word means a different kind of suffering. (227)

Leitner provides a succinct dictionary of *Lager*, in a form reminiscent of an elementary school lesson:

> *Vertreterin* meant kneeling; *Stubendienstkapo*, beating; *Torwache*, kicking…. A *Plus* meant that they might take away your sister into another *Block*. *Mengele* is selecting there in the afternoon. You are looking for your sister, but she is already up in smoke in the *Kremchy*…. *Pritsch* means that fourteen of us are lying on a lice-filled plank of wood. (228)

This brief reflection on camp language, followed by a two-page "*Lager* Lexicon," seems incongruous with the preceding narrative, and it stands out within Leitner's literary corpus. Perhaps, situated in the book after her husband's "last word," Leitner's peculiar reflection on translation is a strategic escape into *Lager* from the neutralizing effects of English in which all of her published accounts were written, and in which the linguistic plurality of her experiences was obliterated. Ironically, it is only in *Lager*, the universal language of camp inmates, rather than in her native Hungarian or in her second language, that Leitner can assert her linguistic mastery and her exclusive interpretive rights to the words which neither her husband "nor God" can comprehend. Leitner's rewritings of her Auschwitz narrative can be seen as an attempt to break out of the silence that her native Hungarian imposed on her when she first tried to write it, and her texts manifest both that struggle and her sense of having succeeded, at least partially, in that endeavor.

In contrast, the story of Izolda Regensberg, recorded by Polish writer Hanna Krall in *Król kierowy znów na wylocie* (2006), is an account of linguistic defeat that leaves the survivor immured in the silence of incomprehension and untranslatability. During the war, Izolda had only one purpose: at any cost, to save her husband Szajek, who was incarcerated in Auschwitz and then Mauthausen. Passing as a Pole, she smuggled goods across the border to make money for the parcels to be sent to her husband. To achieve her goal, she escaped from forced labor in Germany and then from a transport to Auschwitz; she endured repeated rape, imprisonment in the notorious Pawiak prison, and torture at the SS headquarters in Vienna. Izolda's inventiveness and her success in securing help for her husband depended on her knowledge of languages: she could easily pass as Maria Pawlicka because of her flawless Polish; in Germany and Austria, she used her fluent German and French to gain favors or to pretend she was a *Volksdeutsche*; and she secured her husband's final release because she could chat in Russian with an officer of the liberating Russian army. Izolda's story is anything but banal; as the author comments, it is a story fit for an epic Hollywood movie. Yet Krall juxtaposes this image of an adventurous, courageous young woman, who saved her husband's life during the war largely due to her multilingual skills, with a portrait of Izolda in her old age, immobile in her armchair and unable to learn either English or Hebrew. Izolda now lives in Israel, with her two daughters, and while her greatest wish is to tell her story, a linguistic barrier keeps her isolated behind a wall of silence. In a frustrating episode, Krall (2006) shows Izolda asking her daughter to translate her story to her granddaughter, but the truncated version in Hebrew cannot carry the weight of her experiences, and both the daughter and the granddaughter soon grow impatient. With the exception of the narrator, whom Izolda has commissioned to ghostwrite her story in Polish, there is no one with whom to share it. The book ends with a scene of distressing linguistic isolation: sitting at a birthday party in her honor, Izolda reminisces to herself about the past, as if conversing with the ghosts of her long-dead relatives and friends, while the actual conversation in Hebrew floats around her. Izolda's desperation, "Why didn't these people want to listen to her?" (156) and her own inability to understand the guests are underscored by the juxtaposition on the page of the paragraphs in Polish and in Hebrew.[6] Izolda's story starkly exemplifies a translatory impasse, whereby the survivor lacks the linguistic means to tell her story, even though she is surrounded by loving relatives rather than by indifferent or hostile bystanders.

---

6 The translations of the passages from Hanna Krall's *Król kierowy znow na wylocie* are mine.

Striking examples of *traduttore traditore* occur during translation sequences in Claude Lanzmann's documentary film *Shoah* (1985). Unlike in written testimonies, in which survivors' foreign accents disappear, during the film, the viewers are constantly forced to negotiate a variety of cultural markers, signaled by the witnesses' accents. The unique effect of this cinematographic testimony, which frequently includes the presence of translators, lies in its mêlée of languages. By staging the Babel of post-Holocaust memory in front of the camera, Lanzmann evokes Jewish victims' linguistic predicament both during and in the aftermath of the Holocaust. Since, despite the translators' good efforts, many sentences and phrases remain untranslated, the reception of the film depends largely on the viewers' proficiency in the numerous languages spoken by Lanzmann's interviewees, which makes it almost impossible for any single viewer to follow all the linguistic nuances.

Nowhere is the use of English to anesthetize the pain of an intolerable memory more striking than in Lanzmann's interview with Abraham Bomba. In Treblinka, Bomba was a member of the barber *Sonderkommando*, charged with cutting the hair of the women who were ushered into the gas chambers. While other survivors interviewed by Lanzmann speak either German or Hebrew, Bomba is the only major witness who chooses to communicate his experiences in English. During the interview in the barbershop in Tel Aviv, Bomba describes at length the process of selecting the barbers for the work detail and then their gruesome tasks inside the gas chambers. Bomba speaks in a dispassionate tone of voice and with a confident intonation, which strikes the viewer as incongruous with the horrifying content of his account. His fluent performance breaks down, however, when he tries to describe the moment when women from his hometown of Częstochowa walked into the gas chamber, among them the wife and the sister of Bomba's fellow barber. The women started asking Bomba questions; he recalls, "And when they saw me, they started asking me, Abe this and Abe that —'What's going to happen to us?'" At this moment, the protective shield of Bomba's testimony in English crumbles, and Bomba falls silent, struggling for several minutes to regain composure. It seems that, from the start, Bomba's responses in English to Lanzmann's questions (which the director asked in just as heavily accented English) serve to conceal the pain of his memory of the words he exchanged, presumably in Yiddish, with the women whose hair he was cutting in the gas chamber. Significantly, before Bomba resumes his account, cajoled by Lanzmann's insistent "Abe, you have to do it," he mumbles, in a low voice choked with tears, a sentence in Yiddish. In the space where Bomba's English collapses into his mother tongue, on the frontier between languages, the affective "truth" of his experience is conveyed to the viewer.

By contrast, in Lanzmann's interviews with Polish "bystanders," it is French that becomes a neutralizing medium, although in an entirely different way. In the central episode with Szymon Srebrnik, we see the former child survivor of the Chełmno death camp in front of a church in Grabów, in the middle of a group of villagers. The interviews are translated between Polish and French, by an interpreter who is constantly present on the screen. Lanzmann spurs the villagers on with questions about what they knew about the mass exterminations happening nearby, and their answers escalate from expressing joy at seeing "Pan Szymek" to an outburst of voices accusing Jews of deicide. According to Shoshana Felman, this episode stages a reenactment of Polish Christian anti-Semitism, resulting in a re-victimization of Srebrnik, who remains silent throughout the scene. While this is undeniably true, what is lost in a fluent French translation for a viewer who does not know Polish are the background voices of the "bystanders." While Srebrnik is silent most of the time, the translation glosses over brief, direct, even intimate exchanges in Polish between him and several women in the crowd. One of the women, for instance, verifies her memories by addressing short, detailed questions to Srebrnik, to which he responds and then encourages her to speak for the camera: "Please, say it!" The members of the crowd give contradictory answers to Lanzmann's questions, speaking in chorus: "Yes, we remember!" and "I don't remember!", and they continuously vie to correct one another ("you are trying to explain it, but it is all wrong," a man interjects). What disappears therefore is the complexity of this episode as a memory event, as well as Srebrnik's agency in orchestrating it. Undoubtedly, in this scene, his testimony falls victim to mistranslation, despite the translator's competence.

In other scenes in the film, Lanzmann interviews Polish "bystanders" at other sites of German extermination camps, such as Włodawa near Sobibór or Grabów near Chełmno. From behind the voices that become uniformly channeled into the French translation, we hear untranslated fragments of conversations, in which the town inhabitants argue about the details of the events, seek to confirm their recollections, and express their horror at what occurred in their neighborhood. Lanzmann's interlocutors in Polish villages and small towns are not highly articulate. Indeed, their answers to Lanzmann's questions often come out in garbled Polish, although each ungrammatical phrase immediately becomes corrected in the French translation (for instance, the grammatically incorrect "To jest taka morderstwo" instantly becomes "Il était un meurtre"). These grammatical errors, however, are so bizarre that one hesitates to attribute them solely to low levels of literacy among the villagers. Perhaps the awkward manner of speaking also indicates the speakers' inability to come to terms with the reality of murder so close to home, and, at least for some, with their complicity in the events and their indifference to the tragedy of their former neighbors. The former "bystanders'" struggle with the Polish language, which has been hardened by several decades of forgetting, during which the murdered Jewish neighbors remained un-mourned, the difficulty highlighted in their speech by constant (untranslated) repetitions: "To było coś okropnego, coś okropnego!"... "Ja to przeżywałem, przeżywałem!" Lanzmann's questions, however, in which he keeps alluding to the fact that the Poles have profited from the murder of their Jewish neighbors (with a sarcasm that, largely thanks to the translator's tact, remains undetected by his interlocutors), exude a sense of the director's moral superiority, while the Polish language as such stands accused before his camera. Something momentous happens during the numerous, and often distressing encounters between languages in the film. Although this intense sensation resists being translated into one of the languages involved, it persists affectively, bearing witness to a profound failure of communication.

4 The Tower of Babel

Primo Levi writes, "It is an obvious assertion that where violence is inflicted on men, it is also inflicted on language." (1988, 97) The precarious condition of post-Holocaust speech stems directly from the Nazi assault on language as a means of communication, as well as on particular national languages, which were annulled by the decree that those who spoke them should die. As does Leitner in her much later account, in *Survival in Auschwitz*, written in 1946, Levi conceives of the Nazi death camp as modernity's version of the Tower of Babel: "The confusion of languages is a fundamental component of the manner of living here: one is surrounded by a perpetual Babel, in which everyone shouts orders and threats in languages never heard before, and woe betide whoever fails to grasp the meaning." (38) For Levi, the impossibility of communicating—of understanding the orders and obtaining life-saving information from other inmates—is the true force of extermination, more menacing than hunger or physical coercion. Survival depends on one's translating abilities and linguistic talents, which enable one to secure an extra slab of "bread-*Brot-Broid-chleb-pain-lechem-keynér*." (39) In his later account *The Drowned and the Saved*, Levi writes, "The greater part of the prisoners who did not understand German—that is, almost all of the Italians—died during the first ten to fifteen days after their arrival: at first glance, from hunger, cold, fatigue, and disease; but after a more attentive examination, due to insufficient information." (93) As a result of the linguistic dispersion in the camp, the "use of the word to communicate thought, this necessary and sufficient instrument for man to be man, had fallen into disuse." (91) The "drowned" ones perish in the deafening noise from which "the human word did not surface" and where "one finds oneself facing a human being with whom one must absolutely establish communication or die, and then is unable to do so." (93–94)

Levi conveys a sense of incomprehension and linguistic confusion by inserting foreign words into his narrative. The descriptions of the everyday goings-on of the camp are punctuated by German words and phrases that are left untranslated and intrude on every page: "*Tagesraum, Kräzeblock, Alles heraus.*" (33, 70) To every question a *Häftling* must reply "*Jawohl*" because in the camp there is "*kein warum.*" (29) When occasionally Levi provides translation in parentheses, its function is to exacerbate the deadly power of the German words: "a diagnosis of *'dicke Füsse'* (swollen feet) is extremely dangerous." The German language stakes out the linguistic perimeter of the camp, and within it, the respective languages of the inmates are annihilated, reduced to meaningless and inconsequential babble. Ironically, what gave Levi the momentary comfort of feeling "human" in the camp (and what most likely enabled his survival) was passing the chemistry examination in German, as well as being addressed by the examiner in the polite plural form of address ("*Wo sind Sie geboren?*" 1993, 106), after which Levi was recruited for the chemical work detail. After the war, the concentration-camp German will continue to contaminate Levi's native Italian (as well as the translations of his memoirs into other languages), reinforcing the inscription of camp experience in the witness' speech. In Levi's testimony, the barbs of German words continue to wound the narrative and undermine the authority of the language of the account.

The pivotal scene in *Survival in Auschwitz* is Levi's effort to translate passages from Dante's *Divine Comedy* into French for Jean the Pikolo in order to teach him the basics of Italian. Only in the effort to translate Dante in the Nazi camp, as if his life depended on it, does Levi begin to truly comprehend the meaning of the verses that were written in his native Italian. From within Levi's broken French, Dante speaks to him "as if I also was hearing it for the first time: Like the blast of a trumpet, like the voice of God." (113) Translation provides a redemptive moment, in which Dante reminds Levi, via his own translation, "You were made men/To follow after knowledge and excellence." (113) Throughout the translation episode, Levi makes no attempt to supplement German words to aid Pikolo's comprehension, although they both know that language, as if Levi guarded the moment of camaraderie between Italian and French against contamination by the language that has been used by the killers. The association of translation with soup, which is being carried by Levi and Pikolo to feed the members of their *Kommando*, points to its quality as vital nourishment. Levi is filled with its life-giving energy, at least for a brief moment of reprieve, as he searches for the French phrases. In another telling association with nourishment, Levi recalls absorbing foreign words and expressions "like a famished stomach rapidly assimilates even indigestible food." In one episode, Levi trades a daily portion of bread for a lesson of German, commenting that "never was bread better spent." He also recalls becoming conditioned, like Pavlov's dog, to the sound of the Polish words "stergishri steri" (*czterdzieści cztery*), the number preceding his, and he refers to the memory of those words as "the unconscious preparation for survival."

The translation sequence in Levi's narrative, which marks his effort to counter the destructive forces of Babel, is followed by the news of the Allied landing in Normandy, as if the effort of translation and the miracle of communication amid inhumanity were causally related to the German defeat and to the author's eventual survival. The scene also reveals the urgency of the need to translate. Levi pleads, "Here, listen Pikolo, open your ears and your mind, you have to understand, for my sake." (113) Indeed, Levi associates his effort to dredge the fragments of Dante's poem from the depths of memory, which has been dulled by hunger and cold, with the struggle of memory against oblivion, foreshadowing his future destiny as a storyteller from Auschwitz. Translation thus becomes a conduit for recollection: a device that enables Levi to carry the *Häftling* out of the darkness of incomprehension and to translate him back into the human from linguistic chaos.

Like Levi's accounts, Kertész's camp narrative, *Fateless* (1975), recreates the sounds of the mixture of languages in the camps. The narrator, György Köves, the author's young alter ego, is surrounded by the constant noise of incomprehensible words that float around him, which he describes with adjectives that emphasize their strangeness ["that strange language," (93) "some sort of musical language." (140)] Like Levi, Kertész's protagonist arrives in Auschwitz with "a smattering of German" that he picked up in school, which saves his life during the selection because he is able to understand urgent advice from older inmates to lie about his age. In the camp, his fluency in German continues to increase, especially after his transfer to Buchenwald. While at first Kertész phonetically transcribes the German phrases that his narrator does not understand ("*Los ge ma vorne!* he said, or something similar," (65) properly spelled German words and their translations begin to appear in the text with growing frequency ("*Aber Mensch, um Gottes Willen! Wir sind doch ja hier nicht in Auschwitz*" [92]). Yet despite the advantage of comprehending German commands and of being taken care of by a fellow Hungarian inmate, György becomes a *Muselmann* and is left for dead, lying on the ground. Through a series of events that, as he says, he "could never explain," György finds himself in a hospital and is treated by a doctor, a French prisoner, who rewards the patients who speak his language with an additional cube of sugar. While Levi's account implied an association of the knowledge of foreign languages with food, György literally tries to learn a few French words to earn the coveted sugar. He comments, "That's when I realized the truth of what they kept teaching me at home: what an important thing an education is, especially a knowledge of foreign languages!" (143) The narrator's slow emergence from total incomprehension is signaled by his learning of words from different languages, Polish in particular, the language that he previously perceived as "strange" ("*Gyinkuge ... gyinkuge bardz*" ["Dziękuję ... dziękuję bardzo" (Thank you, thank you very much)]; 150), and this process coincides with his physical recovery, followed by the liberation of the camp.

5 The Task of the Translator: Translation as Testimony

Contributing to the debate about the limits of Holocaust representation, Berel Lang argues that these limits depend on cultural and sociopolitical contexts, as well as on a particular community's value systems. This also means that traumatic events are both experienced and remembered against a backdrop of cultural expectations. Let us add that a national language is a medium in which these contexts and values are shaped, and through which a particular community judges the moral weight of what is represented as fact and determines the criteria of inclusion in the official historical narrative. Since the translator moves between different linguistic communities, he or she must take into account the moral consequences of the use of a particular language and consider the linguistic mechanisms of exclusion and repression practiced by a given community.

In his seminal essay "The Task of the Translator," (1969) Walter Benjamin writes that the task of translation is to redeem language's "fallen condition" and to bring languages, dispersed after Babel, closer to what he calls "pure language." Pure language is the "inaccessible realm of reconciliation and fulfillment between languages," (75) which means that languages are a priori interrelated, and translation can bring out their higher kinship. Every language then possesses an inherent quality of translatability, regardless of whether a person capable of translating it may ever exist. The actual work of translation thus reveals the unattainable horizon of linguistic possibility toward which every text is destined. The text always "calls" for a translation, and this call is a promise of future communication. From within one language, translation addresses itself to a wholly other tongue, although its mission is to solicitously watch over both languages. For Benjamin, the life of literary works thus receives "highest testimony" in translation: renditions into other languages bear witness to the work's life but also to its afterlife, its posthumous survival (76). Like memory, translations are always belated, and they mourn the passing of the original text. Translating (*übersetzen*) is always a form of surviving (*überleben*); it is the work's "stage of continued life." (71) For that reason, translations convey the work's demand that it remain unforgotten, even if this claim were never to be fulfilled. But, more importantly, the task of the translator is not only to ensure the mere survival of the text but also to transform it into something more and better, beyond the means of the author.

Ironically, the English translation of Benjamin's essay obscures that the German word for "task," *Aufgabe*, also connotes "giving up" or "failing" (de Man 1986, 80). Although translation engages both the language of the original and the target language, it also necessarily fails to attain the goal of perfect communication. Yet this defeat, this betrayal intrinsic to every act of translation, stems from the lack in the very language of the original, from *its* failure to express what it has always already disarticulated and sent into exile. Translation then reveals "the suffering of the original language": the fact that exactly in the place where we feel most at home and familiar—in our original language—"this alienation is the strongest." (de Man, 84) And this is why, ever since Babel, languages are destined for translation—why the translator's task is to reveal a language's original indebtedness to that which it has always excluded. We do not know to whom the translator is obligated, but it is from the place of this inarticulable alterity inherent in every national language that a work calls for translation. The task of the translator, Benjamin continues, "is to release in his own language that pure language which is under the spell of another, to liberate the language imprisoned in a work in his re-creation of the work." (80) Translation renders the familiar sounds of the native tongue foreign, uprooted from their native soil, *unheimlich*. It exposes the traces of what the language has excluded, yet to which it remains indebted. Instead of striving to preserve the status quo of the target language, the translator must allow a domestic language to be "powerfully affected" (81) by the foreign tongue in order to release the traces of that inscription. Simultaneously, the translator is also the guardian of the frontier between languages, the one who regulates the migrations of meanings: he ensures their safe passage or halts their uncontrolled proliferation. Translation is thus an injunction to a national language to be deeply self-reflective about what it has excluded, and to confront its investments and assumptions.

In the postulate that translation bears witness to the original text, Benjamin's articulation of the translator's task resonates with Emmanuel Levinas's ethical philosophy and its idiom of responsibility. For Levinas, the primacy of the subject is put into question by its ethical relation with the other. The self's existence is primarily testimony to the life of another, while its speech is an echo whose source remains unknown. Translation is a response to the summons from another language, the language of the other. In the context of Levinasian ethics, my obligation to the other is unconditional because I am responsible whether I will it or not. Benjamin's postulate of "pure language" reveals that the translatory imperative is similarly undeclinable and irreducible, and it is valid even if no translator for the work will ever be found. In the border crossings between languages, translation reveals that I come into being as a speaking subject—a member of a linguistic community—because I am indebted to what my language has excluded, to what remains outside its borders, "on the periphery." The translator's mission is to keep a vigil over the target language and to bring out what that language remembers, what it has disowned, and what it will continue to forget.

In arguing that language is primarily constituted by the self's aptitude to respond to the call of the other, Levinas distinguishes between the ethical essence of language (Saying) and language in its communicative function (the Said). The translator is always turned toward the ethical horizon, yet in his everyday practice, he attends with solicitude to the plastic and contextually molded surface of language. Yet what Levinas calls the Said always appears in its concrete manifestation as a national language. Levinas then seems to conceive of Saying as a moment that escapes the totalizing intention of a particular language. Insofar as Saying originates in the call for help that I cannot decline, issuing from the other who always remains outside the horizon of my world, its ethical import resonates with Benjamin's conception of "pure language"—the horizon of communicability between languages, toward which the text is solicited by a call from another language.

It is interesting that throughout his profoundly innovative reflection on the ethical essence of language, Levinas—a Lithuanian Jew, raised in a Yiddish- and Russian-speaking household—never comments on his own displacement within the French language. According to his biographer, Salomon Malka, Levinas's heavily accented French and his struggle with the French syntax bore the mark of "the suffering of language" and signaled his estrangement from the language in which he wrote all of his work. Not unlike the authors of the Holocaust testimonies described above, Levinas remains alienated from his linguistic community. Perhaps the only intentional inscription of this foreignness in his work is the double epigraph in *Otherwise than Being*, which consists of a general dedication to the six million victims, written in French, and a personal tribute in Hebrew to his murdered relatives. The cipher of linguistic and also philosophical alterity (the Hebrew script would have been illegible to a majority of Levinas's philosophical readers) is impressed on the body of Levinas's main work nevertheless. Even if this alterity remains unthematized (in the work dedicated to the discussion of alterity), the epigraph is a sign of a translatory impasse that inflects Levinas's silence on the question of translation. It can be argued that the philosopher's activity as a translator, which likely ensured his survival during the Holocaust, as well as his translatory struggles throughout a lifetime of writing, have profoundly informed Levinas's thinking about language as primarily listening to the other. In a way, for Levinas, "translatability" belongs to language on a fundamental level; in Benjamin's understanding of the term, it means indebtedness to the language of the other and hence its aptitude to reach out and respond to the other's call.

Benjamin's thesis that translation points to an inaccessible region of reconciliation between languages is informed by the cabalistic concept of *tikkun*, that is, messianic mending and restoration. The process of translation is like putting together the fragments of a broken vessel (78); it gathers and rejoins words that have been scattered and abandoned across different languages, or, as in the case of the languages of Holocaust testimony, of words and phrases that have been rendered meaningless by violence. For Benjamin, the sense of translation's "fidelity" to the original is not that it reproduces the original but that it produces an effect of harmony, that it reflects "the great longing for linguistic complementation." (79) In the post-Holocaust context, Benjamin's understanding of translation as a promise of communicability can thus be related to what Canadian philosopher Emil Fackenheim has articulated as *tikkun olam*—a whole and unconditional act of mending that bears upon every aspect of post-Holocaust existence. Fackenheim writes, "It is precisely if the rupture, or the threat of it, is total, that all powers must be summoned for a mending," (253) although he adds that, from the start, we must accept that the post-Auschwitz *tikkun* can only be fragmentary. Orienting itself toward that future, translation announces a pure event of communicability, even if the actual words are always marked and interrupted by strangeness.

In the examples of translatory exchanges in Holocaust memoirs, we have repeatedly seen gestures, not always successful, of trying to mend the broken bonds with the past. If the motif of Babel in these testimonials is emblematic of a radical rupture of language "after Auschwitz" and of the shattering of the human ability to communicate, translation, in its various manifestations, is animated by the promise of the *tikkun* of language, however fragmentary. Because Holocaust translations expose the consequences of violence *on* language as well as violence perpetrated *by* language, they also posit a new imperative, which French writer Maurice Blanchot, in *The Writing of the Disaster* (1980), formulated as "May words cease to be arms." (11) The question of translation is then central to Holocaust testimony because, oriented toward "pure language," it is primarily an articulation of this hope. Its function is to initiate and sustain communication and to transmit the possibility of addressing the other. Tellingly, Benjamin, like Levi, when giving an apparently arbitrary example of language's intention to communicate, chooses the word for "bread," the symbol of nourishment and preservation of life: "The word *Brot* means something different to a German than the word *pain* to a Frenchman.... As to the intended object, however, the two words mean the very same thing." (74) Holocaust testimonials, as they are infused with the translatory imperative, foreground a similar need—not a cognitive desire to impart facts on the reader but an insistent plea: "Are you listening?" In this sense, as Thomas Trezise (2001) has written, "A survivor speaks otherwise," (62) in defiance of the "total linguistic barrier" that Levi says he faced in the camps. In the context of bearing witness to traumatic events, translation also becomes a vehicle of healing, rescuing the words of those who were almost destroyed by the violence of language.

Primo Levi recalls the presence in the camp of a three-year-old boy, paralyzed from the waist down, whom the inmates named Hurbinek. The child kept repeating words that resembled sounds in different languages but which no one in the multilingual crowd of Auschwitz inmates was able to recognize. As Levi notes, because Hurbinek tried so desperately to communicate, "everybody listened to him in silence, anxious to understand, and among us were the speakers of all the languages of Europe." According to Italian philosopher Giorgio Agamben, Hurbinek's attempt to escape from the abyss of non-speech is the true site of testimony, where the witnessing subject comes into being (38). Agamben refers to Hurbinek's nonsensical words as incomprehensible "sounds." What truly matters for the inmates that listen to him, however, which Agamben overlooks, is that these sounds arise in the gaps between languages. Each of the inmates hopes that perhaps they belong to his mother tongue, so that he, in his turn, will be able to respond to the child. Hurbinek, a child without a mother tongue, embodies the orphaned condition of post-Holocaust language, as announced by Kertész. An abandoned, motherless child, Hurbinek is also a symbol of the vulnerability of that language. Yet the testimonial imperative stems from the need to make Hurbinek's non-words comprehensible in the particular languages of those who witnessed his anguished efforts to communicate. This seems to be Kertész's mission: if he writes about the Holocaust because it has no language, he does so in the hope of giving it a language. The space of translation is where the dispersed languages meet, and where the voices whose "paths" would otherwise never cross begin to call to one another and to address one another. There is no "common language" to speak about the Holocaust, and what Holocaust testimonials bear witness to first and foremost is this abyssal, Babelian condition of post-Holocaust speech. Yet, what survivors, their descendants, and those who listen to their stories *do* share is this resounding absence of the common idiom, and they are committed to forging passages across this divide.

Ultimately, Kertesz's comment that the Holocaust has no language points to a unique Babelian predicament inherent in virtually all Holocaust memoirs, even if its manifestations vary significantly. If the Holocaust exceeds the means of verbal representation at our disposal (it is "unspeakable"), it signifies, first and foremost, that it cannot be expressed in the idiom of particular languages. This "unspeakability," however, is signaled and borne witness to in the space of the translatory impasse. Translation is then the means par excellence of searching for new idioms in which to bear witness, and many of the authors of Holocaust testimonies, of which I have discussed only a few, take up the challenge of this "task of the translator."

The accounts of Holocaust experiences, from the death camps, from the ghetto, from the hiding places on the Aryan side, describe states of being for which no words exist in national languages, the lacuna which the writers (and often also their translators) have endlessly tried to express. The Holocaust is extraterritorial with respect to national languages, or, at least in the speech of survivors, it constitutes each language's inassimilable remainder, although those who bear witness in these languages always hope that, in the process of transmission, they will finally "say it right." Witnesses always translate the untranslatable into one of the comprehensible languages and familiar expressions, aware that their speech is a mistranslation, an instance of *traduttore traditore*. Paradoxically, to an extent, translation effaces the very thing it seeks to preserve, and in consequence, it fails to deliver what it has been consigned to bring forth. But what witnesses-translators succeed in conveying, perhaps often against their expressed intention, is both the experience of that failure to translate and the desire for further translation. Here translation is the cipher for witnessing.

The weaknesses of Holocaust testimony—its lack of a specific discourse or narrative and the absence of a national tongue in which it can be properly conveyed—make it vulnerable to appropriation. Within the scope of Levinas's ethics, which I have expanded upon to address the issue of translation, however, this weakness is also its greatest strength in at least two respects. First, the vulnerability and "homelessness" of this language, the intrinsic otherness that is revealed in translatory misencounters, offers a possibility of undoing the linguistic privilege or supremacy of one language over another. This constitutes a credible effort to lend ethical and political content to the clichéd promises of "Never again!" Secondly, Holocaust testimonials foreground the communicative imperative and are structured as an address to another, demanding a response. Since, as I have argued, testimonials always involve some forms of translation, through this summons, they have a potential to create communities of speakers along different, multiple, and intersecting axes of belonging, communities of rememberers yet-to-come.

Bibliography

Agamben, Giorgio. 1999. *Remnants of Auschwitz: The Witness and the Archive*. Translated by Daniel Heller-Roazen. New York: Zone Books.
Améry, Jean. 1986. *At the Mind's Limits*. Translated by Sindey Rosenfeld and Stella P. Rosenfeld. New York: Schocken.
Benjamin, Walter. 1969. "The Task of the Translator." In *Illuminations*, edited by Hannah Arendt, 69–82. New York: Schocken.
Blanchot, Maurice. 1995. *The Writing of the Disaster*. Translated by Ann Smock. Lincoln: University of Nebraska Press.
De Man, Paul. 1986. "Conclusions: Walter Benjamin's 'The Task of the Translator.'" In *The Resistance to Theory*, 73–104. Minneapolis: Minnesota University Press.
Fackenheim, Emil. 1994. *To Mend the World: Foundations of Post-Holocaust Jewish Thought*. Bloomington and Indianapolis: Indiana University Press.
Lang, Berel. 1988. "Language and Genocide." In *Echoes from the Holocaust: Philosophical Reflections on a Dark Time*, edited by Alan Rosenberg and Gerald E. Myers, 341–364. Philadelphia: Temple University Press.
Kertész, Imre. 1992. *Fateless*. Translated by Christopher C. Wilson and Katharina M. Wilson. Evanston: Northwestern University Press.
Kertész, Imre. 2004. *Język na wygnaniu*. Translated by Elżbieta Sobolewska. Warsaw: Wydawnictwo WAB.
Krall, Hanna. 2006. *Król kierowy znów na wylocie*. Warsaw: Świat Książki.
Levi, Primo. 1988. *The Drowned and the Saved*. Translated by Raymond Rosenthal. New York: Vintage Books.
Levi, Primo. 1993. *Survival in Auschwitz: The Nazi Assault on Humanity*. Translated by Stuart Woolf. New York: Collier Books.
Levinas, Emmanuel. 1998. *Otherwise Than Being, or Beyond Essence*. Translated by Alphonso Lingis. Pittsburgh: Duquesne University Press.
Rosen, Alan. 2005. *Sounds of Defiance: The Holocaust, Multilingualism, and the Problem of English*. Lincoln and London: University of Nebraska Press.
Shoah: An Oral History of the Holocaust. 1985. Directed by Claude Lanzmann.
Suleiman, Susan Rubin. 1996. "Monuments in the Foreign Tongue: On Reading Holocaust Memoirs by Emigrants." *Poetics Today* 17, no.4: 639–657.
Szurek, Jean-Charles. 2007. "*Shoah:* From the Jewish Question to the Polish Question." In *Claude Lanzmann's "Shoah": Key Essays*, edited by Stuart Liebman, 149–169. Oxford: Oxford University Press.
Trezise, Thomas. 2001. "Unspeakable." *The Yale Journal of Criticism* 14, no. 1: 39–66.
Wieviorka, Annette. 2006. *The Era of the Witness*. Translated by Jared Stark. Ithaca, NY: Cornell University Press.

Iwona Guść
Ania's Diary: The Polish Translation of the Diary of Anne Frank: Its History, First Publication, and Reception in Post-Stalinist Poland

Since its first publication in 1947, *Het Achterhuis*, a book compiled from the diaries of Anne Frank, a well-known child victim of the Holocaust, has been translated into more than seventy languages and published in numerous editions worldwide. Each edition of the diary, however, deserves to be studied separately, for each translation bears its own peculiarities due to various alternations of the original text made initially by Otto Frank himself, and later on by copy-editors, publishers, and translators. This chapter examines the first Polish translation and reception of the diary published in Warsaw in 1957. It not only brings to light the previously unknown history of this publication, but also some aspects of the reception. It argues that the specificity of the Polish translation needs to be discussed against the background of the political and socio-cultural changes taking place during the post-Stalinist Thaw.

1 *Het Achterhuis:* Anne's Diary and Its First Dutch Edition

On 11 May 1944, Anne Frank wrote in her diary that once the war was over, she would like to publish a book based on her wartime diary. To put plan into action, she started editing and revising her previous diary entries mere days later. This book project, however, remained unfinished. A few months later, on 4 August 1944, all eight people hiding at Prinsengracht 263 were arrested and deported to the camps. Returning home to Amsterdam after the liberation in June 1945,

---

This study was supported by an Early Career Fellowship Grant at the Lichtenberg-Kolleg, the Göttingen Institute of Advanced Studies. It was conducted as a part of the project *The Diaries of Anne Frank: Research—Translations—Critical Edition*. The project was initiated by the Lichtenberg-Kolleg, the Göttingen Institute of Advanced Studies and the Fritz Bauer Institute in Frankfurt/Main. Both institutes provided an ideal academic background in which this work could develop. I am especially grateful to the Lichtenberg-Kolleg for hosting me in the academic years 2014–2016.

https://doi.org/10.1515/9783110550788-012

the family's sole survivor, Otto Frank, learned that Anne's notebooks and notes had been secured. Initially, he hesitated about reading the entries, yet once he discovered that Anne had wanted to turn them into a book, he decided to try and publish her diary. He prepared a typescript containing what he felt were the most essential parts of Anne's diary and shared it with his friends and business connections.[1] Among them was the Dutch historian Jan Romein, whose laudatory article printed on the front page of a former Dutch resistance paper *Het Parool* (3 April 1946), made several publishers take note of the diary of this young Jewish war victim. It was the Contact Publishing House [*Uitgeverij Contact*] from Amsterdam that finally secured the rights to publish the diary under the title coined by Anne herself: *Het Achterhuis* [The Back House] (Van der Stroom 2001, 72–80).[2]

The first Dutch edition of the diary did not contain all the entries that Anne had made during her stay in hiding.[3] It was first and foremost a compilation that Anne's father selected out of the remaining notebooks, following the process of editing started by Anne herself (Lejeune 2009, 237–66). In the hands of editors, this version was, again, slightly adjusted. The Dutch publisher even requested that seven diary entries and a few sentences were omitted from the so-called Typescript II.

With an initial print run of three thousand[4] copies, the book received good reviews but was not immediately a bestseller (Van der Stroom 2001, 74–83). However, in less than three years the book was reprinted five times, and sold

---

[1] There were two subsequent Dutch typescripts. The first typescript was compiled in 1945 by Otto Frank and corrected (in terms of grammatical errors) by his friends. This manuscript was then retyped by Isa Cauvern in 1946. In the Dutch critical edition this typescript is marked as Typescript II. It was this typescript that formed the basis for the publication of the diary in the Netherlands in 1947 and Germany in 1950.

[2] Full title was: *Het Achterhuis. Dagboekbrieven 12 juni 1942 – 1 augustus 1944* [The Back House. Diary Letters 12 June 1942 – 1 August 1944]. All translations from Dutch, German, and Polish are mine, unless stated otherwise.

[3] The critical edition published in the Netherlands in 1986 revealed the differences between Anne's notes, her re-edited version, and the published version. In 2017, Cambridge University Press will publish a new critical edition, containing all of Anne's existing notes and diary texts. This critical edition is a part of the above-mentioned *The Diaries of Anne Frank: Research—Translations—Critical Edition*.

[4] In the literature on Anne Frank, one usually finds information about 1,500 copies of the first Dutch print. Dutch scholar Lisa Kuitert, who studied Contact's documents, has determined that the number was at least twice as high. Contact's documents mention 3,036 copies printed in June 1947 (See Kuitert 2007/2008, 22–23). I also found these numbers in the correspondence between Otto Frank and his literary agent for Scandinavian countries (letter Otto Frank to Greet Berges, 1 June 1948).

over 25,000 copies. The book's increasing popularity and publicity in the Netherlands helped Otto Frank attract the interest of publishers abroad (Graver 1997, 17). The first translations appeared in 1950 in France and West Germany, followed by the English and American markets two years later. The first English translation of the diary was published in June 1952, titled *The Diary of a Young Girl*.[5] To various degrees, all three translations—French, German, and English—were important for the publishing of the Polish edition in the autumn of 1957.

2 *Dziennik Anny Frank:* The Genesis of the Polish Edition of the Diary

The French translation of the diary published by Calmann-Lévy in the spring of 1950, *Le Journal d'Anne Frank*, was a direct translation from *Het Achterhuis*.[6] It was this French edition that brought Jan Parandowski, writer, translator, and chairman of the Polish PEN Club, into contact with Otto Frank. They met in June 1954 during the international PEN-congress held in Amsterdam (Otto Frank's diary, 20 June 1954). The correspondence after their brief encounter in the Netherlands, suggests that Parandowski was extremely impressed by the diary, which he read in French translation.[7] In a letter to Frank, he expressed his wish to see this *"profondément humain"* book published in Poland. Mere weeks after their meeting in Amsterdam, Parandowski revealed to Frank that he had already talked to an editor. Furthermore, he offered to help write a foreword and suggested that his Jewish wife Irena (whom Otto Frank also met in Amsterdam) could possibly translate the diary from French to Polish. It was no secret that Parandowski was rather critical about the foreword written by Daniel Rops for the French edition. He called it "superficial" and "insufficient", stating that a Pole would read such a book differently than a Frenchman or an Englishman because Poles would have frequently been eyewitnesses to similar events during the occupation of their country. He stressed that he himself knew about a Jewish girl who was offered a shelter in the building where he lived. Ac-

---

[5] The English translation was prepared by B.M. Mooyart-Doubleday. The diary was published simultaneously in Great Britain (London) and in the United States (New York).
[6] Tylia Caren and Suzanne Lombard translated the diary into French using the published version of the diary. They therefore copied all the omissions made by Contact Publishing House.
[7] The personal papers of Otto Frank, quoted in this article, have been consulted at the Anne Frank Fonds in Basel.

cording to him, one could quote hundreds of examples of *"les soeurs d'Anne"* hiding in Polish houses (Letter from Parandowski to Frank, 7 July 1954).

Otto Frank was very pleased to hear Parandowski's encouraging words and embraced the prospect of publishing Anne's diary in Poland. Initially, Frank had objections against publishing the diary in communist countries (Kirschnick 2009, 59). After the fall of Stalinism and after establishing contact with some people from the Eastern Bloc, he nevertheless realized that there was enough genuine interest among Eastern Europeans to read the diary and he started supporting this idea.[8] Moreover, his wish to make this book available to a wider public, supported his desire to have it printed in affordable editions in Eastern Europe (Kirschnick 2009, 67–68).

During another PEN Club congress in London in July 1956, Parandowski and Frank met once again, but as Frank notes in their correspondence, they did not have many opportunities to discuss the publication of the Polish version (letter from Frank to Parandowski, 4 January 1957). It is difficult to say what Parandowski's role was in making the publication of the diary in Poland possible, yet it is clear that his interventions did not immediately bring the book to the Polish book market.[9] It was only the European success of the Broadway adaptation of the diary, written by Frances Goodrich and Albert Hackett, that stirred up the Polish interest in the diary.[10] Following its American premiere in October 1955, the play attracted theatrical ensembles across the globe—including those in the Eastern Block. Most impressive was the well-orchestrated premiere in German-speaking countries: on 1 October 1956, *Das Tagebuch der Anne Frank* opened simultaneously in ten cities in Austria, Switzerland, West Germany, and East Germany.

The theater play *Das Tagebuch der Anne Frank* was the first cultural event that united both sides of the Iron Curtain, and as one might expect, this fact did not remain unnoticed in Germany's neighboring country, Poland. Therefore, a mere month later, on 4 November 1956, a popular Polish weekly, *Od A do Z*, published three entries from Anne's diary, translated from German by Krystyna Zbijewska. The lead-in contained a plea for staging a theater play about Anne

---

[8] Here I am pointing mainly to the preserved correspondence between Frank and translator Kurt Harrer. Harrer was a German translator of Polish literature from Dresden. Harrer encouraged Frank to publish the diary in Poland. He also wrote one of the first Polish articles about the German success of Anne Frank's diary. See: Harrer 1956.

[9] I am grateful to Grażyna Pawlak (IBL PAN, Warsaw), who is currently working on a monograph on Parandowski, for her help in finding more background information about the contacts between the PEN-chairman and Otto Frank.

[10] The play opened on 5 October 1955 in New York.

Frank in Poland as soon as possible because of antifascist meaning attributed to the play, especially by East-German commentators. Three weeks later on 18 November 1956, the Polish daily, *Dziennik Bałtycki* [Baltic Daily], published an article about the diary and its success on German stages It also presented the diary as important for the Polish public and urged Polish translators to first and foremost make the original diary text available to Polish readers. The journalist noted that the diary had been successful wherever it was published and that it sold approximately a million copies across different countries. It could be argued, however, that the motivation for translating the diary and staging it as a play in Poland was not so much dictated by the commercial success elsewhere as by its ideological significance.

By the end of 1956, three Polish publishing houses had asked Otto Frank for permission to publish the diary: Silesia Publishing House (*Wydawnictwo Śląsk*) from Katowice, Literary Publishing House (*Wydawnictwo Literackie*) in Kraków, and State Publishing Institute (*Państwowy Instytut Wydawniczy*, hereafter indicated as PIW) located in Warsaw, the largest publishing house in Poland.[11] Vying for the publication rights, all publishers, pushed by competition, hoped for a quick positive response from Otto Frank. Their rush was also possibly motivated by the fact that the story of Anne Frank found its way to Poland at the time of tremendous political and cultural upheaval, known as the Polish October.[12] As a result of a political shift towards liberalization after workers' protests in October 1956, political censorship abated and a more liberal attitude towards foreign literature and publishing policy was adopted. With the limitations imposed on the cultural sector during Stalin's era still fresh in everyone's mind, no one knew how long this situation would last. Consequently, many publishers and cultural institutions were charging forward with newly planned publications and events.

The same urgency can be seen in case of the theatrical adaptation of the diary. At the end of November 1956, Konstanty Puzyna requested the Polish copy-

---

[11] Silesia Publishing House contacted Otto Frank via Kurt Harrer on 18 December 1956. Henryk Vogler from Literary Publishing House first contacted Lambert Schneider Verlag on 20 December 1956 and this letter was forwarded to Frank. Adam Leyfell from the PIW contacted S. Fischer Verlag on 8 December 1956 and this letter was forwarded to Frank. It should be noted that S. Fisher Verlag published in 1955 the bestselling paperback edition in West-Germany. The German edition was, however, for the first time published in 1950 in Heidelberg by Lambert Schneider.

[12] Polish October, also known as October 1956, or (Polish) Thaw, marked a period of radical political changes in post-Stalinist Poland after the new, less Soviet dependent government was established under the leading of Władysław Gomułka during party convention 19–21 October 1956 (for more see Machcewicz 2009, 158–214, 234–53).

rights agency, ZAIKS, to secure the rights and legal agreements in the United States in order to stage Goodrich and Hackett's play in Poland (letter Puzyna to ZAIKS, 24 November 1956). However, the formalities took such a long time that the final agreement with the agency representing American playwrights was not signed until 31 May 1957. Meanwhile, the Polish premiere of the play already took place three months prior, on 8 March 1957.[13]

Unlike the Polish publishers, Otto Frank did not want to rush and preferred to do some more research on the publishers' profiles and reputation. Though he was interested in publishing Anne's diary in Poland, he wanted to ensure that it would be circulated by, as he phrased it, a "first class" publishing house (letter from Frank to Harrer, 2 January 1957). To make a well-informed decision, he not only consulted Jan Parandowski (letter from Frank to Parandowski, 4 January 1957) but also Kurt Harrer, a translator from Dresden he kept in touch with. Harrer advised Frank to accept the offer from the Silesia Publishing House, run by Harrer's friend Wilhelm Szewczyk. However, on 21 January 1957, Frank received a telegram from the Silesian publisher informing him that the state agency supervising press and the publishing sector had assigned the PIW to prepare the Polish edition of the diary. No explanation of this decision followed. Frank immediately informed his contact in Dresden about the situation. Baffled and vexed, Frank could not understand that such a decision had been imposed on him without his approval or without a discussion about the contractual details for the project. Nonetheless, he realized that if he rejected this offer, a Polish edition of the diary might never be published (letter from Frank to Harrer, 22 January 1957). His longing for a Polish version of the diary did not prevent him from complaining to the director of the PIW about being excluded from the decision-making process, but he did not end the negotiations. In part, this choice might have been influenced by a letter that Parandowski sent the day after Frank received the telegram. In this letter, the PEN representative assured Frank that the PIW was the most important publishing house in Poland and publisher of his own books (letter 22 January 1957). In the end, the negotiations between Frank and the publisher in Warsaw went rather smoothly: Otto Frank was even able to negotiate higher royalties than initially proposed by the publisher.

Archival research reveals, however, that Polish authorities did not wait for Frank's consent and their decision to publish the diary at the PIW had already been made by November. Before Otto Frank had even received letters from the

---

[13] The Polish version of the play titled *Pamiętnik Anny Frank* was translated via German by Marian Meller and Konstanty Puzyna, both holding leading functions at the Theatre of the Polish Army in Warsaw. See the play's transcription in the archive of Theatre Institute in Warsaw.

publishers, the translator had already signed an agreement with the publisher in Warsaw on 26 November 1956.[14] Moreover, back in October, the internal reviewer at the PIW, Jerzy Stawiński, praised the diary for its literary and documentary qualities (report dated 13 October 1956). The editorial proposal to translate the diary of Anne Frank was approved by the PIW on 17 October 1956—shortly after the German theatrical premiere of the diary and right in the middle of the Polish October. Before Otto Frank signed the contract with the publisher on 3 August 1957, the Polish edition was already translated and awaiting approval to be printed.[15] In September 1957, printing was finalized and ten thousand copies of the diary found their way to Polish bookstores. On 11 September 1957, a well-known Polish radio performer, Danuta Mancewicz, read fragments of the diary on air. Shortly after, on 29 October 1957, the state radio broadcast the shortened version of Goodrich and Hackett's play, which was still being performed by a Warsaw theatre ever since the beginning of March 1957. The radio programs were clearly part of the publicity campaign of the diary itself, addressed primarily to young listeners.[16]

There are no known sales figures, but according to some press notes the book was very popular.[17] Thus, at the beginning of 1959 the PIW decided to do a reprint, with print run copies doubled in size (letter from Adam Ostrowski to Frank, 28 April 1961). One can conclude that at that moment the book fit into the state publishing plan in Poland particularly well. Meanwhile, different theaters across the country were staging *The Diary of Anne Frank*. This continued up until mid-1961. Theatre scholar Grzegorz Niziołek estimated that, only in the years 1957–1958, sixty thousand people saw the play (Niziołek 2013, 223). The last theatre season of the play, 1960–1961, attracted almost fifty thousand viewers in the region of Kalisz and Wrocław, making it one of Poland's most-visited plays by foreign authors.[18]

---

14 The written agreements with Zofia Jaremko-Pytowska and other internal documents concerning the publication of the diary in Poland have been consulted at the PIW archive.
15 The annotation in the first print of the book shows that it was approved for printing on 18 July 1957.
16 The play was broadcast also after the republication of the diary, on 16 October 1960 and once again on 7 February 1981. See program dossiers in the Polish Radio Archive in Warsaw.
17 According to a note published in *Sprawy i Ludzie* on 2 March 1958, the diary was completely sold out in Wrocław, a capital city of Lower Silesia, the region with a sizeable community of Jews who settled there after WWII.
18 This data has been taken from *Almanach sceny polskiej: Sezon 1960–1961*, 297. In the course of the years 1957–1961, eight different theater ensembles adapted the Anne Frank-play in Poland.

3 *Dziennik Anny Frank* and Its Post-Stalinist Reception

Even before it appeared in Polish in the autumn of 1957, Anne's diary was already an important reference point for the Warsaw play directed by Jerzy Świderski that premiered in the Polish capital in March of that year. Nearly every single theater review stressed that the adaptation prepared by Goodrich and Hackett was based on an authentic diary of a young Jewish girl. Moreover, in addition to background information about the Frank family, pictures of Anne, or photographs of Amsterdam, the theater booklets also often contained fragments from the original diary.[19]

The very existence of the diary authenticated the theater experience and gave the play the special status of a re-enacted document. This was not unimportant because, after the Warsaw premiere, the play was immediately framed within the antifascist discourse. The press was quick to point out that this authentic story of a young Jewish girl represented not only one of the strongest accusations against Nazi Germany but also against the present-day manifestations of fascism. Thus, though Polish reviewers acknowledged the artistic merit of the play, they foregrounded its political significance and the role it could play in stigmatizing anti-Semitism.

After the change in party leadership in October 1956, combating antisemitism became, albeit briefly, an important issue on the political agenda in Poland. This was due, firstly, to the fact that, during internal struggles within the Polish Communist Party, one of the factions repeatedly employed anti-Semitic clichés to discredit Jewish party members. At the same time, in the mid-1950s, the number of anti-Semitic incidents in Poland increased. In April 1956, newspapers reported about various forms of vandalism at Jewish cemeteries. In June 1956, the monument to the Ghetto Heroes in Warsaw was damaged. Furthermore, it was reported that children frequently bullied their Jewish classmates at school. One such case ended quite dramatically: a bullied Jewish girl named Hanka committed suicide. The story was reported by a youth weekly, *Sztandar Młodych* [The Banner of the Youth], in August 1956 (see Michnik 2010).

Following those incidents and the increasing wave of Jewish emigration that they triggered (Węgrzyn, 2016), Polish Prime Minister Józef Cyrankiewicz gave a

---

19 The leaflet of the Warsaw staging quotes fragments published earlier by *Przekrój* and translated by Wanda Kragen. In the leaflets prepared for other theaters (Kraków, Łódź, Szczecin, Bielsko-Biała, Olsztyn, Kalisz and Wrocław) after the publication of the diary, Zofia Jaremko-Pytowska's translations are used.

speech in February 1957, in which he strongly condemned anti-Semitism and anti-Jewish violence in Poland.[20] Shortly after this speech, the Polish press started announcing the theatrical premiere of *The Diary of Anne Frank*, scheduled for 8 March in Warsaw. The emotional appeal of the story about a persecuted young Jewish girl who eventually died in a Nazi concentration camp was immediately recognized as a powerful didactic tool, especially suitable to condemn fascism and anti-Semitism.[21] By that time many Polish intellectuals, concerned about this sudden wave of anti-Jewish violence and hate speech, felt the urge to take a stance in the debate about postwar Polish anti-Semitism and joined discussions in the press (Böhler 2016, 61–65). Subsequently, many theater reviewers took a stance in this ongoing debate, denouncing anti-Semitic sentiments and incidents in Poland and expressing their hopes that this play would have a pedagogical influence on the Polish audience.

During the first three weeks, the play was only performed in the evenings and therefore mostly targeted an adult audience. Yet, at the end of March 1957, the theater started to organize afternoon performances, shifting attention to younger audiences who were now also able to attend. Theater authorities began to understand that the story of Anne Frank was potentially important for educating young people with regards to anti-Semitism. The pilgrimage of West-German youth to Bergen-Belsen to commemorate Anne Frank's death, organized on 17 March 1957, made this point clear. This massive youth gathering was widely covered by the Polish media and, what is more, the newsreel that informed the public about Warsaw's theatrical premiere of *Pamiętnik Anny Frank* was spliced together with footage from the Bergen-Belsen gathering (Polska Kronika Filmowa, 57/15B).

In October 1957, *The Diary of Anne Frank* was staged by *Teatr Młodego Widza* [Youth State Theatre] in Kraków, and the radio adaptation was included in the broadcast cycle entitled *Teatr Młodego Słuchacza* [Theatre for Young Listeners]. Magazines aimed at younger people such as the above-mentioned *Sztandar Młodych*, or the popular monthly for girls, *Filipinka*, published didactic articles about Anne Frank and her diary. As we learn from the reviews, pupils often attended the performances, which meant that teachers were probably encouraged to arrange such theater visits. A letter to the editor of Wrocław-based *Słowo Polskie* [Polish Word] from 24 March 1961, authored by one such teacher, suggests

---

20 Cyrankiewicz's speech was widely covered by the daily press and *Życie Warszawy* printed the entire speech on 27 February 1957.
21 Grzegorz Niziołek also speculates that the Warsaw theater's decision to include *The Diary of Anne Frank* in its repertoire was most probably motivated by the fact that its managers believed it could be used as a tool to combat antisemitism (Niziołek 2013, 235–36).

that school excursions to see the Anne Frank play were undertaken also in subsequent years and not only in Warsaw. In this case, the teacher extolled the play for the profound impression on her pupils, adding that especially the girls sympathized and identified with Anne. This potential of the play was not lost even on the central party paper *Trybuna Ludu*. As Roman Szydłowski points out in his review:

> The didactic impact of this piece is unquestionable; its internationalist spirit and its role in combating persistent manifestations of nationalism, chauvinism, [and] antisemitism are clear and obvious. The youth gathered in the theatre ... will not only be moved by this play but will also be filled with just and noble ideas. (*Trybuna Ludu*, 28 December 1958)

Interestingly, what surfaces in reviews and critical reactions time and again is a certain rhetorical strategy by which reviewers tried to evoke sympathy for the characters of *Het Achterhuis*, connecting their circumstances to the Polish wartime experience. The Frank family was portrayed as a model family that everyone in Poland could identify with and feel sympathy for. Reviewers emphasized universal human values represented by the Franks. Anne was pictured as a lovely, warm-hearted, and talented young girl, while her father, Otto, was often described as a noble, decent, and honest person. Their Jewishness was not omitted altogether, but it was understated. Seweryna Szmaglewska, writer, former prisoner of Auschwitz and one of the few Poles to have testified at the Nuremberg trials, wrote in her review for *Nowa Kultura* in 1957:

> For those who survived the [Warsaw] Ghetto, the face of Anne Frank will have familiar, maybe even Varsovian traces (despite the fact that such events could have taken place almost everywhere in Europe). Those who helped to hide and take care of the persecuted, will recognise their own determination in the behaviour of Miep and Kramer [sic], just as they will see in *Anusia* [Annie] the children they lost during the Warsaw Uprising.

In the light of the above-mentioned engagement of Polish intellectuals in the debate on anti-Jewish incidents, it could be argued that Szmaglewska's framing of the play was intended to make the Polish audience more sensitive to the fate of Jews, and Jewish children in particular. Nevertheless, her attempt to compare Polish losses in the Warsaw Uprising to the Holocaust also displays the Polish competition of victimhood and the tendency to blur the differences between the Jewish and Polish fate under the Nazi occupation. Part of this effect was achieved by means of domesticating Anne by referring to her in the Polish diminutive, as *Anusia* or *Ania*—a strategy common both to Szmaglewska and other reviewers (see Früling 1957, 1355–56, Święcicki 1959, 448–54). Some of them even suggested that it could well have been a diary of a child hidden in Warsaw.

The strategy of domesticating Anne's circumstances for the Polish readers is also reflected in the translation of the book.

4 The Polish Translation of Anne Frank's Diary: A Lexical and Textual Analysis

The first Polish edition of Anne Frank's diary was based on the German translation. In many ways, this is not surprising because until the early 1980s, there were very few translators in Poland who could translate directly from Dutch to Polish. Therefore, Dutch or Flemish books that appeared on the Polish market during the first post-war decades were translated indirectly through other languages: mostly via German and, more rarely, French or English. For this reason, Polish publishers followed the German book market closely and the preserved correspondence suggests a strong relationship between the Polish and West-German publishing worlds during the Cold War period (Dąbrówka 1984, 375–76; Koch 1993, 9–10). Goodrich and Hackett's theatrical version came to Poland via a German translation too, partly because it was easier for theaters in Poland to obtain the German manuscript (letter from Harrer to Frank, 8 December 1956).

The Polish publishing house (PIW) contracted Zofia Jaremko-Pytowska to translate Anne's diary. In the period between 1949 and 1970, Jaremko-Pytowska was working for several publishers, translating fiction and non-fiction from German and French.[22] Her contract, signed with the PIW on 10 December 1956, specified that she would work on adapting Anne Frank's diary from the German version.

The German translation of the diary was originally undertaken for relatives, especially Otto Frank's mother, who lived in Basel and did not understand Dutch. Anneliese Schütz, a Berlin-born journalist, an acquaintance of the Frank family from before the war, and one of the few survivors from Amsterdam's German-Jewish community, offered her help in carrying out the German translation. She based it on the Typescript II that Otto Frank had compiled in 1946 and circulated among his Dutch contacts and publishers. After the success of *Het Achterhuis* in the Netherlands, Schütz' translation was sent to a number of German publishers. In 1950, the Lambert Schneider publishing house in Heidelberg agreed to publish the diary under the title *Das Tagebuch der Anne Frank* in a 4,500 copy print run (Van der Stroom 2001, 83–84; Schroth 2006, 124–25).

---

22 She emigrated to the United States in the 1970s.

It is important to note that, in comparison with the Dutch, French, and English editions, the German version was by far the most comprehensive. It contained seven additional diary entries as well as passages that were omitted in *Het Achterhuis* from 1947.[23] This is because, unlike other translators who used the published Dutch version, Anneliese Schütz worked directly with the Typescript II version (Van der Stroom 2001, 84). Consequently, the Polish translation based on the German version was also more complete than *Het Achterhuis*, *Le journal d'Anne Frank*, or *The Diary of a Young Girl*.

As far as the quality of the translation was concerned, however, Schütz' work was not accurate. She took a lot of liberty in translating Anne's diary entries and she was often heavily criticized for lexical mistakes, factual errors, and the inability to render Anne's style. By the time Anneliese Schütz began working on the translation, in 1946, she was already in her fifties and, because of her age, had limited knowledge of the Dutch spoken by young adults like Anne (Van der Stroom 2001, 84–86; Schroth 2006, 125–26). Schütz' translation sounded more mature, which eventually raised some questions about the diary's authenticity. The inaccurate translation by Schütz was for the first time extensively discussed and analyzed in 1959, during the legal proceedings against a German teacher, Lothar Stielau, who claimed that Anne's diary was a forgery (Heimsath, 2013, 149–58).

Given that the Polish translator quite faithfully followed the German version, various lexical and factual mistakes were copied into the Polish *Dziennik Anny Frank*. For example, on 11 April 1944 Anne speculated about what would happen if someone discovered her family's hideout. If they were exposed by good Dutch people, Anne reasoned, everyone would remain safe; whereas, if they were discovered by the *NSB-ers*, (members of the Dutch National Socialist Party), they would surely have to resort to bribes. Anneliese Schütz, and the Polish translator after her, exchanged the word *NSB-ers* with *Nazis*. What seems like a small alteration raised doubts about the historical accuracy of the diary, since negotiating with the Nazis in a similar situation was basically unheard of.

Another example of an inaccurate translation, which was copied into the Polish version, is even more remarkable. On 9 July 1942, the BBC broadcast a report about "Jews being regularly killed by machinegun fire, hand grenades, and even poisoned by gas." (Van der Stroom 2001, 317) On 9 October 1942, Anne notes that "The English radio speaks about gassing." Revising that entry in the spring of 1944 Anne adds: "Maybe this is after all the quickest method of

---

[23] The German book reprinted the following entries (absent in *Het Achterhuis*): 3 August and 7 August 1943, 20 February, 15 April, 21 April, 25 April, and 11 May 1944.

dying." In the German version the word *gassing* was rendered as *Gaskammern* [gas chambers] and *Vernichtungsmethode* [extermination method] substituted Anne's less explicit *sterfmethode* [method of dying]. The Polish translator only slightly adjusted Schütz' lexical choice, opting for *komory gazowe* [gas chambers] and *sposób zabijania* [killing method] respectively. Although Anne surely realized the process of gassing was a method of killing, we cannot know for sure to what extent she was aware of the exact scale and methods employed by the Nazis. Schütz' choice of words is therefore marked by her post-war knowledge and suggests over-interpretation on her part. What is more, the German translation alters the tone of this passage, by making it sound harsher and more explicit (Schroth 2006, 152).

It is difficult to ascertain why Schütz took such liberty in translating this passage. The assumption that she was determined to point an accusatory finger at the German aggressors is not borne out by the other evidence. In a number of passages, namely, Schütz quite deliberately omitted fragments where Anne voices her anti-German attitude (Van der Stroom 2001, 85; Rosenfeld 1991, 266–69). Interviewed about the translation years later by the *Spiegel*, Schütz explains she did so because she did not believe a book containing "insults against the Germans" could sell in post-war West Germany (*Der Spiegel*, 1 April 1959). She also omitted the sentence "We assume that most of them [deported Jews] are murdered" as well as Anne's reference to the rumors about immorality in camp Westerbork, which led to many pregnancies.

Interestingly, a closer look at the Polish translation of the diary reveals that many of Schütz' alterations had been reversed. The Polish version thus contains the passage about the immorality in camp Westerbork (9 October 1942). Also, Anne's humorous remark about German being the forbidden language in *Het Achterhuis* is present (17 November 1942).[24] Jaremko-Pytowska also retains a passage where Anne imagines the collaborator who could denounce them, picturing him as an evil giant and the worst fascist in the world (20 October 1942). Where the German version elides the word "Germans," the Polish translator brings it back, as in the passage where Anne describes underground activities as "the heroism in war and in struggle against the Germans," (28 January 1944) which Schütz renders as "*Heldenmut im Krieg und im Streit gegen Unterdrückung*" [heroism in war and struggle against the oppression].

---

24 Anne's sentence "allowed are all cultural languages, and therefore no German" was translated by Schütz as *Alle Kultursprachen... aber leise* ["all cultural languages ... but silent"]. The Polish translator reversed it into "all European languages, with the exception of German."

All the adjustments in the Polish version were possible thanks to careful editorial work of the PIW staff and a thorough comparison of the English, German, and Dutch texts that they carried out. We know about this because in April 1957, two months after Zofia Jaremko-Pytowska delivered her translation to the publisher, Adam Leyfell, chief editor at the PIW, sent a request to Otto Frank to provide him with the original Dutch publication. Leyfell mentioned in his letter that, comparing the German and the English texts to each other, their editors discovered some discrepancies.[25] Leyfell hoped that a comparison with the original version would help them correct the German mistranslations (letter to Frank, 5 April 1957). This careful approach towards the German translation might indicate that the Polish editors were suspicious towards publications from West Germany, especially those dealing with the subject of the Nazi German crimes.

At the same time, not all of Schütz' edits were corrected in the Polish version. In one of the entries, Anne states: "there is no greater enmity in the world between two peoples than that between the Germans and Jews." (9 October 1942) Schütz translated it using a more restrictive modifier, *diese Deutschen* [those Germans], and the same solution, *tymi Niemcami,* appears in the Polish edition. Such an emphasis, present in neither the English nor Dutch version, could have been too subtle for Polish correctors to spot, since the Polish language does not have articles. Another omission that remained in the Polish translation is the already mentioned sentence in which Anne expresses the assumption that most of the Jews deported to the East would be murdered. What is more, the word *barbaars* [barbarian] with which Anne refers to the East is likewise omitted in both translations. All things considered, however, the Polish translation contained more anti-German and antifascist references than the text published in Germany.

The original publication of the diary in the Netherlands also contained omissions. Seven of Anne's entries in which she described her sexual development were censored in the Dutch edition, while they were included in the German and Polish ones. In one of the passages Anne writes about the desire to touch her best friend's breasts (5 January 1944), in another, she discusses menstruation (31 March 1944). With regards to the latter, Jaremko-Pytowska either misunderstood the word *unwohl* by the German version and rendered it as *niezdrowa* [feeling unwell], instead of *niedysponowana* [menstruating], or she wanted to censor it. Consequently, several fragments in which Anne writes about her period are

---

25 Already in July 1954, Otto Frank instructed Parandowski to use the English translation of the diary rather than the French one (together with the original version, in Dutch). He believed that the English translation most closely reflected his daughter's style.

not clear to the Polish reader (cf. 29 October 1942, 5 January 1944). By obfuscating Anne's references to her sexuality, the Polish version renders Anne as a more modest and innocent girl.

Some lexical and stylistic choices of the Polish translator are also worth mentioning. For instance, Jaremko-Pytowska decided to domesticate a few proper names: *Peter* becomes *Piotr* and sometimes even *Piotruś* [diminutive of Piotr], Peter's cat *Muschi/Mouchi* is named *Mruczek* [Purrie], Anne's cat *Moortje/Mohrchen* becomes *Murzynek* [Blackie], and another cat, *Moffi* is rendered as *Szwab*.[26] Also, the main protagonist's name is either translated as *Anna*, or, even more frequently, as the diminutive *Ania*. Unlike the English and the Dutch version, the Polish edition also includes two stories written by Anne during her stay in hiding: *Kaatje* and *Katrientje*. Both names are made to sound Polish and, as in the Dutch version, they are rendered in diminutive forms: *Kicia* and *Kasieńka*. Within translation studies, such a strategy by which foreign text is made more familiar to the target audience is referred to as domestication. It aims at making the foreign text more relatable and easily recognizable to its readers, bringing it closer to its audience, often at the expense of losing the original meanings. This strategy is often adopted in order to minimize the foreignness of the source text and maximize its impact on the reader, making it a desirable tool for domestic cultural or political agendas (Venuti 1995, 18–19). Jaremko-Pytowska used this strategy notoriously and not just to adapt foreign names. She also regularly translated emotionally neutral words such as *Vater* and *Mutter* into *tatuś* and *mama* [daddy and mummy]; *Mädchen* into *dziewczynka* [small girl] instead of *dziewczyna* [girl]; *Kater* into *kotek* [little cat]; *dzienniczek* [little diary] instead of *dziennik* [diary]. In Polish, not only nouns, but also adjectives and adverbs have diminutive forms. Hence, the word *sauber* [clean] is translated as *czyściutko*; *ganz leise* [quiet] as *cichutko*, and so on. Diminutive forms of nouns and adjectives are a very frequent feature of Polish language in general, and children's literature in particular (Lockyer 2013, 62–64). However, through the extensive use of diminutives, the entire Polish text sounds more infantile and childlike, certainly more so than its German equivalent.[27] Whether this was the aim of the translator, we can only speculate.[28]

---

[26] *Moffie* derives from *mof* which in Dutch is an offensive word for a German person. The same holds for Polish word *Szwab*.
[27] Interestingly, Wanda Kragen, who translated a few excerpts from the diary for the popular Polish weekly *Przekrój*, domesticated the names of Anne and Peter and that of the cat, but she did not use diminutives. See *Przekrój*, 3 February 1957.
[28] Unfortunately, none of Jaremko-Pytowska's work manuscripts have been preserved in the PIW archive. Migrating to the United States, Jaremko-Pytowska did not take any personal

5 Conclusions

Because of the lexical choices of the translator and the domestication strategies she used, Anne's diary in Poland was perceived as a familiar and accessible text, particularly to younger readers. It helped to diminish the perceived foreignness of German-Dutch Anne Frank. Her Jewishness was neither especially accentuated nor completely silenced, and her image as a universal child victim of fascism was enhanced.

The Polish translation, compared to other versions of the diary published in the 1950s (for example Dutch, German, French, English, or Japanese), corresponded most closely to the original Typescript II. On the one hand because it was based on the already more extensive version of the diary published in Germany, and, on the other, thanks to a careful revision of the major omissions made by Anneliese Schütz, it corresponded more closely to Anne's original entries, as transcribed by Otto Frank.

Another important feature of the Polish publication was that it had a more outspokenly anti-German tone. In terms of language, both Jaremko-Pytowska's and Schütz' translations did not quite capture the informal, childlike style of Anne's writing. However, while the mature and polished language of the German translation raised questions about the authenticity of Anne's diary, the Polish translation, through the extensive use of diminutives, read as if it was written by a child. Only one reviewer voiced his suspicions about the faithfulness of Polish translation to the original. A journalist of the cultural monthly *Odra* [Oder], pointed out that the book was so well written and composed, that he found it hard to believe a fifteen-year-old girl had written it. He therefore raised the following question: "Was the [Polish] translator capable of rendering the original text? Or perhaps she embellished the original text while translating it from German?" (*Odra*, 19 January 1958)

The publication of the diary did not challenge the already established image of Anne Frank as an innocent victim of fascism; it rather reinforced it. By foregrounding Anne's innocence and her charming childlike character and by making her appear more Polish, the book, on one level, stroke to evoke more empathy in its reader for the suffering of Jewish people. However, as we could see above, the tendency to blur the distinction between Polish and Jewish suffering during the Second World War was also present in the Polish reception of the diary. In the early 1960s, the story of Anne Frank, just as the entire discussion

---

work papers with her. Because of her advanced age, health state, and memory problems, she was also not able to answer my questions (E-mail from Bronek Pytowski, 3 December 2014).

on anti-Semitism and the persecution of Jews during the war, slowly faded away from the Polish public debate. Shortly after the diary was reprinted in the spring of 1960, Otto Frank attempted to have Anne's stories published in Poland as well. Although the PIW seemed interested at first, by July 1961 Frank was informed that there was no intention to publish them. All ties between Frank and the publishing house were officially severed in April 1963, when Frank received a letter informing him that the diary was not available in Polish bookstores anymore and that another edition would not be printed. No further explanation followed, yet it is clear that the changing political climate in Poland inspired this decision. In the 1960s, a more nationalist faction within the Communist Party gained power in Poland. Having enjoyed a secondary position within the Party during the Stalinist years, they were now united by strong anti-Stalinist and anti-Jewish sentiments and a worldview combining nationalism and communism. Their agenda took an increasingly anti-Jewish turn. The government they formed no longer expressed the will to combat anti-Semitism. Consequently, addressing Polish anti-Semitism slowly became taboo and was considered "Zionist" or "Western anti-Polish propaganda". In 1964, even the attempt to acknowledge the fact that the majority of inmates of the Nazi extermination camps were Jewish came under criticism as a purposeful attempt to depreciate the memory of non-Jewish Polish victims (Schatz 1991, 288–91, 295–96). Anne Frank's diary, like many other books touching on the subject of the Jewish persecution, disappeared from the Polish book market. It returned only in 1993, after the demise of the People's Republic of Poland, in a new translation, and an entirely new political context.

Bibliography

"Anneliese Schutz overleden." *Het Vrije Volk*, 28 November 1960.
"Oświadczenie premiera J. Cyrankiewicza w Sejmie." *Życie Warszawy*, 28 February 1957.
Bąk, B. 1961. "Ania z amsterdamskiego poddasza." *Słowo Polskie*, 20 February.
Böhler, Jochen. 2016. "'Wer seid und auf welcher Seite steht Ihr?'—Polens literarische Kreise und die antisemitische Stimmung des Sommers 1956." In *1956: (Nieco) inne spojrzenie/ Eine (etwas) andere Perspektive*, edited by Jerzy Kochanowski and Joachim von Puttkamer, 55–72. Warszawa: Neriton.
Csato, E., ed. 1961. *Almanach sceny polskiej: Sezon 1960–1961*. Warszawa: Wydawnictwo Artystyczne i Filmowe.
Dąbrówka, A. 1984. "Toeval en principe in de praktijk van de vertaling: Nederlandse literatuur in Poolse vertaling." *Ons Erfdeel* 27: 375–384.
Frank, Anne. 1947. *Het Achterhuis: Dagboekbrieven 12 juni 1942 – 1 augustus 1944*. Amsterdam: Uitgeverij Contact.

Frank, Anne. 1950. *Le journal d'Anne Frank*. Translated by Tylia Caren and Suzanne Lombard. Paris: Calmann-Lévy.
Frank, Anne. 1956. "Pamiętnik Anny Frank." *Od A do Z*, 4 November, fragments from the diary translated by Krystyna Zbijewska.
Frank, Anne. 1957a. "Droga Kitty! Pamiętnik Anny Frank." *Przekrój*, 3 February, fragments from the diary translated by Wanda Kragen.
Frank, Anne. 1957b. *Dziennik Anny Frank*. Translated by Zofia Jaremko-Pytowska. Warszawa: PIW.
Frank, Anne. 1971. *Das Tagebuch der Anne Frank*. Translated by Anneliese Schűtz. Frankfurt: S. Fisher Verlag.
Frank, Anne. 1981. *The Diary of Anne Frank*. Translated by B.M. Mooyart-Doubleday. London: Valentine Mitchells.
Frühling, J. 1957. "Tragiczny dziennik." *Nowe Książki* 22: 1355–1356.
Graver, L. 1997. *An Obsession with Anne Frank: Meyer Levin and the Diary*. California: University of California Press.
Grodzicki, A. 1957. "Czy należy się śmiać?" *Filipinka*, 6.
Grys, A. 1961. "List w sprawie wrocławskiego przedstawienia Anny Frank." *Słowo Polskie* 6 March.
Harrer, K. 1956. "Dziennik Anny Frank." *Przemiany* 8.
Heimsath, K. 2013. "'Trotz allem glaube ich an das Gute im Menschen': Das Tagebuch der Anne Frank und seine Rezeption in der Bundesrepublik Deutschland." PhD diss., Hamburg, unpublished.
Jarochowska, M. 1958. "Piekło za zamkniętymi drzwiami." *Trybuna Literacka*, 9 February.
Kotańska, M. 1961. "Nauczycielka i jej uczniowie o wrocławskich przedstawieniach *Anny Frank* i *Zawiszy Czarnego*." *Słowo Polskie*, 24 March.
Kirschnick, S. 2009. *Anne Frank und die DDR: Politische Deutungen und persönliche Lesarten des berühmten Tagebuchs*. Berlin: Links.
Koch, J. 1993. *Książka niderlandzka w przekładzie polskim: katalog wystawy w Bibliotece Zakładu Narodowego im. Ossolińskich, Wrocław 12–28 maja 1993/ Het nederlandse boek in Poolse vertaling: catalogus van de tentoonstelling in de Bibliotheek van het Nationale Ossoliński-Instituut, Wrocław 12–28 mei 1993*. Wrocław: Ossolineum.
Krakowski. 1958. "Pamiętnik Anny Frank we Wrocławiu." *Sprawy i Ludzie*, 2 March.
Kuitert, Lisa. 2007–2008. "De uitgave van Het Achterhuis van Anne Frank." *De Boekenwereld* 24: 18–27.
Lejeune, P. 2009. "How Anne Frank Rewrote the Diary of Anne Frank." In *On diary*, edited by J. D. Popkin and J. Rak, 237–266. Honolulu: University of Hawaii Press.
Lockyer, D. 2013. *That Poor Little Thing: The Emotive Meanings of Diminutives in Polish and Russian Translations of Alice in Wonderland* [MA Thesis. Unpublished].
Machcewicz, Paweł. 2009. *Rebellious satellite: Poland, 1956*. Washington, DC and Stanford: Woodrow Wilson Center Press/Stanford University Press.
Minkowski, A. 1956. "Sprawa Hanki." *Sztandar Młodych*, 23 August.
Michnik, A., ed. 2010. *Przeciw antysemityzmowi*, Vol. 2. Kraków.
Niziołek, G. 2013. *Polski teatr Zagłady*. Warszawa: Wydawnictwo "Krytyki Politycznej."
Romein, J. 1946. "Kinderstem." *Het Parool*, 3 April.

Rosenfeld, A. 1991. "Popularisation and Memory: The Case of Anne Frank." In *Lessons and Legacies: The Meaning of the Holocaust in a Changing World*, edited by Peter Hayes, 243–278. Evanston, IL: Northwestern University Press.
Schatz, J. 1991. *The Generation: The Rise and Fall of the Jewish Communists of Poland*. Berkeley: University of California Press.
Schroth, S. 2006. *Das Tagebuch = The diary = le journal: Anne Franks 'Het Achterhuis' als Gegenstand eines kritischen Übersetzungsvergleichs*. Münster: Waxmann.
Święcicki, J.M. 1959. "Pamiętnik Anny Frank." *Homo Dei* 3: 448–454.
Szmaglewska, S. 1957. "Pamiętnik Anny Frank." *Nowa Kultura*, 21 April.
Szydłowski, R. 1958. "Wizyta w teatrach łódzkich." *Trybuna Ludu*, 28 December.
Tom, R. 1956. "Pamiętnik Anny Frank." *Dziennik Bałtycki*, 18 November.
Van der Stroom, G. 2001. "De dagboeken en *Het Achterhuis* en de vertalingen." In *De dagboeken van Anne Frank*, edited by A.H. Paape, H.J.J. Hardy, and D. Barnouw, 69–90. Amsterdam: B. Bakker.
Venuti. 1995. *The Translator's Invisibility: A History of Translation*. London and New York: Routledge.
Węgrzyn, Ewa. 2016. *Wyjeżdżamy! Wyjeżdżamy?! Alija gomułkowska, 1956–1960*. Kraków and Budapeszt: Wydawnictwo Austeria
Zab. 1958. "Dziennik Anny Frank." *Odra*, 19 January.

Archival material

Otto Frank Archive (Anne Frank Fonds, Basel)
Franks' Notebook 1954
Letters:
Parandowski to Frank, 7 July 1954.
Leyfell to S. Fisher Verlag, 8 December 1956.
Harrer to Frank, 8 December 1956.
Harrer to Frank, 18 December 1956.
Vogler to Lambert Schneider, 20 December 1956.
Frank to Harrer, 2 January 1957.
Frank to Parandowski, 4 January 1957.
Wydawnictwo Śląsk to Frank, 21 January 1957.
Parandowski to Frank, 22 January 1957.
Frank to Harrer, 22 January 1957.
Leyfell to Frank, 5 April 1957.
Contract with the PIW, 3 Augustus 1957.
Frank to Ostrowski, 13 October 1957.
Ostrowski to Frank, 28 April 1961.
Ostrowski to Frank, 5 April 1963.

PIW archive (Warsaw)
Internal report on the diary by Jerzy Stawiński, dated 13 October 1956.
Agreement with Zofia (Jaremko)-Pytowska, dated 10 December 1956.

Polish Radio Archive (Warsaw)
Program schedules from 11 September 1957 and 29 October 1957, 16 October 1960, 7 February 1981.
Screenplay of the radio play *Pamiętnik Anny Frank* (1957) directed by Jan Świderski.

Theater Institute Archive (Warsaw)
Theater leaflets and program books from adaptation of The Diary of Anne Frank by theaters in Warsaw, Łódź, Szczecin, Bielsko/Cieszyn, Olsztyn/Elbląg, Kalisz and Kraków.
The Polish translation of Broadway-play *The Diary of Anne Frank*, in Polish titled as *Pamiętnik Anny Frank*. Translated from German by Marian Meller and Konstanty Puzyna.

Online Polish Newsreel Archive (www.KronikaRP.pl)
Polska Kronika Filmowa, "Anne Frank" 57/15B, 1957.

ZAIKS [Polish Society of Authors and Composers] Archive (Warsaw)
Agreement between Frances Goodrich, Albert Hackett, Otto Frank and the ZAIKS, 31 May 1957.
Letter from Puzyna to ZAIKS, 24 November 1956.

Tara Kohn
Translation and Re-Vision: On the Resurgence and Resurfacing of Alter Kacyzne's Photographic Texts

In the years between 1921 and 1929, the Warsaw-based artist, writer, and translator Alter Kacyzne made two visually and thematically intertwined photographs on assignment for New York's Yiddish-language press—two scenes, almost the same but not quite, that he shot at different moments, in different cities, and from different angles.[1] *Old Road-Maker in Ostroleka, Poland* depicts a solitary worker in the middle of an unfinished road strewn with stone.[2] Leaning back against his heels, his knees sink into a patch of bare earth (figure 1). He pauses from his task and gazes calmly into the distance. Wisps of gray hair peek out from beneath the brim of his hat and tangle into a long beard across his chin. The other photograph, *A Jewish Street of Bialystok, Poland*, also depicts a road maker who grips a piece of cobblestone in the palm of each hand as he kneels in the middle of a fragmentary path (figure 2). His sleeves are rolled up to his elbows, and he bends forward along the length of his spine as he aligns pieces of stone in the earth beneath him.

Kacyzne's photographic process, and, in particular, this act of revisiting a scene that he had shot before and framing it, once again, from a different perspective, was deeply entwined with his writerly practice of revision. It was the visual equivalent of coming back to a sentence, editing the syntax, and exchanging one phrase for another; it was like using the lens of his camera, rather than his pen, to inscribe the same idea on a page using different words. Indeed, in every facet of his career, the artist was continually engaged on some level in

---

[1] I borrow the phrase 'almost the same but not quite' from Homi Bhabha's work on mimicry (1994, 127).
[2] Throughout this text, I use spellings that refer directly to the titles of the works I cite. For example, the form of "Ostroleka" here is taken from the caption printed alongside this image in Raphael Abramovitch's *The Vanished World* (1947), a volume at the center of this discussion. When I am not alluding to this particular printed title, I use the more common spelling "Ostrolenka." I have also chosen to use both Jewish and Polish toponyms throughout this essay, a doubling, I suggest, that stands as a rhetorical reflection of the complexity of cultural, visual, and linguistic translation. When referring to the names of this town, I use both the Yiddish "Ostrolenka" and the Polish "Ostrołęka." Similarly, in my discussion of Kacyzne's related photograph *A Jewish Street Paver of Bialystok, Poland*, I pair the Yiddish "Bialystok" with the Polish "Białystok."

https://doi.org/10.1515/9783110550788-013

Figure 1: Alter Kacyzne, *The Old Road Maker in Ostroleka, Poland, 1920s*. From *The Vanished World: Jewish Cities, Jewish People*, edited by Raphael Abramovitch and published by the Forward Association of New York, 1947. YIVO Institute for Jewish Research, New York. Image courtesy of the Forward Association, New York.

the practice of translation. Perhaps better known during his lifetime and in his own country as a Yiddish-language poet, playwright, and essayist than he was as a photographer, he was fluent in Russian, Polish, German, French, and Hebrew. Moving between and across languages in his written work, he transformed the varied tones of spoken language into lines of poetry, adapted great literary works of the past for the Yiddish stage, and altered theatrical works into screenplays. He developed his skill with the camera during the same years he produced his first literary compositions; at the age of fourteen, when he moved to the south of Ukraine to apprentice with a local photographer, he also began to write (Berkowitz and Dauber 2006, 61). As he shifted between linguistic systems and across modes of representation, he worked to maintain the cadences of language and the nuances of memory—to sustain the texture of each word, idea, or vision. In his work as a visual artist, tied, from its inception, to his literary practice, he was able to transcribe the felt experience of loss into his photographic prints.

Figure 2: Alter Kacyzne, *A Jewish Street Paver of Bialystock, Poland*, 1920s. From *The Jewish Daily Forward*, December 14, 1924 (detail). YIVO Institute for Jewish Research, New York. Image courtesy of the Forward Association, New York.

In "The Task of the Translator," Walter Benjamin evokes an image of splintering and mending, of building a whole out of pieces, that echoes the language that emerges in Kacyzne's photographs—in his act of returning to rework one scene of road-making into the other, to edit and refine what he must have realized were significant, metaphorically loaded images of merging pieces. Benjamin suggests that the role of the translator, like the work of the bricklayers who place stones into a web of mortar, is to "glue" "fragments" together, to create a whole out of the splinters and pieces of language. A translation, he suggests, is an emulation, a re-tracing that maintains the structure of a work of art without repeating the contours of each detail (2002, 254). This essay focuses on Kacyzne's work as this kind of translator: as a photographer who returned to revise his images, to articulate the same overarching meaning from a different angle; as a writer whose words, densely visual and distinctly photographic in nature, re-phrased his visions in lines of text; as an artist who adapted his ideas again and again by breaking them apart and splicing them back together in new form. I explore the additional translations that took shape as his photographs were published and re-published, as they resurfaced in new volumes. Kacyzne's images took on new layers of meaning, like layers of sediment on stone, as history unfolded and the site of reading shifted around them. They were transformed with each printed iteration, adapted from records of a vanishing way of life into remnants of a homeland left behind, fragments of a cataclysmic rupture, and slivers of a place that was, for readers looking through them and back across the traumatic break, once lived in and longed for and now brutally destroyed. Each translation of these visions of a world at the edge of despair—each rephrasing and re-writing, each re-surfacing—marks, in Benjamin's words, a "stage of their continued life," a resurgence of meaning and memory, a ghostly remnant of "afterlife" in the midst of dissolution and death (2002, 254).

Kacyzne's photographs of unfinished roads are, in many ways, visual transcriptions. They are traces, copies of cobblestone etched onto a printed surface. Though carefully pieced together through the lens of his camera, arranged and staged, these images appear as records—as material imprints of a world on the verge of disaster.[3] They not only endured the violent destruction of the artist's records, manuscripts, and notes, but also survived the photographer himself, who resolved never to leave his beloved Warsaw even under the threat of escalating anti-Semitism and violence (Web 1999, xvi, xxi). In the wake of such catastrophic loss of life, of materials and documentation, of negatives, they endure only as reproductions—only as translations. As photographs, these images take shape in a visual medium that hinges on its reproducibility; they exist, inherently, as multiples, complicating notions of artistic originality and undercutting our ability to differentiate the original and the copy (Krauss 1999, 76–77). Furthermore, there are no remaining records to indicate which photograph the artist took first and which was the reiteration. *Old Road-Maker* is carefully composed, almost rehearsed in the way it frames the worker in a network of stone and mortar—as if the artist had already learned to set up the shot when he first encountered the scene in Bialystok/Białystok. The faded passage around the old road-paver's head, however, indicates that a section of the negative for *Old Road-Maker* was too dark to produce the even tonal gradations characteristic of Kacyzne's photographic work. It is perhaps more likely, then, that *A Jewish Street Paver* was Kacyzne's effort to make visible what, in Ostrolenka/Ostrołęka, had been obscured in shadow and lost in the translation from the negative to the positive print. In one image, at any rate, he retraced and reinterpreted the other. He maintained its tone and texture, but reframed and rephrased it. He revived and restored, through the act of visual transcription, a traditional Jewish way of life that was already dissolving, already vanishing. He framed, through his photographic practice, significant questions about the nature of translation: about what it means to translate a text that exists in the form of multiples, about what it means to translate a text that has no original.

---

[3] Because handheld cameras were not yet accessible in Poland in the years he was taking photographs on assignment for the *Forward*, Kacyzne used unwieldy equipment and studio techniques to carefully craft and plan his images of the *shtetl* (see Zemel 2015, 33).

When Kacyzne shot and re-shot his photographs of road builders, as the art historian Carol Zemel points out, the diasporic culture of the *shtetl* he framed in the lens of his camera was transforming into an elusive mythological structure; it was becoming a marker of the idyllic past (Zemel 2015, 17, 29). During the 1920s, the *shtetl* was a symbol of a former way of life, woven across the villages of Eastern and Central Europe and bound by religious orthodoxy and spoken Yiddish. It was a sign that was becoming increasingly resonant under the weight of change, of modernization and migration, as customs shifted and threads formed between Jewish families divided by oceans and national boundaries (Zemel 2015, 23–24, 30). For recently resettled immigrant readers, who encountered *A Jewish Street Paver* in the popular Yiddish-language newspaper *The Jewish Daily Forward* on Sunday, December 14, 1924, Kacyzne's work acted as a visual bridge back to this idealized past—to the villages they left behind, to the homelands they longed for.

Pressed up against the edges of photographs of traditional Jewish life, Kacyzne's photograph first appeared in the upper right-hand corner of the Sunday art supplement, printed on a page packed tight with photographs (figure 3). The top of a portrait of Khaim, a ferryman with no documented surname, cuts into the bottom of a marketplace scene, and the corner of that image, in turn, obscures the passage of *A Jewish Street Paver* that extends beyond the worker's downward gaze and his outstretched arms. Intersecting along the physical plane of the page, the photographs were circulated as part of what was, in New York's Yiddish press, the first of its kind: a multi-volume story told in photographs. The high-quality, sepia-toned reproductions, distributed in weekly installments across the span of many years, weave a visual tale of traditional Jewish life in the old country. The photographs, the edges of their frames overlapping on the page, merged to form "national epics," in Zemel's words, "novels," that weave a comforting myth of an unchanging, distant home even as it was shifting and evolving (2015: 27–28).

As he contributed photographic chapters to the story, the novel, that editor Abraham Cahan assembled across the pages of *The Forward* every Sunday, Kacyzne was also writing a novel of his own. Transcribing his visual images into phrases and sentences, he begins his two-volume work of fiction *Shtarke un Shvakhe* (*The Strong and the Weak*) with a written description of stone and mortar that corresponds with his photographs of cobblestone paths. Published in 1929 and 1930, *Shtarke un Shvake* focuses on the residents of the Old Town in Warsaw who cling to their traditional way of life in the midst of change as "the dust of past generations cling to them." The narrative unfolds in a "labyrinth of narrow little alleys between high, gray walls"; it takes shape on a street, broken up, like the unfinished stone-paved trails in Kacyzne's photographs, by

Figure 3: Page layout from the Sunday Art Supplement, *The Jewish Daily Forward*, December 14, 1924. YIVO Institute for Jewish Research, New York. Image courtesy of the Forward Association, New York.

"crooked lines"—on a street that "was disintegrating." These cobblestone paths form the veins of a small Jewish village, a kind of *shtetl*, within, and yet culturally divided from, the bustling streets of Warsaw. It is a place that surfaces in Kacyzne's text as it is slowly, almost imperceptibly, eroding (Kacyzne 2016).

The editor Raphael Abramovitch evoked, in different form, this language of dissolution and decay, of crumbling, when he published Kacyzne's *Old Road-Maker* in 1947, translating the surface of the photograph into a monument to the catastrophic suffering of the Holocaust. Abramovitch printed Kacyzne's photograph in a state of material disintegration, "without embellishment," without "'improv[ing it] by retouching," and without softening its rough edges (Abramovitch 1947, 13). It appears in the pages of the volume *The Vanished World* in a state of falling apart, of corroding. It is scratched and faded, marked with particles of dust and traces of chemical decay. The anthology is a monument constructed out of fragile paper, printed words, and gradually dissolving photographic traces of a world on the verge of atrocity—and not out of durable materials like marble and steel. It is pliant and fluid, a place of remembrance that bends, folds, and fades as time passes. It is a monument as art historian Carol Armstrong, borrowing from Barthes, defines the term: it makes tangible, in "destined-to-crumble pages" the process of aging. It is a monument that, "like footprints, traces in the eroding sand" is also a sign of material dissolution, a marker of "ruins... [and] remains" (Armstrong 1998, 16).[4] Abramovitch articulated his message in *The Vanished World* through what I will term as the rhetoric of dematerialization—through a deliberate choice to lay bare the inevitable process of decay in a way that frames the perceived permanence of physical materials, of memory, even of stone, as illusory.

In the context of *The Vanished World*, *Old Road-Maker* is scratched and discolored, caught on a page of the anthology in an instant in the midst of its own ongoing, inevitable process of physical dissolution. Emerging in the photograph among liver spots, scuffs, and scratches, there is a faded passage around the road-maker's hat that bleeds into the unfinished path behind him, encircling the crown of his head like emanations of holy light.[5] This discoloration, etched around the edges of the worker's aging face without obscuring the details of his features, stands as a mark not of the unrelenting passage of time, but rather of the printing process. The fading is most likely the physical residue of an unsuccessful effort to dodge the image, or to correct the unevenness of the negative by decreasing the exposure for this particular passage—to draw the darkness cast

---

[4] See also James E. Young's discussion of what he describes as the "counter-monument"—memorial spaces that refute conventional understandings of the monuments by making their own material dissolution visible (2003, 244; 1993, 27–48).

[5] In Jewish mystical sources, the concept of Ohr Makif, or encompassing light, describes rays that filter down from God to the earthly realm, but that are not absorbed and remain external to the soul. This light transforms into an aura that cloaks religious seekers and encircles their heads like a halo, revealing their true nature and desire for spiritual enlightenment.

across the center into light.⁶ The fading, though not a sign of physical decline, resonates with, and even, in its conspicuousness, heightens, the effect of Abramovitch's editorial decision to leave raw the photographs in his anthology: his choice to articulate his message through the language of decay.

For the editor, the tarnished, untouched surfaces of the photographs in *The Vanished World* enhanced their power as conveyors of a dark truth, as what he describes in his introduction as "documents" that "record" a world that was once present and is now painfully absent (Abramovitch 1947, 11, 12–13).⁷ The signs of dissolution serve in the book as a kind of evidence, creating for the viewer what Abramovitch hoped would be an experience of "factness." The editor drew upon the rhetoric of dematerialization as part of his project to establish a "rhetoric of fact"—an artistic idiom that "foster[ed] the illusion of actuality" by burying signs of manipulation beneath the perceived naturalness of physical decay (Young 1998, 65, 67–68).⁸ Indeed, his choice to circulate photographic prints without retouching them was a widespread aesthetic strategy in books designed to make the hidden reality of Nazi brutality visible, urgent, and painfully immediate during and just following the War. In *The Vanished World*, however, photographs that trace the swelling of violence that preceded mass destruction are few. They are scattered across the pages as interruptions between visual utterances, fractures and cracks in the central story that the anthology tells: a story set in a more distant past, before the traumatic break. Although Abramovitch frames the book as a disintegrating monument to the millions of victims who "perished from starvation, deportation, epidemics, and as a result of military operations" in what he describes as "the greatest catastrophe known to man," the photographs he selected for the volume rarely picture the horror of torture and mass murder (Abramovitch 1947, 7). They frame, instead, the crumbling stone

---

6 Thank you to the photographers involved in PhotoLab at the University of Texas at Austin and to my brother, Jesse Kohn, for helping me to decipher the marks on the surface of this image.
7 I draw from Roland Barthes' suggestion that photographs are inevitably traces of moments that will end and subjects who will die or who have already perished. Susan Sontag and Marianne Hirsch argue that Roman Vishniac's images of Polish Jews—photographs that were published alongside Kacyzne's work in *The Vanished World*—are particularly affecting because as we can no longer look at his subjects without acknowledging their forthcoming, tragic fate. They are, like all of the images in Abramovitch's volume and others that fall under the category Hirsch terms as "Holocaust photographs"—both images of horror and destruction and photographs of everyday life that are connected to the genocide by context—are inevitably, markers of what no longer exists (see Barthes 1981, 96; Sontag 1973, 70; Hirsch 1997, 20–21).
8 Quoting here from Young's critique of literary realism as a rhetorical device for coping with the loss of the Holocaust, I suggest that his discussion, though grounded in documentary theater, is also a useful framework for considering genocide-related documentary photography.

streets of the *shtetl*, the marketplaces and synagogues of a fading culture, of a distant homeland.

The pain and despair pulses beneath the surface of *The Vanished World*, lurking in the dark spaces between pages, scattered in the few images of destruction, and lingering along the edges of photographs of the life that once existed in Jewish villages. The strangely pale section surrounding the crown of road-paver's head in Kacyzne's photograph, then, is not only a trace of a former presence, of everything that was destroyed, and not only a mark left behind during the printing process. It is also a transcription of erasure, a translation of unthinkable violence that takes form as formlessness, as blankness. It is a sign of what cannot be seen. It obscures our view of the path, wiping away part of the background and rendering it invisible. It is a ghostly outline against which an emptiness takes shape—"photographic evidence of [an] absence." (Gordon 2008, 33) Like the stones that the road-maker holds in his hands—smoothed by "subterranean levels of suffering," "roasted in the heat of some non-human furnace," and containing sedimentary layers and histories we cannot see—the discolored passage in the photograph draws what is buried to the surface. It makes us painfully aware of the invisible (Caillos 1985, 32). It stands as a sign of what, in the sociologist Avery Gordon's words, is "*there and yet hidden*," what is on the verge of disappearance but nevertheless real, what is elusive and ethereal but undeniably present: the very atrocity that the book was designed to memorialize (Gordon 2008, 46, 42).

Two decades earlier, as Kacyzne snapped the shot that would appear in *The Vanished World* and wrote *Shtarke un Shvakhe*, his allusions to erosion and decay, to dissolution, had different resonances, different meanings. His words, the scuffs and scratches that mark the surface of his novel, were not signs of an atrocity seething at the edges of his novel, but rather a means of grasping a world that was slipping away; his descriptions of "shadow people" were a way of clasping onto to the "shadows on the shadowy street," the "shadow of tight alleys between high walls" of the Old Town of Warsaw, the shadows of a dissolving way of life (Kacyzne 2016). Like Abramovitch, however, Kacyzne was interested in how he could use photography, as a medium, to arrest these shadows, this fleeting world; he was attentive to the ways that he could use the camera to transcribe moments, to seize them as they passed, how he could record and document what was, for him, a truth on the verge of disappearing, how he could make loss immediate and tangible across the surface of his prints.

Kacyzne's interest in the capacity of the camera to witness a passing moment emerges as a theme in his novel *Shtarke un Shvakhe*, a piece of writing that opened a space for the author to explore what it meant to translate a dissolving world into photographs, to offer a resurgence of presence under the looming threat of absence. Toward the end of the opening chapter, his central character Shayke—who is struggling, as the author, in his own way, was also striving, to find a direction in his work along the fault line of visual and textual languages—looks up to see a child standing up on a rooftop. In his hand, the child grips a long stick with a rag attached to the end of it. Shayke watches as the child waves the stick back and forth against the horizon, as if he "wanted to paint the entire sky over the Old Marketplace," as if he "waved to the setting sun to make it come back." The child moves the stick back and forth across the darkening silhouette of the sky in a steady rhythm, as if, in Kacyzne's text —his references to silvery shadows and the gradations of black, white, and gray that build up the surfaces of his photographs—the figure in his novel was "conducting a flock of silver pigeons. High, high they circled, sparsely, in an airy, circular ritual. Little silver flowers shadowed by red clouds. He waved down—a smattering of black little rags. He waved up—again, silver flowers." (Kacyzne 2016) In this passage, Kacyzne reveals a desire to trace the contours of a setting sun, a circle of birds in flight, a flower that will one day fade, a desire to hold onto an instant as it dissolves, to record it visually, to use his camera, as the child in the passage uses the end of his stick, to paint the silvery tones of the shifting sky.

As an artist who continually returned to revise his images across languages and expressive forms, Kacyzne was also deeply invested in the rhetorical potentialities of translation—in the ways that transformation and adaptation could serve as a means of evoking what Benjamin describes as "afterlife," new life and a new meaning (Benjamin 2002, 254). His writing, and in particular the narrative form of the novel, allowed him to engage with his understanding of what it meant to be a translator, to address it—as he addressed the capacity of the camera to record a moment as it was fading—through the textual images bound within his unfolding story. The first chapter of *Shtarke un Shvakhe* centers on a discussion between Shayke and his friend Yisroel, who emerges in Kacyzne's writing as a tall, light-haired Jewish man. The conversation revolves around Shayke's search for a path as a wage earner and as an artist. He appears in the scene both as a worker who is negotiating the arduousness of his daily tasks as a house painter and as a "living palette," consumed by his need to create and dressed in a "shirt with pants that were made entirely of paint stains." In the course of the discussion, Shayke makes light of his feelings of failure as a visual artist, laughing as he recounts a conversation with a celebrated fine art painter who had recently encouraged him to "'keep his day job'" after examining his unsuccessful drawings. Shifting the direction of the conversation to his work as a writer, Shayke grips onto a new poem folded in the paint-stained pocket of his pants. Yisroel assures him that his writing would appear, in print, in an upcoming issue of a newspaper at some later vague date, but Shayke shivers with impatience; "his muse didn't wait," there was an urgency to his vision, a need to grasp onto the shadows around him, to give them solidity, before they faded (Kacyzne 2016).

Kacyzne, in tracing his character's search for an artistic language, his need to find a channel for his ideas, delves in this passage into the fissures between visual and written language. In this scene of the novel, they intersect at the edges of Shayke's pocket, the poem he has written tucked just beneath the surface of fabric covered with the marks, the traces of his efforts as a visual artist, the splatters of paint that contain within them his struggle to express meaning in visual form. What emerges at this meeting of the visual and the textual, at the line of frayed fabric that separate the paint and the poem, as it surfaces in Kacyzne's body of work, is the photograph: the artistic medium that catches moments in an instant with a click of the shutter, that most closely approaches the qualities of written language.[9] Mandy Cohen and Michael Casper, who analyzed the texture of Kacyzne's language closely in the process of translating his novel from Yiddish to English, have suggested that Kacyzne's writing is visual in nature, almost photographic. His descriptions of the dark corners of the alleyways cut through by "a beam of sun" and sharp shadows cast by the stone walls, of the "gray" wrinkles of the characters' faces, are analogues of his images composed in words (Kacyzne 2016). These passages, as Eitan Kensky points out, are textual traces, caught in the tonal gradations of darkness and light, of a dissolving world (Kensky 2016). Kacyzne's photographs, conversely, are visual translations of his densely woven language, of the scenes he observed as he moved through and within the crumbling culture of the *shtetl* and captured it on the pages of *Shtarke un Shvakhe*. They are words that he wrote through the lens of his camera, sentences and phrases that he composed using a form of image-making that can literally be translated as "light/writing"—a medium that contains within it, more than painting, more than any other form of visual expression, the practice of inscription (Batchen 1994, 4).

Kacyzne's photographs, his visual translations of partially-paved cobblestone paths, arrest fleeting moments and hold them still, but they transcribe the shadows of the *shtetl* in a fluid language—a language that hinges on the linguistic structures and systems of meaning that unfold around them. The images

---

[9] Many theorists have explored the relationship between photography and writing, suggesting, collectively, that the image-making technology of the camera and the ways that photographs create meaning intersect more closely with language than any other form of cultural production (See, for example, Burgin 1997; Barthes 1980).

retain their solidity, their form, as they surface and resurface in printed form, but their meanings shift in response to the lines of text, the written languages, that surround them.[10] When Cahan published *A Jewish Street Paver* in *The Forward* in 1924—when he translated it into newsprint—he framed it, in the adjacent pages of his newspaper, with breaking reports, political and social commentary, and letters to the editor in a language that was, for many of his readers, both familiar and strange. Yiddish, the mother tongue for many Jewish immigrants filtering into the Lower East Side in the early decades of the twentieth century, had a longstanding oral tradition, but what the newspaper's contributing editor Jacob C. Rich describes as a still-evolving and "uncertain existence" in written form (Rich 1967, 22). A language of storytelling, of daily communication, of struggle and celebration, Yiddish had a vocabulary and a life in Europe's Jewish villages that coincided with, but also diverged from, Hebrew, the language of scripture and religious study (Young 1988, 27; Rich 1967, 21). In *The Forward*, the tone and cadence of spoken Yiddish is approximated in text. It is transcribed, translated, and transformed into strings of Hebrew characters that carry with them resonances of religious roots, allusions to scholarship and prayer. Scattered through these lines were the English words that were permeating steadily into American Yiddish (Rich 1967, 21, 31). The articles in *The Forward*, then, linguistically intertwined the spoken stories with the written narratives, the everyday with the holy, and the traditions of the homeland with the process of assimilation.

Although most of the newly-arrived Jewish New Yorkers who purchased copies of *The Forward* at newsstands across the city were native Yiddish speakers, many of them struggled to understand the written incarnation of the language during the publication's formative years.[11] A substantial sector of the reading public never encountered newspapers or other printed Yiddish-language sources in their former homelands. Many immigrant women, who were often excluded from the religious schooling that was compulsory for their male counterparts

---

10 Allan Sekula has suggested that the photographic image functions as a visual "utterance" that carries with it a message. He suggests that the meaning embedded in the image emerges in the space between the picture plane and the "rhetoric of related utterances" that frame it— the surrounding discourses that render it legible. Photographs, as he suggests, are never transparent; their messages are never wholly contained within the edges of the frame. Rather, they take on significations in relationship to the languages, writings, and systems of knowledge that frame them (1981, 458).

11 By the height of its popularity in the early 1930s, *The Forward* reached over 250,000 loyal readers not only in New York, but also in other major cities across the U.S. and abroad (see Metzker 1971, 11; Rich 1967, 3).

in the old country, were also unfamiliar with the Hebrew letters that compose each Yiddish word in *The Forward* (Rich 1967, 22). Longing for the comfort of familiar places and guidance for their new lives in a strange land, these viewers likely turned past the columns of text to the photo-essays in the Sunday art supplement. They studied pages that, with no written words— aside from titles—told stories about current events, the latest American fashions, Jewish celebrities, and traditional Jewish life in European *shtetlach*.

Kacyzne, in his image *A Jewish Street Paver*, transcribed memories of once-traversed cobblestone paths into an image that served Cahan's audience—immigrant readers who had recently resettled in New York—as a visual bridge from strange, crowded urban streets back to the homeland. The image is a translation not of a spoken language, but rather of lived and felt experiences, of the texture of living in two places at once. *A Jewish Street Paver* stands as a photographic approximation, a visual analogy, of what scholar Ernst van Alphen describes as the cultural experience of the migrant: the "endless process of combining fragmented images and stories from the homeland and places dwelled in after the homeland." (van Alphen 2002, 60) Leaving gaps between each stone, cracks to be filled with mortar, the solitary worker in the photograph creates a pathway out of raw, unwrought stone, a vision of wholeness built out of pieces. His physical toil, the labor of building a road that remains, in the photograph, ever unfinished, alludes to the less tangible process of merging the old world and the new—the unending labor of reimagining a sense of Jewishness, a sense of self, by seeing and "reliving past places" through the lens of an unfamiliar new home. Like the road-maker in the image, who brings pieces together, the readers of *The Forward* were struggling to integrate splinters of the *shtetl* and pieces of New York, to create pathways that extend back to their former homes in Europe, to build a place to stand, to live, in a strange new land (van Alphen 2002, 66–67).

Evoking the metaphors of splitting and doubling, of fractures, of geographical divides, *A Jewish Street Paver* is also, in a more literal sense, a translation of *Old Road-Maker*—an image that though commissioned by Cahan, never appeared in the *Forward*. Both photographs depict a road maker who grips a piece of cobblestone in the palm of each hand as he kneels in the middle of a half-paved road. In one, however, Kacyzne positioned the younger, clean-shaven worker from Bialystok/Białystok in profile, stressing the muscular tension in his subject's forearms as he attends to his task. The other frames not the folds through the length of the worker's trousers, not the curve of his subject's back as he hunches over in work, but rather the expressive details of his weathered face and the buttons down the front of his vest. When Kacyzne returned to rework the first image into the second, it was, for him, a process of revision in

Susan Suleiman's sense of the term: it was a moment of seeing anew, of re-seeing —of re-*vision* (Suleiman 2006, 140).

Stretching the parameters of Suleiman's definition beyond the act of "writing and rewriting," I use her term "re-vision" in the context of this study to encompass also the process of viewing and re-viewing. I suggest, using this theoretical framework, that when Kacyzne shot and re-shot this scene of labor, he set in motion, for his viewers, an experience of seeing again, of return, that spanned two decades (Suleiman 2006, 177). In the act of translating one image to the other, he unwittingly instilled his vision with what Benjamin describes as "continued life," with a significance that continued to surge and resurge in the midst of decay and despair—that continued to transform after his own violent death at the hands of a Ukranian soldier in 1941, that continued to take on new form after the stones of the *shtetl* were soaked in blood (Benjamin 2002, 254 and Web 1999, xxii). *Old Road-Maker* first appeared in *The Vanished World* twenty-three years after *A Jewish Street Paver* was published in *The Forward*, but both publications emerged from the same sources and likely drew overlapping audiences. In fact, Abramovitch, who was himself an important socialist thinker and frequent contributor to *The Forward*, worked in collaboration with Cahan, the newspaper's chief editor, to produce the 1947 volume. As Abramovitch points out in his introduction, they gathered images from many of the newspaper's dedicated readers, whose names he lists in the acknowledgements section of the book (Abramovitch 1947, 14). He supplemented the images submitted by individual readers, societies, and collectives with photographs from the archives of the Yiddish Scientific Institute (now YIVO) the *Jewish Daily Forward,* and a range of photographs that the Russian-born artist Roman Vishniac made on assignment for the American Joint Distribution Society (Abramovitch 1947, 13). Published and distributed, like Cahan's newspaper, by the Forward Association, Abramovitch's volume reached viewers who were, in some cases, longtime, dedicated readers of *The Forward*. As these readers looked through the pages of *The Vanished World*, they did not simply see images of their former homelands on the verge of catastrophe. They saw these images *again*, for the second time.

Turning the pages of Abramovitch's volume and pausing to linger over Kacyzne's image *Grandfather Teaches His Grandson, Biala, Poland*, for example, these viewers may have felt a flash of familiarity that was sparked not only by their nostalgia for the homeland, but also by their vague recollection of seeing the same photograph before (figure 4). Inevitably, the details of the memory of finding the photograph in *The Forward* during the summer of 1926 had faded by the time they saw it pressed up against the edges of a page of *The Vanished World*. The texture of the photograph—the soft curves of the boy's cheek against the book splayed on the table, the folds in the fabric of his grandmother's sleeve,

Figure 4: Alter Kacyzne, *Grandfather Teaches His Grandson, Biala, Poland*, 1920s. Printed in *The Jewish Daily Forward* on July 4, 1926 with the caption 'This is the way, little boy, one studies torah.' Volf Nachowicz...teaches his grandson the abc's and the grandmother looks on with pride (the little boy's father is in America). Re-circulated in *The Vanished World: Jewish Cities, Jewish People*, edited by Raphael Abramovitch and published by the Forward Association of New York, 1947. Yivo Institute for Jewish Research, New York. Image courtesy of the Forward Association, New York.

his grandfather's fingertips bent in response to the angle of his elbow—most likely evoked only a momentary flicker of recognition that was, almost certainly, difficult to place. Perhaps, however, a glimpse of their initial encounter with the photograph came back to them when they saw it again in 1947, and, along with it, traces of the entangled feelings they once experienced—flashes, however fleeting and elusive, of what the image evoked in them when they first saw it as newly arrived immigrants. It is possible that the half-realized recollection of seeing the image before even supplanted the original memory-image, taking hold and taking over the shimmering, ever-waning vision they held from actually *being* in that faraway place. In the pages of *The Vanished World* and through their affective connection with an image they had seen years earlier, tremors of their pasts, of their journeys across oceans and between homes, surged through them.

Although many of the images, repeated and reprinted in *The Vanished World*, remain unchanged, faded and scuffed with age but otherwise indistinguishable from the images circulated in *The Forward*, the site of reading around them shifted. For the viewers who first encountered these photographs in the pages of *The Jewish Daily Forward* as they were struggling to rebuild their lives in New York, the bound, horizontally oriented pages of the 1947 anthology had a different

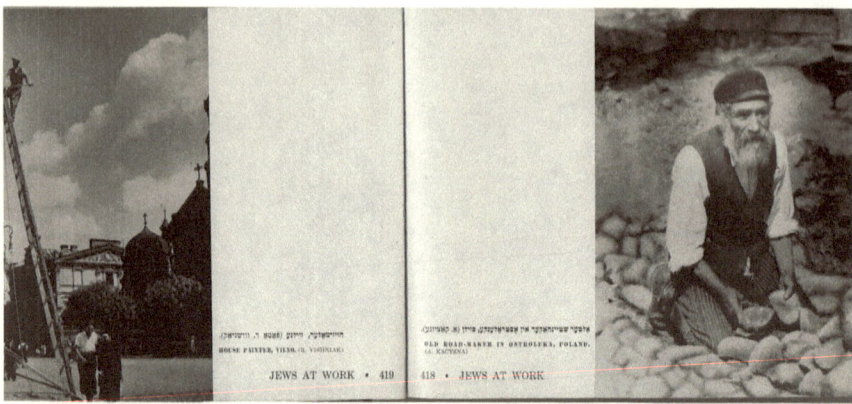

Figure 5: Two-page spread from *The Vanished World: Jewish Cities, Jewish People*, edited by Raphael Abramovitch and published by the Forward Association of New York, 1947. YIVO Institute for Jewish Research, New York. Image courtesy of the Forward Association, New York.

weight and grain than the thin, fragile folds of the newspaper. The pages in *The Vanished World*, hardbound in red fabric with a strip of black running down the length of the spine, turn not from left to right, but rather, echoing traditional Judaic texts, from right to left. *The Vanished World* was designed not only to draw in Yiddish-speaking immigrants, and not only exiles and survivors who crossed national borders to pick up the shattered pieces of their lives in the United States, but also assimilated, American-born Jews who could not read the languages of their ancestors; the essays in the book are translated into two languages and printed in parallel columns. For some readers, the photographs of faraway homelands published in the book are visual conduits back to places where they once lived, places that they left behind in the decades before the war, places where they worked and prayed and managed, by luck or circumstance, to survive. Others, when they look through the book, feel only flickers of connection, flashes of familiarity with places they never knew and only imagined, places they could never reach and find whole.

Whereas the layout of each edition of the Sunday art supplement was packed tight with photographs, overlapping at the borders, Abramovitch isolated a single, large-format reproduction across each page of his volume (figure 5). The publications, produced for divergent reasons, also contextualized the photographs in very different ways. In *The Forward*, these images of Eastern and Central European Jewish villages made a former and fading, yet still achingly familiar, way of life visible and present for immigrant readers once again. The same photographs took on new strata of meaning in *The Vanished World*, becoming also records of catastrophic loss and ghostly specters of everything that was decimated under Nazi persecution. The repetition of images is not merely a faithful, unchanging replication, but rather a repetition with difference, to borrow Suleiman's term from psychoanalytic theory. It allowed for reinterpretation—for a return to a past rupture that was mutable, unstable, shaped by the constant unfolding of history and continual fluctuations of memory (Suleiman 2006, 140). It opened up a space for viewers both to see again and to see anew.

Suleiman suggests that as a literary practice, revision, or the process of rewriting—of editing and altering—can performatively embody the psychological process of working through trauma. Beginning with recent re-readings of Freud's most developed discussion of repetition and recovery, she maps psychoanalytic notions of traumatic and narrative memory onto artistic strategies for registering pain.[12] In her rehearsal of Freud's notion of the "compulsion to repeat," she notes that traumatic memory rips away our sense of chronology. It is associated with stasis, rigidity and endless, ever-unresolved melancholy; it creates in us a need to repeat, to imagine the scene of rupture over and over. Narrative memory, in contrast, remains tied to our understanding of historical time and allows us to place trauma in the past, to mourn it, to work through it, and to move forward into the future and toward healing. Suleiman suggests that through the literary practice of revision, or constant return to and reinterpretation of trauma, writers can enact the psychological process of mending, the working through of trauma and the working toward healing, in cultural form (Suleiman 2006, 43–46, 139–40).

I maintain that Suleiman's argument can be translated from an analysis of the writerly practice of revision into an interpretive scaffold for the experience of re-vision—from the act of reworking lines of text to the act of re-viewing photographs. A site of visual repetition with difference, *The Vanished World* reframes photographs of an abandoned homeland as ghostly traces of catastrophic loss, offering viewers at once a new context for reading them in the wake of destruction and elusive, flickering memories of seeing them in newsprint years earlier. Although it is significant in the context of this essay that Suleiman's analysis—and the theoretical foundations on which she builds—emerge out of the horrors of war and the study of genocide, the visual repetitions in Abramovitch's anthology did not open up a cultural space for mending an unmendable atrocity. Instead, the Holocaust served in his book as a lens through which to re-see an earlier traumatic break: the rupture from the homeland. For readers of *The Vanished*

---

[12] Freud's *Beyond the Pleasure Principle* contains an elaborate discussion of repetition, an idea that he also explores, more concisely, in "The Uncanny." He completed both manuscripts in 1919, but circulated the article before he released the book-length version in 1920 (Freud 1961, xxxviii).

World who had encountered the same photographs in *The Jewish Daily Forward*, the visual *repetition*, the re-printing of images they first saw as they were struggling to build new homes in New York, brought back the loss of leaving the lives they knew behind. The more recent legacy of mass murder, the painful recognition that they could never return to Europe to find their former homes intact, was what created the *difference*. The haunting allusions to the catastrophic cultural trauma, layered beneath and around the edges of each photographic trace of the lives they left behind, allowed readers to see, or rather to see again, their own displacement as a fracture in an unrelenting unfolding of time—a fissure in the broader trajectory of a devastating history.

Each photograph in *The Vanished World* that once appeared in *The Forward* was a repetition, a translation that allowed viewers to re-imagine a difficult personal and familial loss in the context of a catastrophic cultural trauma. Kacyzne's divergent, yet interrelated, images of half-completed cobblestone paths, however, amplified this experience of re-vision. In the fissures and junctures between *A Jewish Street Paver* and *Old Road-Maker*, between the first transcription of the shadows of the *shtetl* and the second, emerged a repetition with a different form of difference. In this instance, it was more than the printed space around the photograph that shifted, more than the captions and framing text, and more than the texture of the paper. There were also changes within the frame itself, photographic revisions, that gave viewers a new angle, a new vantage point from which to see a continually fading past.

Another resurgence, a final translation, a third re-vision of Kacyzne's image of a half-paved cobblestone path emerged in 1963, beneath the large-format, hardbound cover of the *Yizkor Book of the Community of Ostrolenka*. A memorial book published by the Association of Former Residents of Ostrolenka/Ostrołęka in Tel Aviv, the book was compiled as a container of stories—stories written primarily in Yiddish, with some articles contributed in Hebrew, and others, particularly those that trace the history of the town during the Holocaust, translated in both languages for its former residents living in Israel and the United States ("Notes of the Editorial Staff" 2009, 25). Drawn into the web of intersecting tales by the gravitational pull of personal resonance and recollection, these viewers share an immediate, almost dialogical, relationship with the writers (Kugelmass and Boyarin 1983, 14). The lines Chaim Chamel wrote in memory of the day he entered the *heder*, the elementary school, draped in his father's prayer shawl, would have resonated for them in deeply personal ways (Chamel 2009, 189). They would have remembered Icel Sojka, a "quiet and logical" Worka Chassid who married into the family of the renowned writer Fiszel Lachower, opened a fabric store, and, later, ran the flour mill on the corner of Lomza Street (Drezner 2009, 174). Engaging with the descriptions of carefully arranged rows of trees along the shady borders of the city park, they would have remembered walking down the streets that Chaim Nowinski, Awraham Kugel, and the road maker in Kacyzne's re-titled and re-circulated *The Old Street Paver in Ostrolenka*—the same photograph that appeared in *The Vanished World*— "paved with round, unwrought stone." (Kupferminc 2009, 199; Ivri 2009, 59–60)

These viewers—viewers who, in their youth, left their homes in Ostrolenka/Ostrołęka to resettle in New York, who watched the sepia-toned, photographic tale of traditional Jewish life take shape in *The Forward*, who found the same images again in *The Vanished World*—would have felt another shiver of familiarity when they turned a page of the 1963 anthology to uncover, once again, Kacyzne's *The Old Street Paver in Ostrolenka*, translated into a personal, intimate reflection of life in that place, that particular *shtetl* (figure 6). Contained within this image, for them, the entire trajectory of a story, *their* story, the chapters enfolded and twisted together. These readers found in the photograph—in all its translations, in all the tangled layers of meaning it assumed, in vague memories of all the places they had seen it before—the story of fading traditions, of leaving home, of being a stranger in a strange land, of resettling, of horrific loss and destruction, of unbridgeable distances, of building a new life.

Each new printed iteration of Kacyzne's image of stone and shadow, each translation, offered viewers a space to see, and to see again, a fading past: the atrocities of the Holocaust, the familiarity of a homeland left behind and yearned for, a way of life that was shifting and dissolving. As these images surfaced in the pages of the *Jewish Daily Forward, The Vanished World*, and the *Yizkor Book of the Community of Ostrolenka*, the fluctuating photographic language that Kacyzne used to transcribe the *shtetl* took on new form, new meaning; it shifted in response to the lines of text—the stories, captions, and essays—that surrounded them. Photography, as the visual medium that mimics, most closely, the art of writing, was a means of recording ideas that took on particular meaning for an artist who was invested in the act of translation. Kacyzne, who worked within the intersections between text and image, who seized fleeting moments as they passed through the lens of his camera, who translated his visions by breaking them apart and piecing them back together in new form, was a photographer who understood how re-working—re-seeing—could create a form of "afterlife" in the midst of loss (Benjamin 2002, 254). Standing at the edge of a vanishing world, he caught moments as they dissolved, transcribed them into something tangible, and opened up a space for viewers to begin to repair the fractures and fragments of the past—to begin to translate their melancholia into mourning.

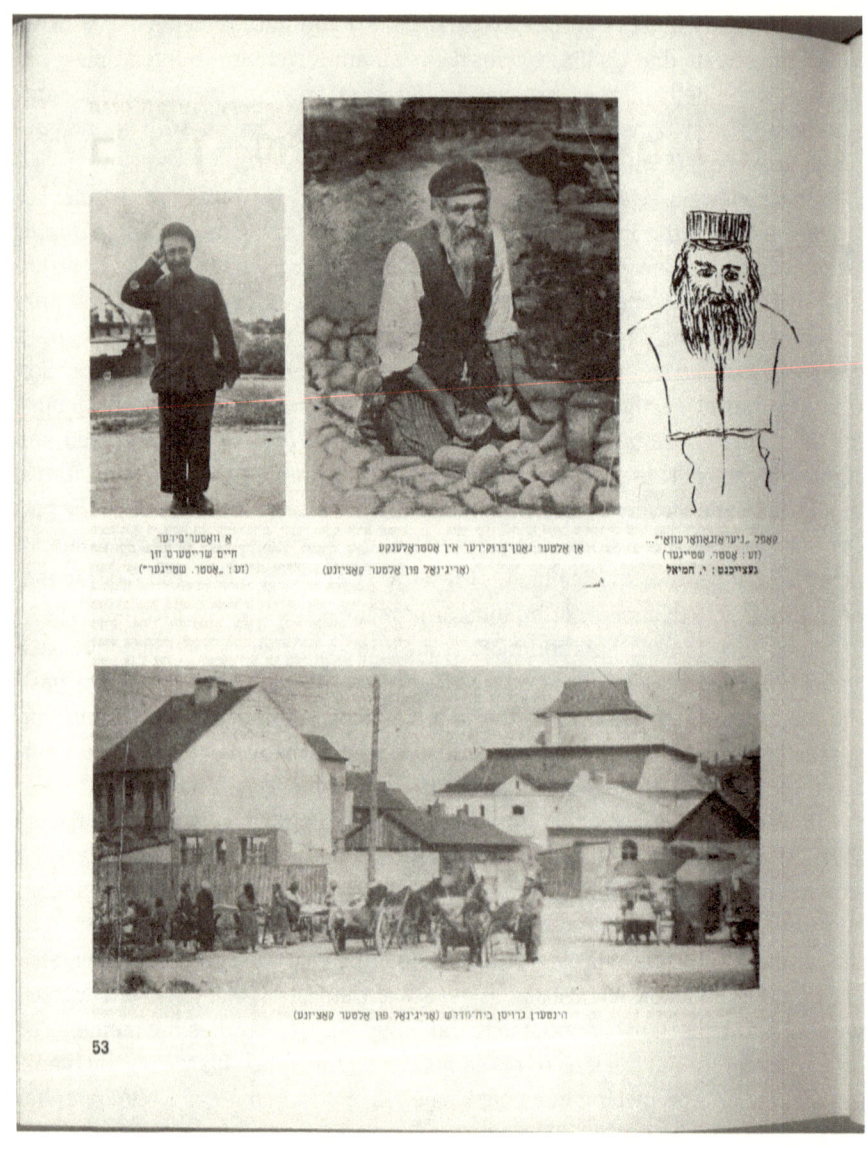

Figure 6: Page layout from *The Yizkor Book of the Community of Ostroleka*, edited by Yitzhak Ivri and published by the Irgun Yotzei Ostrolenka in Israel, 1963 (and in English Translation in 2009). Yivo Institute for Jewish Research, New York. Image courtesy of the Sefer Kehilat Ostrolenka.

Bibliography

Abramovitch, Raphael, ed. 1947. *The Vanished World*. New York: Forward Association.
Barthes, Roland. 1980. "Rhetoric of the Image." In *Classic Essays on Photography*, edited by Alan Trachtenberg, 269–286. New Haven, CT: Leete's Island Books.
Barthes, Roland. 1981. *Camera Lucida*. New York: Farrar, Straus and Giroux.
Batchen, Geoffrey. 1994. "Photogrammatology: Writing/Photography." *Art Documentation: Journal of the Art Libraries Society of North America* 13, no. 4 (December): 3–6.
Benjamin, Walter. 2002. "The Task of the Translator." In *Walter Benjamin: Selected Writings Volume I, 1913–1926*, edited by Markus Bullock and Michael W. Jennings, 253–263. Cambridge, MA and London: The Belknap Press of Harvard University Press.
Berkowitz, Joel, and Jeremy Dauber. 2006. "Translator's Note." In *Landmark Yiddish Plays: A Critical Anthology*, edited by Joel Berkowitz and Jeremy Dauber, 73–80. Albany: State University of New York Press.
Bhabha, Homi. 1994. *The Location of Culture*. London: Routledge.
Burgin, Victor. 1997. "Looking at Photographs." *Screen Education* 24: 17–24.
Chamiel, Chaim. 2009. "Episodes and Memories." In *Yizkor Book of the Community of Ostrolenka*, edited by Yitzhak Ivri, 189–193. Tel Aviv: Irgun Yotzei Ostrolenka in Israel.
Caillois, Roger. 1985. *The Writing of Stones*. Translated by Barbara Bray. Charlottesville: University Press of Virginia.
Drezner, Chaim. 2009. "Icel Sojka." In *Yizkor Book of the Community of Ostrolenka*, edited by Yitzhak Ivri, 174. Tel Aviv: Irgun Yotzei Ostrolenka in Israel.
Freud, Sigmund. 1961. *Beyond the Pleasure Principle*, trans. James Strachey. New York and London: W.W. Norton and Company.
Gordon, Avery. 2008. *Ghostly Matters: Haunting and the Sociological Imagination*. Minneapolis: University of Minnesota Press.
Hirsch, Marianne. 1997. *Family Frames: Photography, Narrative, and Postmemory*. Cambridge, MA and London: Harvard University Press.
Ivri, Yitzhak. 2009. "A Look at the City." In *Yizkor Book of the Community of Ostrolenka*, edited by Yitzhak Ivri, 59–65. Tel Aviv: Irgun Yotzei Ostrolenka in Israel.
Kacyzne, Alter. 2016. "Old Town." Chapter One of *The Strong and the Weak (Shtarke un Shvakhe)*, translated by Mandy Cohen and Michael Casper. In *PaknTreger: Magazine of the Yiddish Book Center*, http://www.yiddishbookcenter.org/old-town (accessed July 8, 2016)
Kensky, Eitan. 2016. "From the Vault: The Yiddish Photograph." http://www.yiddishbookcenter.org/vault/vault-yiddish-photograph (accessed July 9, 2016).
Krauss, Rosalind. 1999. "A Note on Photography and the Simulacral." In *OverExposed: Essays on Contemporary Photography*, edited by Carol Squires, 169–182. New York: New York University Press.
Kugelmass, Jack, and Jonathan Boyarin, eds. 1983. *From a Ruined Garden: The Memorial Books of Polish Jewry*. New York: Schocken Books.
Kupferminc, Aweizer-Drori. 2009. "Figures, Memories, and Deeds." In *Yizkor Book of the Community of Ostrolenka*, edited by Yitzhak Ivri, 198–200. Tel Aviv: Irgun Yotzei Ostrolenka in Israel.
Metzker, Isaac, ed. 1971. *A Bintel Brief: Sixty Years of Letters from the Lower East Side to the Jewish Daily Forward*. Garden City, NY: Doubleday and Company, Inc.

"Notes of the Editorial Staff." 2009. In *Yizkor Book of the Community of Ostrolenka*, edited by Yitzhak Ivri, 25–28. Tel Aviv: Irgun Yotzei Ostrolenka in Israel.

Rich, Jacob C. 1967. *The Jewish Daily Forward: An Achievement of Dedicated Idealists, the Extraordinary Story of a Unique Newspaper and Its Publisher.* New York: Forward Association.

Sekula, Allan. 1981. "On the Invention of Photographic Meaning." In *Photography in Print: Writings from 1816 to the Present*, edited by Vicki Goldberg, 452–473. Albuquerque, NM: University of New Mexico Press.

Sontag, Susan. 1973. *On Photography.* New York: Farrar, Straus and Giroux.

Suleiman, Susan Robin. 2006. *Crises of Memory and the Second World War.* Cambridge, MA and London: Harvard University Press.

van Alphen, Ernst. 2002. "Imagined Homelands: Re-Mapping Cultural Identities." In *Mobilizing Place, Placing Mobility: The Politics of Representation in a Globalized World*, edited by Ginette Verstraete and Tim Cresswell, 53–70. Amsterdam: Rodopi.

Web, Marek. 1999. "Introduction," In *Polyn: Jewish Life in the Old Country*, edited by Marek Web, xi–xxiii. New York: Metropolitan Books.

Young, James E. 1988. *Writing and Rewriting the Holocaust: Narrative and the Consequences of Interpretation.* Bloomington, IN and Indianapolis, IN: Indiana University Press.

Young, James E. 1993. *The Texture of Memory: Holocaust Memorials and Meaning.* New Haven, CT and London: Yale University Press.

Young, James E. 2003. "Memory/Monument." In *Critical Terms for Art History*, edited by Richard Shiff and Robert S. Nelson, 234–250. Chicago, IL: The University of Chicago Press.

Zemel, Carol M. 2015. "Beyond the Ghetto Walls: Shtetl to Nation in Photography by Alter Kacyzne and Moshe Vorobeichic." In *Looking Jewish: Visual Culture and Modern Diaspora*, edited by Carol Zemel, 17–52. Bloomington: Indiana University Press.

Authors and Translators in Conversation

Magdalena Waligórska
The Boundaries of Translation: Polish-Jewish-German Literary Borderlands

"How could what had happened to them be possible in one language, never mind be able to be retold in another?"
Ali Smith, *There but for the*, 2011

If language is a skin with which we rub against the Other, as Roland Barthes (1978, 73) has it in his famous metaphor, a meeting across the language barrier requires a radical effort of shedding our skin and growing a new one. This process is rarely as palpable and as essential as in literary translation. It is through translated literature, after all, that we speak to each other across the borders. And what is hardest to talk about is also the most difficult to translate.

The closing section of this book addresses a particularly difficult area of translation: the Jewish experience as captured in the German- and Polish-language contemporary literature. Both Germany and Poland play a very special role in the history of European Jewry: as important centers of Jewish life and birthplaces of the most important Jewish intellectual, religious, and political movements. At the same time, they feature predominantly in Jewish collective memory as the spaces where the Final Solution was orchestrated and carried out, respectively. To make the issue even more complicated, apart from the stigma of death that taints both countries, Poland and Germany are also linked by a troubled history of conquest and trauma.

In Poland, a country victimized first by the Prussian partitions and then the Nazi occupation, Germans occupy a central place as the negative protagonists in the national martyrology. They are, next to Jews, the other "Others" of Poles; a historical enemy that Poles define themselves in opposition to. Related, Germans often serve Poles as the ultimate reference point in the debates on the Polish complicity in anti-Jewish violence. It can well be said that the Polish-Jewish relations are written into a triangle, with Germans constantly looming in the background. On the other hand, Poland features centrally in the way Germans have remembered Eastern Europe as the cradle of Hassidism and authentic, Yiddish-speaking Jewish life. Literary portraits of *Ostjuden*, by Martin Buber, Joseph Roth or Alfred Döblin have left their indelible mark not only on German-language literature, but also on German imagination. These images linger, even after the world they reference has been annihilated by the German-made killing vortex.

Perhaps paradoxically, Poland and Germany are also linked by a recent wave of interest in Jewish culture that has swept through both countries in the last two decades (Gruber 2002; Polonsky and Steinlauf 2003; Lehrer 2013; Waligórska 2013). This fascination with things Jewish in Poland and Germany is visible also in the realm of translation. One in five German-language books translated into Polish since 2005 within the translation program "*Kroki-Schritte*" [Steps] deals with the history of Jews or includes Jewish motifs. At the same time, Polish authors, such as Hanna Krall, or Henryk Grynberg, whose prose deals almost exclusively with Jewish themes, are very popular in Germany.[1] The same tendency is reflected in popular literature. Some popular Polish novels, such as Maria Nurowska's "Letters of Love" (*Listy miłości*, 1991, German: *Briefe der Liebe*), whose protagonist is a Jewish prostitute from the Warsaw ghetto, sold hundreds of thousands of copies in the German translation (Masłoń 2000).

To what extent, however, is the Jewish experience in Poland understandable for the German-language reader, and vice versa? Are the different collective memories in this Polish/German/Jewish triad mutually translatable at all? What new meanings appear once the text is lifted from its original setting (decontextualized) through translation and inserted into another context (recontextualized) (Bauman and Briggs 1990)? What is lost in such translation, what becomes misunderstood, what causes controversies?

To address these questions, we have invited four pairs of Polish- and German-language writers with their respective translators to share their experiences of portraying Jewish life in Poland, Germany and Austria and rendering them into another language. The interviews that follow were recorded during a series of public talks that took place 2013 in Berlin. The conversations circle around four works that, although formally quite different, share a common preoccupation about the limits of translatability of the Jewish experience into the language of literature. The story of how these literary quests made their way across the language barrier is the focus of the pages to follow.

"Sandy Hill" (*Piaskowa Góra*, 2009) by Joanna Bator (translated into German by Esther Kinsky, 2012) is not only one of the first literary narratives about the predicament of the so-called "new Jews" in Poland, who often find out about

---

[1] So far, 11 books by Hanna Krall have appeared in the German translation, starting with *Shielding the Flame* (*Zdążyć przed Panem Bogiem*, 1977), first published in Germany in 1979 as *Dem Herrgott zuvorkommen*, to *Weisse Maria* (*Biała Maria*, 2011) which appeared in the German translation in 2014. Krall was also awarded a number of German literary awards, among others, Leipziger Buchpreis zur Europäischen Verständigung (1999) and Würth-Preis für Europäische Literatur (2012). Among the writings of Henryk Grynberg that have been translated into German are: *Żydowska wojna* (1965) / *Der jüdische Krieg* (1972), *Kadisz* (1987) / *Kalifornisches Kaddisch* (1993), *Dzieci Syjonu* (1994) / *Kinder Zions* (1995), *Drohobycz, Drohobycz* (1997/2000) and *Prawda nieartystyczna* (1984) / *Unkünstlerische Wahrheit* (2014).

their Jewish roots only as adults, but also a Polish-Jewish love story unfolding against the background of the Jedwabne Pogrom. On the 10 July 1941, the Polish inhabitants of the town of Jedwabne, in north-east Poland, committed a bloody pogrom on the Jewish half of the town's population. After enduring humiliations and beatings, several hundred local Jews were herded into a barn and burned alive. The Jedwabne Pogrom became widely known only after the publication of Jan T. Gross' *Sąsiedzi* in 2000 (the English version *Neighbors* followed in 2001). Gross' revelations sent shockwaves through Polish society, provoking a range of responses: from disbelief and denial to a wave of critical historiography on the Polish involvement in anti-Jewish atrocities during the Second World War (Engelking 2003, 2011; Grabowski 2011; Grabowski and Libionka 2014; Tryczyk 2015). Jedwabne became the symbol of Polish complicity in the Holocaust, and triggered a painful nation-wide debate (Gross 2003; Polonsky and Michlic 2003; Bilewicz 2004; Michlic 2007).

Bator's novel is one of the first literary attempts to confront Jedwabne as a trauma haunting Polish society. It is on the anniversary of the pogrom that the Jewish protagonist of the novel, Ignacy Goldbaum, tragically dies, burning alive in a cottage, set on fire by a Polish partisan. Echoes of Polish violence against the Jews loom large in the background of the plot, even if the novel predominantly plays in the present-day. Bator also skillfully portrays Polish anti-Semitism, as encoded in the very texture of the language. The Polish of her protagonists, filled with pejoratively tainted verbs like "*zżydzić*" or "*użydzić*" (both containing the root "*żyd*" = Jew), would pose a challenge to every translator. Esther Kinsky has masterfully met it, using neologisms and a good deal of lexical creativity to find German equivalents, or render the mockingly disparaging "Jewish" pronunciation (so called "*żydłaczenie*") that also features in the dialogues. Despite all that, the allegory of Jedwabne will be less obvious to a German reader. The afterimage of the burning barn becomes lost in translation. But is collective memory translatable at all? Are Germans ultimately able to understand what specters haunt Poles? Or is each nation sentenced to its own ghosts?

The boundary between the literary and the political seems rather blurred in the case of all four texts discussed here. Literary accounts touching on the painful chapters of national history can arguably resonate even more deeply than works of historiography that reach a limited audience of academic readers. *Gebürtig* (1992, English translation, *Born-Where*, 1995) by the Austrian-Jewish author Robert Schindel certainly offers an interesting case in point. Written at the time of the turbulent Waldheim Affair, the book echoes much of the tension and moral anxiety of that transformative moment. The fact that Kurt Waldheim, elected as president in 1986, was member of the SA during the Second World War sent shockwaves through the international community and triggered a long debate on the questions of Austria's complicity in Nazi crimes (Bunzl 1999; Reiter 2013). Schindel's novel only appeared in the Polish translation two decades later, in 2006, but during an equally turbulent time. The publication of Jan T. Gross' analysis of the Kielce pogrom of 1946 (*Fear*, 2006) aroused heated debates on anti-Jewish violence in post-war Poland (Gądek 2008). Though removed from each other by two decades, the Austrian and the Polish debate had a common feature—they heralded the end of the myth of innocence for both nations.

Schindel's *Gebürtig*, translated into Polish by Jacek St. Buras, speaks about guilt and the impossibility of freeing oneself from history, but also about inheriting trauma. Poles and Austrians, so Schindel suggests in the interview for this section, have grown their own variety of a traditional hostility towards Jews and carry a moral responsibility that will be passed on to the future generations. Only a courageous confrontation with the past, he believes, can heal this condition.

A good example of such a bold confrontation with the past is, without doubt, "A Piece about a Mother and the Fatherland" by the Polish-Jewish author Bożena Keff (*Utwór o Matce i Ojczyźnie*, 2008, German translation by Michael Zgodzay appeared as *Ein Stück über Mutter und Vaterland*, 2010). Its radical language and the richly intertextual, experimental form, which critics classified as an oratorio, unsparingly opens old wounds. A toxic dialogue, or rather two clashing monologues, of mother, a Holocaust survivor, and her daughter violates a number of taboos. "A Piece about a Mother and the Fatherland" is the Polish manifesto of the "second generation," poisoned by the trauma of their parents who survived the Shoah. Keff's starkly autobiographical and iconoclastic work is both an act of rebellion and a means of negotiating her own (Jewish) identity beyond the tight corset of martyrology. Keff's piece is, however, also a study of Polish anti-Semitism. Obscenities, that constitute an important (and difficult to translate) feature of the text, express not only the daughter's rage towards the oppressive parent, but also the Polish hatred towards the (Jewish) Other.

The Polish national phobias, especially the myth of "Judeo-Communism," loom large in Keff's work. The belief that all Jews are communists, and that Jewish communists are responsible for installing state socialism in post-1945 Poland, has been fueling anti-Jewish animosity in post-war Poland (see: Śpiewak 2012; Zawadzka 2016). The greatest paradox of this myth is, however, that it did not save Polish Jews from anti-Semitic purges launched by the Communist Party itself, such as the campaign of 1968, when approximately 20,000 Polish Jews left the country (Stola 2008). Keff, who remained in Poland after 1968, speaks of a Jewish experience that is very specifically Polish, but her reflection on anti-Jewish prejudice that lingers long after the Holocaust and histories of uprootedness and alienation touch a nerve in Germany.

The Second World War and the Holocaust are central legacies in each of the works discussed here, even when they are set in the present day. The final text, however, the bestselling *Aimée & Jaguar* (1994) by Erica Fischer, takes us back directly to the period of National Socialism. Fischer's investigative reportage and Katarzyna Weintraub's excellent Polish translation from 2008 demonstrate that the modes of bearing witness about the Jewish experience of the Second World War remain contested.

In this very intimate account, based on a true story, Erica Fisher attempts to reconstruct the dramatic love affair between Felice Schragenheim, a young Jewish woman, living in hiding in war-time Berlin, and Lilly Wust, the wife of a Wehrmacht officer. In her process of interviewing Wust, searching for witnesses, and consulting archival materials, Fisher did not limit herself to re-telling the story, but instead attempted a deeper reflection on the quest for historical truth and its ultimate unattainability. Richly annotated by Katarzyna Weintraub, the Polish translation introduces the Polish reader into the historical context of war-time Berlin and the daily life of so-called *U-Boote*, German Jews struggling to survive in hiding. The extent to which their predicament differed from that of Polish Jews, living on the so-called "Aryan side," is another indication that seemingly universal concepts like "hiding" also need to undergo cultural translation when used in a comparative perspective.

Perhaps most importantly, though, the story of *Aimée & Jaguar* teaches us that there are multiple truths about the past and that the quest for a formula that can reconcile them and carry them (*translatio*) across the borders is not only a task of historians, but also of writers and literary translators. Without them, we will never be able to grow a new skin—a language of empathy and encounter that enables us to surmount the boundaries between the self and the Other.

Bibliography

Barthes, Roland. 1977. *A Lover's Discourse*. New York: Hill and Wang.
Bator, Joanna. 2009. *Piaskowa Góra*. Warszawa: WAB (German: 2012. *Sandberg*. Suhrkamp Verlag).
Bauman, Richard, and Charles L. Briggs. 1990. "Poetics and Performance as Critical Perspectives on Language and Social Life." *Annual Review of Anthropology* 19: 59–88.
Bilewicz, Michał. 2004. "Wyjaśnianie Jedwabnego: Antysemityzm i postrzeganie trudnej przeszłości." In *Antysemityzm w Polsce i na Ukrainie,* edited by Ireneusz Krzemiński, 248–269. Warszawa: Scholar.
Bunzl, Matti. 1999. *Jews and Queers: Symptoms of Modernity in Late Twentieth-Century Vienna*. Berkeley: University of California Press.

Engelking, Barbara. 2003. *Szanowny Panie Gistapo: Donosy do władz niemieckich w Warszawie i okolicach w latach 1940–1941*. Warszawa: Stowarzyszenie Centrum Badań nad Zagładą Żydów.

Engelking, Barbara. 2011. *Jest taki piękny słoneczny dzień: Losy Żydów szukających ratunku na wsi polskiej 1942–1945*. Warszawa: Stowarzyszenie Centrum Badań nad Zagładą Żydów.

Fischer, Erica. 1994. *Aimée und Jaguar*. Köln: KiWi (Polish: 2008. *Aimée i Jaguar: Historia pewnej miłości: Berlin 1943*. Czarne).

Gądek, Mariusz. 2008. *Wokół Strachu: Dyskusja o książce Jana T. Grossa*. Kraków: Znak.

Grabowski, Jan, and Dariusz Libionka. 2014. *Klucze i kasa: o mieniu żydowskim w Polsce pod okupacją niemiecką i we wczesnych latach powojennych 1939–1950*. Warszawa: Centrum Badań nad Zagładą Żydów.

Grabowski, Jan. 2011. *Judenjagd: polowanie na Żydów 1942–1945*. Warszawa: Stowarzyszenie Centrum Badań nad Zagładą Żydów.

Gross, J. T. 2000. *Sąsiedzi: Historia zagłady żydowskiego miasteczka*. Sejny: Pogranicze.

Gross, J. T. 2001. *Neighbors: The Destruction of the Jewish Community in Jedwabne, Poland*. Princeton: Princeton University Press.

Gross, J. T. 2003. *Wokół Sąsiadów: Polemiki i wyjaśnienia*. Sejny: Pogranicze.

Gross, J. T. 2006. *Fear: Anti-Semitism in Poland after Auschwitz: An Essay in Historical Interpretation*. New York: Random House.

Gruber, Ruth Ellen. 2002. *Virtually Jewish: Reinventing Jewish Culture in Europe*. Berkeley: University of California Press.

Keff, Bożena. 2008. *Utwór o Matce i Ojczyźnie*. Kraków: ha!art (German: 2010. *Ein Stück über Mutter und Vaterland*. Leipziger Literaturverlag).

Lehrer, Erica. T. 2013. *Jewish Poland Revisited: Heritage Tourism in Unquiet Places*. Bloomington: Indiana University Press.

Masłoń, Krzysztof. 2000. "Skoro mnie pokochali..." *Rzeczpospolita,* 25 November 2000.

Michlic, J. B. 2007. "The Dark Past: Polish-Jewish Relations in the Shadow of the Holocaust." In *Imaginary Neighbors: Mediating Polish-Jewish Relations after the Holocaust*, edited by D. Glowacka and J. Zylinska, 21–39. Lincoln: University of Nebraska Press.

Nurowska, Maria. 1991. *Listy miłości*. Warszawa: Alfa (German: 1992. *Briefe der Liebe*. Fischer Verlag).

Polonsky, Antony, and Michael Steinlauf, eds. 2003. *Focusing on Jewish Popular Culture in Poland and its Afterlife*. Vol. 16, *Polin*. Oxford: The Littman Library of Jewish Civilization.

Polonsky, Antony, and Joanna B. Michlic, eds. 2003. *The Neighbors Respond: The Controversy over the Jedwabne Massacre in Poland*. Princeton: Princeton University Press.

Reiter, Andrea. 2013. *Contemporary Jewish Writing: Austria After Waldheim*. New York: Routledge.

Schindel, Robert. 1992. *Gebürtig*. Frankfurt am Main: Surkamp Verlag (Polish: 2006. *Rodowody*. Austeria).

Stola, Dariusz. 2008. "The Hate Campaign of March 1968: How Did It Become Anti-Jewish?" In *1968 Forty Years After*. Vol. 21, *Polin*, edited by Leszek W. Gluchowski and Antony Polonsky, 16–36. Oxford: Littman Library of Jewish Civlization.

Śpiewak, Paweł. 2012. *Żydokomuna: Interpretacje historyczne*. Warszawa: Wydawnictwo Czerwone i Czarne.

Tryczyk, Mirosław. 2015. *Miasta śmierci: Sąsiedzkie pogromy Żydów*. Warszawa: Wydawnictwo RM.

Waligórska, Magdalena. 2013. *Klezmer's Afterlife: An Ethnography of the Jewish Music Revival in Poland and Germany*. New York: Oxford University Press.

Zawadzka, Anna. 2016. "Żydokomuna: The Construction of the Insult." In *World War II and Two Occupations: Dilemmas of Polish Memory*, edited by Anna Wolff-Powęska and Piotr Forecki, 249–280. Frankfurt am Main: Peter Lang.

Joanna Bator and Esther Kinsky
On a Jew in the Attic and Hybrid Identity

Joanna Bator, author of *Piaskowa Góra* ["Sandy Hill"; German title: *Sandberg*], *Chmurdalia* ["Cloudfar"; German title: *Wolkenfern*], and *Ciemno, prawie noc* ["Dark, almost Night"; German title: *Dunkel, fast Nacht*], and Esther Kinsky, her German translator, in conversation with Magdalena Waligórska

Magdalena Waligórska: One of the themes that fascinated me most in Piaskowa Góra *is the subcutaneous otherness of your characters, which they are not aware of. Jadzia Chmura, who embodies almost every stereotype of the Polish mother, is in fact the daughter of Ignacy, a Jew hiding at her mother's place during the war. The miner Stefan Chmura turns out to be the son of Wowka, a Russian travelling circus artist. Both these mysterious father figures—the educated Warsaw Jew who escapes from the ghetto and tries to hide in the Polish not-quite-friendly provinces, and the exotic circus man, who dances with a bear and breaks the hearts of country wenches—represent radical otherness. They arrive in a Polish setting from another world, and aren't really welcome. Are these two secret stories about fatherhood telling us that the ethnically homogenous post-war Poland in fact isn't as homogenous as we think, because otherness is part of our constitution, even if we're not aware of it? Or are these forgotten fathers of Stefan and Jadzia manifestations of our present-day Polish dream of otherness? Wouldn't we all, like Halina Chmura, wish to find an alternative family album with more interesting ancestors?*

Joanna Bator: I think that these motifs can indeed be interpreted as challenging Polish myths—or perhaps rather phantasms—namely that of a homogenous Polishness. It has a complicated sociogenesis and multiple levels. After the Second World War, it had a compensatory function, and at the same time it was used politically. Moreover, the Polish social imagery, and thus also its various representations, exhibit a strong desire for a beautiful linear past, and despite many years of socialist propaganda on the one hand, and some valuable and recognized works in the category of "peasant literature" on the other, it still would be best to have ancestors of noble origins, with fair faces and blue eyes: definitely patriots and insurgents. This of course is an illusion, maintained and even reinforced, as is psychologically understandable, by those who benefited from the post-war social advancement and those who could only live on memories of their past glory. In this sense, these motifs in *Piaskowa Góra* can be read as an indication that this wasn't the case at all. Apart from these beautiful ancestors, there's a Jew in the attic, and the Russian acrobat Wowka, and

https://doi.org/10.1515/9783110550788-015

new generations are becoming more suspicious of stories that seem too beautiful.

That said, *Piaskowa Góra* wasn't meant as a political commentary or a treatise on Polish identity. In a sense, I was forced to write this novel by my own identity: that of a Polish woman born in the "Recovered Territories,"[1] as they are called. I come from a family that lacks a strong linear narrative about the past. There are only traces, fragments. However, they show quite clearly the heterogeneity of that past world, its ambivalence. One possible gesture would have been to select one such fragment, for example the Jewish one, and live with the illusion that this would fix something. And the other possible gesture, which I think is what I've done in *Piaskowa Góra*, was to adopt a hybrid identity and make it into a source of strength.

M. W.: A central motif in the novel is the Jewish otherness as seen by Poles, through Polish stereotypes and prejudices. The language of the protagonists is full of epithets such as Cyganicha *(Gypsy woman),* gudłajka *(kike) or* mojżeszowy *(adjective derived from the name Moses). They speak of* zżydzenie *or* użydzenie *(yidding). How difficult was it to translate this Polish view of the Other and the derogatory colloquial language for German readers?*

Esther Kinsky: Such words simply don't exist in German. Consequently, it was impossible to render these details. Some words are simply untranslatable. This is something that a translator gradually learns to accept. One can't rely on footnotes; one can only hope that the readers show interest or perhaps already have the background knowledge that will allow them to recognize what is implied. In German, these things couldn't be made clear by linguistic means, but if they had been clarified by some artificial means or even footnotes, this would've harmed the text incredibly. Frankly speaking, as a translator, I don't really believe in the strategy of intercultural communication—that is, in communicating all this implied content explicitly. Instead, I'm interested in the book as a linguistic work of art, and of course in the subject matter. I think that by translating a literary text one already prepares ground for awakening interest or drawing the readers' attention to something. In the cases that you mentioned, one could never achieve that level of nuance in German. There's simply no vocabulary.

M. W.: Do you regard footnotes as a failure?

---

[1] Western borderlands of post-1945 Poland that used to be German before the Second World War.

E. K.: Not a failure, perhaps, but I do believe that footnotes have no place in literary texts if they can be avoided. I believe that the text itself must explain things, even when we have to deal with cultural differences.

M. W.: In the novel there's a scene from the Beer Inn, as it's called, where Icek Łapcycek (literally: Yitzhak Tit-grabber) speaks with a Jewish accent and tells Jewish jokes.

J. B.: I've used an authentic text from the Beer Inn—a traditional, less official form of festivity on the Miner's Day, 4th December. The holiday used to be celebrated with great pomp, especially in the time when coal mining was considered the basis of Polish economy. In Wałbrzych, all mines were closed long ago, but former miners still celebrate it. Icek Łapcycek is an actual protagonist of the theater or cabaret part of Wałbrzych Beer Inns. Intrigued by this text, I showed it to experts from the Jewish Historical Institute in Warsaw; they said that it's quite in line with the typical convention of Jewish humor. What isn't in line with it, though, is the figure of Stefan and the way he perceives the Jew; from his point of view, Icek is a copy of a copy, one simple reason being that Stefan doesn't know Jews. The plot takes place in the 1970s, and the last remaining Polish Jews had been "encouraged" to leave the country in 1968. There weren't many left in Wałbrzych either. But after the war there had been some; they worked in the mines.

M. W.: So there were Jewish performers at Beer Inns after the war?

J. B.: Of course, we're talking here about amateur artists, whose performances were based on scripts handed down from year to year. The authorship of these texts was often collaborative. I haven't conducted any proper historical or ethnographic research, but the very construction of the figure of Icek Łapcycek indeed suggests that Jews were involved. After all, this was a miners' holiday.

M. W.: What was difficult about translating this scene?

E. K.: The whole Beer Inn scene was by far the hardest part of the book. I must also admit that I wasn't aware of what Joanna just said. I thought that this was a traditional anti-Semitic sketch, presented by Polish miners at the Beer Inn as a kind of a carnival joke. I didn't know, or I didn't understand, that it was apparently Jewish miners making fun of orthodox Jews. This is actually of secondary importance, though. What is noteworthy, for example, is that Stefan, a miner in the 1970s, still has the word *peyes* in his vocabulary. This illustrates the presence of Yiddishisms in Polish; however, they are absent from German. I doubt that in the 1970s, in the Ruhr region, one would have found miners who had such lexical points of reference. And this of course made this text immensely difficult to translate.

M. W.: Lower Silesia was among the regions where many Jewish Holocaust survivors settled after the war. Are there still traces of Jewish presence in Wałbrzych?

J. B.: One trace that we've already mentioned is Icek Łapcycek featuring in the program of the Beer Inn, in the miners' theatrical productions. Another trace is a neighborhood in Wałbrzych, part of the old district of Sobięcin, that everybody still refers to as "Palestine." In this once-German Hermsdorf, in once-German tenement houses, Jewish survivors settled after the war. They're gone, but the name remains. In my personal microhistory, there's also a word, a beautiful Polish word: *niedobitki*—oddments, left-overs or "underkill." This is how those Jews from Wałbrzych's Palestine were referred to. For me, this word has had such a tremendous power that it returns in my latest novel, *Ciemno, prawie noc*, together with Palestine. There was also a doctor with an uncanny name, uncanny in the Freudian sense: doctor Jedwabny.

M. W.: Piaskowa Góra, *and, to an even greater extent,* Chmurdalia, *are permeated with magic realism. There's Zofia, who lays herself on railway tracks when she finds out she's pregnant, but gets saved by the ghost of her mother. Her daughter Jadzia sees an apparition in the mirror, announcing a great change in her life. In* Chmurdalia, *there are the sirens, in which one can recognize two women who survived a concentration camp. The protagonists also have a premonition of evil. The women in* Piaskowa Góra *can smell burning meat; the smell comes back again and again. The central day in the novel is 10th July, when Dominika has a car accident and her grandparents die in a fire. This day is the anniversary of the Jedwabne pogrom of 1941. It is no coincidence that the arsonist, who kills the only Jewish protagonist, Ignacy, and the woman who saved him, is called Janek Kos, like one of the most popular Polish war heroes from the cult 1960s TV series* Four Tankers and a Dog. *Is this magic dimension, recurring throughout both novels, a kind of encoding that spares us the unbearable truth: that our Polish grandparents, the Janek Koses whom our family stories have presented as heroes, in fact may have also been involved in crimes against the Jews?*

J. B.: Well, it's not that at some point in the narrative one introduces "a moment of magic realism" to camouflage a particular piece of information or opinion. Let me point out two things that I think should be distinguished from each other with reference to this question. Having finished the novel, I was wondering myself where this magic realism comes from; in a sense I was forced to wonder, to find a metalanguage to speak about the book. The thing that critics commonly call "magic realism" shows itself for the first time when I feel that the matter —that from which the narrative is spun—begins to run free, to spin itself out. When I'm writing, I feel very clearly that my hands are full—I can't find a better way of describing it—full of something living, of matter that I need to shape. This was the case in the passage in *Piaskowa Góra* where Dominika's hair begins to grow all over the apartment or the scene where women are crocheting baptism clothes and the yarn entwines the city.

A different situation occurs when the narrative gains such momentum that suddenly the narrator clearly envisages or even knows how the plot is going to unfold. She sees the protagonists so distinctly that they assume supernatural forms; women turn into sirens and say: "faster, faster; all is known already." And as regards Janek Kos, his name was Janek Kos the moment he appeared. I didn't wonder, "Well now, how am I going to call him?" He was Janek Kos right away. Because these horrible things, every single homicide, are perpetrated by ordinary people, with ordinary names, ordinary moustache or ordinary lack of moustache. As for the conclusion, while working on *Piaskowa Góra*, I had no clue where it was going to lead me. I was on a bus, going to the university, and I suddenly remembered doctor Jedwabny. And then everything was clear.

M.W.: Since the year 2000, Jedwabne has been a central image, a lens, a collective experience through which Poles look at the Polish-Jewish past. At the same time, it is a story that a major part of society rejects because it stirs emotions and counters the Polish myth of our nation's wartime martyrdom and heroism. What was your way of making the metaphor of Jedwabne legible for the German reader? Is this Polish experience translatable at all?

E.K.: To an extent, Jedwabne has become part of the discourse about anti-Semitism also in Germany. It would have made no sense to translate it. Jedwabne— much has been said about it here. It would have been pointless to translate the name; into what? One can only hope that these metaphors will be recognized... What do I mean by *hoping*? Well, one should think that an attentive reader interested in Poland and Polish literature would probably get it, one way or another.

M.W.: The "others" in Piaskowa Góra *are not only people, but also objects and places: Jewish or German (*pożydowskie *and* poniemieckie, *literally "formerly-Jewish" and "formerly-German") apartments, curtains, furniture which the Polish settlers painstakingly adapt to their needs, domesticate, and make their own. However,* the newly acquired items and spaces don't bring them luck. The ring that Kazimierz Maślak had swindled out of Ignacy Goldblum, a Jew he betrayed, perishes in mysterious circumstances together with his unhappy wife. The apartment with "wardrobes that belonged to the Nazis" and "Gestapo toilet seats," as Stefan Chmura calls them, is not a place where he'd feel well. One can't sit comfortably at a "once-German table," though one can't really tell why either. In their manifesto of the fictitious Jewish Renaissance Movement in Poland, Sławomir Sierakowski and Kinga Dunin claim that the only remedy for the specters of "others" haunting Poles in their nightmares would be to symbolically return the once-Jewish possessions to their owners. In Yael Bartana's film Nightmares, Sierakowski speaks about an elderly Polish lady who suffers from insomnia, because she sleeps under a duvet that used to belong to a Jewish household, and she would like to give it back. Your novel suggests that by getting rid of, losing, throwing away, or destroying these once-German or once-Jewish objects, the protagonists can experience a kind of catharsis. Do you believe that Jewish and German items in Polish houses are a curse?

J. B.: I'm more interested in my own personal microhistory, which gave rise to this book. In my microhistory, there are no objects that used to be Jewish. Luckily. There are some formerly-German ones. Naturally, the attitude towards things left by the Germans must be different from the attitude towards things left by the Jews. About once-German objects it was possible to say that we were somehow "entitled" to them. True, a certain claim or even demand is foregrounded here, but *poniemiecki* was also used in a purely descriptive sense, to identify particular items. They were not only German; they were left behind by Germans—involuntarily, but this didn't matter so much. We lived among them and with them, they would gradually grow into our everyday life, they became "ours" without necessarily losing their ambiguous status. One had to domesticate them somehow.

Imagine being uprooted against your will from your old place; often there's no returning to this place, because it was destroyed or appropriated by others. After all, people resettled from their homes in the eastern part of pre-war Poland or those who had to seek a new place didn't land in a desert. They took over other people's homes, especially just after the war; they would find beds which had belonged to others, their household items. And even if this wasn't the case, the new empty space had to be furnished with what was available— with "once-German" things. An existentially shattering situation; uncanny in the Freudian sense of the word. We also need to remember that right after 1945 this had a different dimension than at the turn of the 1970s. But even if in the beginning there was a discernible rhetoric of conquest or rectification of wrongdoing, at the level of the unconscious it served as a rationalization of the feeling of unfamiliarity, which evolved with time and assumed new overtones. I grew up among once-German objects. At some level, I've always asked myself—though perhaps back then I wasn't quite as aware of this question as I am now—whether we were entitled to them. That's probably why for all these years, through all my apartments, I dragged along a once-German punch bowl. It was really a rather unwieldy thing to carry along. Another such object is a photo album; it appears in *Piaskowa Góra*, too, but the one I once got was empty. Someone took out all the pictures; some German woman did, it must've been a woman. She took the photos out before leaving Waldenburg/ Wałbrzych.

The question of who this album belongs to reminds me of Lidia Ostałowska's book *Watercolours*, which tells the story of a Jewish woman, death camp prisoner, who painted portraits of Roma inmates for doctor Mengele. These watercolors were found and in put in a museum. After many years, the author wanted them back. Who owns Roma portraits painted in the camp? The woman who painted them because otherwise she would've lost her life? The commissioner? Or those who were killed there in gas chambers?

M. W.: The Polish adjective pożydowski *is unique, not to be found in any other Central- or Eastern-European language, not in Czech or Russian or Lithuanian. How is it possible to communicate to the German reader the complex nature of words such as* pożydowski *or* poniemiecki *and the connotations they have in Polish?*

E. K.: First of all, these particular words might be exclusively Polish, but as a category of coinage, as word-building possibility, they potentially exist in all Slavonic languages. One can always combine *po-* with an adjective; as a translator, however, one must try and see what can be done with it, because German is nowhere near as productive and creative as Slavonic languages. Both these words were among the most difficult ones right at the start of my work as a translator; I had to confront myself with them. I can remember very well that this was the case in Stefan Chwin's wonderful essay *Hitler's Gardens*, which still hasn't been translated in whole. It's about a real confrontation with German aesthetics in Oliwa district of Gdańsk/Danzig. These words recur in almost all texts that I've translated from Polish. In this respect, I'm well familiar with this vocabulary; however, over the years I haven't found a better solution but to say *ehemals deutsch*, "formerly/once German," or adapt it each time depending on the context. Of course, in terms of grammar this can't be used as an adjective so easily as in Polish. But there's simply no other way.

M. W.: At one point in Piaskowa Góra, *you write that Halina Chmura, who comes to the Recovered Territories, becomes "a resettler (Polish:* przesiedleniec*), and resettler doesn't even have a feminine form."*[2] *Was it difficult to find an accurate language with which to describe the experience of migrants, especially women?*

J. B.: I didn't have to search for it. It's my inherited language, my mother tongue. It's my first language. I've heard it around since childhood. My father's parents were resettlers. Mom came to Wałbrzych from a different part of Poland. In my family, everyone came from somewhere, they had to move somewhere else. Apart from *przesiedleniec*, there are many other words in Polish which don't have a feminine equivalent. Sadly. But we're slowly creating them.

E. K.: As regards translation problems, this lexical issue had already been addressed by Olga Tokarczuk; I have translated a great many texts where such vocabulary is problematized. And it's not that German lacks it. I think the problem with its application is rather that many people in Germany are not even aware that such mass resettlement from former eastern Poland to present-day western Poland took place. To this day, this historical fact has hardly been described and is little known to German readers—these many layers of trauma, which build up geographically.

translated into English by Zofia Ziemann

---

2 All Polish nouns are gender-marked: masculine, feminine or neuter [translator's note].

Robert Schindel and Jacek St. Buras
On Naming the Dead and Splinters of Truth

Robert Schindel, author of *Gebürtig* (*Born-Where*), and his Polish translator Jacek St. Buras in conversation with Magdalena Waligórska and Magdalena Marszałek

Magdalena Marszałek: Your novel Gebürtig, *published in 1992 with Suhrkamp, adapted into a film ten years later, and translated into Polish in 2006 by Jacek St. Buras,[1] was written in the 1980s. Despite all political and social differences between them, during this decade Austria and Poland did have something in common. In both countries, changes in the politics of memory were in the air. In Austria, the scandal around Kurt Waldheim was a turning point in this respect; it basically marked the beginning of the "reappraisal" of the National Socialist past. In the People's Republic of Poland, the political opposition made first attempts to remind the society about the history of the Jews and the Holocaust, countering the official communist politics of memory and state anti-Semitism, identified with the ruling Polish United Worker's Party since 1968. In both countries, Jewishness increasingly became a literary subject. In mid-1980s, Hanna Krall published her novel* Sublokatorka *(The Subtenant), where she postulated the impossibility of articulating Polish-Jewish identity, showing that the culturally accepted Polish biographic narratives leave no room for the Jewish experience. Your novel* Gebürtig, *in turn, whose plot takes place in Vienna in early 1980s, "dramatizes" the differences between Jews and non-Jews in Austria and their mutual incapability of understanding the other. Looking back twenty years after the publication of the book, what's your view of this constellation? Do bloodlines or origins still have the same (fatal) significance?*

Robert Schindel: Given the monstrosity of the Holocaust, the confrontation between Jews and non-Jews—which no longer concerns the first generation, but presently takes place in the second and third generations—will certainly last into the seventh generation. In Austria, the focal point of this confrontation has shifted, fixating on a substitute object: the justifiability of the State of Israel. This is of course a very difficult and complex issue, which I won't address here in detail. Naturally, just as with any other state, criticism of Israeli politics is always justified and even desirable. However, in Germany and Austria, the countries of the perpetrators, this justified critical stance can be used to mask very particular

---

[1] English edition: *Born-Where*, trans. and afterword Michael Roloff, Riverside, CA: Ariadne Press 1995.

agendas, aversion and xenophobia, which continue to exist, now under a different name. This confrontation often has to do with who the victim is. When critics of Israel are accused of anti-Semitism, they immediately adopt the position of victims, lamenting that "Nowadays you're not allowed to say a word against the Jews." And then we're back to square one. Recently, at an event in St. Stephen's Square, a Viennese man shouted in my face, "In Austria you can't achieve anything unless you're a Jew!" In the 1980s, it was harder for the anti-Semites to assume the role of victims; nowadays it's much easier, because meanwhile the escalation of the conflict in the Middle East has created a very good backdrop for a renewed manifestation and justification of Austria's traditional and notorious anti-Semitism. The bottom line is that in Austria we like dead Jews best, Jews of the past, the great Jews of literature, but when it comes to living issues, such as the justifiability of a Jewish homeland, there reveals itself, in a new and old light, so to say, the old problem.

M.M.: Mr Buras, your translation of Robert Schindel's book came out in 2006, in a country very different from the People's Republic of Poland of the 1980s: after the political transformation and distressing debates about Polish-Jewish relations during the Holocaust and the issue of Polish complicity. How do you think this context has influenced the reception of Gebürtig *in Poland?*

Jacek St. Buras: The book appeared in a series called *Kroki/Schritte*, established in 2005 and dedicated to literature from German-speaking countries. As co-editor of this series, I selected *Gebürtig*, because I believed it was very important in the Polish context. Apart from the fact that it's brilliantly written, of course the subject matter was vital. However, it's not that the novel was published in Poland for the particular reason that the much belated debate about Poland's role in the Holocaust erupted in the twenty-first century. That was rather a coincidence. And I have to add that, regrettably, the Polish edition hasn't won so much attention as I'd hoped it would and as it deserves.

You said that a debate about these things began back in the 1980s. At that time I wrote a theatre play set in the Warsaw Ghetto. It was about young people who lost their lives there. It served as a metaphor for our situation in 1980s Poland. Years passed by, and we also felt that we were being deprived of something, even though the two situations are not really comparable. Teatr Dramatyczny in Warsaw staged the play, but there were protests against it within the ensemble. I hadn't expected such resistance; it was a rather traumatic experience for me. Sadly, a resistance, sometimes strong, against this kind of literature still exists in Poland, and this is because, to put it bluntly, in certain circles blatant anti-Semitism reigns—in the absence of Jews. I have no reason to defend

Austrians for their attitude towards the Holocaust, but I spent a total of ten years living in Austria, and, unlike in Poland, I never heard anyone make an anti-Semitic remark. Nor have I ever witnessed something like that in Germany. Of course it hurts and annoys me that, in contrast to the Germans, the Austrians keep denying any responsibility for the Holocaust. But it also hurts that a significant number of Poles, who, as a nation, obviously weren't responsible for the Second World War or the Holocaust, completely deny or make light of their actual participation, however limited or incidental.

Magdalena Waligórska: Your protagonists can't escape the past; they are poisoned with history, and they can't be themselves because they still carry within them the traumas of their parents. The suffering caused by the traumatic history is so intense that it becomes physical, too. There's a scene in your novel with a son of Holocaust survivors, Emanuel Katz, who having listened to his parents' stories for years, ends up at the point when he feels poisoned by death. On learning that his father died, he "vomited a green, spreading corpse directly in front of his mother's feet." This image reminded me strongly of a picture from Art Spiegelman's Maus, *where we see the author at work, drawing a comic while sitting on a pile of dead bodies. Did you also think about your dead ones when writing* Gebürtig?

R. S.: Collective memory, which functions in such a way that the names of those remembered have gone lost because there's an anonymous mass of victims, demands naming. But then we can't describe the crime without trivializing it. Every direct description is inadequate. In general, language is insufficient to communicate, even approximately, what really happened. And so one must take a detour. Literature always takes detours when it wants to be true. For me, one such detour was to take this infinite number of people who were killed not knowing why, only due to their ancestry, and give them names, name them, find a fate and *invent* a fate for them. I believe that my own family history gave me a certain sense of what it means for people who are not involved in politics to be taken away from Vienna one day, transported across Europe, to end up in some Russian or Baltic forest shot through the belly. I inherited a sense that something like this can happen. This can't be exactly translated into words. One has to wake people up to life, one has to invent a story, and this story must take place in the present. *Gebürtig* is not a novel about the past; it's a contemporary novel of the 1980s, when the things that I've spoken about so far were ingrained at a meta-level in the biography of all people from that generation: Jews and non-Jews. And that past played itself like a mute symphony in Austria—and also Germany—because Austria and Germany were the countries of the perpetrators, there's no changing that. A vast majority of German and Austrian citizens at least accepted the unfolding events, even if they didn't participate. Hence in my generation this mute symphony of the past was present in every single individual, whether politically engaged or not. When you talked with someone and suddenly he would mention his father, "who had been in Stalingrad but was no Nazi, and he wasn't aware of anything"—there we were. The past immediately became present, and therefore it was necessary to ask about lines of ancestry. In this way, the mute symphony of the Shoah acquired a current tone, so that one could try to figure: What does it mean for the next generation? How much does the past interfere with the present, to an extent influencing the future as well?

This is a special story for Austrians and Germans of the second and third generation. In the case of Poland, it's actually more complicated. The death toll of the Polish nation was particularly high in the Second World War. Poles both actively opposed the Germans and, in some cases, persecuted the Jews. They were by no means National Socialists; perhaps some were Polish nationalists and anti-Semites. The Austrians, in turn, identified themselves with Germany. I think this is a decisive difference. Only after the war did they say, "We've got nothing to do with that. We are Austrians; we were attacked, we were the first victim." This justification has been present throughout the Second Austrian Republic.

M.M.: In your novel, Jews and non-Jews meet largely on the erotic plane. The passion between Danny Demant and Christiane Kalteisen, which on the one hand is based on irresistible attraction, but on the other fails due to Christiane's inability to understand the Jewish experience, appears to be an allegory of the relationship between Jews and non-Jews in Austria. Do you find the language, the imagery of the erotic especially suitable for speaking about this relationship?

R.S.: This should be up to the reader to judge. In my view, it's in the delicate things in life, in intimate moments, that differences between people become most striking. If, in an intimate situation, a woman draws her finger over her lover's nose ridge, saying "I love this Jewish nose of yours," then of course this stereotype may well stir up certain things in him. Love strikes where it strikes, paying no attention whatsoever to people's different origins. However, these differences will become clear in things that happen beyond the control of our consciousness or will. Misunderstandings between Jews and non-Jews in an intimate situation can be depicted more vividly than, say, those surfacing when two people talk about Jews having too much money. In love, one is also open, and an unintentionally discordant tone caused by the different background of the lovers will hit a vulnerable spot. In my novel, Käthe Richter has no idea what she's saying. But anti-Semitism that is not recognized as such by the speaker hurts even more, because then one must take a position and show that one was actually a victim; one must try explaining oneself. And would one want to say of his or her own accord that he or she is a victim or a child of victims? One doesn't want that at all, certainly not in a romantic relationship. And then suddenly one blow opens up a chasm that has always been downplayed in Austria. After the war we've been hearing: "there are no differences," "our Jewish fellow citizens," "we all know one another." But it's not like that, because it takes seven generations, if you allow me a biblical reference, to get rid of this pinching in the soul.

M. W.: Transformations, doublings and ambiguities, combined with very complex narrative structure, play a central role in your novel. It opens with an image of a "double lamb": "There stands the two-headed lamb/ Wants both to blanch and blush/ But to do that, and not exhaust itself,/ It needs both heads." Does one need two first-person narrators to tell a story that is otherwise untellable? Is this because there are limits to realism when one describes trauma?

R. S.: I don't know if *one* needs two narrators, but *I* did. On the one hand, an omniscient narrator is very practical. You sit there and tell the world your little tale, and everything is known, one is present everywhere, one peers through every keyhole, lies under every bed, hears everything, and knows exactly what the other thinks, better even than the other person him or herself. This has certain advantages for the narrative technique, but results in an increasingly diminishing plausibility. Now, I'm not a trained literary scholar, but I'd say that it's not in vain that modern literature has overthrown the authorial narrator. There's the split "I" and similar techniques which make it possible to tell a story from different perspectives. In this way, it becomes clear that there's no one single truth, but rather many splinters of truth. By having the first-person narrator wander from one character to the other, I found my way of tackling this relatively complex problem.

J. St. B.: The author may disagree with me here, but I think that the problem of identity is absolutely central to this novel. After all, during the Second World War, the question of identity became very problematic indeed for the Jews. Many people with a Jewish background have nothing to do with Jewish culture, and yet their background does play a role. And then one asks oneself, "Who am I actually?" The question of identity certainly exists in post-war generations. Even when I know nothing about this culture, this language or religion, I somehow feel connected to them, being aware that I come from people who lived this culture and nurtured it. The problem of identity is, I think, crucial not only for this book but also for post-war history in general.

M. W.: The Polish edition is titled Rodowody, *which could be translated as "bloodlines," "genealogies," "ancestry," "lineage," or even "pedigrees." The original title must have posed a significant challenge to translators, since their solutions vary greatly. The English version is called* Born-Where, *the Slovenian—*Gebirtig, *the Italian—*Gli ultimi testimoni *(The last witnesses), the French—*Le mur de verre *(The glass wall). What options did you consider when looking for a Polish title?*

J. St. B.: I always try to keep as close to the original as possible. In my opinion, the German title reflects the content of the novel very accurately. This form can't be exactly repeated in Polish, but its meaning can. Family origins are imprinted on every character in this book; they play a very important role. I had published one chapter of *Gebürtig* in a literary journal under a slightly different title: *Rodowici*, "die Gebürtigen," "the native ones." I thought it sounded a bit odd, however, so in the end the book edition was titled *Rodowody*, using a noun rather than an adjective. I believe that the Polish title corresponds well with the content of the book and the author's original idea. Only the semantic link between the title and the name of one of the characters, Herman Gebirtig, was lost in translation.

M. W.: You once said that the translator is a servant of his author, and should follow him as closely as possible. Here you had to follow an author who writes in a very poetic language, full of neologisms, metaphors, oxymorons and intertextuality. Translating Gebürtig, *you had to interpret a lot on your own, find an adequate language, sometimes also invent things, as in the case of neologisms, while at the same time making sure that you don't reduce the complexity of the original and that you keep its various interpretive possibilities open for the Polish reader. This sounds like a very dynamic process, which required considerable creativity and autonomy on the part of the translator. How to reconcile your advice to serve and follow the author with the challenges that sometimes require that the translator should go his own way?*

J. St. B.: A translator mustn't go his own way. This is a misunderstanding. A translator must strictly follow the author and make the best of it. This is simply part of the profession; you know how to do it or you don't. And if you don't, you better let it be. Of course, when translating as complex a book as this one, one has to master various ways of speaking and talking, thinking and expression. It's not that one can always enjoy full success, though. At times, it's necessary to compromise something. Compromises are unavoidable; we've mentioned some already. That said, I don't see this particular case as fundamentally problematic; after all, literature is full of difficult texts.

M.M.: Mr Schindel, Doron Rabinovici once said that you don't shrink from mésalliance, creating a new language out of "the classic and the modern, standard German and Viennese dialect, yidding and yodelling." Jewish-German literature often explicitly problematizes German language, the language of the perpetrators. Does your style also signify such an approach? Should we interpret your sophisticated language as a means of a certain detachment or as a specific marker of the Jewish-Austrian voice?

R. S.: It's hard for me to answer this question, because in a sense my language is a given. It's my own language; it comes out from within me, and I work my way through it. It's only afterwards that I notice certain things: "What? Did I write that, is that what came out of me?" As a novelist, if you're close to your characters, if you love them, if you defend them, if you try to avoid narrative unfairness, if you immerse yourself in the rhythm of a character's life, then this character speaks his or her own language. The character forces itself on me; I must write down whatever it says. And I must follow wherever it wants to go. And sometimes it wants to run out on me, and I must try to capture it, because I still need it. In principle, if the character is well constructed and coherent, it has its own life. This is, so to say, the secret of poetic or literary writing, if you will. Any author will tell you that when he or she succeeds in creating a character. Why it is so and why things come out well, one doesn't know. But one often knows why they don't.

M.M.: Mr Buras, how have you dealt with Robert Schindel's style, in particular the Yiddish elements in his writing? Was it easy to render it into Polish?

J. St. B.: Robert Schindel's literary style is very peculiar and not particularly easy to translate into Polish due to his original and sophisticated manner of presenting meanings, views and emotions that often are already highly complex. However, for a literary translator such challenges are the daily bread, and the struggle to find a Polish equivalent that would be as adequate as possible is, in my view, the greatest appeal of this profession. In this sense, working on this novel wasn't more difficult, but also no less fascinating, than working on, say, the novels of Christoph Ransmayr or dramas of Thomas Bernhard.

As regards translating Yiddish expressions, it wasn't so hard either, because many Jewish or Yiddish words passed into Polish, perhaps more than into German. Until the 1960s, this vocabulary was still relatively popular and it was actually used without any inhibitions. This kind of language featured for example in cabaret sketches; in spite of the Holocaust, this wasn't considered a big problem and hardly anyone took issue with it. Things changed only after 1968, after the anti-Semitic campaign. Ever since then, people stopped using Yiddish words (it was almost exclusively single words that functioned in Polish). At least that's my impression. I don't think that today anyone would dare tell a Jewish joke in a Polish cabaret. This could easily be criticised as ridiculing Jews. Today, this manner of speaking is thus as good as forgotten in the younger generation, and it would also be regarded as inappropriate to employ it. I was born in 1945, so for me it's still familiar, and I'm able to reproduce it. In fact, though, there's not much Yiddish in *Gebürtig*. Wherever a word of this kind was absent in Polish, I left it in the original form, and explained it in a short glossary at the back of the book. My glossary is in fact much shorter than the author's, because in Poland many terms don't need additional explanation. Every more or less educated person will know the meaning of words such as *mezuzah* or *Yom Kippur*. There's one particular passage, though, where the poet Hirschfeld sits in a bar and says with a Yiddish accent: *Ä Chund hat geschissen. Is das git far die Jidden?* (A dog took a dump. Is this good for the Jews?) I translated it in such a way that a reader familiar with this manner of speaking will hear behind the text the typical pronunciation and intonation of a Polish-speaking Jew. However, for an uninitiated reader this pronunciation and intonation aren't of course recognizable in the written text itself.

translated into English by Zofia Ziemann

Bożena Keff and Michael Zgodzay
On Mother, Fatherland, and the Judeo-Communist Nation

Bożena Keff, author of *Utwór o Matce i Ojczyźnie* ("A Piece on Mother and the Fatherland"[1]), and Michael Zgodzay, the German translator of this text, in conversation with Magdalena Waligórska and Magdalena Marszałek

Magdalena Marszałek: Five years since the publication of Utwór…, *what do you think of the blasphemous, heretical and provocative power of your text? It has inspired many events: conferences, two theater plays, and an exhibition. Has anything surprised you about the reception of your text in Poland? And, from your point of view, how important has its Jewish subject matter been in the reception of the work?*

Bożena Keff: You've raised a couple of points here; let me begin with taboo transgression. Unfortunately, it's impossible to remove a taboo—for that you'd need a more serious attack than just one person's—but of course it's possible to try and violate it. And I've certainly done that, first unconsciously, and later quite deliberately. The problem is, first of all, is that the burdened figure in my text, who is perceived very negatively, is the mother. This is further complicated by the fact that she is a Jewish survivor who managed to endure the Holocaust—if not in its harshest form, for she spent those years in Russia (this is important, too). In brief, I was very well aware that this was a difficult combination. Such an attack on the mother, not only as a person, but also as the institution that is called Mother, constitutes a violation of a taboo. The mother in my text is both a real-life and a metaphorical figure. She is a parent figure, and in the patriarchal system, the parent—even if it's not the father, but only the mother—has very extensive authority, in this case even too extensive.

Fatherland, which in Polish as well as German contains the word "father," is the other parent, the opposite pole of the mother, so to say. Since this fatherland is described from the point of view of a person who was a stigmatized child and then, in adulthood, "not-quite-a-Pole" but "probably-a-Jewess," it's a fatherland-foreignland, full of anti-Semitic prejudices. It's oppressive, suffocating, demanding obedience, excluding dialogue—for dialogue assumes equal rights. In a nutshell, the fatherland is patriarchal, too. In this way, the oppressed mother, who

---

[1] The translator would like to thank Mateusz Chaberski for sharing his unpublished English version of the text: *A Piece on Mother and the Fatherland*, 2014.

uses certain prerogatives accorded to the mother figure in Polish culture, is in a relationship with the oppressive fatherland. And this couple isn't really that absurd; I'd say it's rather typical.

In my view, the situation in Poland was ripe for me to express rage against the authority, in this case: against a parent. My text is drama-laden, but at times also very funny, crude or grotesque, and it's actually rather digestible, it's edible. However, it wasn't originally written for the stage, so I was surprised that it attracted the interest of theater circles. I was lucky indeed, because it was staged by two very good directors, Marcin Liber and Jan Klata. Of course, each told the story in his own way. For example, Klata cut out the anti-Semitic theme. His adaptation couldn't disregard it completely, because it's ingrained in the text, but my piece rather served him to address Polish national stereotypes and Polish problems, which are his passion. Thus, although he used my words, his theatrical text was different from my poetic text. Marcin Liber's earlier adaptation was close to my message, but still not quite mine. It's very interesting indeed to have your text interpreted by others, and I'm grateful to both directors. As a poet, I couldn't dream of such wide reception as the text has had thanks to theater.

You also mentioned the Jewishness of the text. Well, it's a difficult question, because I'm not sure what Jewishness might be, and I certainly don't believe that there's one version of it, just as there's no one single version of Polishness or Germanness. I wasn't brought up in the Jewish culture, language, or with a deeply felt Jewish identity. My knowledge of or sense of belonging to what is Jewish, however we define it, used to be very superficial. In my case, this meant that I had to undertake the effort of self-definition. And that's what I did, in post-1968 Poland, after the last and biggest wave of forced emigration of Polish Jews. Frankly speaking, it was pure accident that I didn't leave. Not because I decided to stay. I didn't really make any choice at that time. I was aware that I should probably go. It's just that various things in my life combined in such a way that this didn't happen. For a long time, I felt offended by the country in which I lived. I guess I still do.

As regards defining Jewishness, I think I'm closest to seeing this problem the way Imre Kertesz does; for him, Jewishness means being in the situation of a Jew, with all that this entails outside Israel. What does it mean to be in the situation of a Jew in Hungary, in Poland? For me, it's a situation that one hasn't chosen; one is simply in it. One can shirk it or take it on. I took it on, probably due to the grudge, disappointment, and alienation from Polish identity that I felt after 1968. You could say that I'm an émigré who hadn't left. I don't want to tell tales about having an especially deep Jewish identity back then. This wasn't the case. In Poland, the nation that I hail from is referred to as *żydokomuna*, "Judeo-Communism." Of course there's no such thing, nothing like that exists; it's a Polish phantom which equated Jews with communism when, after the war, some of the remaining ones who survived, and a minority of the majority who left Poland in the aftermath of the Kielce pogrom, became part of the power apparatus at various levels. And so, because of that part of the remainder and that minority of the majority, historians speak of a Jewish overrepresentation in the authorities of the People's Republic of Poland. But the thing is that those Jews who stayed, hoping that the new political system would bring equality, were an "overrepresentation" themselves, because other Jews were murdered or fled the country. After the war, the Jews who deliberately decided to stay—if they did—were communists or had very leftist views. This was the case with my father, and largely also my mother and my stepfather. Thus, if I were to speak of any nation, this would be my nation, my people, if a rather small one, with its own significance in history and the future. Judeo-Communism is like another tribe of Israel, except that it's from Poland and it represents certain attitudes. Today, this tribe of Israel is a name that draws hateful attacks, because its calling is to carry responsibility for the period of the PRP. As opposed to the "innocent Poles," who aren't to blame for anything. Let's put it in more serious terms, though: perhaps it's only now that there begins a more thoughtful discussion about what kind of people Judeo-Communism actually was. This discussion doesn't quite present this people from its own perspective, that is, in universal, Marxist or political categories, but rather proceeds in the spirit of social psychology.

M.M.: *In Poland, your text has been compared to Art Spiegelman's* Maus. *They both depict a child's ambiguous relationship with a parent who survived the Holocaust. I've noticed a significant difference, though: I'd categorize* Maus *as testimonial literature, because the son's narrative ultimately serves to tell the story of the parents, whereas in your* Utwór..., *the survivor's story is present, but the speaking I is adamant in rebelling against her mother's testimony. Here, the mother as a witness is targeted with an attack. Therefore, in my view, your text goes beyond the definition of testimonial literature, and rather belongs to "post-testimonial literature," in which testimony is an important subject, but the very gesture of bearing witness is no longer present. Would you agree?*

B.K.: Yes and no. Of course, the "gesture of bearing witness" was overused to such an extent that it became an object of ridicule and rebellion; that said, there is some testimony in my text, only it's separated from the language of the mother. I love *Maus*. I think Spiegelman acted subversively, too; he was one of the first to show that suffering doesn't ennoble anyone, and that parents who had suffered aren't necessarily wiser, better or more empathetic because of that. I'd even venture to claim that perhaps they rather lack something. Anyway,

Spiegelman's work is also about the story of Art, the son; it's in the background, but it's there. In my text, mother is not challenged as a witness. What is challenged, though, is the psychological strategies she employs as a mother and a human being. As an author, I tell mother's story precisely in such a way as to avoid the manner in which my real mother would've told it. This is why, for example, the history of the Nazi-Soviet war is told in the convention of Tolkien's Fellowship of the Ring. I've done this in order to get away from the thrall of the oft-repeated story and to lead it elsewhere, where my protagonist and I wanted to take it. In this sense, it is "post-whatever-was before".

M.M.: Michael, you worked on the German translation very long and hard… What was the biggest challenge here? What fascinated you about this text? Which passages did you regard as potentially difficult to understand for German readers?

Michael Zgodzay: This translation project began quite by accident. I first met Bożena as a poet and lecturer when I was a student at the Humboldt University in Berlin. She totally took my colleagues and me by storm, also with her poetry. We started corresponding with each other, discussing her collection of poetry, among other things. These are wonderful texts. I found them especially empowering, emancipatory; one can also see that they're underlined with a strong historical awareness and, above all else, they take a theoretical and political stance. This is also true about *Utwór…* I guess I was rather naïve about this undertaking. At first, I was just very attracted to the idea of being entrusted with the task of translating such an important book. And then I became aware of the difficulties, because *Utwór…* is very multi-dimensional. First of all, it's autobiographical, so one needs to find one's own special language for that. Secondly, it refers to a historical context—not only to the most recent history of Poland, though, but also to the history of the fight for liberation elsewhere. Then there's the Jewish context, and many, many more. Although I grew up in Poland, I haven't lived there since 1989, so I had to laboriously track down most of the references. The chief problem was that I was dealing with a poetic text, a very dense text in which all the above-mentioned dimensions can merge in one line. This means that I had to translate into German a number of different languages at a time. I think this was the greatest difficulty. My solution was simply to have very, very long discussions about the book with Bożena.

Magdalena Waligórska: Critics have described Utwór… *as a cross between an opera, a drama and an oratorio. In the afterword to the Polish edition, Maria Janion and Izabela Filipiak write that perhaps you've even created a new genre: a narrative poem for voices. Rather than in the definition itself, I'm interested in the cre-*

ative process behind this heterogeneous literary form, that is the process of translating the experience of Polish "second generation" into a structure and language that hadn't been known in Polish before.

B. K.: You're right; the second generation doesn't have a voice. The parents have had a history, the children haven't. What sort of history is it if one just went to kindergarten, then school, ate porridge or didn't, went to university, perhaps left the country or not, married perhaps, perhaps got a divorce. Let's face it, this doesn't count as history. The point is to get a history, one's *own* history, which, in the human sense, would be equal to the history of the parent generation.

As regards polyphony, it's a means of defense against unambiguity, but also against very painful feelings. I believe that it's better to laugh, then cry and curse, cry again, then bite someone subtly and then harder—than to just cry the whole time. This text is very autobiographical. Having found myself caught up in the web of somebody else's language, I felt a very strong need to extricate myself from it and not to reproduce it. Besides, I'm not the kind of person who would relish in telling a personal story. But if you decide to do it after all, you need very strong armor. Otherwise, you're defenseless. For me, poetic language serves as such armor, but also as a kind of armament. I'm using it both for attack and defense.

M. W.: Your text features characters from Greek, Aztec, and Persian mythology. Why is it that in this tragedy, which is not only very Polish, but also expresses something about Poland, we hear voices from behind the masks of "foreign" gods?

B. K.: But I don't consider them foreign at all! There's nothing foreign in Aztec gods, who are terrifying and who must be fed with blood, who must be given blood to drink, for the existence of the cosmos depends on that; otherwise, they won't get down to work. This may seem absurd or cruel, but European history is no less absurd or cruel. As a child, I grew up with all these gods. In school, I was totally fascinated with Greek mythology. Later, other gods came along, on various occasions. Here Kore and Demeter, there Zeus, here Pasolini's films, there Lara Croft, and elsewhere also Aztec gods or stories about slavery in the US. You go out into the street and you see posters from Tarantino's *Django Unchained*. We're living in this; it's all around! At least I have certainly lived surrounded by all this and in this sense it belongs to my world.

M. W.: The names of the main protagonists, Usia and Meter, pose a major translation challenge already at the level of form, because they exemplify the extraordina-

ry diminutive-building capacity of the Polish language. Usia *is a truncated form of* Korusia, *a diminutive derived from* Kora, Kore. Meter *is short for* Demeter. *We have to do with two goddesses here. You decided to call them* Ohrinchen *and* Mater. *The mythological reference is lost here, and* Ohrinchen, *whose name is a German diminutive of* Ohr, *ear, is identified with the act of listening, which in the text is presented as a form of violence. Becoming a passive* Ohrinchen, *doesn't the Polish* Usia *lose her divine power of vengeance?*

M. Z.: The myth about Demeter and Kore is about a drama between two women, mother and daughter. In *Utwór...*, the mother exercises violence against her daughter, but also against herself. That's why both names are mutilated in a way; both these women are victims. It was very difficult to render this into German. I decided to use a German diminutive. Why? The text is very direct; it uses the language of pop-culture, which makes it easy to read, and it contains all these diminutives. But it is also very sound-oriented. Poles have a particular taste for diminutives, and this is where cultural differences come into play. I always say that Polish diminutives are like the touch: they can signify a gesture of kindness, but also appropriation. This is exactly the case here. The mother owns Kore/Usia, and that's why she calls her daughter in this way, even *Córusia, Korusia, Srusia,* "little daughter, little Kore-Shmore." We ran through this from A to Z. In this instance, Bożena could only help me by reproducing the original sound pattern, which made me none the wiser, so I just had to settle for something. In the end I simply went for the ear variant, because I believed it would be recognizable for the German reader. After all, lending the ear is Usia's/Ohrinchen's function in the text. I figured that the motif of revenge would manifest itself elsewhere. The most obvious place is the myth of Orestes; there's a direct reference to it when Usia decides to raise her hand against the mother.

B. K.: In fact, it was only thanks to the German translation that I learnt that Usia has something to do with the ear (Polish: *ucho*, plural *uszy*)! It never crossed my mind before. It was just a diminutive that can have various Polish names or nouns for a basis: *Martusia* (from the name *Marta*), *Córusia* (from *córka*, daughter), *Bożusia* (from *Bożena*). But I liked this discovery very much!

M. M.: I find it incredibly brave of you to be so open about the autobiographical nature of this text. Was it a kind of a coming out for you? If so, what kind?

B. K.: Tough question. I'd say it was a coming out of silence, of not having a biography, of respecting sacrosanct things that aren't saintly in the least.

I already tried such an approach in my poetic book *Nie jest gotowy* ("It's not ready"), but that text wasn't even remotely as insolent. There's a short story written in Yiddish in the Warsaw ghetto in 1941, probably authored by Lejb Goldin, who was killed a year later. It's a very beautiful story and when I read it in Polish translation, I felt an urge—not really to find myself in that horrible reality of the ghetto, perhaps, but to try and break the taboo that emerges when one regards that past as somehow untouchable. Thus, my narrator in a sense follows Lejb Goldin walking in the Warsaw ghetto, and offering some rather biting comments. It was an important exercise, because it allowed me to open a kind of a flow between my contemporary history and that period, which indeed is untouchable because it's so horrific.

In Spiegelman's book, Art has been listening to Vladek's stories his whole life, but when he sets out to write *Maus*, he grabs a tape recorder and goes to visit his dad to ask him how it was. Art doesn't remember. To put it briefly, the narrative, the story that had been force-fed to the listener without asking, must go silent so that any interest can be awoken in the first place. This was certainly true in my case. I'm among those people who did not learn anything substantial about the situation of Jews in occupied Poland until rather late in life. This was not only because I was terrified with this spot in history that is like a black agonizing hole into which no one would want to step of his or her own accord, but also because this channel in my head was jammed, something was there already. Thus, I had to begin by clearing this channel to make room for my interest. And let me tell you, I wasn't very eager to do it. It was a kind of coercion, and it involved work, too. You know, this knowledge comes at a cost. When you read archival records in the Jewish Historical Institute in Warsaw, every kilogram of documents is worth three months of depression. There's no way around it.

M.M.: Did the autobiographical aspect of this text make a difference to you as a translator? You'd been in close contact with the author while working on the German version. Could you tell us a bit more about this experience? What role did the exchange with the author play in your work?

M.Z.: Well, it's just really great to be able to watch someone trying to express her identity. For me, it was more of a learning process than a translation process. I was simply excited about getting to know Bożena's biography. I really can't tell you more.

M.W.: Utwór... is a story about a toxic relationship between mother and daughter, but it's also a space of resistance that plays out at the level of language. Swear words have an important function here, and so do onomatopoeias. The text growls, howls, sighs, screams, hurts, offends, causes discomfort. How did you manage to draw out this blasphemous aggressive language, which not only shocks, but also inflicts pain?

B. K.: I prefer concrete to abstract things, and I definitely believe in translatability. That's why I get really annoyed with the argument of inexpressibility, put forth in some research on Holocaust texts. I hate this notion, and I especially hate the aim it serves, namely that under the semblance of a solemn, respectful behaviour, certain terribly sad topics are simply pushed away.

It's not everywhere that I play with onomatopoeia, but in this case I constructed my text in such a way as to make it very concrete and close to my biography, but at the same time universal at some level. That's why it features a hyena's barking and howling, but also a piece of feminist discourse delivered in a pseudo-Marxist style. In brief—I'm playing here, playing in the good sense of the word. I hate it when the reader gets bored. I hate getting bored myself, too.

M. W.: The text screams with verbal abuse, sometimes even strung together as in this example: Czarna małpo, pedale, żydzie, wyrzutku, bezbożniku, zdrajco, cwelu, bolszewicki ryju! *("you black ape, faggot, yid, outcast, heathen, traitor, sissy, you bolshevik snout you!"). These are of course culturally specific words, very Polish indeed. In the German version (*Negeraffe, Schwuchtel, Saujude, Abschaum, Verräter, Bolschewiken-Fresse!*), you skipped two elements:* bezbożnik *(godless person, heathen, infidel) and* cwel *(sissy, pansy, prison whore, fucker). Why did you give up here? Does one say different things to insult in German than in Polish?*

M. Z.: That's actually the only place in the text where I omitted two expressions. Indeed, I think that in the German language, people give insults in a different way. In Germany, you can insult someone by saying just anything, depending on the context. In this case, the plantation owner alias Meter/Mater addresses her slaves or Usia/Ohrinchen. I felt that if you call someone *gottlos* (godless) or *Atheist* in German, it won't hurt quite as much as in Poland. It's sheer pragmatics. Even in Poland, atheist is not really an insult. *Cwel*, in turn, belongs to prison lingo; it signifies a man at the bottom of the hierarchy, who is sexually abused by other inmates. I researched it and found out that Olaf Kühl, the German translator of Andrzej Stasiuk's novel *Mury Hebronu* ("The Walls of Hebron"), translated it as *Pupe*, a word that also denotes for example a male prostitute or simply a homosexual man, so there are several partly overlapping meanings here. I didn't find this idea helpful; in fact, I'm not sure if the term functions well in Stasiuk's text. Bożena told me that the Polish *cwel* is the worst you can call a man. I decided that this emotional charge is present in the word I used earlier in this cluster, *Schwuchtel* (swish, faggot). I think that's the only functional solution in German.

M. W.: Utwór... has a really rich soundscape; it contains numerous onomatopoeic expressions. Mother sighs, daughter moans, mother's soul howls like a hyena. It's not easy to render such material into another language. How did you look for the right sounds in German?

M. Z.: I'm not sure whether it's something I should openly share... With the hyena, I remember experimenting a very long time. I was looking for a link between the sound and the name of the animal; the very word *Hyäne* (Polish: *hiena*) is very interesting sound-wise. I also decided to listen to the actual sounds a hyena makes, I'm not joking.

M. W.: You went to the zoo?

M. Z.: Today you can find everything on the Internet. Crucial for me here was the way a hyena laughs. It's a totally mad laughter, a laughter that can mean different things. In the text, mother doesn't really laugh; it's only as a hyena that she does.

M. W.: The text is set against the backdrop of Poland's recent history. Not only does it contain numerous references to historical events, such as the rise of nationalism in pre-war Poland, the beginnings of the People's Republic of Poland, the founding of the Solidarity movement, but it also draws on historical myths such as Judeo-Communism, a Jewish conspiracy against Poland, smear campaigns against allegedly Jewish politicians. What was more difficult to translate: history or mythology?

M. Z.: Both were difficult. Poland's most recent history is permeated with this mythology, for example the myth of *żydokomuna* or Judeo-Cumrnunism, and yes, it was difficult indeed. When it comes to myths such as *żydokomuna*, the question was how to render this into German without simply reaching for the vocabulary of National Socialists or fascists. In such cases I usually opted for the simplest variant, using those anti-Semitic expressions that I found to be still rampant in contemporary German. *Żydokomuna* is of course very hard to translate. There are many options, for example *Bolschewismus* or *Judäobolschewismus*, but they didn't seem to work for me. There exist even reference works specifying how this term should be translated into German. We settled for *Judenkommune*.

M.M.: It's bitter indeed that it is precisely this cultural context that enables communication, though not reconciliation, between mother and daughter. What is the role of Polish anti-Semitism in the identity of your protagonists? What role does it play in your life?

B.K.: It's a very significant factor in their identity. And since the story is told from the daughter's perspective, anti-Semitism is particularly significant for her. The question about how I feel about Polish anti-Semitism is terribly painful to answer. I wrote a book about this (*Antysemityzm: Niezamknięta historia* [Anti-Semitism: Unconcluded History], Czarna Owca, 2013), meant as an educational reference text for high school and university students, and other readers. But to talk about anti-Semitism or its history is one thing; to live with this phenomenon, which in Poland surfaces very often, is quite another. That's why I think that very many Polish Jews—there are next to none anyway, so I should rather say very many of the very few—choose not to see it, it's their strategy. To put it in learned terms, they speak the language of the majority, under conditions imposed by the majority.

For me, however, if I am to live in Poland, then speaking about the fact that anti-Semitism is there, that it's deranged, paranoid, that it was there during the war, too, and that it provided a very strong motivation for various actions, is the only way in which I can remain a Polish citizen. Although there's a certain problem with the idea of citizenship, too, for in Poland it doesn't really enjoy particular respect.

translated into English by Zofia Ziemann

Erica Fischer and Katarzyna Weintraub
On Searching for the Truth and Translation that Gets under the Skin

Erica Fischer, author of *Aimée & Jaguar* and *Himmelstrasse* [Road to Heaven], and her Polish translator Katarzyna Weintraub in conversation with Magdalena Waligórska and Magdalena Marszałek

Magdalena Marszałek: Aimée & Jaguar *is both an atypical love story and a political book. Publishing it in 1994, you addressed two political themes relevant in early 1990s Germany, combining them into a highly precarious entanglement. On the one hand,* Aimée & Jaguar *made a very important and extraordinary contribution to the new wave of literary (and not only literary) confrontations with Germany's past—from the point of view of the "second generation." At the same time, your book corresponded with critical feminist discussions about women's complicity, not only in patriarchy, but also in National Socialism. Looking back after twenty years, what's your view of the reception of your book in Germany? What did you, as a politically engaged person, find most important back then, in the book itself and its reception?*

Erica Fischer: I often get asked how I came across this story. Well, my then publisher, Kiepenheuer & Witsch, served it to me on a platter. I've been waiting for another such wonderful story ever since... Having acquainted myself with the material, I immediately realized that it deeply resonated with two aspects of my personality and my personal story. As a feminist, I'm of course very much interested in women and their stories. And it was right at the time that I began researching this story that I also started tackling my own Jewish background.

The process of exploring one's family past wasn't easy in Germany, and yet it was more difficult in Austria. It was only in the second half of the 1980s that people like me—the second generation—began to confront their Jewishness and their family history. I moved to Germany in 1988, in part because of that horrible anti-Semitic mood that spread in Austria when Kurt Waldheim was elected president. I just wanted to leave, and actually it was only in Germany that I could begin to tackle my personal history; the distance made it easier, and so did the fact that at that time in German society this confrontation with the past was much more intense than in Austria.

And so I thought: it's such a beautiful romantic love story, and it's also an opportunity to say quite a lot about the situation of Jews in 1930s and 1940s Berlin. In this way, I managed to reach two groups of readers. I addressed those who were already interested in Jewish history and the Holocaust, and who had read extensively on the topic. For them, this was probably nothing new. However, I also reached young women, possibly lesbians, too, who were looking for a romantic story of love between women. They learned a lot through this love story. I took part in many meetings with the readers, and I would always be approached by eighteen- or nineteen-year-old girls, who said, "I had no idea what it was like." I was rather surprised to hear that, because I thought such things are taught at schools, but apparently they found this living story much more powerful than what they had learned in school. I made every effort to keep the historical realities in the book as close as possible to the original story. I focused on everyday life in Nazi Berlin: how Jews were no longer allowed to visit non-Jewish hairdressers, how they had to hand over their pets, how they were banned from listening to the radio. I showed this collective experience through the individual story of a young Jewish woman, Felice Schragenheim. I think it worked out well, and I'm very glad about this.

Magdalena Waligórska: In your preface to the Polish edition, which came out only in 2008, your write that thanks to your collaboration with Katarzyna Weintraub, this translation is special, even "more complete" than the German original. It's not every day that the translator gets such compliments from his or her author, so I'd like to hear more about your cooperation. What's so special about the Polish Aimée & Jaguar?

E. F.: The Polish translation is the twentieth. It's quite telling, too, that in Poland it took so long to translate it. In the meantime, the text had been revised a number of times. Letters and new information from readers kept coming, and I would integrate this material in every subsequent German edition. Thus, the upside of Poland having waited so long to publish *Aimée & Jaguar* is that the Polish translation is the most complete. Moreover, in no other case did I cooperate so closely with a translator. Of course this is largely due to the fact that we live in the same city [Berlin—editor's note], we know each other, we're friends. But Kasia is also tremendously meticulous, and she pointed out inconsistencies in my own text. That's the ideal situation indeed: when the translator, who must look at the text very closely, notices things that the author herself has missed.

M. W.: What I found fascinating in the book is the literary process of searching for the truth. As an author, you have undertaken a kind of translation task, too: you have combined various, sometimes mutually exclusive narratives, recollections and testimonies into a coherent story, which is supposed to present "real events."

If we follow the story closely, however, it turns out that many questions remain open. Was there a Hitler bust in Lilly's apartment or not? Was she an anti-Semite, or—as she herself claims—she wasn't? How difficult was this translation process, putting together various sources? And how did you deal with the impossibility of reconstructing the truth in any definitive way?

E. F.: I realized rather soon that oral history can be problematic. I was writing the book more than five decades after the events that it describes, and we know how the past retrospectively changes itself in our memory. I figured that the best method to encourage the reader to reflect on this would be to leave contrasting observations without any comment. First, I met Lilly Wust; she made a huge impression on me and I believed every word she told me. But then I started talking to other people involved with this story, and they were telling me something completely different. Sure, I felt really confused at first; I didn't know how to go about it. My solution was simply to juxtapose these things. One could say that it's this narrative thread that constitutes my subjective truth. I reconstructed and fictionalized this story the way I believe it happened. Then I intertwined it with a number of interviews, which indeed partly contradict one another. As for the famous Hitler bust—I think it was a relief, not a bust—I believe she did have one, although she denied it. And of course I had to include this in the book, too, that she claims not to have had one. That was the case with several motifs. One of the consequences was that different camps formed among my readers; the reception was split. There were the young lesbians who longed for a romantic love story and saw their own grandmothers in Lilly Wust; they didn't want any suggestions that she might have done something bad. It made them angry that in my original afterword—later turned into a foreword—I took a critical stance towards Lilly. They didn't like that at all; they thought it was outrageous. And then there was also a group of Jewish women, centred around a Holocaust survivor who was among my interviewees. They, in turn, believed that it was unjust of me to help make Lilly Wust, a Nazi, famous. I was stuck in-between, so to say, and tried to defend myself depending on the direction of the attack.

M. W.: What I immediately noticed about the Polish edition was a significant number of translator's footnotes. You provide information on various institutions of the Nazi state, but also indicate references to German popular culture, which the Polish reader would likely have missed, and offer additional comments on historical events, as well as bibliographic references. Reading Aimée & Jaguar *in Polish, I was wondering how the footnotes influenced my reception of the book, and I must say that I feel they conditioned me to place the text on the continuum between fiction and documentary much closer to the documentary pole.*

Katarzyna Weintraub: I'd describe *Aimée & Jaguar* as a fictionalised in-depth investigative feature. Thus, for me it's a piece of documentary rather than belletristic writing, and in this sense the footnotes are justified. Secondly, I'm aware that Polish people have considerable gaps in the knowledge about the realities of wartime Germany. Of course they are well familiar with the details of the situation in occupied Poland in that period; as regards the life of Berlin citizens in 1942 or 1943, however, they know very, very little. They are acquainted with the history of the Third Reich at a very general level, but not with the political, military and other state structures. Consequently, the Polish reader might find many things in the book rather confusing. Take this passage: "'Following the heinous assassination in Paris, no German teacher can be expected to give instruction to Jewish schoolchildren,' read the decree issued by the Reich Minister of Education."[1] What assassination in Paris? What's it all about? I'm not even sure whether German students know that. And so I added a footnote here, explaining the context of this story and its reference to Poland.[2] I found it especially important to explain what triggered the Crystal Night and that there was a Polish connection.

M.M.: Lilly is a highly ambiguous, and thus an extremely interesting character. In many respects, she's an enigma. In Polish Holocaust literature, we've had some quite ambivalent love setups: between the victims and their saviors, but also between the victims and their persecutors (for example in Hanna Krall's short stories). Where do you see the "truth" of the figure of Lilly, Ms Weintraub? In love? In her political blindness? To me, it seems that what Polish readers may find surprising is precisely Lilly's naïveté (when she was naïve), which would be hardly imaginable in Nazi-occupied Poland, given that people who were hiding Jews lived under the threat of death.

---

[1] *Aimée & Jaguar: a love story, Berlin 1943*, translated from the German by Edna McCown, London: Bloomsbury 1995, p. 71.

[2] The passage refers to the assassination of German diplomat, Ernst vom Rath, in Paris on 7 November 1938. The assassin, young German-born Jewish student Herschel Grynszpan, might have been motivated by the predicament of his parents who, as Polish citizens, were expelled by the German authorities into Poland, where they were stranded in a no-man's land on the German-Polish border. The event triggered the so-called *Kristallnacht*, on 9 November 1938.

K. W.: For me, the only thing that makes Lilly the way she is, is her love for Felice. Had it not been for this love, Lilly would've been just another ordinary bystander. Not an active participant of the events, so not a Nazi in this sense of the word, but she certainly wouldn't have paid any more attention to the fate of the Jews than others did; that's entirely clear to me. Lilly sometimes allowed herself to make openly anti-Semitic remarks, and she saw nothing wrong in that. They just slipped out. I think that as regards this kind of indifference, it is comparable to the indifference of Polish society. Of course the Poles were in an entirely different situation, but still—indifference is indifference, at least that's how I see it. In any case, I think that in Poland this lesbian love attracted more attention, perhaps because there hadn't been any such books before.

M. W.: In Poland, Aimée & Jaguar *was identified as lesbian literature—it was reviewed and recommended for example in lesbian forums—but also as a Holocaust novel, showing contexts little known to Polish readers, such as Berlin's emancipated Jewish bohemia. But it was also regarded as a story about Germans. One review was even entitled "The bad love of a good German woman." Do you believe that there really was a chance that the book would change Polish stereotypes about Germans?*

K. W.: No book is capable of doing that. Polish stereotypes about Germans are ingrained so deeply that changing them would take years and years of social processes, two or three generations. What this book certainly does offer, however, is a closer look at the daily reality of the Third Reich, the war years in bomb-shattered Berlin. It shows the reader how people used to live here, what they used to do, how they obtained food, how food was rationed and so forth. These realities are set against the background of all those decrees and announcements. It's incredibly interesting and I must say I've learned an awful lot from this book.

E. F.: I can't say much about the reception of *Aimée & Jaguar* in Poland, but I'd like to refer to a conversation I had with a Hungarian journalist from a gay magazine; his eyes almost swelled with tears as he was telling me how much I'd done with this book for the LGBT movement in Hungary. I think we shouldn't underestimate the importance of this book in countries where homosexuals are discriminated against. In Russia, *Aimée & Jaguar* is not available at all. Even though it has been translated into Russian, it is only sold in sex shops. This shows that in certain places homosexuality is still seen as problematic. I can imagine that the book played a similar role in Poland, too.

K. W.: In Berlin, I once met a gay couple from Poland. When I told them my name, their reaction was, "Oh! So it's you who translated *Aimée & Jaguar* into Polish!" They came to Berlin to enjoy some freedom in this "Gay Land," to go to gay bars and so on. They were super excited to meet me; it seemed important for them. Looking at the Polish discussion about same-sex marriage or partnership, I think and I hope that it's only now beginning to become normal to talk about these things. Something's already changed over the last few years; I really think it's about time.

M. W.: One of the characteristics of Aimée & Jaguar *is the vocabulary used in Nazi Germany. There's the language of racism and anti-Semitism, with terms such as* Weltjudentum *(world Jewry),* Rassenkunde *(racial science),* arisch, halbarisch, nichtarisch *(Aryan, half-Aryan, non-Aryan),* halbjüdisch, vierteljüdisch *(half-Jewish, quarter-Jewish),* judenrein *(Jew-free). There's even a children's prayer to Adolf Hitler: "Fold your hands, bow your head,/ Think of Adolf Hitler only./He gives us our daily bread/And leads us out of worry."[3] To what extent did the language of German fascism get through into Polish? Is it recognizable for Polish readers? And how did you go about this historical slang, which can't be familiar to Polish readers, also because it reflects the experience of German Jews, which was different from that of Polish Jews?*

K. W.: This problem was always at the back of my mind. The thing is, we have two different cultures of memory here. Nazi terminology in the occupied countries, including Poland, differed considerably from the words and names used on a daily basis in the Third Reich. Since we've already mentioned footnotes, I must add that I also tried to explain terms to the Polish reader that were important for Germans during the war. As regards the prayer, I had to think something up; I'm not great at rhyming.

As regards this original terminology, for example *Nazisse*, I have to say that in Poland *naziści*, the Nazis, was not a widely used term; the more common way of referring to them was to say simply *Niemcy*, Germans. The German *Nazisse*, Nazi woman, sounds disparaging, so I translated it as *hitlerówka*, "Hitler woman"/"Hitlerette," rather than *nazistka*, because it's similarly derogatory. *Nazistka* foregrounds Nazism over being German; *hitlerówka* seems optimal to me. Another specific term was *U-Boote*, denoting people who lived in hiding. The lit-

---

[3] In German original: "Händchen falten, Köpfchen senken, nur an Adolf Hitler denken./ Er gibt uns das täglich Brot und führt uns aus aller Not."

eral translation, *łodzie podwodne*, submarines, wasn't functional, so I simply called them *nurkowie*, divers.

Working on this translation, I also learned that there's no German-Polish dictionary of Nazi or Third Reich terminology. Trying to find Polish equivalents for the names of various institutions and organizations, I naturally consulted a number of reference works, but to no avail. There's an online platform called *Learning from History*, available in six languages including Polish, but I came across very many mistakes there. You can also forget Wikipedia, where everyone translates as he or she feels like. The only reference work which I can really recommend is two large volumes by Professor Eugeniusz Cezary Król, a long-time director of the Centre for Historical Research of the Polish Academy of Sciences in Berlin, who specializes in the history of National Socialism. He translated all abbreviations, which was very helpful, because the Nazi lingo had an abbreviation for every term, however minor. In Poland, only several names of camp types are recognized: *KZ* (concentration camp), *Arbeitslager* (labour camp), *Stalag*, *Oflag* (POW-camps), and *Vernichtungslager* or death camp, although death camps were not "camps" in the technical sense, but rather "centres." In fact, German has eighteen camp categories, some of which are hardly decipherable today, so I'm very glad to have found such a reference work in Polish; it made my work much easier.

E. F.: I faced a similar problem in 1991, while doing research for this book. I tried to identify German names of towns and villages in Lower Silesia, part of Polish "Recovered Territories"; it was a nightmare. Today it's not a problem anymore, but back then it was an incredibly difficult task. I can still remember poring over my ancient atlas from the time of the Austro-Hungarian Empire; places such as Trachenberg (present-day Polish name: Żmigród) were marked there, but I had no way of locating them on the contemporary map.

M. W.: More than a decade after Aimée & Jaguar, *you published* Himmelstrasse, *another book in which you reconstruct a personal history, but this time it's the history of your own family, and the last days of life of your brother. Like* Aimée & Jaguar, Himmelstrasse *has a collage-like structure; it contains for example excerpts from old letters and your descriptions of your bother's drawings, some of which were found only after his death. One can also sense the same drive to find the truth, to reveal and explore it, however painful it might be. In what way did your work on* Aimée & Jaguar *influence* Himmelstrasse? *Did these two processes of literary reconstruction of the truth differ from each other?*

E. F.: Working on *Aimée & Jaguar* definitely strengthened my self-identification as a Jewish woman. I mean both the writing itself and the research. I'm not a historian, but when I approach a story, I begin to investigate it, gathering all materials that look useful to me. During the working process—and also afterwards, in the discussions—I had to position myself clearly as a Jew. And so my identity grew clearer and clearer to myself. This was certainly the foundation that gave me the ability to write the story of my own family. *Aimée & Jaguar* was also my first attempt at literary writing. Before that, I had authored non-fiction; I interviewed people for my books and then somehow combined the interviews with facts. For *Aimée & Jaguar*, I timidly wrote up small scenes, including sex scenes, picturing them the way I thought they might have taken place. And this is the form with which I've worked ever since then, more or less, and which I also employed in *Himmelstrasse*. Unfortunately, in the end the publisher marketed the book explicitly as a family history rather than a novel. I hate such labelling! If the cover says "a novel," the book must contain dialogues and a certain percentage of fictitious events. If it says "The story of my family"—as in the case of *Himmelstrasse*—it must all be true. I'd much rather have nothing on the cover, as in the Polish edition. First of all, I find these categories obsolete, and secondly, I can't decide between them anyway!

M. W.: The Polish edition also has a different cover design. Could you tell us what it shows?

E. F.: The original cover shows charming photos of myself at different ages, and my parents, who were a very attractive couple; the whole thing is quite lovely indeed. Yet the story itself is very, very sad and dark. Its point of departure is the disappearance of my brother; he went missing, and after a year his body, or rather a pile of bones, was discovered in Vienna Woods. In between, I write about Treblinka camp, where my grandparents were murdered. Definitely not a delightful family story... The cover of the Polish edition shows my brother's drawings; they feature inside the book, too. My brother expressed himself in this way. For Polish readers, his drawings are an inherent part of the book. The German Publisher, Rowohlt Verlag, found them too brutal. They thought that the book wouldn't sell if it contained such images. The Poles are bolder.

M. W.: Ms. Weintraub, Erica Fischer left Austria, and you left Poland after 1968. Was this shared experience of escaping an oppressive homeland helpful in translating Himmelstrasse?

K. W.: Not *Himmelstrasse*, no, but it did help me very much with *Aimée & Jaguar*. We didn't have the same experiences, Erica and I, although we both belong to the second generation. Our Jewish mothers were communists; their wartime experiences were radically different, though. Erica's mother immigrated to England, while my mother spent the whole war at Ravensbrück concentration camp as a guinea pig in medical experiments. Erica grew up in a free country, in Austria, and left it in an act of rebellion. My home was Poland. I grew up in a totalitarian state, but I felt at home there, it was my country—up until the moment when I was told that I was a foreigner. I was forced to go, because I didn't want to live in a place like that. I left, but it was a terribly difficult experience and it seriously affected my whole life. Therefore, we can't really speak of a shared experience here.

Going back to my translation work, though, let me explain why I feel more attached to *Aimée & Jaguar*. There's a passage in the book where Erica describes how Felice tried to leave the country before the war, and met with countless little hindrances. I identified myself with her at that point. She grew up in Germany as a normal little girl, until one day someone told her that she was an unwelcome element and an enemy of the state. Of course, there's no one-to-one correspondence between my experiences and hers; after all, the anti-Semitic campaign of 1968 was not life-threatening. However, in the beginning Felice didn't know that the situation could become life-threatening. This was before the decision about the Final Solution; at first, there were only these tiny instances of oppression. Just like Felice, I had to draw up endless lists of items that I wanted to take with me, obtain countless certificates from the tax office and housing authorities. We had to clear out and hand over our apartment. We had to give away our possessions to friends, sometimes parting with our favourite things. My father once gave me the Brockhaus Encyclopedia in seventeen volumes. I wasn't allowed to take it along, because it was published in 1908, and only books that came out after 1945 were permitted. Later, in Leipzig, I heard from someone who survived the "*Polenaktion*," the deportation of Polish Jews from Germany in 1938, "Imagine, Ms Weintraub, that people were only allowed to take ten Reichsmarks." I could imagine this very well indeed. "Yes," I said, "we were only allowed to take five dollars." I left the country with a document that was valid for one month; it said "Mrs Katarzyna Weintraub is not a citizen of the Polish People's Republic." I'm sharing all this to say how close Felice's story has been to me, and that I was really translating it with a lump in my throat. Of course I found *Himmelstrasse* very interesting, too; it allowed me to get to know Erica better, to learn about her family history and its difficult relationship with Poland. But what really got under my skin was *Aimée & Jaguar*.

Translated into English by Zofia Ziemann

Contributors

Joanna Bator is a Polish author, columnist and academic. She has lectured in London, New York, Tokyo and Warsaw and published in *The National Geographic* and *Voyage*, among others. She is the author of *Japoński wachlarz* (2004), *Piaskowa Góra* (2009), *Chmurdalia* (2010), *Wyspa łza* (2015), *Rok królika* (2016) and *Purezento* (2017). She is laureate of numerous literary awards, among others, the Nike Literary Award for her novel *Ciemno prawie noc* (2012).

Jacek St. Buras is a Polish translator, author, and literary critic. Since 2005, he has been Chief Editor of the Polish-German Translation Project *Kroki/Schritte*. He has translated works by Gottfried Benn, Bertolt Brecht, Thomas Bernhard, Paul Celan, Friedrich Dürrenmatt and Joseph von Eichendorff, among others, into Polish. He has been awarded by the Bosch Foundation (1989), the Polish Translators Association (1993), and others. He is also the recipient of the Austrian National Award (2004).

Erica Fischer is an Austrian writer, translator and journalist. She was one of the towering figures of the Austrian feminist movement and founder of the feminist magazine *AUF*. She is the author of the bestselling *Aimée & Jaguar* (1994), translated into over twenty languages. Her most recent novels include *Himmelstraße* (2007), *Mein Erzengel* (2010) and *Königskinder* (2012).

Dorota Glowacka is Professor of Humanities at the University of King's College in Halifax. Her fields of interest include Holocaust and genocide studies, and critical theory. She is the author of, among others, *Po tamtej stronie: świadectwo, afekt, wyobraźnia* (2012), *Disappearing Traces: Holocaust Testimonials, Ethics and Aesthetics* (2012), and co-editor of *Between Ethics and Aesthetics: Crossing the Boundaries* (2002) and *Imaginary Neighbors: Mediating Polish-Jewish Relations after the Holocaust* (2007).

Iwona Guść is a Postdoctoral Research Fellow at the Center for Holocaust Studies at the Institute for Contemporary History in Munich. She was one of the contributors of the project of critical edition of Anne Frank's diaries at the Göttingen Institute for Advanced Studies. Her fields of interest include transnational cultures of memory, anti-Semitism in post-World War II Europe, and wartime film and literature. She is the author of *'Polished' Cinema: over de receptie van het werk van Andrzej Kondratiuk in Polen en het groteske* (2012).

Mahmoud Kayyal is Senior Lecturer at the Department of Arabic and Islamic Studies at the Tel Aviv University. His main field of research is the study of intercultural contacts between Hebrew and Arabic cultures. His most recent monograph, *Selected Issues in the Modern Intercultural Contacts between Arabic and Hebrew Cultures: Hebrew, Arabic and Death*, appeared with Brill in 2016.

Bożena Keff is a Polish poet, columnist, film critic, translator and scholar. She also lectures in Gender Studies at the University of Warsaw. She is the author of, among others, *Postać z cieniem: Portrety Żydówek w polskiej literaturze od końca XIX wieku do 1939 roku* (2001) and

Antysemityzm: niezamknięta historia (2013). Her *Utwór o Matce i Ojczyźnie* [A Piece on Mother and the Fatherland] (2008) was nominated for the Nike Literary Award.

Esther Kinsky is a German author and translator. She was awarded for her translations with the Paul Celan Award (2009) and the Karl Dedecius Prize of the Robert Bosch Foundation (2011). She has translated writings by Ida Fink, Hanna Krall, Ryszard Krynicki and Aleksander Wat, among others, into German. She is also the author of *Sommerfrische* (2009), *Banatsko* (2011) and *Hain* (2018), as well as a volume of poetry *Naturschutzgebiet* (2013).

Tara Kohn is the Andrew W. Mellon Postdoctoral Fellow in Art History at Bowdoin College. She is a scholar of the art of the United States with an emphasis in the history of photography, the politics of identity, and trauma studies. Her work has been supported by the United States Holocaust Memorial Museum, and she has published essays in *American Art* and other periodicals.

Wojciech Kosior is a scholar of religion and a psychologist. He teaches at the Center for Comparative Studies of Civilizations at the Jagiellonian University in Kraków. His fields of interest include the Hebrew Bible, early rabbinical literature, angeology and demonology. He has published in *The Polish Journal of Arts and Culture*, *The Polish Journal of Biblical Research*, *Studia Judaica*, and others.

Natalia Krynicka is a scholar of Yiddish literature and a translator. She is the Chief Librarian at the Medem Library-Paris Yiddish Centre and teaches Yiddish and Jewish literature at the Sorbonne. Her PhD thesis addressed the Polish-Jewish cultural relations in light of Polish-Yiddish translations between 1885 and 1939. She regularly publishes translations from Yiddish literature.

Magdalena Marszałek is Professor for Slavic Literature and Culture at the University of Potsdam. Her fields of interest include Polish literature of the 19th and 20th centuries, Polish-Jewish cultural history as well as Polish-Russian and Polish-Ukrainian cultural contacts. She is the author of *Życie i papier: Autobiograficzny projekt Zofii Nałkowskiej: Dzienniki 1899–1954* (2004) and co-editor of *Nach dem Vergessen: Rekurse auf den Holocaust in Ostmitteleuropa nach 1989* (2010). Her most recent publications include the German anthology of Maria Janion, *Die Polen und ihre Vampire* (2014).

Kenneth B. Moss is the Posen Associate Professor of Modern Jewish History at the Johns Hopkins University. His first book, *Jewish Renaissance in the Russian Revolution* (Harvard 2009), received the National Jewish Book Council's Sami Rohr Prize for Best Work of Jewish Literature in 2010; a Hebrew translation will appear from Mercaz Zalman Shazar. He is currently working on a second book entitled *The Unchosen People: the Polish Jewish Condition and the Recasting of Jewish Political Imagination in the 1930s*. He coedits the journal *Jewish Social Studies* and is coediting volume 7 of the *Posen Library of Jewish Culture and Civilization*. His work has appeared in the *Journal of Modern History*, *Jewish Social Studies*, *Jewish History*, the *Journal of Social History*, and many other venues.

Agnieszka Podpora is a PhD candidate at the Department of Hebrew Studies of the Warsaw University. Her fields of interest include Polish and Israeli post-Holocaust literature, contemporary Israeli literature and culture as well as history and art of European Jews. She has published in *ResPublica Nowa*, *Krytyka Polityczna*, *Cwiszn*, *Zagłada Żydów*, and others. She also teaches Hebrew and translates Israeli literature into Polish.

Orr Scharf teaches at the Cultural Studies M.A. Program at the University of Haifa. He has edited *Vorlesungen über Judentum und Christentum* (volume 5) in the critical edition of Martin Buber's works. His monograph, *Thinking in Translation: Scripture and Redemption in Franz Rosenzweig's Thought* is forthcoming from de Gruyter (2019). Together with Ishay Rosen-Zvi he has also translated Tractate Sotah for the *Oxford Mishnah Project*.

Robert Schindel is an Austrian author, poet and film director. He has been awarded with the Erich Fried Prize (1993), the Eduard Mörike Prize (2000), the Literary Award of the City of Vienna (2003) and the Heinrich Mann Award (2014), among others. He is the author of *Kassandra* (1970), *Gebürtig* (1992), and *Der Kalte* (2013). He has also published several volumes of poetry, including *Geier sind pünktliche Tiere* (1987), *Fremd bei mir selbst* (2004) and *Mein mausklickendes Saeculum* (2008).

Joachim Schlör is Professor for Modern Jewish/non-Jewish Relations and Director of *The Parkes Institute for the Study of Jewish/non-Jewish Relations* at the University of Southampton. His fields of interest include urban studies, migration studies and memory studies. He is the author of *Nachts in der großen Stadt: Paris, Berlin, London 1840–1930* (1994), *Das ich der Stadt: Debatten über Judentum und Urbanität, 1822–1938* (2005), *'Liesel, it's time for you to leave:' Von Heilbronn nach England: Die Flucht der Familie Rosenthal vor der nationalsozialistischen Verfolgung* (2016) and the editor of *Jüdisches Leben in Berlin 1933–1941* (2012).

Na'ama Sheffi is Associate Professor at the Department of Communication, in Sapir College, Sderot. Her book *The Ring of Myths: The Israelis, Wagner and the Nazis*, was published in Hebrew (1999), English (Sussex Academic Press, 2001; revised edition 2013), and German (Wallstein Verlag, 2002). Her previous research *German in Hebrew: Translation from German into Hebrew in Jewish Palestine, 1882–1948*, was published in Hebrew (1998) and German (2011). Currently she researches the images on Israeli banknotes together with Prof. Anat First.

Marek Tuszewicki is a lecturer at and the vice-director of the Department of Jewish Studies at the Jagiellonian University in Kraków. Apart from his academic pursuits, he also translates Jewish literature into Polish and teaches at the Jewish Community Center in Kraków. His fields of interest include Ashkenazi folk culture and Hassidism as well as their response to modernity. In 2015 he published his post-doctoral book on Jewish folk medicine *Żaba pod językiem*. He has co-edited *Polskie tematy i konteksty literatury żydowskiej* (2014), and his work appears in *Kwartalnik Historii Żydów* and other important publications.

Magdalena Waligórska is Assistant Professor for East European History and Culture at the University of Bremen. Her fields of interest include the revival of Jewish heritage in post-Holocaust Europe, representations of Jews in Polish and German popular culture, as well as Holocaust commemoration and nationalism studies. She is the author of *Klezmer's Afterlife: An Ethnography of the Jewish Music Revival in Poland and Germany* (2013) and co-editor of

Music, Longing and Belonging. Articulations of the Self and the Other in the Musical Realm (2013).

Katarzyna Weintraub is a Polish journalist and translator. Her most important literary translations include Erica Fischer's *Aimée i Jaguar: Historia pewnej miłości* (2008), *Droga do nieba* (2009), as well as Aleksandra Maxeiner's *To wszystko rodzina!* (2012), Wolfgang Büscher's *Hartland: Pieszo przez Amerykę* (2013), and Pola Kinsky's *Usteczka* (2014).

Michael Zgodzay is a literary scholar and translator of Polish literature. He teaches at the Department of Slavic Studies at the University of Potsdam. His literary translations include Bożena Keff's *Ein Stück über Mutter und Vaterland* (2010) and Jolanta Brach-Czaina's *Die Geschäftigkeit* (1999). He also published in *Manuskripte*, *Magazyn Materiałów Literackich Cegła* and *Der Tagesspiegel*.

Index

'Abbāsī, Maḥmūd, 204
'Abd al-Fattāḥ, Nāzik, 200
Abramovitch, Raphael, 285–87, 292–95
Abramovitsh, Sholem-Yankev (Mendele Moykher-Sforim), 113, 116–17
Agamben, Giorgio, 256
Aggasi, Eliyahu, 198
Aharon, Zakkay, 198
al-Baḥrāwī, Ibrāhīm, 201
al-Dāwūdī, Salīm, 195
aliyah, *see also* migration 177, 217, 219–20, 227
al-Shāmī, Rashād, 200
American Joint Distribution Society, 292
Améry, Jean (Hans Mayer), 182, 242
angels, 25, 27–28, 140
An-ski, Sh., 69, 74, 84, 91, 97–104, 137–42, 146
anti-Semitism, 113–16, 123, 127–30, 179, 199, 266–68, 282, 305–6, 320–23, 327–28, 335–36, 341–42
anti-Semitic campaign 1968, 306, 326, 345
'Arāyidī, Naʿīm, 202
Arendt, Hannah, 159, 168–69
Asch, Sholem, 124–27, 213
assimilation, 99, 113, 118–23, 126–28, 167, 239

Ballas, Shimon, 205–7
Banasiewicz-Ossowska, Ewa, 137
Bartmiński, Jerzy, 145
Bayādsī, Maḥmūd, 204
Benjamin, Walter, 4, 173, 176, 184, 240, 252–56, 281–82, 288, 292, 297
Berlin, 7, 153–69, 187, 304, 307, 338–43
Bialik, Haim Nahman, 69–70, 77–78, 84–105, 214
Bialystok/Białystok, 279–82, 291
Bible
– exegesis, 24–30, 56–59, 224
– translations of, 2, 17–35, 39–59, 173
Blücher, Heinrich, 155–69
Brenner, Yosef Haim, 4, 6, 213–33

Brzozowska, Małgorzata, 145
Buber, Martin, 39–59, 128, 303

Cahan, Abraham, 283, 290–92
Célan, Paul, 241–42
Christianity, 2–5, 7, 39–59, 114–16, 124–26, 135–37, 248
communism, *see also* socialism, 102–3, 206, 262, 266, 275, 306, 327–35
correspondence, 44, 160–63, 214, 260–62, 269

deparochialization, 82–106
diary, 183, 243, 259–75
Diaspora, 72, 103, 136, 166–67, 203, 215–20, 223–24, 227–28

Eliach, Yaffa, 240
Exilcafés, 160

Fackenheim, Emil, 255
Feldman, Wilhelm, 122–23
Folks-Farlag Publishing House, 70–71, 92–98
Frank, Anne, 259–75
Frank, Otto, 259–75
Freud, Sigmund, 295, 314
Frishman, David, 70, 76–81, 85, 88–98

Ghanāyim, Muḥammad Ḥamza, 202, 204
ghetto, 128, 238, 266–68, 304, 311, 320, 333
Gilbert Finnegan, Marianne, 157
Gilbert, Jean, 155
Gilbert, Robert, 7, 153–69
Głos Żydowski (Warsaw, weekly), 128
Goldberg-Mulkiewicz, Olga, 137
Gressmann, Hugo, 57–58

Ḥaddād, ʿEzra, 198–99
Ḥaddād, Meir, 198
Ḥammād, Aḥmad, 199
Hebraism, 69–79, 91–101

Heymann, Werner Richard, 154–55, 160
Hofshteyn, Dovid, 86–91, 97
Holocaust, 4, 10–11, 181–86, 238–58, 269, 296, 307, 320–22, 335, 339–42

Iliad
– Jewish Translations of, 74–75
intelligentsia, 9, 68–71, 86, 96, 99–104, 117–22, 125, 216–17, 227
Isaiah, 25–27, 33–34, 54–58
Israel, 28, 46–47, 55, 88, 91, 168, 174–88, 193–209, 319–20
Izraelita (Warsaw weekly), 116–25, 128–29

Jedwabne, 305, 314–15
Jesus, 9, 45–47, 54, 57, 136
Jewish place(s), 153
Joseph, 140–41
Judaism, 39, 44–55, 135, 199, 227
Junosza, Klemens (Szaniawski, Klemens), 6, 113–25

Kacyzne, Alter, 279–98
Kapeliuk, Menahem, 196–97
Kertész, Imre, 7, 237–42, 251, 256–57, 328
Kiever Farlag (publishing house), 70, 92–97
Kirszrot, Jan, 127
Klausner, Joseph, 70, 74, 83, 87–88, 104–5
Knox, Israel, 238
Krall, Hanna, 237, 246, 304, 319
Kultur-Lige, 70, 92–97

languages
– Arabic, 3, 40, 187, 193–209
– Dutch, 259–61, 269–73
– English, 3, 128, 153–69, 182, 187, 238, 243–47, 290
– French, 3, 120, 239–42, 248, 250–56, 261
– German, 3–4, 39–59, 75, 82, 122–25, 128–30, 153–69, 173–88, 242–53, 269–74, 303–18
– Greek, 2–3, 17–35, 43, 75
– Hebrew, 2–4, 17–35, 39–59, 67–105, 173–88, 193–209, 213–29, 290–91
– Hungarian, 7, 126, 241–45
– Italian, 249–51

– Polish, 113–30, 136, 213–29, 248–52, 259–75, 303–7, 311–45
– Russian, 4, 71–72, 75–87, 99, 101–2, 145, 187, 246, 341
– Yiddish, 2–11, 67–106, 113–30, 137–47, 177, 229, 238–39, 247, 280–83, 290–96, 325–26
Lanzmann, Claude, 4, 247–49
Leitner, Isabella, 244–45, 249
Leopoldi, Hermann, 153–69
Levi, Primo, 238–40, 249–52, 256
Levinas, Emmanuel, 240, 253–58
Lew, Henryk, 119–20
Libera, Zbigniew, 135
Liliental, Regina, 119, 138, 144–46
Litai, A., 67–73, 76–78, 94–95, 99–100, 104
Litvakov, Moyshe, 70, 72–86, 89–98, 102–3, 105
Loewe, Frederic, 162–63
Luther, Martin, 40, 43, 56, 173

Mallūl, Nissīm, 195
Mann, Thomas, 179–85
memory, 154, 229, 241–53, 280–85, 292–96, 303–7, 319–22, 342
Mendelssohn, Moses, 3, 40, 173–77
Michael, Sami, 205
migration, *see also aliyah* 2–7, 128, 153–69, 177, 194–98, 203, 217–25, 266–67, 283, 328
musical comedy, 158

New York, 11, 80, 94, 153–69, 279–84, 290–98

Ohr, Jerzy, 123–24
Ojczyzna (Lvov monthly), 120–22
Omanut (publishing house), 70, 92–100
operetta, 155–60
Ostrolenka/ Ostrołęka, 279–82, 296–98

Palestine, 31, 78, 95, 102, 187, 197, 213–33, 314
Paris, 153–58
People's Republic of Poland, 275, 319–20, 329, 345

Peretz, Yitskhok-Leybush, 86, 121–24
Persits, Shoshana, 76, 92, 95, 97–100
poetry, 72–79, 86–96, 101, 104–5, 128–29, 161–69, 280
prayer, 47–51, 126, 137, 291, 343
prose, 78–80, 121–23, 127, 129

readership, 40–42, 79–80, 113, 193, 205–6, 218
Rivlin, Joseph Joel, 196
Rosen, Alan, 238–41
Rosenstock-Heussy, Eugen, 43–47
Rosenzweig, Franz, 39–59
Rozenfeld, Moris (Rosenfeld, Morris), 128

Schneider, Lambert, 43, 270
Septuagint, 2–3, 17, 39, 56
Shammas, Anton, 202–5
Shamosh, Tuvia, 198
Shoah, *see also* Holocaust, 4, 247, 323
Shteynman, Eliezer, 70, 73, 82–84, 92, 97–98, 104
socialism, *see also* communism, 92, 218–20, 307
Somekh, Sasson, 205
Stomma, Ludwik, 135
Stybel publishing house, 70–79, 94–100
Suesser, Ignacy, 120–22
Szofman, Józef, 6, 214–34

Testament
– Old, 44, 47, 57, 147
– New, 27, 44, 54
testimony, 4, 185, 238–58, 330–31, 339
The Forward Association, 281–82, 285, 293–95
The Star of Redemption, 48–49
Torberg, Friedrich, 165

Tshernikhovsky, Shaul, 74–75, 79, 82–83, 87–88, 91–92

underworld, 20–22, 28–34

vernacular, 40–41, 49–50, 116, 126, 142, 168–69, 175–76, 204, 218
Vienna, 153–54, 156–57, 160–63, 247, 320–22
Virgin Mary, 9, 136
Vishniac, Roman, 287, 293
Vulgate, 40, 56

Waldheim, Kurt, 306–7, 320, 338
Warsaw, 80, 94, 129, 214–16, 239, 260–69, 280–88, 305, 321–22, 334
Weinreich, Max, 74–75, 137
Weys, Rudolf, 157–59, 162
Wieviorka, Anette, 240
witness, witnessing, 4, 34–35, 166, 238–58, 289, 307–8
World War
– First, 4, 117, 155, 223–26
– Second, 4, 162, 180–82, 187, 266, 275, 306–8, 322–24

Yiddish literature, 67, 72–76, 79–91, 95, 113–30
Yiddish Scientific Institute (YIVO), 293
Yiddishism, 68–74, 86, 92–99, 104–6, 315
Yiddish-Polish translations, 113–30
yishuv, 4, 103, 178–83, 216–18, 220, 223, 226, 229–34
Yizkor Book, 136, 297–99

Zionism, 100, 127–28, 177–88, 194–209, 216–22, 227–32
Zweig, Stefan, 179–82